Rethinking the Novel/Film Debate

The relationship between books and film has been one of the key topics of cinema studies. Much of this criticism, however, has been inherited from eighteenth-century debates on poetry and painting and thus has fostered false and limiting paradigms in which words and pictures are opposed. *Rethinking the Novel/Film Debate* historicizes and critiques the central paradigms of this debate. Testing theory against practice and uncovering the hidden agendas, Kamilla Elliott creates new critical models that can be applied to the novel/film issue in an effort to transform the field for future inquiry. In the process, she mounts a major critique of novel theory and film history and theory, demonstrating how rivalries have shaped and falsified each discipline when considered separately.

Kamilla Elliott is Assistant Professor of English and American literature at the University of California, Berkeley, where she teaches literature, film, and Victorian studies.

Rethinking the NOVEL/FILM DEBATE

Kamilla Elliott
University of California, Berkeley

CAMBRIDGE
UNIVERSITY PRESS

PUBLISHED BY THE PRESS SYNDICATE OF THE UNIVERSITY OF CAMBRIDGE
The Pitt Building, Trumpington Street, Cambridge, United Kingdom

CAMBRIDGE UNIVERSITY PRESS
The Edinburgh Building, Cambridge CB2 2RU, UK
40 West 20th Street, New York, NY 10011-4211, USA
477 Williamstown Road, Port Melbourne, VIC 3207, Australia
Ruiz de Alarcón 13, 28014 Madrid, Spain
Dock House, The Waterfront, Cape Town 8001, South Africa

http://www.cambridge.org

© Kamilla Elliott 2003

First published 2003

Printed in the United Kingdom at the University Press, Cambridge

Typefaces ITC New Baskerville 10/12.5 pt. and Bodoni Poster Compressed
System LaTeX 2ε   [TB]

A catalog record for this book is available from the British Library

Library of Congress Cataloging-in-Publication Data is available.

ISBN 0 521 81844 3 hardback

To George Bluestone,
forerunner and mentor,
with respect and gratitude

Contents

List of Illustrations

Acknowledgments

A book is never the production of a single person, least of all an academic book. *Rethinking the Novel/Film Debate* builds on the work of many scholars before me and benefits from the astute input of many insightful readers. Foremost of these, Elizabeth Abel, Seymour Chatman, and Joss Marsh read more than one version of the manuscript and offered invaluable feedback as well as staunch personal support. Katie Snyder, Robert Stam, and John Glavin offered excellent feedback on an early draft of the manuscript, as did several anonymous reviewers who must, therefore, remain unnamed. Mitch Breitweiser has been a mentor in every sense of the word, offering astute comments on portions of the manuscript as well as advice on its broader presentation. Russell Merritt, Colleen Lye, Celeste Langan, Catherine Gallagher, and Sharon Marcus gave indispensable input on single chapters. Ryan McDermott lent meticulous proofreading skills.

Elaine Scarry, Philip Fisher, and George Bluestone supported and informed my research in its earlier dissertation stages, but their hand and influence remain. Scarry blended astute insights with immaculate attention to detail, suggesting the most rigorous of revisions with the most velvet of gloves, and providing constant encouragement along with ever higher goals. Scarry subsequently lent polishing touches to this book in its final stages of development. Fisher offered early challenges and focus. And Bluestone, whose book *Novels Into Film* (1957) marks the starting point of novel and film studies proper, was enormously generous and supportive even from retirement.

I am further indebted to the film archivists and technical staff of the Motion Picture Reading Room at the Library of Congress (Madeleine Matz, Rosemary Hanes, and Joe Balian) and of the National Film Archive at the British Film Institute in London (Ros Cranston, Alison Strauss, and Kathleen Dickson), whose professionalism made research a pleasure. My thanks too to the Bancroft Library at the University of California, Berkeley, the Margaret Herrick Library at the Academy of Motion Picture Arts and Sciences, the British Film Institute (especially Nina Harding), and to Patrick Fay at University Copy in Berkeley, California, for provision of and assistance with the illustrations. Without the assistance of dissertation grants from Harvard University and the Whiting Foundation and from the University of California's Committee on Research, I would never have been able to amass the base of archival research that underlies this project or to make my arguments with such confidence in their wider applicability. And without my research assistants, Arun Nevader, Marguerite Nguyen, Joe Nugent, and Nicole Asaro, this book would have been at least a year longer in the making.

I am also indebted to friends and family for their unflagging encouragement, support, and patience. Joss Marsh has been a stalwart friend as well as a mentor and collaborator. Sharon Doublet-Thompson offered perspective and unfailing humor at even the most dismaying twists and turns of the process. My brother, Kenton Sparks, provided financial assistance for additional research trips and earthquake insurance for the manuscript, receiving and storing countless e-mail versions of it far from the Hayward fault. Other family members and friends too numerous to name provided a constant stream of encouragement and support. Most of all, I wish to thank my children, Lucas and Christina Denman, for their unwavering confidence in my ability to complete this book, which spans a good part of their lifetimes, and for their blithe faith in its contents without reading a single word of it.

Introduction

This is not the book I intended to write, although that book haunts the margins of this one. The original book (on Victorian novels and their film adaptations) was stymied by problems, paradoxes, and polarizations in novel and film studies more generally. Recent publications on the subject express a mounting dissatisfaction with the paradigms and methodologies that govern the field. At the heart of the novel and film debate lies a particularly perplexing paradox: on one side, novels and films are diametrically opposed as "words" and "images," at war both formally and culturally. J. Dudley Andrew, the most widely reprinted scholar of literary film adaptation, is one of many to argue "the absolutely different semiotic systems of film and language."[1] On the other side of the paradox, novels and films are integrally related as sister arts sharing formal techniques, audiences, values, sources, archetypes, narrative strategies, and contexts.[2] Oddly, interdisciplinary scholars do not adhere to one or the other side of the paradox: they rather occupy both.

Unable to discover the roots of the paradox inside novel and film studies, I turned to prior word and image discourses, where I found its recent origins in the two main branches of the eighteenth-century poetry and painting debate. One branch categorically differentiates poetry and painting along word and image lines, classifying the two arts as separate species, as in Lessing's famous distinction between poetry as temporal and painting as spatial. The other identifies them as sister arts, setting up rhetorical family resemblances through interart analogies, as in Simonides of Ceos's frequently cited analogy: "Poetry is a speaking picture; painting is a mute poem." Categorical differentiators recommend separate spheres for poetry and painting; interart analogizers foster sibling incest and sibling rivalries. Chapter 1, "Analogy and Category," ponders the problematic application of the eighteenth-century poetry and

1

painting debate to the study of novels and films. Given the hybrid verbal–visual nature of illustrated novels and worded films, the wholesale application of categorical tenets developed for poetry and painting to novels and films is at worst inappropriate and at best partial. It is further demonstrated in Chapter 1 that category and analogy are not so opposed as they at first appear but rather collude to foster the word and image divide, even in hybrid word and image arts. Indeed, Chapter 2, "Prose Pictures," and Chapter 3, "Film Language," delineate how word and image wars wage within as well as between illustrated novels and worded films, most intriguingly in analogies that speak of words as pictures and of pictures as language. While these analogies imply affinities, they more often foster word and image wars. Chapter 2 outlines how novelists, reviewers, editors, and literary critics have used analogies of prose as painting and illustration as commentary to subjugate, denigrate, and excise novel illustrations. Chapter 3 traces how, in a similar vein, filmmakers, reviewers, critics, and historians have used analogies of film images as language to minimize, excoriate, ignore, and exile film's words. In both discourses, analogy joins with category to press novels and films into word and image camps as "pure" word and image arts. They are proclaimed categorically pure, but paradoxically so, by interart analogies.

Chapter 4, "Cinematic Novels/Literary Cinema," carries the examination of intra-art analogies into a discussion of interart analogies. It examines the paradox that novels are deemed "cinematic" when novels are defined as "words" and words are decreed "uncinematic." It shows how, among all branches of novel and film studies, literary film adaptation places the greatest pressure on the debate's central paradox. From the categorical side that opposes novels as words and films as images, adaptation emerges as a theoretical impossibility, for words and images are everywhere declared untranslatable, irreducible, *a priori* systems – even by poststructuralist critics like J. Hillis Miller. But from the analogical side that speaks of "cinematic novels" and "literary cinema," adaptation appears as the logical, even inevitable, outcome of interart analogies, as cinematic novels *become* cinema – the discursive word made aesthetic flesh.

Interart analogy and interart adaptation feature prominently in this book as highly revelatory points of interdisciplinary rhetorical and aesthetic exchange. Furthermore, because of its pivotal position between the eighteenth-century poetry and painting debate and the twentieth-century novel and film debate, the nineteenth-century novel features prominently in this book. If interart analogies like cinematic novels and literary cinema cast novel and film as sister arts in the twentieth and twenty-first centuries, analogies of cinematic nineteenth-century novels construct a strangely anachronistic ancestral relationship between them. In the 1940s, Sergei Eisenstein forged a widely followed argument that "from Dickens, from the Victorian novel, stem the first shoots of American film esthetic."[3] In the 1970s, Christian Metz concurred and expanded:

> Inasmuch as it proposes behavioural schemes and libidinal prototypes, corporeal postures, types of dress, modes of free behavior or seduction, and is the initiating authority for a perpetual adolescence, the classical film has taken, relay fashion, the historical place of the grand-epoch, nineteenth-century novel (itself descended from the ancient epic); it fills the same social function, a function which the twentieth-century novel, less and less diegetic and representational, tends partly to abandon.[4]

The idea expressed here is not simply that the nineteenth-century novel influenced western film, but that it in some sense *became* film, while the modern novel evolved in a different direction. This aesthetic history place film in the literary family tree, giving the nineteenth-century novel filmic as well as literary progeny. Metz's contrasts between these media place film in a literary critical context, in that they resemble nineteenth-century comparisons of poetry and prose. For example, J. S. Mill wrote in 1833: "The truth of poetry is to paint the human soul truly; the truth of fiction is to give a true picture of life . . . the novelist . . . has to describe outward things, not the inward man."[5] Such theoretical and rhetorical lineages require interdisciplinary scrutiny.

The Victorian novel plays a central role in mediating these discourses, as well as in the aesthetic practices fed by and feeding these discourses. It is not to my mind coincidental that British Victorian novels and novellas have been more frequently adapted to film than any other body of literature, including Shakespearean plays (and Shakespeare is the only author from his period to be so frequently adapted). I have located over 1,500 film and television adaptations of British Victorian prose fiction (1837–1901). Given the erratic nature of film records, this list can only be a partial one. Numerous Victorian novels have been filmed more than 20 times – some over 100 times. This fact renders film adaptations of Victorian novels particularly rich and variegated places for examining interdisciplinary exchanges across decades, genres, and nations. Chapter 5 examines multiple adaptations of a Victorian novel, Emily Brontë's *Wuthering Heights*, not only to illustrate these multiple variables but also to grapple with a second dogma that has plagued novel and film studies: adaptation and the problem of content. Adaptation lies between the rock of a post-Saussurean insistence that form does not and cannot separate from content and the hard place of poststructuralism's debunking of content, of original and local signifieds alike. If words and images do not and cannot translate, and if form does not and cannot separate from content (whether because of their mandated insoluble bond or because content is simply an illusion), then what remains to pass between a novel and a film in adaptation? Scholars are faced with two choices: they must either treat adaptation as a theoretical impossibility (though adaptation's cultural ubiquity renders those who do so ostriches with heads buried in the sands of philosophical and semiotic abstraction), or they must find some way to account for what passes between a novel and film in adaptation without committing semiotic heresy. This critical bind is, to my mind, largely responsible for many of the problems plaguing adaptation studies in particular and novel and film studies in general and for the pervasive sense that adaptation scholars lag behind the critical times. For example, Robert B. Ray regrets the lack of "distinguished work" and the absence of a "presiding poetics" and Brian McFarlane ascertains that "it is depressing to find at what a limited, tentative stage the discourse has remained."[6] Chapter 5 highlights a number of heretical ways in which critics, filmmakers, reviewers, and audiences have dared to split form from content in the criticism and practice of adaptation and investigates ways in which these heretical spaces have been used to foster additional interdisciplinary rivalries far more fraught and insidious than those arising from categorical distinctions of novels and films. These heretical splits are by no means limited to formal concerns: they open up spaces in which cultural, historical, and contextual concerns also enter interdisciplinary exchange.

Although heresies run rife in the rhetoric and practice of adaptation, officially, critics adhere to both dogmas: to the unbridgeable word and image divide and to the indissoluble form and content union. As a result, a structurally constrained model of analogy has been the only officially sanctioned model of adaptation from film's earliest days, for it is the only one to account for adaptation while avoiding semiotic heresy. Under this model, films locate analogous, already complete signs in their own lexicons that approximate literary signs: hence, content need not be split from form to pass from novel into film and words do not metamorphose into images. This model rejects any essential or inherent connections between novels and films apart from structural ones. In so doing, it strengthens the word and image divide, for it typically mandates that films find visual equivalents for verbal signs, ignoring the transfer of novel words to film words or novel illustrations to film pictures. Chapter 6, "Adaptation and Analogy," demonstrates the limitations and problems of this officially sanctioned model as well as two other unofficial analogical models of adaptation (the literalized analogy and the psychoanalytic analogy). It concludes by recommending a new (but also old) analogical model for adaptation: the looking glass analogy. This recommended model is not an abstract philosophical one, but a model gleaned from interart rhetoric and aesthetic practice, from interart analogies and certain interart adaptations. My research indicates that a model so gleaned will prove more valid than abstract ones in a field where theory and practice have been so greatly at odds. It moves toward resolving the analogical/categorical paradox, toward bridging the word and image divide, and toward opening a credible space in the form and content fusion.

There are of course limitations to such a study. In dealing chiefly with mainstream and hegemonic rhetorical and ideological currents, it, of necessity, omits many individual and minority voices. But in focusing on problems that persist across several centuries, disciplines, arts, technologies, and many theories, it aspires to clear ground for new critical voices and approaches and for those voices, protesting unheard, to be heard. A second limitation is that, in tracing specific threads from various interart and intra-art discourses into the novel and film debate, there was neither time nor space to follow the poetry/painting debate into the nineteenth, twentieth, and twenty-first centuries, to address the rarified practice of book illustration later in the twentieth and twenty-first centuries, or to investigate a host of other word and image forms, like magic lantern shows and comic books, that fed into film.

Recent critics of the novel and film debate argue that formal approaches have been overdone, need no more doing, and require undoing by cultural studies and poststructuralist scholarship.[7] However, these newer approaches have done little to bridge the word and image divide or to resolve adaptation's problem of content. The problems of the field cannot be resolved by exchanging new theories for old. Indeed, such changes may serve only to exacerbate the problems. Feeding novel and film studies into some recent theoretical paradigms would exacerbate word and image polarizations. For example, to gender words male, images female, and hybrid arts androgynous, after feminist models, or to read literary film adaptation as a subversive subjugation of the phallic to the presymbolic realm under psychoanalytic rubrics, or to feed canonical literature and popular film into Marxist class categorizations of high and low art would not serve to unravel false oppositions of novels and films, but would rather intensify them and place them in the service of new ideological oppositions. Thus, although my study is significantly informed by postmodern theory and cultural studies and draws on some of their methodologies, it does not espouse them as overarching structures.

Rather, it demonstrates their limitations in resolving the field's central problems.

If this book does set up a methodology, it is one that tests aesthetic theory with aesthetic practice. It shows repeatedly how theory has obfuscated a clear understanding of aesthetic practice and of intra- and interdisciplinary dynamics. Novel and film studies are particularly hospitable to a critique of theory from practice, since there is often no clear demarcation between theorists, academic critics, novelists, filmmakers, reviewers, and reader-viewers. For example, Sergei Eisenstein, who mainstreamed both the analogy of the cinematic novel and of film "language," was theorist, critic, and filmmaker. Novelists like Joseph Conrad, F. Scott Fitzgerald, and William Faulkner became screenwriters. Novelists like Fitzgerald, Leo Tolstoy, and Virginia Woolf have written about the novel's relationship to cinema. Other novelists are academics: semiotician Umberto Eco wrote a novel, *The Name of the Rose*, and later critiqued its film adaptation; Anthony Burgess has been professor, novelist, screenwriter, film reviewer, and adapter of literature to theater and film – he even composed music for a theatrical adaptation of one of his novels, *A Clockwork Orange*. Moving across this fluid continuum from abstract philosophers and elite artists to mainstream novelists and filmmakers to popular reviewers and mass audiences enabled me to probe some of the field's contradictions between abstract theory and actual aesthetic practice: for example, the paradox that adaptation is theoretically impossible yet culturally ubiquitous. But the methodology has proven constructive as well as deconstructive: studies of aesthetic practice not only debunk critical paradigms, they also suggest new ones.

Another limitation of this book's focus on the novel and film debate is that it, of necessity, shares in many of the debate's imbalances. I am fully aware that film is not merely a word and image art, but that it draws on other artistic forms and technologies. While my last case study does pay some attention to film music, additional studies of film music are needed to put further pressure on film's synecdochal definition as "images," as are analyses of other arts and technologies on which film draws. Similarly, in the course of my research it became manifestly clear that theatrical adaptations of novels form crucial intertexts between novels and their film adaptations – many early film adaptations record theatrical adaptations – but such intertexts receive short shrift in this book, just as they do in the novel and film debate. Chapter 4, however, does reopen the question of film's relationship to theater. Recent critics rightly protest novel and film studies' neglect of pulp fiction, screenplays, novelizations, and films that adapt other films, which this book too must minimize in order to maintain its focus on the central problems of the debate.[8] This book further shares the debate's preoccupation with the Victorian novel, and does so to excess in order to exorcise some of its ghosts. The Victorian novel looms monolithic: first, as the link pin between poetry and painting and novel and film debates; second, as film's most immediate and loudly proclaimed parent; third, as a particularly problematic, anachronistic locus of cinematic novel analogies; and fourth, as a body of literature offering multiple adaptations of single novels. While many twentieth-century novels have been adapted, it is rare to find one that has been adapted more than once. None has been adapted anywhere near the number of times as the average canonical Victorian novel. Finally, *Rethinking the Novel/Film Debate* shares the debate's imbalanced attention to Anglo-American films and Anglo-American criticism, though like that debate, it does ponder a handful of French critics, a few films from other continents, and some television adaptations. In spite of these necessary limitations, it is my hope that this book will clear ground for future scholars to foray freely among all of these neglected areas.

Another limitation of this book lies in my decision to limit the number of novels and films used for the case studies. Researching hundreds of films and dozens of novels over the course of a decade, I determined that any number of novels and films would serve equally to problematize and expose theory and rhetoric from aesthetic practice. It was tempting to cite multiple texts and films in order to showcase (show off) my painstaking and extensive research. However, because this book addresses a wide historical swath and several interdisciplinary discourses, I discerned that citing multiple books and films would tend to create analytical scatter and encyclopedic gloss, while sustaining fewer case study materials in depth and detail across centuries and discourses would maintain greater clarity and force of argumentation, provide clearer continuity and connections between the various debates, and enable greater analytical depth and interpretive nuance. While each case study is, as far as any case study can be, representative of the dynamics it illustrates – indeed, some are especially so – each inevitably contains idiosyncratic elements. However, standing on an extensive base of primary and secondary materials, I am confident that any idiosyncrasies do not affect the central arguments of this book. While other case study materials would certainly provide variations on the themes, they would not essentially change or undermine them. Without recourse to a multivolume format, these were choices I had to make.

A Note on Terminology

I resist the dominant terminological trend that makes films and books alike "texts" on two counts. First, it obviously confuses an interdisciplinary discussion. Second, I join numerous film and visual arts critics in opposing the colonizing application of terminology derived from language and linguistics to film and pictorial arts. I cite some of these critics and explain this objection further in Chapter 1.

1 | Analogy and Category

The tendency to speak of one art analogically in the terminology of another is an ancient one traced so often to Horace's *ut pictura poesis* ("as is painting so is poetry") that the phrase has become the general epigraph, title, or slogan of many essays on poetry and painting. Although scholars refer to the arts in terms of each other in various ways, interart analogies – in which one art takes on the primary and literal labels of another in a secondary and figurative sense – have proven versatile not only for pressing sibling resemblances, after the ancient sister-arts tradition, but also for fostering sibling rivalries between the arts. In 1713, for example, Sir Richard Blakemore asserted that, in many respects, "Poetry exactly resembles her sister Painting." He then wrote of them in the language of each other: "The painter is a poet to the eye, and a poet a painter to the ear. One gives us pleasure by silent eloquence, the other by vocal imagery."[1] The opening of C. A. Du Fresnoy's *De Arte Graphica* similarly follows a declaration of poetry and painting's sibling resemblance with an interchange of aesthetic rhetoric:

> True Poetry the painter's power displays;
> True Painting emulates the poet's lays:
> The rival sisters, fond of equal fame,
> Alternate change their office and their name;
> Bid silent Poetry the canvass warm,
> The tuneful page with speaking picture charm.[2]

But with the rise of Linnaean systems of classification, aesthetic theorists sought to emulate the sciences. In Chapter 18 of his *Laocoön: An Essay upon the Limits of Painting and Poetry* (1766), Gotthold Ephraim Lessing challenged the dominant analogical strain of interart discourse, defining poetry and painting according to categorical differences instead of sibling resemblances. Against interart analogies that maintained shared sources of inspiration, aesthetic principles, and techniques, Lessing pressed the higher priority of the bond between form and content, arguing that poetry is a temporal art and should therefore limit itself to representing temporal action, while painting is a static and spatial art and should limit itself to representing static bodies in space.[3] Thus Lessing classified the classical sister arts as separate species whose attempts to imitate and emulate each other were as misguided as performing animals trained to do tricks that nature never intended.

While Lessing's categorical approach won out over the analogical approach in the twentieth century, in the nineteenth century, interart analogies resurged with a vengeance, in bold defiance of Lessing's categorizations. Fueled at one end of the century by romantic theories of a shared artistic imagination and at the other end by emphases on form over content (so that exchanges between aesthetic forms were of more interest than bonds between form and content), interart analogies permeate nineteenth-century interart discourse to such an extent that Irving Babbitt denounced it as "the greatest debauch of descriptive writing the world has ever known."[4] To cite a few of the more famous interart analogizers, John Ruskin addressed the "coloring" of Rembrandt, Caravaggio, Salvator, Scott, Byron, Keats, and Tennyson in a single paragraph and elsewhere discussed the "language of lines" in painting, and Walter Pater wrote of "literary architecture" and of "the mere melody of Greek architecture."[5] Analogies extended to aesthetic principles: Ruskin argued that the "laws of expression for language were just the laws of expression in colour" and Pater averred that in the best kind of writing, "The elementary particles of language will be realised as colour and light and shade."[6]

Martin Meisel documents conventional, stylistic, and aesthetic intersections between novels, pictures, and plays in nineteenth-century Britain, demonstrating the role that interart analogies played in criticism and practice of the arts. "All three forms," he writes, "are narrative *and* pictorial; pictures are given to storytelling and novels unfold through and with pictures."[7] Serial paintings are described as drama; drama is referenced as "speaking pictures" and "moving pictures"; narrative paintings "tell" stories; and novels "paint" pictures. Nineteenth-century interart analogical rhetoric extended to interart aesthetic practices. In dramatic *tableaux*, for example, theater froze into painting; conversely, in *tableaux vivants*, paintings were embodied by live actors. In the novel, prose writers sought to create visual effects through ekphrasis and illustrators strove for dramatic and rhetorical as well as pictorial effects.

In the first half of the twentieth century, interart critics joined Irving Babbitt in denouncing interart analogies and adaptations as "confusions" of the arts. Babbitt's *New Laocoön*, published in 1910, pressed for a restoration of Lessing's categorical rigor after the rampant interart analogies of the nineteenth century, which he deplored as self-indulgent "half-truths."[8] Most twentieth-century interart critics followed suit. René Wellek and Austin Warren's influential chapter on "Literature and the Other Arts" (1942) set the standard for decades of interart criticism. It dismisses interart analogies as "vague metaphor[s]" that "never lend themselves to verification."[9] W. J. T. Mitchell encapsulates the general twentieth-century consensus: "We tend to think . . . that to compare poetry with painting is to make a metaphor, while to differentiate poetry from painting is to state a literal truth."[10] Even though figurative rhetoric has more recently gained critical substance under deconstructive and psychoanalytic theories, these theories have done little to redress analogy's reputation for deception and half-truth. If analogy proved too rhapsodic, impressionistic, unverifiable, and partial for earlier critics, for postmodern scholars it is calculating, manipulative, agenda-driven, and deceptive. Mary Jacobus is representative: "analogy is a term that elides or erases metaphoricity by attempting to claim an actual or essential reality for what is figurative." As such, she argues, it functions in especially pernicious ways to foster social and political injustices.[11] Thus, even though analogical rhetoric pervades the novel and film debate, categorical approaches have dominated its theorization.

The Celluloid Laocoön

It is readily apparent how much twentieth-century novel and film studies owe to eighteenth-century poetry and painting studies. George Bluestone, unilaterally designated the father of novel and film studies, entitled the first chapter of his 1957 *Novels into Film* "The Limits of the Novel and the Limits of the Film," after Lessing's subtitle to his *Laocoön: An Essay upon The Limits of Painting and Poetry*. In this chapter, he follows Lessing's categorizations of poetry and painting, designating the novel as conceptual, linguistic, discursive, symbolic, and inspiring mental imagery, with time as its formative principle, and the film as perceptual, visual, presentational, literal, and given to visual images, with space as its formative principle.[12] Just as Lessing had done, Bluestone presses for a separation of representational spheres on the basis of these differences: "The film and the novel [should] remain separate institutions, each achieving its best results by exploring unique and specific properties."[13]

Where Bluestone neglects a central eighteenth-century distinction between poetry and painting, other scholars breach the gap. For example,
James Monaco in 1977 echoes Samuel Johnson's claim in 1745 that "The
business of the poet . . . is to examine, not the individual, but the species;
to remark general properties and large appearances: he does not number
the streaks of the tulip" with his identical argument that the word "rose"
refers to no particular rose, but rather to the general category of rose,
while a film must show a specific rose. Here, he even replicates Johnson's
floral illustration.[14]

While Lessing's classifications waged war on interart analogies,
Bluestone aimed his against the practice of literary film adaptation. The
two are integrally connected. Interart analogies speak of one art in terms
of another, as though they were in some way each other; adaptation purports to fulfill such analogies by making one art into the other. Bluestone's
categorical distinctions, set in opposition to literary film adaptation, find
their epitome in the maxim pervasive in critical, practitioner, and lay
discussions of novels and film that "You can't make a good film from a
good book." First advanced on New Critical grounds by film scholar Béla
Balázs in 1952, the maxim builds on the concept that "the adaptation of
a content to a different art form can only be detrimental to a work of art
if that work of art was good. In other words, one may perhaps make a
good film out of a bad novel, but never out of a good one."[15] Balázs's arguments were subsequently promulgated by filmmaker François Truffaut
and novelist Anthony Burgess. Truffaut's declaration that "a masterpiece
is something that has already found its perfection of form, its definitive
form" is regularly juxtaposed to Burgess's claim that "brilliant adaptations
are nearly always of fiction of the second or third class."[16] The maxim is
so widely accepted that it appears as fact rather than myth in *The Complete Film Dictionary*'s definition of "adaptation": "Great novels have always
been more resistant to adaptation."[17]

Bluestone is as widely cited in his field as Lessing is in his. But, unlike
poetry and painting studies, which debate Lessing's premises,[18] novel and
film studies have maintained Bluestone's taxonomy without demur: even
postmodern scholars who deplore the political dimensions of formalist
agendas cite Bluestone as an authority on formal matters.[19]

More important than emulating challenges to Lessing within poetry
and painting scholarship, however, is questioning why categorizations
developed for purely verbal and purely visual arts have been applied without modification to hybrid verbal/visual arts – to illustrated novels and to
worded films. Novels are not poems; films are not paintings. Novels have

been illustrated: nineteenth-century novels in particular are brimful of pictorial initials, vignettes, full-page plates, frontispieces, and endpieces. Films abound in dialogue, intertitles, subtitles, voice-over narration, credits, and graphic words on sets and props. Yet scholars continue to designate the novel "words" and the film "images" and to define them according to Lessing's categorizations of poetry and painting. This application has broader implications than those of the novel and film debate since, in the twentieth century, Lessing's categorizations of poetry and painting came to emblematize distinctions between the verbal and the visual more generally.

In the mid-1970s, Robert Scholes did suggest that, if Lessing "were brought back to life again today, he would recognize in cinema the reconciliation of the parts of his divided world."[20] Yet Scholes's more plausible application of Lessing's work had no lasting impact: Bluestone's more problematic application holds sway. To cite just a few examples from among hundreds, in the late 1970s, Keith Cohen set up detailed and complex narratological categories and codes under which to study novels and films, yet wrote of literary film adaptation more crudely as "seeing words changed into images."[21] Cohen's representation of adaptation as "words to images" takes into account neither the word-to-word transfer of a novel's dialogue or narration nor the ways in which illustrations have been copied by filmmakers nor a host of other similar interchanges. Similarly, in the 1980s, J. Dudley Andrew, one of the most widely reprinted scholars of literary film adaptation, wrote of "the absolutely different semiotic systems of film and language."[22] Andrew's assertion of "the absolutely different semiotic systems of film and language" does not offer any account of verbal language in film. In the 1990s, after acknowledging that film draws on a combination of visual, aural, and verbal signifiers, Brian McFarlane continued to designate the novel linear, the film spatial, the novel conceptual, and the film perceptual, after Lessing's categorizations of poetry and painting.[23] Logically, however, if films contain words and if words are linear, temporal, conceptual, and symbolic, then film must to some degree be linear, temporal, conceptual, and symbolic as well.

These categorizations hold fast even when novels and films are discussed separately. Indeed, as subsequent chapters argue, theories of the novel and of the film within their separate disciplines appear to have been significantly influenced by interdisciplinary rivalries and their feeding into ancient word and image wars. No theory of the novel to date offers any account of novel illustrations. In the 1960s, Christian Metz eliminated film words from his otherwise thoroughgoing and detailed semiotics of film, arguing that "a true definition of 'cinematographic specificity' can...only be made on two levels: that of filmic discourse and that of image discourse."[24] Apart from word and image rivalries, such a claim is unaccountable in the work of such a meticulous scholar.

Clearly, the designation of novels as "words" and of films as "images" is neither empirically nor logically sustainable: rather, it participates in ancient representational rivalries. W. J. T. Mitchell has demonstrated that "the history of culture is in part the story of a protracted struggle for dominance between pictorial and linguistic signs."[25] In spite of their verbal–visual hybridity, novels and films have become just so much more fodder in the word and image wars. Everywhere, novels and films are seen to wrangle in a relationship that Bluestone describes as "overtly compatible, secretly hostile."[26] In the end, however, novels and films tend to unravel the very word and image divide they have been conscripted to uphold, since novels contain pictures and undertake pictorial effects and films contain words and undertake verbal effects. And, as Chapters 2 and 3 detail, the battle between pictorial and linguistic signs rages inside illustrated novels and inside worded films as well as between them.

By contrast, the analogical strain has received short shrift in twentieth-century interart metacriticism. Henryk Markiewicz's survey of the poetry and painting debate focuses almost exclusively on its categorical strain, omitting any discussion of nineteenth-century British interart theory.[27] Mitchell – the single twentieth-century scholar to suggest that interart analogies have not been taken far enough – and I agree with him – also skips over those unruly Victorians and their tumultuous interart analogies, moving directly from the Romantic period to the twentieth century in the case studies of his *Iconology*.[28] Even those who specialize in Victorian interart theory and practice are skeptical of Victorian interart analogies. Although Meisel acknowledges that "where the arts are concerned...analogy is a legitimate mode of action," he nevertheless warns that it is "the work of the imagination, and risks degradation from the imaginative to the imaginary," lamenting that "unregulated analogy" has been the "plague" of serious scholarship.[29] In a similar vein, Elizabeth Abel, who argues compellingly for a "diachronic approach" to interart theory, warns of the "dangers of impressionistic" nineteenth-century interart analogies, demonstrating that they do not hold up under rigorous stylistic comparisons.[30]

Yet outside the humanities in the cognitive and natural sciences, analogy garners considerable respect as a mental and pedagogical model. There is a growing consensus that

Analogy and similarity play a central role in conceptual change. Analogy allows the application of preexisting conceptual structures to new problems and domains, and hence supports the rapid learning of new systems. Of all the learning processes, analogy is the only one that offers a mechanism for the acquisition of substantial knowledge structures in a brief span of learning. By contrast, other learning processes, such as generalization, differentiation, accretion, or compilation, offer ways of refining, adding to or consolidating an existing system of beliefs.[31]

In this account, differentiation (which includes categorical differentiation) feeds existing systems of belief, while analogy enables understanding across systems and the rapid learning of new systems. Analogy should thus constitute an ideal model for interdisciplinary discourse – for learning across systems and for discovering new ways to approach interart criticism.

But despite its higher valuation in the sciences, only a structurally constrained model of analogy is allowed there. Dedre Gentner and Michael Jeziorski chronicle the evolution of analogy in the sciences, rejecting older analogical models, like those of medieval alchemists, as "chaotic metaphor." They favor a structurally constrained model of analogy, which they define as one maintaining structural consistency, relational focus, and systematicity, allowing no extraneous associations or mixed analogies, making clear that analogy is not causation, and representing no essential connections between the analogically related entities, – only structural ones. Gentner and Jeziorski figure the shift from medieval analogy to structural analogy as scientific progress, implying a connection between false analogies and false scientific theories and between "true" analogies and "true" scientific theories. Alchemical analogies, which claim the interconnectedness of all things, they argue, were proven false by the alchemists' failure to transmute base metals into gold. The authors further attach the misguided belief in the interconnectedness of all things to base, mercenary motivations, in contrast to the objective, high-minded scientific inquiry of modern scientists.[32]

Intriguingly, Babbitt's excoriation of interart analogies distinctly resembles Genter's and Jerziorski's castigations of alchemical ones. He too lambastes analogies for representing false relations between the arts and for promulgating false aesthetic theories, viewing them as self-indulgent emotional rhapsodies rather than indicators of objective, intellectual academic inquiry. Where Gentner and Jeziorski welcome structural constraints on analogy, Babbitt recommends "the broad, masculine, and vigorous distinction" of categorization to remedy the excesses of analogy.[33] But as the following case study indicates, categorical distinctions bring as much confusion to novel and film studies as the most impressionistic of analogies. In illustrated novels and worded films, pictures can operate according to the features and functions traditionally assigned to words, and words can function according to the features and functions conventionally assigned to pictures.

Picturing Words/Wording Pictures

One of the most striking points of dislocation from my initial research occurred when, bred on Bluestone and (unknowingly then) on Lessing, I turned to illustrated novels and intertitled silent films to clarify just exactly how words and pictures represent in each medium. I assumed that the sharp divisions of prose and illustrations in illustrated novels and of verbal intertitles and filmed scenes in silent films would provide a baseline of categorical word and image operations from which to consider the more complex visual/verbal blends of verbal imagery, visual symbolism, symbolic gestures, and film images interacting with dialogue on soundtracks. But the material immediately thwarted this plan at even the most surface levels: words appear in novel illustrations and in filmed scenes; pictures embellish the initial letters of prose chapters and garnish film intertitles. Determined to establish some kind of baseline, I turned doggedly to points where words and pictures purport to represent the same character, plot, event, location, or concept, after narratological models. I quickly discerned that such analyses would fail to offer any account of interactions between words and images inside or between novels and films. My readings instead produced an effect of autopsy or taxidermy. But when I turned to examine points of interchange between words and images and other verbal and pictorial forms, a lively exchange emerged in which categorical differentiations unraveled and new interdisciplinary dynamics emerged.

While illustrated novels and intertitled silent films offer ample support for traditional verbal/visual differentiations, they defy their universality at points where words take on properties conventionally associated with images and where images take on properties conventionally associated with words. At other points, traditional categorizations used to distinguish words from images instead distinguish words from other words and images from other images. In yet other instances, both sides of a traditional categorical visual/verbal distinction coexist within a single verbal or pictorial sign.

Visual/verbal categorizations break down at every level in the hybrid arts of illustrated novels and worded films: at the level of the whole arts, at the level of whole signs, and at the level of pieces of signs. As an example of the first, early film intertitles often frame their words in borders resembling painting frames and place artist signatures in the bottom right-hand corner of these frames after painting conventions. For example, each narrative intertitle of Edison's 1915 *Vanity Fair* is framed by a plain white border and signed "The Edison Studios" in the bottom right corner. In this practice (common to many early films), words are framed as pictures. The filmed scenes, however, are not accorded such pictorial frames. Conversely, the signs and gestures of actors in the filmed scenes turn pictorial representation into language. Fingers point, "Get out!" or "He went that way"; heads shake "No" or "Yes"; open palms demand, "Give me that!" or offer, "Here, take this"; clenched fists denote "I'll be revenged!"; and kisses say, "I love you." In such early film conventions, film words cross-dress as pictures and film pictures cross-dress as words.

Hybrid arts raise more philosophical vexings of word and image differentiations. For instance, Samuel Johnson's claim that images represent specifically, while words represent generally, echoed in James Monaco's discussion of novels and films two centuries later, finds both support and contradiction when words and images interact in hybrid art forms. Supporting the distinction, the verbal intertitles of Cecil Hepworth's 1913 *David Copperfield* describe a general state of affairs for which the filmed scenes provide specifics. One such intertitle reads: "My earliest recollections are those happy days spent with my mother." The ensuing scene specifies this general state of affairs, showing young David (Eric Desmond) skipping out of his house, joining his mother (actress uncredited) in their garden, plucking a rose, pinning it on her dress, hugging her, kissing her, and sitting on her lap.[34] Here, we even find Monaco's illustration of the aesthetic principle dramatized: the film does depict a specific rose.

But in other cases, an exactly opposite dynamic operates: words specify generic images. In Vitagraph's 1911 *A Tale of Two Cities*, intertitular words particularize generic actor bodies: an intertitle identifies a shot of an old man, a middle-aged man, and a baby in indeterminate historical dress as "Doctor Manette, his servant Defarge, and his infant daughter, Lucie." Throughout the film, and in silent films of this period more generally, intertitle words make ambiguous spaces specific places ("In England"; "In Paris"), specify undefined passages of time ("Eighteen years after the events of Part 1"), represent the exact words spoken nebulously by silently moving mouths ("Take this estate for the benefit of the people"), and explain the significance of uncertain scenes ("Darnay acquitted" follows indeterminate shots of a courtroom).

In between the two poles – the one, where images specify words, the other, where words specify images – lie more complex intersections. For example, when an intertitle dubs a handful of well-fed actors "The starving populace" in Vitagraph's *A Tale of Two Cities*, it pulls a specific group of actor bodies toward a larger historical significance at the same time that it lends a specific narrative significance to a generic group of actors.

Hybrid art forms put pressure on Lessing's most central categorization: the temporal and spatial dichotomy of words and images. Illustrated novels and worded films undermine this contradistinction at even the most superficial levels of analysis. While the more temporal thread of the narrative runs through the prose of illustrated novels, it runs through the pictorial scenes of early films. Concomitantly, illustrations appear as frozen moments in novels, while verbal intertitles emerge as frozen moments in films. Thus, words and pictures change temporal places. Indeed, the kinship between book illustrations and film intertitles is readily apparent in the widespread critical and reviewer rhetoric that makes book illustrations "distractions" from the prose and film intertitles "interruptions" of the scenes. Donald Hannah, like many critics before and after him, complained in 1966 that the illustrations of *Vanity Fair* are "distractions" from the prose.[35] This term occupies a definitional place in discussions of book illustration: illustration historian Edward Hodnett, for example, defines "an illustration [as] a distraction."[36] A film reviewer complained similarly of intertitles in 1912:

> One often has a feeling of irritation at having a scene interrupted, and when the scene is resumed, it often takes one an appreciable time to readjust one's mind. The continuity of the scene is broken and the illusion is spoiled.[37]

In a similar vein, a reviewer of F. W. Murnau's *The Last Laugh* rejoiced in 1926 that "there are no subtitles at all to interrupt the mood [of the pictures]"[38] – and I stress that these passages represent only a few voices from among hundreds.

Just as a novel's prose carries the temporal narrative, with illustrations pulling out single frozen moments for visual and spatial contemplation, so too, the scenes of silent films carry the bulk of the temporal narrative, with intertitles "illustrating" (I use the phrase here in its earlier sense of verbal annotation).[39] For example, an intertitle in the 1912 film *Little Nell*, which adapts scenes from Charles Dickens's *The Old Curiosity Shop*, reads: "Nell's grandfather robs her of the money she has saved." The scenes that follow present a far more temporally extensive narrative than do the words: they depict the grandfather stealing Nell's purse from the fairground booth, fleeing, meeting a group of gamblers, entering a gaming shanty with them, gambling away the money, and being mocked and ejected from the game.[40] Moreover, compared to the sequential dramatic scenes, the present tense of the intertitle renders the verbal portion of the film far more of a present tense affair than the film images, further rupturing Lessing's categorizations of verbal and visual signs. The pictures of novels and the words of early films occupy the more temporally static position in each form, appearing as stop-action moments excerpting, amplifying, annotating, and illustrating the moving prose and film scenes, respectively. In these hybrid arts, we see especially clearly that stasis and movement are relative effects not essentially tied to verbal or visual forms.

The disintegration of Lessing's temporal/spatial opposition runs within hybrid arts as well as between them. Although Lessing's distinction seems to hold in illustrated novels, where the main thread of temporal narrative runs through the prose and where illustrations appear as frozen moments, this categorical distinction also unravels at points. The vignettes of Thackeray's *Vanity Fair*, for example, are combinations of movement and freezing – instances where Lessing's categorical opposition of movement and stasis merge in a single pictorial form. Interspersed between lines of moving prose, they at times seem to leap out from that movement, carrying with them both the mobility of the prose and their own mobile pictorial leap from it, freezing momentarily before diving into the prose stream again. But even this freezing does not constitute total stasis, for the mobile lines and vigorous strokes of vignettes suggest captured motion rather than stop-action. If they do freeze a moment, part of what they freeze is the temporal mobility of that moment.

The notion of vignettes as arrested mobile moments leaping from a stream of fluid prose and then plunging back into it finds continuities in early film. In 1896, Maxim Gorky documented the practice in which early films began with freeze frames and then plunged into cinematic movement:

> When the lights go out in the room in which Lumière's invention is shown, there suddenly appears on the screen a large grey picture, "A Street in Paris" – shadows of a bad engraving ... you anticipate nothing new in this all too familiar scene, for you have seen pictures of Paris streets more than once. But suddenly a strange flicker passes through the screen and the picture stirs to life. Carriages coming from somewhere in the perspective of the picture are moving straight at you ... somewhere from afar people appear and loom larger as they come closer to you. ...[41]

Like the mobile vignettes of novels, the *tableaux* of nineteenth-century theater that froze scenes before the curtain fell, and the *tableaux vivants* that arrested live actors in the poses of famous paintings, early films share an oscillation between static and mobile representation.

Temporal contrasts exist between various forms of pictures as well as between a hybrid art's words and pictures. The full-page plates of *Vanity Fair* generally appear less mobile than its vignettes. The steel-plate technology of their production required them to be set apart from the prose: thus, they do not leap from words midparagraph or midsentence, but rather remain in their own discrete space. The steel-plate technology further allows for finer graphic lines and a more formal, finished look, while the wood-engraving technology of the vignettes results in a rougher, sketchier effect, more likely to suggest motion. In keeping with these technological and draughting differences, characters on full-page plates are generally more formally posed than for their vignettes. They have stopped moving to sit for their portraits; they have arrested themselves for the picture, rather than been arrested by the picture. By contrast, the vignettes more commonly appear to have captured characters in motion through swift sketching.

Nowhere are such contrasts more apparent than in the vignette and full-page plate representing *Vanity Fair*'s Miss Swartz (Figures 1 and 2).[42] In her vignette, she seems to spring from the very prose line that describes her into the picture that depicts her. The almost seamless leap is aided by various formal techniques. Just as film quickly learned to cut on character movement to hide transitions between shots, so too, Thackeray makes his "cut" from prose to vignette on Miss Swartz's movement, on her spinning round on a stool, which she does in both prose and picture. And, just as early filmmakers deduced that matched shots – adjoining shots matching one or more elements, such as camera movement, camera angle, character position, or shot size – effect smoother, less jarring transitions, so too, Thackeray transitions smoothly from prose to vignette and back again on referential matches between words and pictures, gesturing alike to Miss Swartz, her movement, and the music stool. Moreover, her lips in the vignette are parted in a formulation of the prose speech that appears on either side of the illustration, so that a piece of prose appears to have flown from prose to picture and back to prose again. That both prose and vignette can represent the uttered syllable with graphic shapes connects word and picture even more closely. The verbal syllable is read as a grapheme and pronounced as a phoneme; the pictorial syllable is seen on the depicted lips as a phonetic shape. The reader thereby shifts fluidly from prose reading to lip reading, from the graphic–phonetic elements of prose to the graphic–phonetic elements of picture.

182   VANITY FAIR.

The sisters began to play the Battle of Prague. "Stop that d—— thing," George howled out in a fury from the sofa. "It makes me mad. *You* play us something, Miss Swartz, do. Sing something, anything but the Battle of Prague."

"Shall I sing Blue Eyed Mary, or the air from the Cabinet?" Miss Swartz asked.

"That sweet thing from the Cabinet," the sisters said.

"We 've had that," replied the misanthrope on the sofa.

"I can sing Fluvy du Tajy," Swartz said, in a meek voice, "if I had the words." It was the last of the worthy young woman's collection.

"O, Fleuve du Tage," Miss Maria cried; "we have the song," and went to fetch the book in which it was.

Now it happened that this song, then in the height of the fashion, had been given to the young ladies by a young friend of theirs, whose name was on the title, and Miss Swartz, having concluded the ditty with George's applause, (for he remembered that it was a favourite of Amelia's), was hoping for an encore perhaps, and fiddling with the leaves of the music, when her eye fell upon the title, and she saw "Amelia Sedley" written in the corner.

"Lor!" cried Miss Swartz, spinning swiftly round on the music-stool,

1. William Makepeace Thackeray's vignette of Miss Swartz, in Chapter 21 of *Vanity Fair* (London: Bradbury & Evans, 1848). Courtesy of the Bancroft Library, University of California, Berkeley.

Within the vignette itself, the lines flow with far more motility than those of the decorous full-page portrait that depicts Miss Swartz's dressing by the Osborne sisters. In the vignette, the lines of her gown cascade in multidirectional swirls. By contrast, the Miss Swartz of the plate is more sedately posed, the lines of her dress lines falling evenly and unidirectionally, evincing only a tiny ripple where an Osborne sister adjusts the skirt.

Miss Swartz rehearsing for the Drawing Room

2. William Makepeace Thackeray's "Miss Swartz Rehearsing for the Drawing-Room," a plate in Chapter 21 of *Vanity Fair* (London: Bradbury & Evans, 1848). Courtesy of the Bancroft Library, University of California, Berkeley.

The widely discussed lines of her racial caricature also vary from mobile vignette to posed full-page plate. In the vignette, her caricatured features exude a vitality and spontaneity that spread through the lines of her costume. In the plate, however, her features are frozen in a half-wild glare, in striking contrast to her sedate and formal dress. The plate, then, points to an incongruity between her racially coded body and her culturally coded clothes: her face peers out from her couture as an untamed region in an otherwise Westernized body. In the vignette, however, Miss Swartz's expressive vitality (also racially coded) sweeps Western accouterments into its own flow, dominating and refiguring them.

Just as mobility and stasis vary between types of pictures, so too, they vary between types of prose. While this point has, of course, been widely established elsewhere, certain aspects of it bear more pertinently on verbal/visual categorizations of novels and films. It is well documented that film inherited many conventions from many art forms. Intertitling practices are no exception, deriving from multiple sources: from theatrical scene headings, painting titles, opera, ballet, and mime synopses, newspaper headlines, and more, as well as from chapter titles in novels. In keeping with this book's focus on relations between novels and films, I can address only this last connection and only in terms of the temporal/stasis dichotomy at hand. My research indicates that temporal relations between novel chapter titles and novel chapters resemble those between early film intertitles and early film scenes. Thackeray's *Vanity Fair* again serves as an illustrative and representative example. Its chapter titles (when they bear any tense at all) are cast in the present tense, as in "Miss Sharp Begins to Make Friends," "In Which Mr. Osborne Takes Down the Family Bible," and "In Which the Reader Is Introduced to the Very Best of Company." The narration of the chapters themselves, however, is cast in various past tenses, with one exception: those places where the narrator steps outside of the story to address the reader. What we see here is that reading and reader occupy the present tense, as do narration and narrator, while the story's characters live and its events occur in the past tense. That the present tense of a novel's chapter titles differs little from the present tense of a film's intertitles calls into question widespread claims that film has only a present tense and that this present tense differentiates film from literature.[43] There is nothing to stop us from regarding film scenes as past deeds presently narrated, just as we do in novels. Practically speaking, film scenes are recordings of past deeds performed before a witnessing camera, which presents them to present viewers. Indeed, one might argue that film's present tense derives from the novel rather than existing in contradistinction to it.

Temporal patterns that place narration and reading in the present tense and what is narrated in the past tense not only deconstruct contrasts between novels and films and words and pictures, but also concepts of time and space. In Chapter 1 of *Vanity Fair*, the narrator narrates the story in the past tense:

> ... when the day of departure came, between her two customs of laughing and crying, Miss Sedley was greatly puzzled how to act. She was glad to go home, and yet most wofully [sic] sad at leaving school. . . . She had to make and receive at least fourteen presents, – to make fourteen promises of writing every week ...

But pondering his readers, the narrator shifts to a strangely mixed future and present tense:

> All which details, I have no doubt, JONES, who reads this book at his Club, will pronounce to be excessively foolish, trivial, twaddling, and ultra-sentimental. Yes; I can see Jones at this minute (rather flushed with his joint of mutton and half-pint of wine), taking out his pencil and scoring under the words "foolish, twaddling," & c., and adding to them his own remark of "quite true."[44]

While Jones begins as a projected future reader, the present tense of reading is so strong that he is sucked into its vortex "at this minute." The present tense of reading here emerges as a universal present that swallows up all other tenses, whether past writing, present narration, or future reading. It impinges on authorship itself, yoking past writing and printing with future annotation in the voracious present acts of narrating and reading.

Thackeray reinforces this conjuring of past writing, present narrating, and future reading into present presence by interjecting a vignette of Jones reading the very book that describes him, writing in the very book that has written him (Figure 3). The narrator's "I can see Jones at this minute" passes into a visual representation of him for the reader-viewer, who can also see him now, at this minute. In this pictorial translation (a translation in two senses – of prose to picture and of future reader to present annotator) we see not only that illustration can do exactly what prose does – unite many tenses – but also that it can do so along spatial as well as temporal axes. Temporally speaking, Jones reads the book that has predicted him as a future reader, a book that has already been written, printed, and sold. His future presence thus casts a long shadow into the past, which in turns casts a long foreshadow into the future. Spatially speaking, Jones holds the book that holds him and writes in the

A NOVEL WITHOUT A HERO. 5

and good-natured a person. As she is not a heroine, there is no need to describe her person; indeed I am afraid that her nose was rather short than otherwise, and her cheeks a great deal too round and red for a heroine; but her face blushed with rosy health, and her lips with the freshest of smiles, and she had a pair of eyes, which sparkled with the brightest and honestest good-humour, except indeed when they filled with tears, and that was a great deal too often; for the silly thing would cry over a dead canary-bird, or over a mouse, that the cat haply had seized upon, or over the end of a novel, were it ever so stupid; and as for saying an unkind word to her, were any one hard-hearted enough to do so,— why, so much the worse for them. Even Miss Pinkerton, that austere and god-like woman, ceased scolding her after the first time, and though she no more comprehended sensibility than she did Algebra, gave all masters and teachers particular orders to treat Miss Sedley with the utmost gentleness, as harsh treatment was injurious to her.

So that when the day of departure came, between her two customs of laughing and crying, Miss Sedley was greatly puzzled how to act. She was glad to go home, and yet most wofully sad at leaving school. For three days before, little Laura Martin, the orphan, followed her about, like a little dog. She had to make and receive at least fourteen presents,—to make fourteen solemn promises of writing every week: "Send my letters under cover to my grandpapa, the Earl of Dexter," said Miss Saltire (who, by the way was rather shabby): "Never mind the postage, but write every day, you dear darling," said the impetuous and woolly-headed, but generous and affectionate Miss Swartz; and little Laura Martin (who was just in round hand) took her friend's hand and said, looking up in her face wistfully, "Amelia, when I write to you I shall call you Mamma." All

which details, I have no doubt, JONES, who reads this book at his Club,

3. William Makepeace Thackeray's vignette of Jones, in Chapter 1 of *Vanity Fair* (London: Bradbury & Evans, 1848). Courtesy of the Bancroft Library, University of California, Berkeley.

book that has written him. These impossible temporal and spatial representations serve to undermine temporal and spatial conventions. The temporal Jones future reads the temporal Jones past reading the temporal Jones future, *ad infinitum*. The pictorial Jones holds the book that holds a vignette of him holding the book, and so on, into spatial infinity. Temporal omniscience thus allies and intersects with spatial infinity, pressing the verbal away from the temporal qualities accorded it and the pictorial away from the spatial boundaries that Lessing and others bestowed on it.

Despite the voracity of the present tense, Jones is, paradoxically, never really present. He is prescience, not presence; he is possibility, not actuality, despite his vivid presentation. In much the same way, chapter titles, though grammatically cast in the present tense, are not solidly and simply present either: rather, they are blends of past and future – they are foreknowledge of upcoming narration that will presently be narrated as past. To put the equation more spatially, chapter titles are like packet labels detailing ingredients: they point to what has been already packaged and to what the reader can expect to consume as well as to what is present in the package.

Even from these brief introductory analyses (and I could indicate a thousand more were that the sole purpose of this book), it is readily apparent that the words and images of illustrated novels and early films exhibit far more variable features and engage in far more complex functions than the Lessing-derived categorical model allows. That in some cases, categorical tenets reverse and that in others, they are relative and variable places in question the validity and usefulness of these paradigms for the novel and film debate. Pressing this even further, one wonders if traditional distinctions between words and images are variable to the point of collapse in hybrid word and image arts: what maintains them between so-called pure arts? Indeed, one questions whether "pure" arts have been valued more highly precisely because they preclude such testings and underminings of word and image oppositions and, concomitantly, whether the long-standing resistance to hybrid arts (whether their aesthetic excoriation or the denial of their very existence in aesthetic theories of novels and films) is motivated chiefly by the challenges they present to word and image oppositions. At this point, one is tempted to throw out categorical approaches altogether but, as we will see, such a step is premature if one would understand relations between novels and films and between analogical and categorical approaches to their study.

Categorizing Analogies/Analogizing Categories

We have seen that Lessing propounded categorization of the arts to counter eighteenth-century interart analogies, that Babbitt recommended their categorization to counter the excesses of nineteenth-century interart analogies as well as interart adaptations, and that

Bluestone advocated categorization to redress the practice of literary film adaptation, which literalizes interart analogies by making so-called cinematic novels into cinema. It appears, then, that interart categorization separates the arts, while interart analogy and adaptation link them. But categorizing and analogizing are not so essentially opposed as they at first appear.

Many categories are based on analogies. Mitchell astutely observes that categorical distinctions between poetry and painting are themselves founded on analogies between formal signs and abstract concepts:

> ...the differentiation of the arts follows the classic pattern of figurative discourse: it tries to explain something we think we don't understand (...the difference between text and image) by comparing it to something we think we do understand (the difference, say, between the natural and the conventional, or the temporal and the spatial).

He concludes: "The theoretical discriminations between text and image serve more to mystify than to clarify the difference."[45]

What's more, Lessing based his categories on analogies between form and content. A line in *Bullinger's Decades* (1577) indicates that this form of analogy was operative much earlier: "Analogie is an aptnes, proportion and a certaine conuenance of the signe to ye thing signified."[46] Lessing's turn toward categorization, then, does not abandon analogy, but rather privileges analogies between an art's form and its content over analogies between art forms.

Looking further, one discovers that many interart categories were once interart analogies. In 2000, Monaco wrote: "Ever since the beginning of film history, theorists have been fond of comparing film with verbal language ... but it wasn't until a new, larger category of thought developed in the late fifties and early sixties [semiotics] ... that the *real* study of film as a language could proceed."[47] Changes in semiotic theory and rhetoric, then, have turned interart analogies (half-truths) into "real" categories, into "truth." "New, larger categor[ies] of thought," it seems, have power to substantiate analogies as "real." In this way, categorization functions as a laundering system for analogies, legitimating them for scholarly circulation.

Promotions of implicitly "false" and illegitimate analogies to "real" and legitimate subjects of scholarship have served primarily to place some arts in subjection to others. In the instance of the film language analogy, the categorical legitimation of film as a "real" language subjugates it to methods and models derived from linguistics. Metz objects to the dominance of linguistics in film semiotics: "In theory, linguistics is only a branch of semiotics, but in fact semiotics was created from linguistics."[48] Such a subjugation is by no means the unproblematic matter that many scholars, who write blithely of films and books alike as "texts," assume. Once films are decreed "texts" in a literal rather than analogical sense, they become subject to textual evaluations and textual concerns. David Bordwell complains that Roland Barthes's application of semiotics to film implicitly makes language the master system.[49] While culturally speaking, Barthes's recategorization of nonverbal representations as "texts" has had certain leveling and democratizing effects, in terms of interdisciplinary dynamics, his rhetoric continues the long-standing favoring of words over pictures and subjugates pictorial signs to linguistic paradigms. Interestingly, interart analogies play a major role in Barthes's subjection of the pictorial to the verbal: "Pictures become a kind of writing as soon as they are meaningful: like writing, they call for a *lexis* ... a photograph will be a kind of speech for us in the same way as a newspaper article." Meaning for Barthes is here synonymous with verbal language. While photographs become speech to be studied with literary methods "in the same way as a newspaper article," nowhere in this essay does Barthes suggest that writing be conversely and reciprocally subjected to pictorial terms and parameters. Barthes's theorization is unidirectional: "This generic way of conceiving language is in fact justified by the very history of writing: long before the invention of our alphabet, objects like the Inca *quipu*, or drawings, as in pictographs, have been accepted as speech."[50] But these very pictographs made speech pictures just as much as they made pictures speech.

When narratology replaced semiotics as the dominant critical model of novel and film studies, the categorical subjugation of pictorial forms to verbal paradigms through interart analogy continued. Keith Cohen's decree that "narrativity is the most solid median link between novel and cinema, the most pervasive tendency of both verbal and visual languages" turns interart analogy into an overarching category derived from literature (narrative) under which film is subsumed. Cohen's reference to "verbal and visual languages" links novels and films under a shared noun category, differentiating them only adjectivally.[51] Calvin Pryluck is one of several critics to protest such subjection, arguing that "language-based units, terminology, and analysis can by reduction direct attention from those aspects that may be unique to film."[52] Mitchell holds any verbal criticism of visual art in suspicion: "The very notion of a theory of pictures suggests an attempt to master the field of visual representation with a verbal discourse."[53]

Further confusing oppositions, categories and analogies frequently muddle at various levels of categorization. Cognitive theorist Eleanor Rosch has shown that categorical distinctions hold most firmly in cognition at what she calls the "basic level of categorization," defined as the one at which category members are recognized most rapidly, the highest level at which category members share perceived shapes, the highest level at which an image can stand for the category, the level coded earliest in the language, and the level learned first by children.[54] So, in a vertical categorical chain that descends from everything to physical objects to organisms to vertebrates to mammals to cats to domestic cats to tabby cats to my tabby cat, "cats" would constitute the basic level of categorization. More relevant to this discussion (though a little more unruly and arbitrary than a biological chain), in a categorical line that descends from everything to physical objects to representational objects to books to novels to illustrated Victorian novels to *Vanity Fair* to my copy of *Vanity Fair*, "books" would constitute the basic level of categorization. Similarly, in a line that runs from everything to physical objects to representational objects to films to fiction films to dramatic fiction films to literary film adaptations to film adaptations of *Vanity Fair* to the 1935 adaptation of *Vanity Fair* to my videocassette copy of the 1935 adaptation of *Vanity Fair*, "films" would be the basic level of categorization. It is at these basic levels of categorization – the levels of "books" and "films" – that categorical opposition appears greatest. Higher up at the level of representational objects or lower down at the level where novel and film share the title *Vanity Fair*, categorical oppositions weaken. At higher levels, categorical difference vanishes entirely: at the level of representational objects, for example, books and films belong to the same category. Here they are likely to be considered sister arts, sharing a categorical surname; at the basic level of categorization, however, they are more likely to be classified as different species.

We have seen that Lessing's categorizations of the visual and the verbal are relative and deconstructible. Here, we see that categorization itself is relative and deconstructible. Overarching categories prove unstable in other ways. One could argue that semiology and narratology – two overarching categories into which novels and films are regularly cast – also constitute subcategories of books and films, since they account for only some aspects of each. Even that monolith of an overarching category, cultural ideology (as pervasive in postmodern scholarship as ether once was in medieval philosophy), can be configured as a subcategory of books and films.

Far from representing "literal" truth in contrast to the half-truths of analogies, categories prove less elucidating of interdisciplinary interchanges and criticism than analogies, as this book will show. Indeed, categorical claims that falsely consign novels and films to word and image camps in defiance of aesthetic practices yield very little insight into anything except word and image rivalries – and they hide a great deal of the workings that word and image analogies reveal. The myths and half-truths of analogy paint a sharper picture of interdisciplinary exchanges and have shaped the practice, criticism, and theory of novels and films inside each discipline as well as their interdisciplinary engagements. In the final analysis, the relationship between categorical and analogical modes of criticism emerges not so much as a binary opposition as an analogy itself. Categorical claims to literal truth intersect with the figurative claims of analogies to create a larger analogy between novels and films: a play between perceived literal and nonliteral dimensions that resembles the play between literal and nonliteral dimensions of analogies.

2 Prose Pictures

Between the twentieth-century novel and film debate and the eighteenth-century poetry and painting debate from which it gleaned so many of its tenets and methodologies, lies another relevant word and image discourse. Art historian Richard D. Altick ascertains that "Missing from the art criticism of the Victorian era was much mention of the old *ut pictura poesis* concept, which was now a dead issue.... Replacing the theoretical issue of the sisterhood of the arts ... was the related one of illustration."[1] All sorts of books were illustrated in the nineteenth century. This chapter can only address illustrated novels, for these and the discourse on these run most directly into the novel and film debate.[2] While critics continue to make categorical distinctions between prose and illustration to the present day, this chapter focuses primarily on the discourse's neglected analogical interart rhetoric that speaks of prose as painting and of illustration as commentary.

Prose Painting/Illustration Commentary

In his preface to the second edition of *Oliver Twist*, Dickens refers to his writing by analogy to painting: "I had read of thieves by the score ... But I had never met (except in Hogarth) with the miserable reality. It appeared to me that to *draw* a knot of such associates ... to *paint* them in all their deformity ... would be a service to society."[3] Everywhere one turns in the nineteenth century, one finds novel writers aspiring to painting via similar interart analogies. To cite just a few examples, in 1843 Edward Bulwer-Lytton declared: "To my mind, a writer should sit down to compose a fiction as a painter prepares to compose a picture"[4]; in 1859 George Eliot opened *Adam Bede* with an analogical display of the magical hieroglyphic powers of her ink; in 1872 Thomas Hardy subtitled his

novel, *Under the Greenwood Tree*, "A Rural Painting in the Dutch School"; in
1881, Henry James published his prose *Portrait of a Lady*; in 1897 Joseph
Conrad wrote that fiction "must strenuously aspire . . . To the colour of
painting."[5] The reference to prose as painting is so pervasive that Mario
Praz nominated *ut pictura poesis* "the golden rule . . . of nineteenth-century
narrative literature."[6]

Similar rhetoric pervades periodical reviews of novels from the 1830s
into the early twentieth century. Indeed, it is difficult to find a review
that does not speak of prose in terms of painting, of characterizations as
portraits, of the novel as a canvas, of prose style in terms of painting techniques, or of writers by analogy to well-known painters. Critics have tested
the foundations for such analogies – particularly prose writers' aspirations
to realist, visual, and empirical modes of representation – and have found
them both plausible and wanting.[7] They have traced changing relations
and rivalries between authors and illustrators through correspondence,
contracts, salaries, reviews, popular responses, and even suicides.[8] But
no one has yet addressed how prose painting analogies, together with
counteranalogies that made illustrations verbal affairs, constructed theoretical and publishing relations between a novel's prose and illustrations
and later fed into the discourse on novels and films, constructing their
relation to one another as well.

My research into eighteenth-century poetry and painting debates,
nineteenth-century novel illustration debates, debates on the verbal intertitles and filmed scenes of early film, and twentieth-century novel
and film debates indicates that interart rhetoric and theories often follow dominant contemporary scientific theories. As we saw in Chapter 1,
Lessing adopted Linnaean methods of classification against classical concepts, fueling interart analogies. Similarly, early nineteenth-century interart analogies based in romantic theories of a shared imagination
derived an organicist impetus from contemporary scientific theory. Later
nineteenth-century discussions of novel illustration shift from analogies
based in organic imaginative unity to those favoring Darwinian dynamics,
where shared traits intensify competition, sister arts become sibling rivals,
and closely related species battle for the same territory. P. G. Hammerton's
1888 fictional debate on book illustration featuring an archetypal Poet
("representative of imaginative literature generally"), an Artist, a Critic,
and a Scientist, expresses just such a sense of territorial competition:

> . . . if illustrations are appreciated for high artistic reasons they are the
> more dangerous as rivals, and we who write have the stronger reasons for
> keeping them out. I say nothing against pictorial art in its own domains,

that is, on the walls of an exhibition or in a portfolio of prints, but I want to keep it out of ours.

In contrast to Lessing's grounds for separate spheres – categorical differentiations expressing essential differences recommending, in turn, different functions – here, the argument for separate spheres rests on essential similarities, similar functions, and shared rival territory. Hammerton's inclusion of a Scientist in this debate reinforces the link between interart and scientific theory. It is the Scientist who tells the Critic: "The conflict you speak of cannot be avoided. It is in the nature of things. But what strikes me is that when literature and art are put together it is generally literature that suffers."[9]

Analogies are particularly hospitable figures for Darwinian rivalries and usurpations predicated on "genetic" similarities. Before Dickens aspired to Hogarth in his preface to *Oliver Twist*, a review of his earlier *Sketches by Boz* had praised him by analogy to the then more celebrated illustrator, George Cruikshank: "Boz is the Cruikshank of writers."[10] Dickens subsequently secured Cruikshank to illustrate *Oliver Twist* and, after its initial success, aspired to greater analogical heights – as we saw earlier – to Hogarth himself, in whose style and after whose school Cruikshank drew. Hitherto it was Cruikshank who had been dubbed "the modern Hogarth."[11] Now Dickens shared these laurels by analogy. A review of *Oliver Twist* placed Dickens in rivalry with Cruikshank as Hogarth's successor: "What Hogarth was in painting, such very nearly is Mr. Dickens in prose fiction."[12]

More generally and pervasively, nineteenth-century authors and critics attached prose to painting by analogy in ways that undermined, trumped, and finally justified the excision of illustrations from novels. By likening prose to the higher, finer art of painting, critics raised it above the humbler art of illustration. First, authors and critics decked prose in the language of painting reverently and emulatively in a secondary and figurative sense. Subsequently they pressed the analogy with such frequency that it assimilated a more primary, literal, and conventional sense. These same critics invoked counteranalogies that made illustrations "commentaries" and other such verbal affairs. But far from equalizing the field, these analogies and counteranalogies combined to claim both the pictorial and the narrative redundancy of illustrations, contributing to their excision in publishing practice.

Before I turn to an examination of these rhetorical dynamics, two pictorial representations of author–illustrator relations at opposite ends of the nineteenth century – one published in 1827, the other in 1890 – forge an epitomatic pictorial "statement" of the case. An 1827 frontispiece for *Facetiae and Miscellanies* depicts author William Hone and illustrator George Cruikshank working at a shared desk, Hone writing prose with a pen, Cruikshank drawing illustrations with a pencil (Figure 4). Gerard Curtis reads in this illustration that "Writer and artist have equal weight in what are seen as analogous activities."[13] There are, however, subtle imbalances in these "analogous activities": while Cruikshank looks to Hone, Hone looks slightly away, indicating the dependence of illustrator on author for inspiration in contrast to the independent inspiration of the author. By 1890, author–illustrator representations had changed considerably. In George Du Maurier's drawing, the realist workaday setting of professional collaboration is reconfigured as a fanciful fencing match between a pen-wielding author and a pencil-wielding illustrator, their weapons decidedly enlarged – or they themselves decidedly diminished (Figure 5).[14] Author and illustrator are of equal stature and equally engaged. They look directly at each other: the focus is no longer on their work, but on their rivalry. No more are they joined by a shared work space or by an invisible thread of inspiration running through their eyes to an outer source. Rather, they are both conjoined and divided by the spine of the book, as each, quite literally, stands his occupational ground, the author adamant on his page, the illustrator resolute on his plate. Their battle is illuminated by a sun rising from (or setting behind?) an enormous ink pot. I read this enigmatic, bulbous, effulgent ink pot as representative of the flurry of critical discourse on the illustrated novel.

While many reviews of many Victorian novels offer similar evidence for this analysis, after pondering many candidates, I settled on William Makepeace Thackeray's *Vanity Fair* and its criticism as a case study. *Vanity Fair's* invocation in so many nineteenth-century writings on illustration indicates that it was a representative and exemplary case study in its own century. The relatively early publication, popularity, and many editions of *Vanity Fair* between 1847 and 1899 further present a wide array of reviewer commentaries across many decades, allowing one to trace changing attitudes toward prose and illustration, evolving fashions, theories, and technologies of illustration – changes that emerge more clearly when the reviewed novel remains constant. One could certainly trace many of these changes across other authors and illustrators, as J. R. Harvey has done. One could begin with Dickens and Cruikshank, progress to Trollope and Millais, then to Morris and Burne-Jones and Wilde and Beardsley. But such a study would be a book-length project in itself. *Vanity Fair* serves to coherently and succinctly pull out major rhetorical threads that feed into the discourse on early film and into the novel and

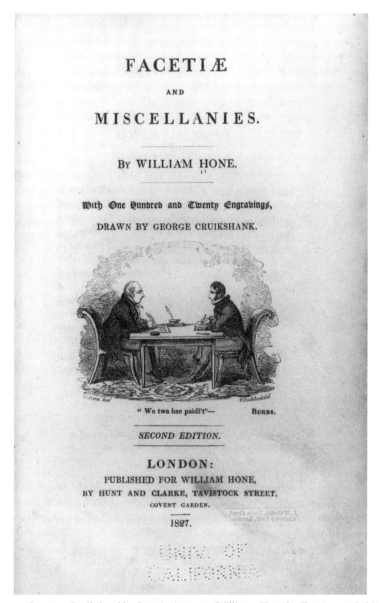

4. George Cruikshank's frontispiece to William Hone's *Facetiae and Miscellanies* (London: Hunt and Clarke, 1827). Courtesy of the Bancroft Library, University of California, Berkeley.

(*Drawn by George du Maurier. Engraved by J. Swain.*)

5. George Du Maurier's "An Edition de Luxe!", from his "The Illustrating of Books from the Serious Artist's Point of View" (*The Magazine of Art* XIII (1890): 375).

film debate. *Vanity Fair* is a special as well as a representative case, in that few authors illustrated their own novels. But for the purposes of this investigation, Thackeray's dual role as writer and illustrator is a distinct advantage, for it reduces the biographical variables that must be considered when authors and illustrators are different persons, allowing for a more intense and direct focus on prose–picture relations, both in the critical rhetoric used to describe them and in their interactions within the novel. Thackeray's dual role intriguingly literalizes analogies of the prose-writer-as-visual-artist, in that he is both. In addition, his pictorial initials test criticism and theory from aesthetic practice as analogies of prose pictures are tested against that form of pictured prose. The number and variety of *Vanity Fair*'s pictorial initials offer a rich range of material from which to test both these analogies and categorical distinctions made between verbal and pictorial signs.

Penning the Pencil: Prose Criticism of Illustrations

The subtitle of *Vanity Fair*'s first edition, "Pen and Pencil Sketches of English Society," yokes novel writing and novel illustration under the contemporaneous visual arts analogy "Sketches." From one angle of view, the placement of "Pen" within "Pen-cil" and the shared noun, "Sketches," place writing inside the domain of graphic art.[15] From another angle, the subtitle asserts the precedence of pen over pencil. Placed before "Pencil" as well as within "Pen-cil" as a *bona fide* word in its own right, "Pen" makes "Pencil" appear derivative and dependent, like a "Mrs." following a "Mr."[16] The matrimonial simile is by no means an arbitrary one in discussions of nineteenth-century illustration or in word and image studies more generally.[17] In 1842, the first issue of *The Illustrated London News* announced that it had made art the bride of literature.[18] An 1888 article on book illustration spoke similarly of "the [art] of the draughtsman ... married to immortal verse."[19] In 1899, a reviewer adduced: "we have in 'Vanity Fair' probably the finest example of the intimate wedding of pen and pencil, in the case of a novel, ever produced."[20] In *Vanity Fair*'s subtitular wedding, pen and pencil merge, yet remain distinct and vie for rhetorical dominance. On the one hand, the bride remains subjugated by her derivative title as well as by the cultural gender differential it expresses; on the other, the groom lies embedded in the bride's name and takes her surname, "Sketches," a word that describes her literally and him only analogically. These subtitular wranglings are representative of larger currents in illustration discourse.

By the time Thackeray's *Vanity Fair* was published, analogies of prose to painting and of novel writers to painters were so commonplace as to be conventional in reviews of novels, illustrated or not. Written character descriptions are "portraits," prose is "painting," books are "canvases," and prose styles are defined by analogy to painting styles. Reviews of *Vanity Fair* offer representative examples; similar analogies can be found everywhere in reviews of novels from the 1840s into the early twentieth century. In 1848, Elizabeth Rigby praised Thackeray's verbal characterization by analogy to *plein air* portraiture: "There is that mutual dependence in his characters which is the first requisite in painting every-day life: no one is stuck on a separate pedestal – no one is sitting for his portrait."[21] George Henry Lewes agreed: "We feel that he is painting after Nature."[22] In the same year, Robert Bell extended the analogy, equating the novel with a canvas: "Into this picture all sorts of portraits are freely admissible. There is nothing too base or too low to be huddled up in a corner of the canvass [sic]."[23] A writer for the *North British Review* comparing Dickens to Thackeray in 1851 determined that "it will assist us very much in our discriminations if we call to mind, by way of illustration, the leading distinctions of style and faculty in the kindred art of painting." Likening Thackeray to Hogarth, Wilkie, Maclise, and Watteau and comparing Dickens to Landseer, Leech, Wilkie, Rembrandt, and Maclise (rejecting, interestingly, the Dickens–Hogarth connection), this reviewer designates

Thackeray an artist of the "Real School of Low Art" and Dickens a writer in the "Ideal School of High Art."[24]

Such analogies persist in reviews of later editions of *Vanity Fair*. *Blackwood's Magazine*'s review of the 1855 edition notes that "There are certain portraits which convince us that they are admirable likenesses"; an 1881 reviewer declared Thackeray "a fine artist in words"; an 1898 reviewer claimed: "Thackeray's style, whatever we may determine of its absolute merits, is unquestionably discursive, and requires a large canvas for proper exercise"; and, in the next year, another reviewer likened Thackeray's "ease of style" to "Raphael's line."[25] These examples are representative rather than exhaustive, both of reviews of *Vanity Fair* and of Victorian novels more generally.

Prose painting analogies impinge on and limit the language that can be used to discuss novel illustrations. In 1848, Robert Bell devoted 13 pages to *Vanity Fair*'s prose and only a brief paragraph to the illustrations (this was typical). His account of the prose abounds in painting analogies:

> The life that is here painted is not that of high comedy, but of satiric farce ... He knows his sitters well and has drawn them to life ... he seizes upon the small details which make up the whole business of the kind of life he paints with a minuteness, precision, and certainty, and throws them out with a sharpness of outline and depth of colour rarely if ever equalled.

When Bell turns to the illustrations, he abandons the language of the fine arts, representing them in technological and generic terminology:

> We ought to say something about the illustrations of our artist-author, for he gathers laurels in both fields. The humour of the plates is broad and sketchy, and full of the same cynical spirit which pervades the text. The characterization is equally keen and striking. Becky is especially excellent ... [and] the grotesque Dobbin, the surly Osborne, the radiant O'Dowd, are all capital, and hit off at the top of their peculiarities with a bold and brilliant pencil.

The illustrations are not "pictures" but "plates" – a term emphasizing their technological reproduction rather than their artistic production (their drawing). The label further casts them hierarchically below "prose painting" on a visual arts spectrum as applied rather than fine art.[26] Alternatively, drawings of characters are not "portraits," but more generally and generically "characterization," again eliminating their artistic means of production.[27] While the final reference to the pencil does restore a glimmer of the illustrations' genesis, as does the reference to them as

"illustrations," both position illustrations below prose, which is "painting."
Adding to this hierarchical effect, pencil illustrations were often perceived as sketchy, preliminary stages of painting. Gleeson White, in 1897,
is one of many to document the condescending admiration that decreed
an illustration "a composition worthy of being painted."[28] That from an
objective empirical standpoint printed prose looks far less like painting
than does illustration attests to the power of analogy to override visual perception. Similar terminological usurpations extend across the century.
In 1881, Henry James's *The Portrait of a Lady* claims "portrait" for prose,
while Oscar Wilde's *The Picture of Dorian Gray* in 1891 adopts the more
generic term "picture" to describe a painted portrait. The overuse of "portrait" for prose characterization evidently required such a clarification.

Prose painting analogies grew more hostile and militant in the latter
decades of the nineteenth century. Again, reviewer responses to *Vanity Fair*
offer points of comparative and representative focus. Mid-nineteenth-
century reviewers do not generally engage in comparative criticism of
Vanity Fair's prose and illustrations. When they do, they either value the
drawings more highly ("Mr. Thackeray's pencil is more congenial than
his pen")[29] or, more commonly, equally with the prose ("he gathers laurels in both fields . . . The characterization is equally keen and striking";
"Mr. Thackeray can handle the pencil as well as the pen").[30] Reviewers in
the first half of the 1860s emphasized the collaborative and harmonious
relations of pen and pencil through analogies to other things or other
arts, avoiding usurping prose picture analogies. Henry Kingsley, for example, wrote of "these wonderful woodcuts" as "a key to the text"; John
Brown proclaimed: "how complete is the duet between the eye and the
mind, between word and figure."[31] Such analogies express complemen-
tary and egalitarian dynamics.

By the end of the century, however, reviewers emphasized prose –
illustration rivalries over their collaboration, both categorically and analogically. While some earlier critics compared Thackeray's drawings unfavorably to Cruikshank's, later critics invariably denigrated Thackeray's
illustrations by comparison to his prose. In 1899, George Somes Layard
adduced:

> Thackeray was a great humourist sent forth to war against the foibles
> and follies of our human nature, armed with two weapons – the [pencil]
> weak and faulty, the [pen] puissant and of sterling temper; the [pencil]
> inelastic and flaccid, the [pen] resilient and proof.

Layard's placement of the weakness in the pencil itself, rather than in its
wielder, points to a more essential hierarchical evaluation of prose and

illustration. Layard turns subsequently to appraise illustration, regardless of its artistic merit, in relation to prose: "Not that I would wish in any way to belittle the services rendered by the few good illustrators of books, but it must never be forgotten that they are, in a sense, but 'journeymen' compared with the originators of the thoughts which they are employed to interpret."[32] Layard's assessment establishes a class distinction between prose and illustration: illustrators are hired "journeymen" paid patronizing critical compliments for "services rendered," while writers are mystified as patriarchal "originators of thoughts" rather than mere practitioners of prose – their salaries, writing tools, and representational functions evaporated. That such a view appears in a piece on illustration in an art magazine indicates the overwhelmingly higher valuation of prose in the late nineteenth century.

Several factors contributed to such changing evaluations. *Vanity Fair* is again illustrative. The latter 1850s and 1860s ushered in "The Golden Age of English Illustration," a new style marked by greater mimeticism, a preference for ideal beauty, and an emphasis on technical polish, with John Everett Millais's illustrations for Anthony Trollope's novels offering prime examples. As illustration historians attest, it took some time for the new style to gain critical support; thus, evaluations of Thackeray's drawings in the early 1860s do not yet reflect these changes. Later critics, however, disparage Thackeray's illustrative technique along with the whole Hogarthian and Gillrayan school in which he drew. It took some years for the critical tide to turn fully against Thackeray's illustrations. His fame, the popular nostalgia associated with reeditions of his works, and *Vanity Fair*'s swift entrance into the literary canon afforded him a longer twilight than many others drawing in the same school. As late as 1880, a reviewer called *Vanity Fair* "one of the best illustrated books in the world." Yet the same reviewer, referring to an illustrated poem by Thackeray, pronounces: "The verses describe a beauty: the illustration gives a deformity, a monster."[33]

Increasingly, however, earlier styles of illustration came to be viewed as primitive precursors of the fuller, more detailed Golden Age and later realist styles, in much the same way that illustrations had been subordinated to prose "painting" as preliminary sketches or unfinished paintings. Russell Sturgiss describes Thackeray's illustrative style as one might a child's: as not "too accurate, not showing very profound insight ... never highly finished, never technically skillful, but generally full of a certain naive vigor, and often expressive and significant."[34] By the end of the century, changing illustrative fashions led to a complete rejection of Thackeray's style. Although he frequently suffered unfavorable comparisons to Cruikshank in every period of the nineteenth century, by the 1890s, the critical tide swept Cruikshank and Thackeray away in a single reviewer sentence that decreed both "simply rubbish."[35] Gleeson White, the best-known Victorian scholar of "Sixties Illustration," uses Thackeray as his chief example of what was wrong with pre-1860s styles of illustration. Of Thackeray and his ilk, he writes: "Their purpose seems to have been caricature, not character-drawing, sentimentality in place of sentiment, melodrama in lieu of mystery, broad farce instead of humour" and of their school of illustration, he adduces:

> Its "drawing" is often slipshod, and never infused by the perception of physical beauty that the Greeks embodied as their ideal .... Indeed, as you study the so-called "immortal" designs which illustrate the early Victorian novels, you feel that if many of the artists were once considered to be as great as the authors whose ideas they interpret, time has wreaked revenge at last.

In this period, advocates of prose and of newer styles of illustration allied to trounce older modes of illustration. "Time" in Gleeson's assessment appears to refer to a change in fashion that renders earlier fashions aesthetically "bad." Again, White turns to *Vanity Fair* as the proof text for his argument:

> If a boy happens to read for the first time Thackeray's *Vanity Fair* with its original illustrations, the humour and pathos of the masterpiece lose half their power when the ridiculously feeble drawings confront him throughout the book. This is not the case with Millais' illustrations to Trollope, or those by Fred Walker to Thackeray.[36]

Such critical views influenced publishing practice: a number of later editions of *Vanity Fair* replace Thackeray's illustrations with illustrations in the Golden Age style or in later nineteenth-century mimetic, realist, and photographic styles.[37] Very little has occurred subsequently to reverse these judgments against earlier styles of illustration. In 1970, illustration historian J. R. Harvey similarly compared Thackeray's drawings unfavorably with the Golden Age style and no subsequent critic has sprung to defend their pictorial merit.[38]

However, another defense of Thackeray's illustrations and illustrations in the Hogarthian school more generally has been mounted by the very critics who dismiss their pictorial value: a defense that poses counteranalogies to prose – picture analogies. Returning to Layard's 1899 evaluation of *Vanity Fair*, we find disparaged illustrations rescued from pictorial disrepute via verbal analogies:

> Who can forget the sense of fitness which has recommended to him
> these drawings, weak and insufficient in themselves, but so evidently
> imbued with the living literary conception?...So profound, indeed, is
> the intimacy of the two modes of expression that at times an illustration
> becomes an integral part, a phrase, so to speak, of the sentence itself.[39]

In Layard's rhetoric, the drawings are weak "in themselves" – that is, as
pictures – but rise to life and "fitness" through "literary conception" and
through analogies that make them "phrases," pieces of prose sentences.
Such counteranalogies, however, by no means equalize prose and illustration. Prose's analogy to painting leaves its narrative power unchallenged,
even as it lends prose a superadded pictorial capacity. By contrast, the
only value accorded the illustrations is through analogy to literature and
language. Their pictorial value is summarily dismissed ("weak and in-
sufficient *in themselves*"); subsequently "*themselves*" are swallowed up (via
analogy) into "the sentence *itself*." Such displacements lend metonymic
dimensions to analogies.

Twentieth-century critics of Victorian book illustration have followed
Layard, valuing illustrations primarily – often exclusively – for their narrative, semantic, and commentating aspects, rather than for their pictorial
dimensions, while they continue to praise the pictorial capacities of prose.
John Sloan, who for over 50 years pronounced *Vanity Fair* "the best example of book illustration ever printed," qualifies his praise: "I do not
make the claim that Thackeray's work is superior to that of his master
John Leech....Nevertheless, these drawings by Thackeray are autobi-
ographic commentaries: a running comment upon...his own brain
children."[40] Sloan devalues the drawings pictorially, valuing them purely
for their verbal functions – again, by analogy. Similarly, Joan Stevens,
arguing compellingly for a restoration of Thackeray's illustrations as they
were in the first edition, founds her argument on a claim that the illustrations are essential to the "meaning" of the text, valuing their semantic
rather than their pictorial effects.[41] In 1993, Christopher Coates also
warned that "the absence of Thackeray's pictorial text seems to coincide
with a misreading of the written one";[42] two years later Judith Fisher
valued Thackeray's illustrations analogically as "visual dialogues, which
develop into voices echoing the narrator."[43] Although the illustrations
certainly possess semantic and narrative functions, critics have by and
large valued them for these functions alone. As we saw in Chapter 1, before 1820, the term "illustration" referred primarily to written marginal
annotations or illustrative verbal examples of larger textual claims. In this
analogical rhetoric, book illustrations are pressed back to their earlier etymological roots away from their pictorial dimensions.

At the turn of the twentieth century, analogies of prose to painting and counteranalogies of illustration to verbal narrative cooperated with changing illustrative fashions and technologies to bring about the virtual excision of illustrations from novels written for adults. Charles Lamb described Hogarth's pictorial style as "books," bearing "the teeming, fruitful, suggestive meaning of *words*."[44] Numerous critics have commented on Thackeray's illustrations for *Vanity Fair* in this vein, designating them "symbolic drawings," "visual explanation," and "ironic commentary," stressing their metaphoric, punning, allegorical, allusive, and analogical operations.[45] Such readings offer substantial grounds for analogies that make illustrations quasi-verbal affairs. To offer one such interpretation of my own in this well-established tradition, Chapter 47's vignette of Lord Steyne's children seated reading beneath a breastplate stuffed with swords aimed at their heads plays metaphorically on and literalizes the more abstract prose that describes them: "The absent lord's children meanwhile prattled and grew on quite unconscious that the doom was over them too ... The stricken old grandmother ... watched sickening for the day when the awful ancestral curse should come down on them" (Figure 6). "Doom" and "ancestral curse" gain a pictorial concretism in the clutch of weapons: arms that should protect the children are turned against them. The coat of arms is literalized as a breastplate of arms (the nearest armor gets to a coat), with its arms menacing rather than embracing its brood. The pun, paradoxically, disarms the armor: there are no arms to the sleeveless "coat" – the "coat of arms" is thus lacking that which defines it. In its place, violent arms of another kind protrude.

Some drawings go further to contradict the prose, creating pictorial – verbal narrative dissonances. The most frequently discussed illustration of *Vanity Fair* in this regard is its penultimate full-page plate, "Becky's Second Appearance in the Character of Clytemnestra," in which Becky hides behind a curtain, apparently clutching a knife, as Jos confides fears for his safety to Dobbin (Figure 7). The prose text, however, places Becky out of the house during this discussion and does not say how Jos dies – only that his insurers find his death suspicious. Elizabeth Rigby, who reviewed the novel in 1848, was incensed by this plate, exclaiming: "Who can, with any face, liken a dear friend to a murderess? ... We should, therefore, advise our readers to cut out that picture."[46] Even at this early date, the point is clear: when pictures conflict with prose, they should be excised. Intriguingly, late-twentieth-century critics, like Fisher and Coates, take a contrary stance, asserting that pictures are truer than prose. In between, ameliorating critics welcome both positions as reinforcing the narrator's famous ambiguity.[47] Teona Tone Gneiting goes further to argue that such

A NOVEL WITHOUT A HERO.   423

the father's family, long before Lady Steyne's sins had begun, or her fasts and tears and penances had been offered in their expiation. The pride of the race was struck down as the firstborn of Pharaoh. The dark mark of fate and doom was on the threshold,—the tall old threshold surmounted by coronets and carved heraldry.

The absent lord's children meanwhile prattled and grew on quite unconscious that the doom was over them too. First they talked of their

father, and devised plans against his return. Then the name of the living dead man was less frequently in their mouths—then not mentioned at all. But the stricken old grandmother trembled to think that these too were the inheritors of their father's shame as well as of his honours : and watched sickening for the day when the awful ancestral curse should come down on them.

This dark presentiment also haunted Lord Steyne. He tried to lay the horrid bed-side ghost in Red Seas of wine and jollity, and lost sight of it

6. William Makepeace Thackeray's vignette of the Steyne children, in Chapter 47 of *Vanity Fair.* Courtesy of the Bancroft Library, University of California, Berkeley.

Becky's second appearance in the character of Clytemnestra

7. William Makepeace Thackeray's plate, "Becky's Second Appearance in the Character of Clytemnestra," in Chapter 67 of *Vanity Fair*. Courtesy of the Bancroft Library, University of California, Berkeley.

illustrations threaten the realist representational claims of prose more generally.[48] Whatever the interpretation, however, critics are unanimous that Thackeray's illustrations compete and conflict with his prose, rather than merely decorating, supplementing, or supporting it.

Golden Age illustrations, as well as later photographic realist, art nouveau, aesthetic, and arts-and-crafts styles of illustration that followed them, tend to offer less basis for verbal counteranalogies because they emphasize pictorial over rhetorical functions. Because of this, scholars have frequently castigated such illustrations as narratively redundant, retracting verbal counteranalogies from them and denying their narrative value, even as their pictorial merit is reckoned more highly in art circles. For example, in 1896, Laurence Housman complained of realist illustration that told readers "twice what they need only be told once."[49] In 1970, Harvey argued that mimetic styles of illustration have "no real function in the novel, though they may be decorative."[50] In 1993, surveying the photorealist illustrations that replaced Thackeray's in later editions of his works, Coates concludes that "they are smooth and unobtrusive; they do not narrate, but 'decorate'."[51] Together with the rhetorical shifts that made prose painting and illustrations commentaries, shifts in illustrative style offered support to perceptions that illustrations were redundant and demanded that they thus could and should be excised from novels. This practice in turn led increasingly to a twentieth-century redefinition of "the novel" as pure prose, as though it had never been illustrated or as though illustrations had never been an integral part of the novel. The vast majority of twentieth-century readings treat illustrated Victorian novels as though they had never been illustrated, and no theory of the novel takes illustration into account.

There is no need to establish or detail here the decline in novel illustration that illustration historians have so amply documented. Although some argue that this decline was simply "a matter of economics and fashion," having nothing to do with prose and illustration rivalries, the proliferation of illustration everywhere else throughout the twentieth century into the twenty-first – in children's literature, nonfiction books, encyclopedias, posters, advertisements, magazines, visual aids, postage stamps, product packaging, television graphics, film animation, computer graphics, and Internet graphics – renders such an argument dubious. If these other forms could manage the economics, why not the novel? And why should the "fashion" change here and nowhere else?[52]

As demonstrated in Chapter 1, the profusion of nineteenth-century interart analogies led to calls for renewed categorical rigor in interart discourse. Critics like Irving Babbitt called for rigorous segregation and an end to interart analogies and interart adaptations.[53] Nowhere was the battle more marked than in efforts to separate verbal and visual arts. Altick documents late-nineteenth-century reactions against "literary" painting; William Morris, pioneering new theories and practices of book illustration during this period, declared himself utterly opposed "to rhetorical, retrospective, or academical [visual] art."[54] Hammerton's dialogue on book illustration likewise pressed for a separation of spheres:

> POET: I can attain to indifference when the Fine Arts keep to their proper place, and illustrate subjects of their own; I mean subjects that the artist finds for himself in nature, and especially on the condition that the illustrations be kept out of the books and exhibited separately as pictures are at the Royal Academy, or like etchings that are published by themselves.
> ARTIST: We have here, as it seems to me, a case of jealousy.
> CRITIC: In this case I think the poet may reasonably be jealous, as the illustrator, under the pretext of doing honour to the poet, really gets upon his shoulders and attracts most of the public attention to himself.
> POET: We can do without illustrators as ships can do without barnacles.[55]

Despite rampant prose painting analogies, prose was losing the pictorial battle to illustration. In the 1890s, technological improvements in printing led to a mass market flooded with affordable illustrated books in styles that combined the mimetic polish of Golden Age illustrations with photographic realism. If illustrations had once appeared sketchy by comparison to prose "painting," prose "painting" now appeared sketchy by comparison to photographic styles of illustration. Moreover, the many prestigious painters who now engaged in book illustration pressed book illustration toward high art, even as hack writers and Grub Street authors pushed prose toward low art associations. As celebrated artists like John Everett Millais, Dante Rossetti, Edward Burne-Jones, and Frederick Leighton turned to book illustration, the author–painter analogy suffered competition from this more literal painter–illustrator affiliation. In 1896, Henry Blackburn documented a rising analogy between illustration and painting, recommending that illustrators be designated "painter-etchers" and receive "recognition as original artists." Further threatening to prose's claims to represent fully and independently, Blackburn's theory of illustration has illustrations appearing "where words fail to express" or where "words fail to communicate the right meaning." In these cases, "pictorial expression should come to the aid of the verbal."[56] In this theory, the very appearance of an illustration implies a failure of prose's representational power and self-sufficiency.

At the end of the century, prose often took second place to illustration, particularly in the popular gift book and "the Book Beautiful." Here bindings and illustrations were "the thing": books of this kind were collected as visual and tactile artifacts rather than as verbal narratives, and more attention was paid to the lettering, font, and borders than to the semantics of the text. Here, pictures appeared for pictures' sake, not for words' sake. They did not illustrate, but rather eclipsed the word. Hammerton's Scientist, who only advances facts in the exchange, is, significantly, the one to claim that "when literature and art are put together it is generally literature that suffers. People do not read splendidly illustrated editions, and the fewer and more insignificant the illustrations the better is an author's chance of being read."[57] It is a claim that no other dialoguer, not even the Poet, counters.

It was in this context that author-critics like Henry James marshaled prose painting analogies for a final coup of novel illustrations, claiming the novel for prose alone. As we have seen, newer mimetic styles of illustration had frequently been declared narratively redundant: now they were to be decreed pictorially so. In 1884, James claimed that "the analogy between the art of the painter and the art of the novelist is, so far as I am able to see, complete."[58] But James refers to a one-sided completion, in which prose has aspired to and attained all the functions of painting, not one in which illustrations have aspired to and attained all the functions of prose. Twenty-five years later, as new styles of illustration continued to draw popular attention away from prose, James urged a more annihilating triumph of the prose painting analogy, declaring prose sufficiently pictorial to do without illustration at all. James here enters a wider debate, noting that "the very question itself [is] at large – that question of the general acceptability of illustration coming up sooner or later, in these days." He complains that "the author of any text putting forward illustrative claims (that is producing an effect of illustration) by its own intrinsic virtue [finds] itself elbowed, on that ground, by another and a competitive process" – that of illustration.[59] Again in contrast to Lessing's bid for a separation of visual/verbal spheres on the basis of their essentialist differences, James urges prose's segregation from illustration on grounds of their competitive overlap. In a letter to a *Century* editor, he deplores: "Ah, your illustrations – your illustrations; how as a writer one hates 'em; and how their being as good as they are makes one hate 'em more! What one writes suffers essentially, as literature, from going with them, and the two things ought to stand alone."[60]

James, conceding the popular and critical consensus of his day that "The essence of any representational work [verbal or visual] is of course

to bristle with immediate images," declares an illustrative "picture by another hand on my own [prose] picture" to be "a lawless incident . . . that
relieves responsible prose of the duty of being, while placed before us,
good enough, interesting enough and, if the question be of picture, pictorial enough, above all *in itself,* [thereby doing] it the worst of services."[61] A
far cry from Layard's patronizing recognition of illustrative "services rendered," this metaphor implies that such services militate against a solid
prose work ethic.

James's use of prose picture analogies to argue for the excision of literal
pictures pressed the novel toward an aesthetic of pure prose. As historians
attest, book illustration suffered a gradual decline in this period until, by
the 1930s, it appeared rarely in adult novels. Strikingly, as novel illustrations declined, so too did prose painting analogies. As late as 1916, James
Joyce nominated his prose characterization *A Portrait of the Artist as Young
Man.* Subsequently, the titular rhetoric of prose portraits and painting mi-
grated from novels to historical and biographical works, where portraits
of ages, cities, communities, decades, and generations, of generals, pres-
idents, revolutionaries, and other historical figures, proliferated. (Most
of these books are illustrated.)[62]

Returning to our central case study, we discover that verbal "illustrations" (annotations and commentaries) increasingly take the place of
visual illustrations in twentieth-century reeditions of nineteenth-century
novels. While the 1898 biographical edition of *Vanity Fair* contains "illustrations by the author and a portrait" of the author (the portrait here is a
visual arts rendition),[63] the 1943 edition substitutes a verbal "biographical sketch of the author" for his portrait (the analogy "sketch" is pointed
in the context of this discussion).[64] Most twentieth-century editions of
Vanity Fair contain no illustrations; the few that do by and large represent only a few plates. By contrast, almost all twentieth-century editions of
Vanity Fair contain illustrations in the older sense of verbal annotation and
commentary. While nineteenth-century bibliographical descriptions of
Vanity Fair typically append subtitular statements like, "with illustrations
on steel and wood by the author,"[65] twentieth-century editions characteristically bear bibliographical subtitles like, "with an introduction by G. K.
Chesterton,"[66] "with an afterword by V. S. Pritchett,"[67] "with an introduction and notes by Geoffrey and Kathleen Tillotson,"[68] "with commentary
by Nicholas Pickwood and Robert Colby,"[69] and "backgrounds, contents,
and criticism edited by Peter Shillingsburg."[70] Frequently such editions
are advertised as "a new critical edition," "an approved edition," or as "an
authoritative text."[71] Chapter 5 ponders the continuum between illustration and criticism in the theory and practice of literary film adaptation:

here the point to glean is that verbal illustration by and large displaces pictorial illustration.

But this is not the end of the story. The rhetoric used to oust illustrations from novels reappears in discussions of the novel and film in relation to one another, particularly in the discourse on literary film adaptation.

Prose at the Pictures

Surprisingly, after his unequivocal objection to illustration, Henry James allowed photographs to illustrate the very novel whose preface voices the objection. James asserts somewhat bafflingly that the photographs illustrating *The Golden Bowl* comprise "a contribution in as different a 'medium' as possible" from the prose. Even so, he exerted rigorous control over the photographs, selecting the scenes photographed by A. L. Coburn and insisting that they exhibit a "discreetly disavowing emulation" and that any "reference . . . to Novel or Tale should exactly be *not* competitive and obvious . . . that of the images always confessing themselves mere optical symbols or echoes, expressions of no particular thing in the text, but only of the type or idea of this or that thing."[72] Nominating illustrations "optical symbols" subordinates their pictorial to their symbolic functions since the latter garners the substantive noun and the former only the modifying adjective. Moreover, designating photographs "echoes" renders them derivative aural aftermaths of phonetic prose, echoes faded further since they express "no particular thing in the text."

James is by no means alone in aligning prose with photography against drawn illustrations. Scholars document the allied threat that prose and photographs posed to book illustrations at the turn of the twentieth century. Henry Blackburn in 1893 and Joseph Pennell in 1896 both identify photography as a major factor in "the collapsing role of, and the lack of respect for, the pictorial image, illustration, and the graphic artist."[73] Before this, photographic reproductive technologies had made the engravers who "translated" drawn illustrations for the press redundant. Critics hailed such technological advances as reducing the number of steps between "nature" and the art of the illustrated page. Photographic illustration was similarly and subsequently hailed as rendering illustrators themselves obsolete, eliminating one more intermediary step between nature and its representation. Moreover, just as illustrations had once been likened to preliminary stages of painting, now even the most mimetic and detailed illustrations appeared sketchy in comparison to photography. Addressing the popular preference for the full and finished photograph over the suggestive sketch, illustration historian James Thorpe concludes that, "With the coming of the photographic camera and the development of its powers the interest in black-and-white art has sadly declined."[74]

James was short-sighted, however, in thinking that photographs would guarantee and maintain the pictorial supremacy of prose fiction over visual art (this belief itself turns out to be a "prose fiction"). Prose may have won the battle with book illustrations, but film – that near relation and descendant of photography – was to prove an even more formidable rival to prose's pictorial claims. James was less prescient than Stephane Mallarmé, who suggested that cinema might one day replace the illustrated book – both its prose and its illustrations.[75] Film's temporal capacities – its pictorial mobility and syntax of editing – lent it superadded narrative powers that rivaled those of prose. Periodical reviews of early films affirm the narrative rivalry between literature and film. A 1926 reviewer of G. W. Pabst's *Secrets of the Soul* asserts: "This picturization is vastly more provocative and downright informative and clarifying than any row of books on a shelf could be . . . it is a triumph of the pictorial."[76] Beyond such reviews, historians of Western book illustration largely agree that literary film adaptation replaced the illustrated book in the early years of the twentieth century. Reviews of early films of *Vanity Fair* are representative. A review of Edison's 1915 *Vanity Fair* decrees that "the reels make a set of illustrations superior to the conventional pen-pictures of a deluxe edition."[77] *The New York Dramatic Mirror* presses the displacement further to include both prose and illustrations: "The photoplay production of *Vanity Fair* is an actual visualization of the novel."[78]

Several historians, including Philip James, go further to argue that film in general (not just literary film adaptation) replaced illustrated fiction: "Illustrated fiction, once a source of rivalry between all the great publishing houses and the illustrator's main occupation, has now given way to screen fiction."[79] At times, early film reviewers hailed films as outdoing both illustrated novels and performed plays. One *New York Times* review attested in 1921: "[this film is] much more worth seeing than all the illustrated novels and plays turned out in a year."[80] This and reviews like it do not express rivalries between literature as words and films as images, but rather between three hybrid narrative art forms: illustrated novels, performed plays, and intertitled films.

Prose fiction writers in the 1920s and 1930s were as concerned about film's threat to the novel as their recent predecessors had been about illustration's threat to prose in the 1900s and 1910s. In the 1930s, F. Scott Fitzgerald echoed Henry James's 1909 concern that visual competition threatens the novel. James concludes his preface to *The Golden Bowl* with a worry that illustrations "may well inspire in the lover of literature certain lively questions as to the future of that institution."[81] Similarly, Fitzgerald worries: "As long past as 1930, I had a hunch that the talkies would make even the best-selling novelist as archaic as silent pictures." Fitzgerald does not express this threat from films as images to novels as words, but rather from a hybrid "art in which words [are] subordinate to images."[82] As Chapter 3 details, film subjugates words to images as novels have subjugated images to words. Hybrid arts that favor images over words are particularly threatening to entrenched hierarchies of word over image, for they daily showcase the dominance of images over words. It is easier to maintain hierarchies between so-called "pure" arts with rhetoric and theory. But when words and images mix within art forms, they frequently disregard and contradict the theories concerning them, as we have seen.

While novels have not become extinct in the wake of illustrations or film, they have, nevertheless, had to "adapt" to film in the evolutionary sense of that word. With considerably more prescience than James or Fitzgerald, Leo Tolstoy wrote on his eightieth birthday in 1908:

> You will see that the little clicking contraption with the revolving handle will make a revolution in our life – in the life of writers. It is a direct attack on the old methods of literary art. We shall have to adapt ourselves to the shadowy screen and to the cold machine. A new form of writing will be necessary. I have thought of that and I can feel what is coming.
>
> But I rather like it. The swift change of scene, this blending of emotion and experience – it is much better than the heavy, long-drawn-out kind of writing to which we are accustomed. It is closer to life.[83]

Modernist prose fiction writers have by and large adapted to film's superior pictorial capacities by abandoning their own pictorial aspirations. Although prose won the battle with illustrations over the production of images in the novel, increasingly in the first half of the twentieth century, interdisciplinary critics and literary voices cede images to painting and to film.[84] Bluestone ascertains that, in the wake of film's ability to so vividly and immediately represent visual and dramatic narrative, "The novel has tended to retreat more and more from external action to internal thought, from plot to character, from social to psychological realities."[85] Although literary critics continue to claim that mental images aroused by literary words are superior to actual pictures,[86] Ellen J. Esrock has documented a concomitant relinquishment of even mental images by twentieth-century literary critics, many of whom consider imaging while reading "a harmful fall from the reading process" and a violation of the abstract representational essence of prose.[87] Such critical tendencies, coupled with widespread assertions that the high modern novel is un-filmable, carve out separate territories for novels and films.[88] The novel's retreat from its own pictorial and theatrical aspirations, then, is followed by a taunt that film cannot follow.

Two essays by Virginia Woolf – one on "Pictures" and the other on "The Cinema" – illustrate and amplify prose fiction's surrender of the pictorial to visual arts as well as the continuum forged between painting and early film. Woolf's essay, "Pictures," authorizes the prose retreat from picto-rial description, conceding painting's superior pictorial powers: "words began to raise their feeble limbs in the pale border-land of no man's language, to sink down again in despair. We fling them like nets upon a rocky and inhospitable shore; they fade and disappear. It is vain it is futile . . . The silent painters, Cézanne and Mr. Sickert, make fools of us as often as they choose." Woolf goes further to reject the realist pictorial mandate that had dominated novel aesthetics for so long on vague aes-thetic grounds: "We can say for certain that a writer whose writing appeals mainly to the eye is a bad writer . . . he is incapable of using his medium for the purposes for which it is created, and is as a writer a man without legs." The rhetoric here is moralistically judgmental ("bad") and ridiculingly scornful rather than descriptive or analytic. In making her point, Woolf rejects the prose painting tradition: "it is extremely doubtful whether [the writer] learns anything directly from painting." She then proceeds to lambaste the narrative painting tradition: "painters lose their power directly they attempt to speak . . . A story-telling picture is as pathetic and as ludicrous as a trick played by a dog." She concludes with a by now familiar call for a separation of verbal and pictorial spheres: "something must separate [writers] from [painters]."

Woolf's essay on "The Cinema" places film in the visual arts tradition and sets both in contrast and opposition to the prose novel. She equates visual art with the eye functioning primitively apart from the brain. Film audiences are "the savages of the twentieth century" at "no great dis-tance . . . from those bright-eyed naked men" whose eyes "lick up" the screen while their brains lie dormant. If writers who aspire to picto-rial effects are legless men and pictures that aspire to narrative effects are ludicrous performing dogs, film for Woolf lies somewhere between maimed human and trained animal. It is Neanderthal man, an art that has not yet learned to "walk erect."[89] In each essay, Woolf mounts moral-istic, dogmatic, even histrionic defenses of verbal territory. In "Pictures," she snaps: "with half a sheet of note-paper we can tell all the stories of all the pictures in the world"; in "The Cinema," she commands: all "which is accessible to words and to words alone, the cinema must avoid."[90]

Juxtaposing the two essays furthermore highlights the integral connection between interart analogies and interart adaptations. "Pictures" rejects interart analogies; "The Cinema" rejects interart adaptation. The latter essay argues that the alliance of film and the novel in literary film adaptation "is unnatural. Eye [used by film viewers] and brain [used by novel readers] are torn asunder ruthlessly as they try to work in couples . . . the brain knows Anna almost entirely by the inside of her mind. All the emphasis is laid by the cinema upon her teeth, her pearls, and her velvet."[91] The novel holds the higher organ, the brain, while the film garners only the sensory, bestial, and materialistic eye.

Subsequent discussions also link older verbal/visual rivalries to new ones and attempt to excise interart analogies with excoriations of interart adaptations. Attacks on literary film adaptation frequently draw on rhetoric used in attacks on novel illustration. Slurs representing adaptations as "mere" moving book illustrations are everywhere. They mount a double-edged attack on film, as they both subjugate film to prose fiction under older rhetorical and conceptual models and reduce film's pictorial vivacity, photographic realism, color, sound, temporality, and mobility to a sketchy static visual art. William Luhr's essay, "Dickens's Narrative, Hollywood's Vignettes," for example, represents MGM's 1935 adaptation of *David Copperfield* as a plural miscellany of that clinging vine of illustration, the vignette. It is not itself allowed to be narrative.[92] More central to adaptation discourse, Geoffrey Wagner's hugely influential categories of adaptation rank "transposition" – subtitled "book illustration" – lowest as the "least satisfying" and, to his mind, regrettably the most common form of adaptation. Significantly, Wagner draws on literary criticism of book illustrations to denigrate this mode of adaptation. Citing I. A. Richards's famous claim that "all illustrations are disappointing," he extends this evaluation to the majority of film adaptations, noting condescendingly, "They usually are, except to children; and Hollywood was for long making films for children of all ages."[93] Here Wagner seizes on illustration's wholesale banishment to children's books to relegate popular film adaptations and their audiences to the nursery. In so doing, he replaces Woolf's biological primitivism with a psychological one.

Analogies that figure adaptation as book illustration persist throughout the first century of film. In 1992, John Orr suggested that the term "picture-book" replace the more common designation, "literary film adaptation." The "picture-book" is to be deferent to prose: "At its most powerful, it illustrates the power of the text by persuading us to read it … it graphically reminds us of textual power." The picture-book does not exist to gesture to its own power. It does not even illustrate the text, only the power of text, a power that implicitly includes the text's power over the film as well as over the reader-viewer. The rhetoric here accords film adaptations an almost magical or religious power to turn viewers into readers, whether by spell or conversion.[94]

Aesthetic practice and consumption bore out Orr's prescription long before he made it. Historians of illustrated novels attest to the power of illustrations to sell prose; sales of books bearing film stills indicate similar effects.[95] More copies of *Wuthering Heights* sold in the single year following the MGM film adaptation than in the nearly 100 years between the book's publication and the film's release.[96] A 1985 survey found that 46% of viewers had bought or borrowed a book as a direct result of seeing a television adaptation.[97] Contrary to Hammerton's dialoguers, who worry that buyers of illustrated books do not read the prose of their picture books, and to James's and Fitzgerald's fears about literary extinction in the wake of illustration and film, it appears that the more direct the competition (that is, when prose and illustration or novel and film claim to represent the same characters and events), the more eager consumers are to consume both forms. It appears that consumers are not champions of separate spheres: that only academics and artists are, and from territorial and economic motives. In rhetoric and practice then, the film adaptation is not the "picture-book": rather, novel and film adaptation together constitute the picture-book, the illustrated book, which consumers consume as they once did illustrated books. The same principle holds for novelizations of films. These "picture books" – books of motion pictures – also sell extremely well.

Other connections between novel illustration and novel adaptation to film emerge. In some cases, theatrical adaptations form intriguing intertexts. Stills from nineteenth-century theatrical adaptations of novels frequently replaced novel illustrations in tie-in editions, just as film and television stills serve as novel illustrations in the twentieth and twenty-first centuries. For example, Langdon Mitchell's 1899 theatrical adaptation of *Vanity Fair, Becky Sharp*, was produced in conjunction with Harper's tie-in "Becky Sharp edition" of the novel (also 1899) and contains stills from the play instead of Thackeray's illustrations. A century later in 1999, a new edition of *Vanity Fair* placed stills from a BBC television dramatization in place of Thackeray's drawings.[98] Tangling connections between novel, theater, and film still further, Langdon's play featured Mrs. Fiske in the title role. She later starred in the 1915 Edison film of *Vanity Fair*.[99] By placing adaptation stills as illustrations, publishing practice aligns with and literalizes the analogical critical rhetoric that makes film adaptation "book illustration." Here, aesthetic practice functions as criticism and fosters interart rivalries. Stills from the adaptation displace the novel's illustrations, but not one word of the novel's prose. The clear implication of this practice is that adaptation can take the place of illustration, but not of prose. Moreover, the stills quite literally still performance and moving images in both senses of the verb – they both freeze mobile actors and silence their dialogue, reducing them to poster children for the prose. These publications become stilling fields of live theatrical performance and mobile sound film. Paradoxically, such publishing practices foster divisions of novels and films into word and image camps even as they create new hybrids. They present the film as pure images and strip the novel of its illustrations to pure words. They never represent the words of films or the illustrations of novels.

When novels are thus reduced to words and films to static images, intraart word and image exchanges are obscured. Without an understanding of such intraart dynamics, there can be no clear comprehension of interart word and image dynamics. The next section examines the aesthetic practice that literalizes the prose picture analogy – the pictured prose of pictorial initials – to test both the validity of interart analogies against an aesthetic practice that purports to fulfil them and to examine verbal/pictorial dynamics inside the illustrated novel. This case study can only begin the enormous task that novel and film scholars must undertake to understand intradisciplinary word and image dynamics and, subsequently, interdisciplinary word and image relations.

Pictured Prose: The Victorian Pictorial Initial

Like a looking glass, which appears to mirror exactly, but in fact inverts right and left fields, "pictured prose" rhetorically inverts the left–right orientation of the "prose picture" analogy, carrying us from prose that is spoken of analogically as picture to prose that is literally and categorically pictured. Part of what a *Saturday Review* critic referred to as "the new hieroglyphics" sweeping Victorian publishing, pictorial initials derive in part from medieval illuminated letters, whose role was to cast light on the prose text, both in the sense of interpreting and of making it illustrious.[100] My discussion focuses on a different sort of illumination: the illuminating exposé of prose picture analogies by pictured prose. The pictured prose of pictorial initials parodically punctures prose's analogical claims to painting and challenges categorical distinctions made between words and images. Not only does it subject interart analogy and interart category to the scrutiny of looking glass inversions, it also subjects itself to the same inverse processes, almost endlessly.

Penciling the Pen: The Pictorial Initials of Vanity Fair

If the prose criticism of illustrations constitutes a "penning of the pencil," then pictorial initials comprise a "penciling of the pen." In these titles and in the discussion that follows, aesthetic practice turns critical rhetoric, looking glass fashion: the inversion of left and right parts of speech here points to a more substantial inversion, mockery, and debunking of prose picture analogies and of word/image distinctions. This section holds the critical rhetoric regarding the prose and illustrations of *Vanity Fair* up to the mirror of Thackeray's pictorial initials, selected as particularly inter-woven and embedded points of verbal–pictorial encounter by a single author–illustrator. Unlike full-page plates, vignettes, and endpieces, pic-torial initials harness grapheme to graphic to such an extent that they frequently run, quite literally, along the same lines. Not only does their production by one author-illustrator limit the variables that otherwise must enter such a discussion (one cannot presume that the author and illustrator fought to trump each other since author and illustrator are one), their universal acclaim by art critics who otherwise disparage Thackeray's illustrations also removes another variable. Critics have fre-quently argued for the excision of Thackeray's illustrations on grounds of their poor aesthetic quality, dislocating the argument from more central interart rivalries. But Thackeray's pictorial initials have received nothing but praise from the art world.[101]

Pictured Prose versus Prose Pictures. We have seen the ubiquity of prose painting analogies in Victorian novel criticism and the use of these analo-gies early in the twentieth century to press for the excision of illustrations. Certain pictorial initials in *Vanity Fair* play on and undermine prose paint-ing analogies when they make the grapheme a picture frame for the picto-rial elements of the initial. The **C** and **O**[102] that open Chapters 25 and 26 form cameo frames for characters and scenes, enhancing the picturesque-ness of the picture rather than contributing verbal or narrative dimen-sions (Figures 8 and 9). In a pictorial system, the frame is subservient to the picture, a packaging that defers to and showcases the picture's more central contents. These initials undermine prose's analogical aspirations to painting, for prose is rendered subservient to illustration in a pictorial system as picture frame rather than picture. If interart analogies frame prose as painting (I use the term here in the sense of "to devise falsely"),

ONDUCTED to the ladies, at the Ship Inn, Dobbin assumed a jovial and rattling manner, which proved that this young officer was becoming a more consummate hypocrite every day of his life. He was trying to hide his own private feelings, first upon seeing Mrs. George Osborne in her new condition, and secondly to mask the apprehensions he entertained as to the effect which the dismal news brought down by him would certainly have upon her.

8. William Makepeace Thackeray's pictorial initial, in Chapter 25 of *Vanity Fair* (New York: Heritage, 1940).

then pictorial initials that frame pictures with prose call their bluff. The hierarchical pretensions of verbal prose painting "frames" go topsy-turvy in a punning literalization of pictorial framing. Here an interart pictorial pun punctures and subjugates prose's aspirations to picture.

Such deflations and prose rallies against such deflations unfold further through the double articulation of pictorial initials in both pictorial and verbal systems. The dynamics in these dual, dueling contexts present further challenges to critical concepts and rhetorical positionings of the verbal and the pictorial. The **C** and **O** frames form parts of linguistic sentences as well as picture frames. Viewed from their verbal context, the letters appear less subordinate to the pictures – even predatory on them: the **C** scoops and the **O** swallows the picture into the words of each opening line: "Conducted to the ladies ... "; "On quitting Brighton .... " From the verbal context, the picture lies inside the letter, contained by it, smaller than it, swept into a tide of other letters that overwhelm it. Neither context, however, ever entirely overrides or eradicates the other: in their pictorial context, the letters remain subordinate to the pictures; in their verbal context, the pictures remain contained by the letters.

N QUITTING Brighton, our friend George as became a person of rank and fashion travelling in a barouche with four horses, drove in state to a fine hotel in Cavendish Square, where a suite of splendid rooms, and a table magnificently furnished with plate and surrounded by a half-dozen of black and silent waiters, was ready to receive the young gentleman and his bride. George did the honours of the place with a princely air to Jos and Dob-

9. William Makepeace Thackeray's pictorial initial, in Chapter 26 of *Vanity Fair* (New York: Heritage, 1940).

The double articulation of these initials also presents a challenge to categorical distinctions made between words and images, not only to the categorization of the verbal as temporal and the pictorial as spatial, but also beyond this to temporality and spatiality themselves. The pictorial **C** creates a temporally and spatially illogical relationship between prose and picture. The chapter's opening sentence has Dobbin "Conducted to the ladies," a group that includes Amelia, while the textual Dobbin thus directed moves, paradoxically, away from the pictorial Amelia through the left-to-right direction of prose reading. The scooping shape of the pictorial **C** frame, meanwhile, has the effect of conducting the pictorial Amelia toward the prose Dobbin, even as he moves away from her toward the prose Amelia. Directional confusion accelerates to nonsensical temporal-spatiality as the prose paragraph carrying Dobbin away from pictorial to prose Amelia keeps snapping back toward her picture with the return of each line of prose to the left margin, bringing Dobbin to the right edge of the pictorial initial, but never quite to her image. Like the lovers on Keats's Grecian urn (and most theories of words and images), prose Dobbin and pictorial Amelia can never, never meet. But in this instance the effect derives less from a frozen temporality or from essentialist and irreducible differences between the two forms and more from a delicious play on the incongruous temporal and spatial relations between prose and picture in a hybrid form.

Dramatic Analogies: Character Character. As I noted in the introduction, one of the novel and film debate's central omissions lies in the relationship of each to theater and in considering theater's mediating role between the two. The metacritical and historical priorities of this book do not allow it to adequately fill the gap (it would take many books to do so), but at several points, it turns to address aspects of the gap. While prose picture analogies are pervasive in illustration criticism, a thinner strain of dramatic analogies mediates at times between a novel's words and illustrations. Thackeray's own prefatorial analogy for *Vanity Fair* is of a puppet show: the narrator is a stage manager, the narration is a play, the characters are puppets, and the illustrations are candles lighting the prose performance. Some of *Vanity Fair*'s pictorial initials literalize the dramatic analogy, depicting fairground sideshows, performers,[103] and costumed actors.[104] At times, graphemic characters form theatrical backdrops, stage sets, and props with which pictorial characters interact. These initials forge dramatic encounters between prose and picture. For example, Chapter 3's initial **A** forms a backdrop against which Jos poses for his first appearance (Figure 10). The shadows cast by the letter and Jos clearly

VERY stout, puffy man, in buckskins and Hessian boots, with several immense neckcloths, that rose almost to his nose, with a red striped waistcoat and an apple green coat with steel buttons almost as large as crown pieces, (it was the morning costume of a dandy or blood of those days) was reading the paper by the fire when the two girls entered, and bounced off his arm-chair, and blushed excessively,

10. William Makepeace Thackeray's pictorial initial, in Chapter 3 of *Vanity Fair* (New York: Heritage, 1940).

indicate that they are both three-dimensional objects sharing a space. Chapter 60 positions its initial **C** as a piece of scenery over which one character must step to reach another, the floor boards in this initial both literally and metaphorically representing a stage – "the boards" (Figure 11). Chapter 37's clown balances a letter **I** as a theatrical prop on his nose (Figure 12).

In the first of these initials, Jos makes his pictorial debut against his letter of introduction. The letter diminishes him, as does the prose of the paragraph the letter initiates. The prose buries Jos and his claims to dignity and dandyhood in suffocating clothes: "A very stout, puffy man, in buckskins, and Hessian boots, with several immense neckcloths, that rose almost to his nose, with a red striped waistcoat and an apple green coat with steel buttons..."(21). But these are prose clothes and prose diminutions: he looks less ridiculous in the picture. The neckcloths do

OOD fortune now begins to smile upon Amelia. We are glad to get her out of that low sphere in which she has been creeping hitherto, and introduce her into a polite circle; not so grand and refined as that in which our other female friend, Mrs. Becky, has appeared, but still having no small pretensions to gentility and fashion. Jos's friends were all from the three presidencies, and his new house was in the comfortable Anglo-Indian district of which Moira Place is the centre. Minto

11. William Makepeace Thackeray's pictorial initial, in Chapter 60 of *Vanity Fair* (New York: Heritage, 1940).

N the first place, and as a matter of the greatest necessity, we are bound to describe how a house may be got for nothing a-year. These mansions are to be had either unfurnished, where, if you have credit with Messrs. Gillows or Bantings, you can get them splendidly arranged and decorated entirely, according to your own fancy; or they are to be let furnished; a less troublesome and complicated arrangement to most parties. It was so that Crawley and his wife preferred to hire their house.

Before Mr. Bowls came to preside over Miss Crawley's house and cellar in Park Lane, that lady had had for a butler, a Mr. Raggles, who was born

12. William Makepeace Thackeray's pictorial initial, in Chapter 37 of *Vanity Fair* (New York: Heritage, 1940).

not rise to his nose. Though the towering letter and subsequent prose reduce him, the pictured character maintains a degree of dignity and counterpoint to the prose ridicule. Once again, the picture reveals not only itself, but also the exaggerations of prose.

The stage set piece over which one character must step to reach another in Chapter 60's initial poses a textual obstacle between pictorial characters, yet it is also the prose **G** that brings the "Good fortune" that has come to "smile upon Amelia." The stranglehold of the Osborne circle, the **O**, has opened to a less closed circular **G**. Amelia enters into possession of the Osborne fortune through the opening accorded by two Osborne **G**eorges – her husband and her son. The smiling gentleman stepping into the space vacated by George senior and opened by George junior is a personification of smiling good fortune, which arrives in the form of new social bonds for Amelia – "the polite circle" she now inhabits. But just as the **G** does not form a complete graphic circle, so too, the polite circle is qualified as "not so grand and refined as that in which our other female friend, Mrs. Becky, has appeared." Partial circles, then, can be lacking as well as opening. The graphemic character here thus constitutes both an obstacle and an opening for characters. Semiotically speaking, it is both subservient to drawn characters in a dramatic interart analogy as a piece of a stage set and representative of dynamics between those characters (literally).

The third instance of dramatic relations between alphabetic character and drawn character, between an initial **I** and the clown-narrator who opens Chapter 37, shows the pictorial character master of the written character. The initial **I** is encapsulated in a pictorial picture frame rather than forming a frame for the pictured character. Thus it is a central rather than a supporting character in a pictorial system. But the framing

IR PITT CRAWLEY was a philosopher with a taste for what is called low life. His first marriage with the daughter of the noble Binkie had been made under the auspices of his parents; and as he often told Lady Crawley in her life-time she was such a confounded quarrelsome high-bred jade that when she died he was hanged if he would ever take another of her sort at her lady-ship's demise, he kept his promise, and selected for a second wife Miss Rose Dawson, daughter of Mr. John Thomas Dawson, ironmonger, of Mudbury. What a happy woman was Rose to

13. William Makepeace Thackeray's pictorial initial, in Chapter 9 of *Vanity Fair* (New York: Heritage, 1940).

also contains the verbal in a pictorial system, so it is in another sense subjected to the pictorial. In a dramatic system, the alphabetic character is decidedly subservient to the drawn character, a mere prop supported by a far more central pictorial actor-character. The alphabetic character becomes a prop showcasing the abilities of the pictured character and of the pictorial over the verbal character. The clown smiles complacently, his arms crossed ("Look! No hands!"), his flexible legs expressing ease as he balances the **I** on his ample nose. The mastery here extends beyond the initial: the clown-narrator's dexterity spills from the initial into the ensuing prose as the narrator skillfully explains what appears to be impossible: "In the first place, and as a matter of the greatest necessity, we are bound to describe how a house may be got for nothing a-year."

Even in less blatant theatrical contexts, numerous pictorial initials in *Vanity Fair* set alphabetic characters (letters) in dramatic interaction with pictorial characters (drawn people), dramatizing semiotic relations as well as the narrative. Chapter 9's pictorial initial gives pictorial characterizing weight to the alphabetic character that begins the name of its drawn character. Sir Pitt Crawley sits smoking on the **S** that begins his title, "Sir Pitt Crawley" (Figure 13). The letter initializes his verbal characterization as well as his name – "Sir Pitt Crawley was a philosopher with a taste for what is called low life" – and pictorially constitutes his "seat," both symbolically and literally. As a pictorial object, the letter lifts him literally off the ground, literalizing the verbal effect of his title, the "Sir" that lifts him symbolically and socially. Yet his position on the sloping lower curve of the **S** suggests that the high title on which he has risen paradoxically and simultaneously points him toward "low life." The pictorial initial suggests that his high title simultaneously supports and enables his low life. Like a parodic inversion of the game Snakes and Ladders,[105] the "ladder" on

UR duty now takes us back for a brief space to some old Hampshire acquaintances of ours, whose hopes respecting the disposal of their rich kinswoman's property were so wofully disappointed. After counting upon thirty thousand pounds from his sister, it was a heavy blow to Bute Crawley to receive but five; out of which sum, when he had paid his own debts and those of Jim, his son at college, a very small fragment remained to por-

14. William Makepeace Thackeray's pictorial initial, in Chapter 39 of *Vanity Fair* (New York: Heritage, 1940).

which he has risen doubles as snake – as likely to send him sliding down as to raise him up. Everything in the drawing beyond his initial elevation by his title letter connotes downward movement: his slumping posture, weighty corpulence, and the pot of ale at the base that calls him down to drink. Not even the pipe smoke rises – in defiance of physical laws, it too floats downward. On one level, the pictorial initial suggests a conspiracy between high titles and low living: the title both belies and enables the slovenly corpulence and indulgent consumption of the depicted body. Thus, while the characterization of Sir Pitt Crawley here is a paradoxical one, verbal and pictorial elements create a perfectly consonant (in both senses of the word) characterization.

Other pictorial initials set prose representation at odds with pictorial representation. The pictorial initial **O** that opens Chapter 39, "A Cynical Chapter," illustrates tensions between the novel's author, illustrator, and narrator. In the opening sentence, the narrator announces his immediate narrative duty in steady prose, indicating pleasant familiarity with his readers and appropriate sympathy with his characters: "Our duty now takes us back for a brief space to some old Hampshire acquaintances of ours, whose hopes respecting the disposal of their rich kinswoman's property were so wofully [sic] disappointed." But inside the initial **O** of this sentence sits a maniacally grimacing caricature of Thackeray the author (as opposed to the harlequin or clown narrators of other pictorial initials) – teeth clenched, eyes bulging, huddled limbs clutched together in a dark, cavernous frame (Figure 14).[106] The illustrator represents the body of the author cramped and confined by the letter that initializes the narrator's easy prose. The facial grimace is decidedly ambiguous. It could denote the author's secret glee at his characters' disappointment – a glee the narrator slickly masks. The title of the chapter certainly supports such an interpretation. ("Chapter" and "capital" are, by the by, etymological siblings.) On the other hand, it could represent the author's reluctance to fulfill his narrative duty and his sense of being constrained by the letter, by the verbal duty that the narrator undertakes without complaint. Both readings, which can coexist, point to a dramatic relationship between author and narrator, one that the illustrator reveals and mediates. The illustrator depicts an author swallowed by his verbal duty, resisting bodily, even as the narrator's words flow relentlessly forward. This pictorial initial reminds one that "the novelist" is as a composite of writer and illustrator and, by extension, that "the novel" is a blend of prose and illustration.

More generally, pictorial initials highlight the verbal–visual hybridity of this and other nineteenth-century novels. Victorian critics show little of the twentieth century's categorizing tendencies, accepting pictorial initials as junctures of verbal and pictorial art. An 1856 reviewer is characteristic, designating them "full of real [visual] art *and* poetical comprehension."[107] Nearly 150 years later, J. Hillis Miller acknowledges their hybridity, yet views them as a battleground for words and images rather than as a harmonious plenitude:

> There is an element of picture in every letter, and an element of writing in every picture. In an illuminated capital the one runs into the other. They are superimposed or interwoven. The place where one stops and the other begins can scarcely be detected. Where would one put an illuminated capital on my spectrum from pure picture to pure letter? It seems to be at both ends at once, therefore the locus of a battle between extremes.[108]

He does not situate pictorial initials at the midpoint of his word and image spectrum, but rather has them leaping frenetically from one end to the other in a bipolar war. The 1856 critic, by contrast, considers them a word and image plenitude, without a hint of conflict.

Although he is a poststructuralist, Hillis Miller shares mainstream twentieth-century structuralist convictions that words and images are irreducible, untranslatable, *a priori* elements eternally in conflict with each other: "A picture and a text juxtaposed will always have different meanings ... Neither the meaning of a picture nor the meaning of a sentence is by any means translatable. The picture means itself. The sentence means itself. The two can never meet."[109] This is why pictorial initials must occupy both ends of Hillis Miller's word and image spectrum, rather than meeting in the middle.

By and large, twentieth-century scholars share Hillis Miller's view. Roland Barthes concludes that "there is never a real incorporation since the substances of the two structures (graphic and iconic) are irreducible."[110] Michel Foucault presents "statements" and "visibilities" as pure, *a priori* elements.[111] And, although W. J. T. Mitchell has argued convincingly that the word and image opposition is culturally constructed rather than essential, he nevertheless claims their opposition as an essentialist principle: words and images are always opposed, for they "are not merely *different* kinds of creatures, but *antithetical* kinds."[112] Thus, when words and images do engage, modern and postmodern critics insist that they can only do so in rivalrous, parasitic, hierarchical, or subversive ways.

Although one can certainly locate points of conflict, opposition, parasitic exchange, and hierarchical dominance between the graphemes and graphics of pictorial initials, these are by no means the only operative dynamics. There is as much breeding ground and playground as battleground: there are points of fusion and of copulating representational fecundity, and points where graphemes and graphics change places. Thus pictorial initials challenge not only traditional categorical distinctions but also postmodern figurations of word and image dynamics.

Although about half of *Vanity Fair*'s 66[113] pictorial initials position the initial letter separately from the drawing in the upper right-hand corner, like a stamp mailing itself into the prose paragraph, in many instances the jettisoned letter is given a pictorial role in the drawing as well as a leading alphabetical role. Just as the word "Pen" both stands alone and is also embedded in the word "Pencil" of *Vanity Fair*'s original subtitle, so too the grapheme of each pictorial initial stands self-sufficient as a letter and yet is also embedded in a drawing. The handwritten appearance of these letters positions them halfway between picture and print, emphasizing the graphic dimensions of writing.

Most readings of words and pictures to date emphasize their semantic and referential functions. Such readings sublimate pictorial lines to what pictorial lines represent, just as they do graphemes to what graphemes represent, favoring the symbolic over the graphic aspects of both text and picture. In both processes, graphics are sublimated to symbolic signification. Cognitive scientist Nicholas Wade explains:

> ...the written form of language and graphics have more in common than is often supposed. That is, the processes in the visual system that recognize the objects in the environment and pictorial images operate in a similar manner to recognize the diverse written symbols we produce...Written words form graphical images that are rarely acknowledged as such because their significance is defined almost entirely at the mental image level.[114]

It is my contention that the tendency to see the verbal and the pictorial as untranslatable and to subjugate images to words derives as much from

UR old friends the Crawleys' family house, in Great Gaunt Street, still bore over its front the hatchment which had been placed there as a token of mourning for Sir Pitt Crawley's demise, yet this heraldic emblem was in itself a very splendid and gaudy piece of furniture, and all the rest of the mansion became more brilliant than it had ever been during the late baronet's reign. The black outer-coating of the bricks was removed and they appeared with a cheerful blushing face streaked with white: the old bronze lions of the knocker were gilt handsomely, the railings painted, and the dismallest house in Great Gaunt Street, became the smartest in the whole quarter, before the green leaves in Hampshire had replaced those yellowing ones which were on the trees in Queen's Crawley avenue when old Sir Pitt Crawley passed under them for the last time.

A little woman, with a carriage to correspond,

15. William Makepeace Thackeray's pictorial initial, in Chapter 44 of *Vanity Fair* (New York: Heritage, 1940).

this cognitive sublimation of graphic lines to symbolic signification as from any other factor. In the shared lines of pictorial initial graphemes and graphics, there is at times no need for translation from one to the other, for one is already graphically if not symbolically the other. Nor from a graphic point of view can either be clearly subjugated to the other when they run along the same lines.

Picture Symbols/Symbol Pictures. Some pictorial initials put pressure on the central categorization that makes phonetic graphemes arbitrary, symbolic, and conventional, and pictorial graphics iconically and mimetically referential. These categorical lines fuse and confuse in pictorial initials where the letter forms a pictorially mimetic sign. In the pictorial initial that opens Chapter 44, for example, the grapheme **O** shares an identical outline with a graphic full moon (Figure 15). Although the **O** as letter leads into a different (geo)graphical and semantic context, away from the pictured mythological seascape to a verbal cityscape ("Our old friends the Crawleys' family house, in Great Gaunt Street"), the fusion of mimetic moon and arbitrary letter in the **O** shape unites verbal and pictorial systems literally along the same graphic lines. The full moon is a found shape in nature, preexisting alphabetic constructions, and the word "moon" bears an arbitrary relationship to its referent. However, its two middle letters do not, and even its **m** and **n** can be configured as so many curved half-moons. Although such mimetic congruences are themselves arbitrary, they demonstrate (quite deliciously) that letters can be arbitrarily mimetic as well as symbolically arbitrary.

WE must pass over a part of Mrs. Rebecca Crawley's biography with that lightness and delicacy which the world demands—the moral world, that has, perhaps, no particular objection to vice, but an insuperable repugnance to hearing vice called by its proper name. There are things we do and know perfectly well in Vanity Fair, though we never speak them: as the Ahrimanians worship the devil, but don't mention him: and a polite public will no more bear to read an authentic description of vice than a truly-refined English or American female will permit the word breeches to be pronounced in her chaste hearing. And yet, Madam, both are

16. William Makepeace Thackeray's pictorial initial, in Chapter 64 of *Vanity Fair* (New York: Heritage, 1940).

Indeed, in the pictorial initials for *Vanity Fair*, symbolic/mimetic distinctions run across the whole spectrum from purely symbolic to purely mimetic lines: for instance, a series of varied **W** initials. Chapter 64 offers the least pictorially mimetic **W** in the initial gallery: its thin two-dimensional lines evoke no mimetic object, only handwritten script (Figure 16). Nevertheless, even as pure letter, the handwritten form places it closer to drawing than to the typeset letters of printed prose, the curlicues pulling away from the symbolic toward purely decorative lines. The **W** of Chapter 20 carries more pictorial substance as a three-dimensional collection of overlapping sticks. But its position close to the prose paragraph and its elevation above the more grounded objects in the picture situates it closer to the symbolic than to the mimetic end of the pictorial initial spectrum (Figure 17). In Chapter 27's pictorial initial, similar sticks form a **W** pair of stilts on which a costumed child-actor balances,

WITHOUT knowing how, Captain William Dobbin found himself the great promoter, arranger, and manager of the match between George Osborne and Amelia. But for him it never would have taken place: he could not but confess as much to himself, and smiled rather bitterly as he thought that he of all men in the world should be the person upon whom the care of this marriage had fallen. But though indeed the conducting of this negotiation was about as painful a task as could be set to him, yet when he had a duty to perform, Captain

17. William Makepeace Thackeray's pictorial initial, in Chapter 20 of *Vanity Fair* (New York: Heritage, 1940).

HEN Jos's fine carriage drove up to the inn door at Chatham, the first face which Amelia recognized was the friendly countenance of Captain Dobbin, who had been pacing the street for an hour past in expectation of his friends' arrival. The Captain, with shells on his frock-coat, and a crimson sash and sabre, presented a military appearance, which made Jos quite proud to be able to claim such an acquaintance, and the stout civilian hailed him with a cordiality very different from the reception which Jos vouchsafed to his friends in Brighton and Bond Street.

18. William Makepeace Thackeray's pictorial initial, in Chapter 27 of *Vanity Fair* (New York: Heritage, 1940).

lending each further substance as a supporting alphabetic character in a theatrical context (Figure 18). The lines of the **W** initiating Chapter 1 take wooden stilts back to their natural source – trees – and, concomitantly, away from constructed theatrical representation to naturalistic pictorialization (Figure 19). Chapter 27's and Chapter 1's initials thus undermine symbolic/mimetic and conventional/natural differentiations of verbal and pictorial modes at the level of both signifier and signified – of both **W** shape and of what that shape signifies. However, Chapter 1's tree branches appear unnaturally boxy and truncated in comparison to other shrubs in the picture, indicating a degree of concession to the unnatural alphabetic world. But the **W** branches that open Chapter 12 are as mimetic and naturalistic as any pictorial lines in the drawing, so that the **W** requires more searching to identify it as the initial letter of the sentence and to extract it from the branches of the pictorial world for prose purposes. In the pictorial context, the bodies of the walking lovers faintly echo the shape of the **W** branches, pulling the lines of the

HILE the present century was in its teens, and on one sun-shiny morning in June, there drove up to the great iron gate of Miss Pinkerton's academy for young ladies, on Chiswick Mall, a large family coach, with two fat horses in blazing harness, driven by a fat coachman in a three-cornered hat and wig, at the rate of four miles an hour. A black servant, who reposed on the box beside the fat coachman, un-

19. William Makepeace Thackeray's pictorial initial, in Chapter 1 of *Vanity Fair* (New York: Heritage, 1940).

E MUST now take leave of Arcadia, and those amiable people practising the rural virtues there, and travel back to London, to inquire what has become of Miss Amelia.

"We don't care a fig for her," writes some unknown correspondent with a pretty little hand-writing and a pink seal to her note. "She is *fade* and insipid," and adds some more kind remarks in this strain, which I should never have repeated at all, but that they are in truth prodigiously complimentary to the young lady whom they concern.

Has the beloved reader, in his experience of society, never heard similar remarks by good-natured female friends; who always won-

20. William Makepeace Thackeray's pictorial initial, in Chapter 12 of *Vanity Fair* (New York: Heritage, 1940).

grapheme away from the alphabetic world toward their affinities with similar pictorial shapes (Figure 20).

Such pulling, however, can run in either direction. The pictorial initial that opens Chapter 41 (Figure 21), for example, sports an **S**-shaped pictorial whip, which is elected over a conventional alphabetic **S** (the final **S** of "OMNIBUS" on the back of the carriage) to open the paragraph. The effect is to pull pictorial lines toward prose and to keep symbolic letters in the picture. Within the picture, the alphabetic functions of the **S** whip are pressed on both sides – it is pulled by its twin in "OMNIBUS" to the left and by the prose sentence to the right. This pictorial initial further distresses any clear delineation of picture as mimetic and letter as symbolic when one notes letter shapes scattered all over the foreground: an **O**, a **V**, a cursive **Y**, and various **S** and **W** shapes, to name only the more legible

O the mourning being ready, and Sir Pitt Crawley warned of their arrival, Colonel Crawley and his wife took a couple of places in the same old High-flyer coach, by which Rebecca had travelled in the defunct Baronet's company, and on her first journey into the world some nine years before. How well she remembered the Inn Yard, and the ostler to whom she refused money, and the insinuating Cambridge lad who wrapped her in his coat on the journey. Rawdon took his place outside, and would have liked to drive, but his grief forbade him. He sate by the coachman, and talked about horses

21. William Makepeace Thackeray's pictorial initial, in Chapter 41 of *Vanity Fair* (New York: Heritage, 1940).

ones. Like handwritten drafts preceding a final printed text, they appear
as rejects from the paragraph, prose litter embellishing pictorial ground.
Their role here is not, however, semantic, but purely graphic. The choice
of the **S** whip over the picture's more textual **S** further troubles reading
conventions. Reading from the whip into the paragraph, one slides along
the mobile whip into the prose at the right. Had the final **S** of OMNIBUS
been the selected initial letter, the cognitive process would have been a
leap from boxed word to boxed word – which is precisely what readers
do normally: they leap from boxed word to boxed word along sentences.
Here, far from words and images being separated by an unbridgeable divide, the journey from picture to word flows more smoothly than it does
from word to word.

Although the effect of **O** moon, **W** branches, and **S** whip is more one
of double articulation in two sign systems than a total deconstruction of
mimetic and symbolic distinctions between words and images, the selection of the mimetic whip over the symbolic letter nevertheless demonstrates that the mimetic–symbolic divide is itself arbitrary, conventional,
and variable and that there are lines – quite literally – that run words and
images together. Thackeray demonstrates that **O**, **W**, and **S** shapes occupy
no exclusive or essential position in either verbal or pictorial systems.
Rather, the reader-viewer sees the picture in the letter and the letter in
the picture, finds the moon in the **O** and the **O** in the moon, the **W** in the
branches and the branches in the **W**. To do this, the reader-viewer must
engage in a double process of sublimation: sublimating picture to letter
to read the sentence, and letter to picture to view the pictorial lines, a
sublimation from which s/he surfaces only to sublimate again.

Returning to Rosch's theory of categorization outlined in Chapter 1, we
find that categorizations of verbal and pictorial systems hold less strongly
at categories above or below the basic level of categorization ("words"
and "pictures"). In a vertical chain of categorization that runs from everything to signs to verbal signs to paragraphs to sentences to single words
to graphemes to fragments of graphemes, "words" comprises the basic
level of categorization.[115] Similarly, in a vertical chain of categorization
that runs from everything to signs to pictorial signs to discrete pictures to
pictorial lines to pieces of pictorial lines, "pictures" constitutes the basic
level of categorization. As Rosch has shown, it is at these basic levels that
contrasts between vertical chains hold most strongly. Higher up at the
level of "signs," words and pictures share more features and functions
and appear less categorically opposed. Most interdisciplinary studies of
literature and film have been conducted at these or at other higher levels of categorization, like "representations" or "narratives" or "cultural

FEAR the gentleman to whom Miss Amelia's letters were addressed was rather an obdurate critic. Such a number of notes followed Lieutenant Osborne about the country, that he became almost ashamed of the jokes of his mess-room companions regarding them, and ordered his servant never to deliver them, except at his private apartment. He was seen lighting his cigar with one, to the horror of Captain Dobbin, who, it is my belief, would have given a bank-

22. William Makepeace Thackeray's pictorial initial, in Chapter 23 of *Vanity Fair* (New York: Heritage, 1940).

ideologies." Few, however, have addressed lower levels, like graphemic and pictorial lines, where categorical differences also hold less firmly. Far from being separated by an unbridgeable chasm, in some instances verbal and pictorial systems run along exactly the same lines. These shared lines open up, somewhat paradoxically, both more integral relations and more varied dynamics between verbal and pictorial systems than purely oppositional models have provided.

The Ends of the Spectrum. If at one end of the graphemic–graphic spectrum lie points of merger that turn the "confusion of the arts" bemoaned by Babbitt into a fusion, at the other end lie points of multifarious fragmentation, in which pictorial and verbal significations bounce (nearly) endlessly back and forth, creating multiplicative copulating representations, as when two mirrors face each other and produce an infinite number of reflections. In contrast to the **S** whip initial, which boasts an excess of graphemes, the pictorial initial of camel and rider that opens Chapter 23 appears at first glance to be entirely devoid of graphemes (Figure 22). Most of Thackeray's pictorial initials place the desired letter in the upper right hand corner: in Chapter 23's initial, this corner remains blank. The reader-viewer may begin to hallucinate letters, as I did, discerning an **I**-shaped rifle, an **S**-esque camel's head and neck, and a tangle of camel legs that appear alternately as **A**, **H**, or **M**. It was only through reading the opening sentence, "HAT is the secret mesmerism which friendship possesses . . . ?" that I made sure of the letter: a **W**-shaped saddle embedded in the center of the drawing. I identified it, not on the basis of its shape (since there are other letter shapes or else no letter shapes in the picture, depending on one's angle of view and capacity for alphabetic hallucination), but rather on the basis of what is lacking in the prose sentence.

My process immediately evoked deconstructive accounts of how linguistic meaning is predicated on lack and absence. It also recalled Hillis Miller's differentiation of verbal absence and pictorial presence – words "are by nature the presence of an absence. In the presence of the thing itself words are not needed. A painting is there, here and now."[116] But pictorial initials create a presence-in-absence that unravels such contrasts. The pictorial initial is both a pictorial tab that pushes aside the text and a part of that displaced text: it is thus both pre-text and text. Not only does it figure literally and spatially as pre-text, in some cases it assumes an additional pretextual function as an allusive initial, referring to prior texts and pictures – to ancient mythologies and old family crests, to recent histories (like Napoleon's), and to earlier historical periods, like the Elizabethan Renaissance or the late eighteenth century.[117] In another sense, all pictorial initials function as pre-text in that their hieroglyphic form renders them contemporaneous pseudo-precursors of phonetic language, a role that playfully brings out the second sense of "pretext" – that of pretense – as hieroglyphics aspire to pure prose.

Such hieroglyphic pretenses to prose create a presence-in-absence that connects as much as it opposes the two signifying systems. The desertion of the verbal for the pictorial represented by all pictorial initials intensifies in the example under consideration, where the grapheme poses as a mimetic pictorial object, hiding its "letterness" in the picture. It plays a game of hide-and-seek, in which the hiding is always seen and yet never fully outed by the seeking: the grapheme is continuously sought by the sentence and continually found hiding in the picture. While it at first appears that the grapheme's absconding from the verbal creates a surplus representation in the picture and an absence in the text (such an interpretation would resemble conventional deconstructive readings), on further examination, surplus representations run through both systems as a result of their shared lines. Ostensibly the sentence lacks a **W**, while the picture contains both saddle and **W**. But in the verbal context, the letter **W** is burdened with extra lines and shadings, so that it can never be fully assimilated into the typographic verbal sentence. The surplus here is semantic as well as pictorial. The pictorial **W** is paradoxically more semantically resonant than the graphemic **W**: the latter is a meaningless grapheme beginning a word all but empty of referential substance – "What" – whereas the **W** picture represents a saddle, a whole word and a concrete referential noun at that. The pictorial saddle is thus far richer semantically than the **W** that shares its lines, but this richness must be discarded by the verbal system, which seeks only the **W** shape of the saddle and the "w" sound the symbol evokes – not the idea of saddle or the word "saddle" or the shading of the saddle. One does not read "W**saddle**HAT is the secret mesmerism that friendship possesses . . . ?" or "W[shaded lines]**HAT** is the secret mesmerism that friendship possesses . . . ?" Yet sublimation is never entirely identical with excision in such dynamics, so that one does carry the saddle into the sentence, though it makes no sense, and the "WHAT" lurks in the picture.

An additional tension pulling against traditional verbal and pictorial categorizations in this and other pictorial initials lies between the grapheme as graphic and the grapheme as phoneme. These tensions put pressure on categorizations of language as belonging to the ear and pictures as belonging to the eye. As the pictorial context pulls the **W** toward pictorial functions and loads it with pictorial lines, the initial emphasizes the graphic over the phonetic aspects of writing. Yet even as the phoneme seems to vanish into a pictorial vortex, the **W** tinges the pictorial with its phonetic properties, lending it aural as well as visual dimensions, and further swelling the initial's representational surplus. In pictorial initials, letters are pictures, pictures are symbols, phonemes are graphic, and pictures are audible. As such, pictorial initials restore the sound lost from pictures and the sight lost from language when hieroglyphs separated into phonetic and visual parts.

In the face of such practices, assertions regarding the irreconcilable, *a priori* differential nature of words and images begin to crumble. While there may be no semantic translation between the shared lines of a **W** saddle and the **W** of "WHAT," in a pictorial context, **W** and "saddle" are graphic synonyms, sharing nearly identical lines. We have been looking at the irreducibility and untranslatability of words and images from only one angle – from that of semantics, signs, and referents – when all along pictorial bridges have run between words and pictures.[118] Discussing a lecture by Paul de Man on translation, Eve Tavor Bannet notes:

> Translations focus on pure language and translate literally, word for word, word *instead* of word, to [in the words of de Man] "disrupt the ostensibly stable meaning of a sentence and introduce in it a slippage by means of which that meaning disappears, evanesces, and by means of which all control over that meaning is lost."[119]

In the pictorial initial, a different kind of translation exists within the original itself: a translation from line to line, where original meaning is neither lost nor destroyed, but rather multiplied in both pictorial and verbal contexts. In such a configuration, hierarchies of original and copy are circumvented, though not through deconstructive methods.

HAT is the secret mesmerism which friend-
ship possesses, and under the opera-
tion of which a person ordinarily
sluggish, or cold, or timid, becomes
wise, active, and resolute, in another's
behalf? As Alexis, after a few passes
from Dr. Elliotson, despises pain,
reads with the back of his head, sees
miles off, looks into next week, and
performs other wonders, of which, in
his own private normal condition, he
is quite incapable; so you see, in the
affairs of the world and under the
magnetism of friendship, the modest
man become bold, the shy confident,

23. William Makepeace Thackeray's pictorial initial, in Chapter 13 of *Vanity Fair* (New York: Heritage, 1940).

As evidence of this multiplicative, copulating effect, I turn to the other end of the spectrum that fractures word–image binarisms into multiple mirrorings. In the pictorial initial that opens Chapter 13, pictorial and verbal signs copulate and reproduce multiple resonances, shattering dichotomous models into shards of multifaceted signification. The I of this initial begins a sentence that reads: "I fear the gentleman to whom Miss Amelia's letters were addressed was rather an obdurate critic" (Figure 23). In an immediate fissuring of representation, the I claims two referents and two narrative spaces and temporalities. The I of the textual sentence refers to the narrator in present time and extradiegetic space; the I of the picture represents "the gentleman," the diegetic, past-tense George Osborne, in a most uncritical state, gazing at himself and a single letter with which he is evidently in love. In the verbal context, I narrator and I George diverge; in the pictorial one, George and his I coincide perfectly, as narcissistic self-love fuels George's gaze on himself and on the I. In a more mixed pictorial-verbal reading, they also coincide, as George's narcissism is the source of his obdurate criticism of Amelia's letters: the letter with which George is in love is the letter I, representing himself, just as the portrait he prefers to gaze on (even while Amelia worships his) is his own mirror image. The I takes on a third verbal signification: it seems to grow from the reflection of his head in the mirror, like a monosyllabic, monographemic monologue framed in the dialogue balloon of the I-imaging glass.

Ironically, this is only the beginning of this monomaniacal, solipsistic grapheme's many significations. In giving the I so many other referents, the author-illustrator mirrors George's self-magnification, so that this single grapheme contains all the world. Yet at the same time, the multiplied

referents undermine the **I**'s solitary stance and George's egotistical appropriation of it, in that it refers to so many things that are not George.
The narrator injects himself as the shared object of George's loving gaze
at the **I**. The playful placement of the **I** on George's head renders it a pictorial horn as well as a grapheme, a mythological allusion strengthened by
a verbal reference to George as "a devil of a fellow" in the adjoining paragraph. That single horn is plausibly realistic given the angle of the picture
(which could obscure a second horn) and egocentrically asymmetrical,
extending the joke of George's single-minded self-absorption through
his single bachelor status and stated preference for short love letters
(**I** represents the shortest *billet-doux* of all). At the same time, the single
horn provides a pseudo-erection and pseudo-castration of these allegorical and mythological appendages (the horn he has and the horn he lacks)
or, for those who find Freudian symbolism as unacceptably anachronistic
as silent filmmaker Hugo Ballin found Thackeray's costumes, it presents
an image that suggests a happily solipsistic self-cuckolding.

The addition of the horn, together with subtle differences between
George's mirrored and unmirrored faces, creates a further asymmetry
that fissures mimetic realism and allegorical reference. The unmirrored
face of the dashing, fashionably groomed young bachelor becomes in the
mirror a smirking, sinister face with a hint of mythological devil. The **I** as
devil's horn protruding from the mirrored head is reinforced by subtle
omissions and additions in the facial lines that metamorphose the original
George's groomed sideburns into a devilish goatee in the reflection. The
reflection further evokes a more subjective self: George's body has all but
vanished through the looking glass and his head floats without a neck.
Not only does this detachment of head from body symbolize his solipsistic
disconnectedness from his context: the lines of the mirrored face also
indicate the content of that subjective self-absorption. The unreflected
face is proudly posed, as for a portrait, while the mirrored face smirks
with self-satisfaction – as if the reflection is admiring the original rather
than the other way round.

The asymmetry of the reflection extends to the absence of the letter **I**
on the unmirrored side of the picture. While the pictorial lines of the
reflected George are fewer and lighter, the letter **I** is, by contrast, gar-
ishly thick. The letter is too loud in the picture – even louder amidst the
more lightly sketched lines of the mirror world – its very presence mocking the mirror's claim to mimeticism, revealing instead the influence of
subjectivity on perception and the impingement of the verbal on the
pictorial, whether of the noisy grapheme or the presiding literary traditions that inform the picture's allusions. Yet the pictorial lines also assert

independence in their refusal to construct George by the other allusive names accorded him in the adjoining prose – Don Giovanni and Apollo. Beyond this refusal, numerous pictorial lines in the initial resist verbal interpretation and construction. To read the shadings, hatches, lines, and curls I have not yet discussed in verbal terms is certainly possible – one could note, for example, the heavy preponderance of random and unassigned vertical lines, echoing the vertical **I**. But the verbal cannot entirely express the pictorial. To read pictorial lines to such verbal excesses begins to partake of the verbal narcissism that the letter mocks. One must also read the pictorial lines in terms of each other, in terms of pictorial rather than symbolic considerations – crossed lines at odds with each other, lines opening up light and space, lines closing them down, lines representing nothing but themselves (like the vertical stripes on the wall), lines refusing to differentiate objects (the lines of George's trousers merge with the lines of his dressing table).

What we see in these readings, which represent only a few of many possibilities, is that pictorial initials not only challenge distinctions between words and images, but also reveal dynamics that are far more aesthetically fecund than the deceptive, railroaded, agenda-driven rhetorical analogies of "prose painting." We see here too the limitations imposed on the novel by partial theories that treat it as though it had always been pure prose. The excision of illustrations from reeditions of novels and from most academic considerations of them is responsible not only for major omissions in novel criticism (one could argue that every reading of an illustrated novel should take its illustrations into account, regardless of the argument), but also in understanding the novel and film debate. The next chapter traces similar tendencies in film theory that press film toward an identity of pure image through a similar but inverse use of interart analogies.

3 Film Language

Film Pictures as Language

This chapter highlights continuities between prose painting analogies in the nineteenth century and film language analogies in the twentieth and twenty-first to probe how theories of the novel and of the film have evolved in relation and reaction to one another. Just as novel prose was decreed "painting" throughout the nineteenth century, film images were decreed "language" throughout the twentieth century, continuing into the twenty-first. From the early 1900s, when reviewers heralded film as a cure for the Tower of Babel, to the early 2000s, when Landmark Company theaters preface each screening with the words, "The language of film is universal," the analogy pervades public, artistic, and academic discourse. More than this, film images have been proclaimed a universal language, rooted in the idea here articulated by Christian Metz, that "visual perception varies less throughout the world than languages do."[1]

It should come as no surprise at this juncture to learn that film inherited this rhetoric from painting. Analogies of painting as language surface regularly in painting discourse and receive a particularly robust airing in nineteenth-century art criticism.[2] Most famously, John Ruskin propounded: "Painting, or art generally, with all its technicalities, difficulties, and particular ends, is nothing but a noble and expressive language."[3] Others, like Mary Barton in 1890, further designated painting not simply a language but a "universal language."[4] And in 1921, Edmund J. Sullivan extended this phrase to book illustrations.[5] Now illustrations speak a universal language, in contrast to prose's specific one.

Critics, however, insist that film "language" more closely resembles verbal language than painting. Christian Metz argues that "To go from one image to two images, is to go from image to language."[6] It is editing or montage, according to filmmaker, theorist, and critic Sergei Eisenstein, that constitutes film's "language," "diction," "syntax," and "speech" as cuts between shots function like spaces between words and create syntactic relationships among them.[7] (In order to avoid confusion in this discussion, I use "film language" to refer exclusively to the analogical language of film's images and "film words" to refer to its literal verbal words.)

Just as prose painting analogies were marshaled to subordinate the novel's literal pictures, its illustrations, to prose pictures, so too have film language analogies been used to subordinate film words to film images. The essay "Film Language," in which Eisenstein most influentially advances the film language analogy, begins thus: "I do not propose to talk of the talking film – or, more exactly, of its talking portions. It speaks for itself. It even screams."[8] For Eisenstein, the analogical "language" of image montage requires a spokesman precisely because it is not literally language, while film's verbal language is deemed self-explanatory. Were such an argument followed in literary studies, there would be none. It is intriguing that both novel illustrations and film words are accused of a hyperliterality that mandates little or no critical attention and leads to suggestions of their excision or minimization in aesthetic practice.

Similar attitudes to film words pervade film criticism. Ralph Stephenson and J. R. Debrix's *The Cinema as Art* (cited here both as representative and as one of film studies' most widely reprinted texts) devotes only 5 of its 270 pages to verbal language, in spite of the fact that most films are full of words – dialogue, voice-over, intertitles, words on sets and props, foreign language subtitles, song lyrics, and credits, to say nothing of the verbal bases (treatments, scenarios, screenplays) of almost all films. Equally telling, much of the scant attention accorded words in Stephenson and Debrix's book represents them as threats to filmic visuals and seeks to diminish their signifying power by subordinating them to nonverbal film elements, particularly images. Words in Stephenson and Debrix's account "interfere with and disturb the image." "The shooting script" is "a technical blue-print for putting together bits of sight and sound (of which speech is only one element among several)" – the parenthetical reference here graphically epitomizing the overall minimizing and subjugation of film words in film studies generally. More than this, the script is denuded as a verbal form and turned by analogy into a technical visual arts form, in much the same way book illustrations were chiefly treated technologically as "plates" or by verbal analogy as "commentaries" in the previous century. The authors further denude film words of their verbal dimensions: "there is beauty in speech and acting apart from the meaning of the words . . . when we do hear the words and their meaning

matters, the sound and intonation and the appearance of the characters as they say them may . . . be of as much or more significance."[9] The
rhetoric strips speech of its narrative and semantic functions and, even
when these do resurface, they remain subjugated to film visuals and,
adding insult to injury, to film's nonverbal aural elements. These critical
and rhetorical tendencies show no signs of abating (though there have always been unheeded dissenting voices, represented parenthetically here
to indicate their effect on the criticism).[10] Near the turn of the twenty-
first century, 50 percent of the 14 pages addressing "Spoken Language"
in Louis Giannetti's *Understanding Movies* (1999) is devoted to film stills,
which seems to mount a looming objection to even the scant amount of
attention accorded film words.[11]

The subjugation expresses a fierce territoriality reminiscent of turn-
of-the-twentieth-century book illustration criticism. Just as Henry James
opposed illustration as a pictorial rival to prose "painting," so too, filmmakers and critics object to film words primarily as rivals to film's visual
"language." Henri Colpi lamented in the 1960s: "Today montage has practically lost [its] power. The word explains everything, it slows down the
progression, it waters down the emotional impact of the image. The camera is no longer concerned with making the objects or faces speak."[12] As
we have seen, montage is film's primary claim to language. The speech
of the word in this account has usurped the "speech" of the images – the
wordless significations of objects and faces. Just as novel illustrations are
deemed too pictorially loud, disrupting prose reading and blocking out
mental imaging, so too, film words are seen to shout down and slow down
the visual "speech" of film images.

Just as illustration historian Henry Blackburn recommended in 1896
that illustrations appear only where "words fail to express," filmmakers
and critics recommend a similar rationing of words in film.[13] Director
Rouben Mamoulian is typical: "The less dialogue the better the film . . .
when you cannot express it visually, then you put in words."[14] If every
appearance of a word marks film "language's" failure to represent, this
can only heighten word and image hostilities.

The changing fortunes of screenwriters in the twentieth century resemble those of illustrators in the nineteenth. Like British book illustrators
of the 1820s and 1830s, screenwriters of 1920s and 1930s Hollywood en-
joyed a period of moderate prestige and creative credit. But in the 1950s,
extensions of the film began language analogy combined with new theories of film began to change the balance of power. The *Cahiers du cinéma*
movement made the director, rather than the screenwriter, the author
(*auteur*) of the film. The screenwriter lost the language of authorship,

and screenwriting, like book illustration, was increasingly referenced in technological terminology or through analogies to nonverbal arts. The camera became a *caméra-stylo* and the screenplay frequently became a "blueprint," as we have seen. In the 1920s, the camera–pen analogy had been reserved for screenwriters, particularly the famous novelists and playwrights recruited by producers like Adolph Zukor to heighten the prestige of film: "famous authors actually in the studios writing new plays for Paramount Pictures, advising with directors, using the motion picture as they formerly used the pen."[15] Screenwriters were so important in this period of film history that Rex Beach adduced: "The author is now contesting with the star for supremacy." As late as the 1930s and 1940s in Hollywood, the director was not recognized as the film's major creative power. As Gore Vidal explains:

> . . . the ambitious man became a producer (that's where the power was). The talented man became a writer (that's where the creation was). The pretty man became a star . . . the directors were, at worst, brothers-in-law; at best, bright technicians. All in all, they were a cheery, unpretentious lot, and if anyone had told them that they were *auteurs du cinéma*, few could have coped with the concept, much less the French.[16]

In 1939, producer Irving Thalberg said: "The writer is the most important person in Hollywood, but we must never tell the sons of bitches."[17] The *auteur* movement changed even such behind-the-scenes perceptions.[18] Today, even when a director is also the screenwriter of a film, it is his/her role as director rather than as screenwriter that defines him/her as the film's author, just as it is Thackeray's role as prose writer rather than illustrator that defines him as a "novelist."

In the 1960s and 1970s, Roland Barthes, Marie-Claire Ropars-Wuilleumier, and others extended the *auteur* analogy from practice to academic theory and criticism, advancing cinematic visuals as *écriture*, labeling films "texts," and subjecting cinema to semiotic methods derived from linguistics and literary study.[19] As noted in Chapter 1, the scholarly treatment of the film language analogy as though it were a literal fact (in James Monaco's phrasing, "real") led, against all filmic agendas, paradoxically, to a subjugation of cinema to literary scholarship.[20] Well into the 1970s, semiotic methodologies derived from literary studies dominated film studies. However, it was precisely this literal application of semiotics to film that ultimately unveiled the fallacies and limitations of the analogy. The discussion is amply documented elsewhere: semiotic scholars found film language too unruly to conform to the finite set of grammatical structures and limited sets of operations that characterize verbal languages.[21] Monaco summarizes the failure of the film language analogy's claim to identity, diluting analogy to the weaker rhetorical figure of simile: "Film is not a language, but it is like a language."[22] Gilles Deleuze argues that cinema is "not a language, but a visual material which is the utterable of language."[23] Metz led the retreat from semiotics to Lacanian psycho-analysis, a theoretical framework emphasizing visual and scopic cognitive processes in film viewers, one that presses language underground toward the unconscious and toward analogy and simile in its central assertion that the unconscious is structured "like" a language. Other film critics turned to structuralist, narratological, and cultural studies approaches (these remain the most popular approaches to novel and film study) and, as we saw in Chapter 1, they sidestep the problems of analogy and category by working at higher levels of categorization, like "signs," "representations," "narrative," and "ideology."

Yet despite film "language's" dilution to simile, its relegation to the un-conscious, and its burial in larger categories, the film language analogy persists. Metz's *Film Language* and James Monaco's *How to Read a Film*, two of the most influential books on film, are regularly reprinted, and new publications, like *Film as Text* (1991) and *The Language of Cinema* (1998), reinscribe the analogy for new generations of scholars.[24] Even critics who challenge the film language analogy, like Deleuze, continue to subordi-nate film words to film images: "the talkie, the sound film . . . [is] *a new dimension of the visual image, a new component . . .* a fourth dimension of the visual image, supplementing the third."[25] Here, just as illustrations were not allowed to be pictures but were considered analogically as supple-mentary verbal matter – "commentaries" on the prose – so too film words are not allowed to be words but are rather supplements of the image. Thus, these analogical dynamics persist in spite of changes in critical theories.

The two discourses not only run parallel, they also intertangle. That literati grew most eager to purge novels of illustrations precisely as film was gaining popular ascendancy in the early decades of the twentieth cen-tury is, to my mind, no coincidence. As James and others pushed novels toward a new aesthetic of pure prose, film critics pressed film toward an aesthetic of pure image, carving up verbal and pictorial territory between them. Part of this shared imperative came from a wider preference for aesthetic purism, as Babbitt's *New Laocoön* attests. But purism also serves interart rivalry. Pure arts are not only "better"; they can also claim territory another hybrid art has abandoned in order to press its own purity. Thus, as the novel pushed toward pure prose, the film pushed toward pure image. David Bordwell *et al.* document that film without verbal intertitles was a prevalent ideal between 1913 and 1916.[26] The ideal resurfaced in the late 1920s during the heyday of silent film: "It can hardly be claimed that the promiscuous meeting of words with pictures leads to purity," wrote a 1928 aesthetician; "pictorial form ought not to be given place beside the literary form – and here is at least a start towards chaste reasoning."[27]

But most filmmakers have been unwilling or unable to do without words. Film's inability to excise its words to my mind accounts for the persistence of the film language analogy, even as the prose painting analogy died slowly along with book illustration. Indeed, it is neither legal nor economically advisable for films to contain no credits or copyright. Film and television, therefore, display credits, but often they do not allow viewers time to read them. This is especially the case with television credits and the credits following film previews. However, it is also the case with the closing credits of some feature films. Even a rapid reader has only time to catch a few actor names from the credits list at the end of *In the Bedroom* before the frame cuts to another list. Thus, though film cannot and does not excise all its words, it may just as well have done so in these instances. Here, words appear as visual images, seen but not read or heard their semantic capacities hobbled and mocked.

Film criticism also achieves an effectual rhetorical if not literal excision of film words when it treats film words as though they do not belong to film – as "uncinematic." This rhetorical bastardizing, however, requires some probing. "Cinematic" comes from "cinematography," which represents only one aspect of film art – the camera work. Yet this one part comes synecdochally to describe the whole – "cinema." In the early days of film, however, "Screen Play" referred to the entire film. Now it refers only to one part of film: to the written text on which the film is based. Thus what was once the whole has been reduced to a part (Screen Play to screenplay), and what was once a part has been inflated to the whole (cinematography to Cinema).

These displacing and usurping terminologies extend to critical configurations of the relationship between screenplay and finished film – or between screenplay and Screen Play. Most consider the process simultaneously as a birth through, and abortion of, language. John Harrington is representative:

> Because of film's emphasis on visuals, the verbal language recorded in a script tells little of the ultimate impact of a film . . . Necessary as a blueprint is, the film image is of ultimate importance . . . film scripts receive scant attention. Primarily only film buffs read scripts . . . The fact that few people read scripts signals the rightful dominance of the medium of film.[28]

This last phrase is particularly revealing: "the medium of film" here excludes film words. But film theory goes further than this to define film as something that has purged itself of words. It is not simply "not words" but words eradicated and converted to images. In 1998, Bernard F. Dick put it this way: "the script recedes into the background as it changes from a verbal to a visual text, so that by the time the film has been complete, the words have been translated into images."[29] Such a theory of filmmaking does not accord with aesthetic practice, for most screenplays consist primarily of dialogue, which transfers directly into film as words. Moreover, "translated" is not quite the right term. Like those film adaptations that begin with dissolving shots of their founding novels, films in general base their creative process on a visual dissolution of their words. The process of filmmaking is one of deverbalizing, deliterarizing, and de-wording verbal language to make film "language." This is not translation but evisceration into images. Indeed, one could argue that the destruction and dominance of the word constitutes a principal aesthetic of film theory.

Film Words as Literature

If film words are not "cinematic," then what are they and where do they belong? William H. Phillips's 1999 book categorizes original screenplays with other written sources of film – with novels, plays, short stories, biographies, histories, and news articles.[30] Phillips's configuration of the screenplay as literary source points to a wider idea that film words do not belong to film at all, but are rather literary encroachments on film. If the film language analogy claims the other, language, as filmic self, the film-words-as-literature analogy disowns film's actual language as literary other.

The tendency to cast film words as literature and to resent them as encroachments on film appears early on. In 1928, Ukrainian theorist Leonid Skrypnyk complained: "Cinema has to humiliate itself and seek compromises [with literature]. Intertitles constitute the first major compromise."[31] In 1923, Ernst Lubitsch similarly perceived that, "In our titles we borrow from the stage or the novel. Later we will have discovered the motion picture style.... I try to exclude titles wherever possible ... [and] have every scene speak for itself."[32] The word "borrow" indicates perceptions that words do not belong to film, but rather constitute temporary loans until film's visual "language" can "speak for itself." The analogy here strikingly echoes Henry James's polemic that prose be "pictorial enough in itself."[33] And, like James, Lubitsch engages a rhetoric and aesthetic practice of exclusion.

The graphic rivalry between film images and film intertitles eased with the coming of the synchronized soundtrack. As in Western language generally, verbal graphics were subjugated to phonetics as written words became aural words. Film images held a monopoly on the eye, while the word was relegated to the less acute sense of the ear. Nevertheless, critics and filmmakers attacked sound dialogue as though it were a reinfestation of film by literature, rather than a new invention of film technology or an integral component of an evolving medium. The synchronized sound-track was hailed simultaneously as a rescue from the verbal tyranny of intertitles (of graphically represented words) and as a new verbal oppres-sor (of aurally represented words): "the sound film had liberated the cinema from its thirty-year bondage to the printed word," says one histo-rian. "The task now was not to re-shackle the medium to the spoken word of the talkie."[34] Again, quite strikingly, "the medium" excludes words and stands in opposition to words. No such objections are made to the music or sound effects that the synchronized soundtrack also brought to film.

The literary arch-villain in film history has always been theater, a subject I address further in Chapter 4. Film historian Gerald Mast laments:

> Although the post-Griffith silent film had declared its independence from the stage, the early sound film became the vassal of the theatre once again. . . . The moving picture stopped moving and stopped us-ing pictures. Critics and directors sang a requiem for film art and said amen.[35]

The rhetoric of liberation, slavery, and religion here signals a competitive and mythological aesthetics rather than a tangibly empirical one. "Film art" is again reduced to cinematography and film words are represented as hampering that art.

Arthur Knight's account of early sound is perhaps the most marked in its use of political rhetoric. Just as prose writers and critics had com-plained of book illustration by observing that "when literature and art are put together it is generally literature that suffers," so too Knight com-plains that "the new emphasis on dialogue was robbing the screen of its visual impact."[36] Before sound can be Knight-ed as a *bona fide* part of film art under a subheading, "The Art of the Sound Film," it must first traverse Knight's other subheadings: "The Tyranny of Sound," "Lib-erating the Camera," "Mastering the Sound Track," and "Exploring the New Medium." "The Tyranny of Sound" posits sound as an aural tyrant ravaging and imprisoning visual images; the other three subheadings describe the cinematographic liberation, dominance, and conquest of sound in a rhetoric of revolution and expansionist colonization.[37]

The concept of film words as literary other, to be overthrown, mastered, and colonized, is by no means limited to film's formative years. Sarah

Kozloff documents both "the conventional notion that films caught voice-over (like the measles?) from novels" and the vociferous objection to any narrative voice not subjected to the scrutiny of the image.[38] Richard L. Stromgren and Martin F. Norden represent two among hundreds of critics declaring any kind of verbal narration in film "uncinematic."[39] Their central objection is to a mastering, omniscient narrative verbal voice, for such a voice smacks too much of verbal dominance over the image.

In addition to criticism that casts film words as literary, uncinematic other, film visuals have frequently allied with literature proper to undermine film words further, a process resembling alliances of prose with photography against book illustration. Film critics not only castigate film words as "uncinematic," they also attack them as "bad literature." Just as Dickens sought to elevate his writing by analogy to famous painters,[40] so too, Eisenstein urged "film-workers" to emulate the "speech and word" of "the great masters of literature" in their "montage and shots," developing each "montage sequence with as much care as a line of poetry is admitted into a poem." His argument, however, pits great literature against film words: the verbal portion of film, "even before cinematically appraising it, contains so much poverty of a purely literary sort that its film claims may be put aside."[41] Film images are to aspire to great literature; film words are condemned as bad literature. Literary judgments thus govern the aspirations of film images and the condemnations of film words alike. The film language analogy is marshaled with dazzlingly unjust brilliance not only against film words, but against any theory or criticism of film that would even consider these words worthy of study.

Such unfavorable comparisons of film words to great literature by no means originate with Eisenstein. A 1920 advertisement for the Irving System of Photoplay Writing decrees: "Millions of People Can Write Stories and Photoplays and Don't Know It! Don't you believe the Creator gave you a story-writing faculty, just as He did the greatest writer?"[42] Such leveling claims set film writers apart from contemporaneous literary cults that worship the "greatest writers" as rarefied geniuses. A 1927 account of these advertisements adds impairment to insult: "No physical exertion required – invalids can succeed. Learn in five days' time."[43]

On the other side of the film-words-as-literature analogy, producers like Adolph Zukor sought to improve and elevate screenwriting with an infusion of literary talent. In an attempt to raise the quality of film scripts, Hollywood hired famous novelists and playwrights, including James Barrie, Joseph Conrad, and F. Scott Fitzgerald. The experiment was a dazzling failure: whose, however, depends on which side of the

interdisciplinary fence one sits. Author and critic Edmund Wilson blamed
Hollywood for the early deaths and wasted talents of Fitzgerald and
Nathaniel West: "both West and Fitzgerald were writers of conscience and
with natural gifts rare enough in America or anywhere and their failure
to get the best out of their years may certainly be laid partly to Hollywood, with its already appalling record of talent depraved and wasted."[44]
But film critic Bernard F. Dick takes an opposite viewpoint, declaring
Fitzgerald a bad screenwriter who simply could not succeed at that genre
of writing and who drank himself into an early grave.[45]

Even apart from literary luminaries, film writers of the early 1920s
aspired to greater "literary" heights. Notes a 1921 essay:

> Picturegoers of to-day who can recall the early days of the kinema in-
> dustry will retain memories of the crude and ugly explanatory sub-titles
> [another term for intertitles] that once disfigured the silver sheet. In
> those days the sub-title was regarded as a necessary blemish on the face
> of the film, and no attempt was made towards either literary or artistic
> improvement.[46]

"Literary improvement" refers to the increasingly prolix, florid intertitles
of later silent films. Livid purple prose burgeoned in the late 1910s and
early 1920s, ranging from bad puns ("Mr. Sowerberry, the Undertaker,
whose need of five pounds provides Oliver a chance to study a grave
occupation") to overwrought metaphors ("And each night Oliver sought
rest amid the terrifying souvenirs of eternal sleep") to moralistic, melodramatic attempts at elevated prose:[47]

> Eighteen years have passed since Honoria Barbary became Lady
> Dedlock. In the magnificence of her surroundings, and under the sooth-
> ing touch of time, her former romance has faded into a sad memory.
> [*shot*] The impulsive girl of years ago is now a cold and haughty leader
> of society, concealing her womanly emotions behind a mask.
>
>   *Bleak House*, Ideal Pictures, 1920

Such prolixity was not limited to literary adaptations. Peter Milne complained in 1925 of prolix intertitles more generally:

> A situation calling for a simple fact such as the passing of a night is liable
> to blossom forth in such a literary hemorrhage as:
> 'Came the sweet-voiced harbingers of a new day, putting to rout the
> somber blackness of the night.' . . .
> 'The next day' becomes 'Comes another rising sun and the troubles
> of yesterday are forgotten in the brilliant new avenue of opportunities
> it unfolds.' . . .

If titles continue to progress from brevity to superverbosity we expect to see 'Passed by the National Board of Review' appear as 'Pronounced worthy of the gods and of the great American public by the venerable men and women who make up that great and august body . . . guardian of the public morals . . . the National Board of Review.'[48]

Intertitles, then, were condemned either way. As necessitous informative labels, they were castigated as "crude and ugly." As literary aspirants, they were attacked as "literary hemorrhages" blighting the screen.

The Word in Silent Cinema

Although one can analyze relations between film words and film images at any point in film history to reveal fallacies in the film language analogy, the most historically contiguous and formally connected place from which to establish a parallel critique between illustrated novel and worded film lies in so-called silent films, divided into verbal intertitles and dramatic filmed scenes. This section parallels the previous chapter's section on illustration criticism: it examines intertitle criticism and undertakes case studies of silent films to test critical rhetoric against aesthetic practice.

Titling Cinema: Silent Film Intertitle Criticism

Although novel illustrations are less critically regarded than novel prose, at least whole books have been devoted to them: no such criticism has yet been accorded the intertitles of silent film.[49] In his 1928 *Anatomy of Motion Picture Art*, Eric Elliott is typical: "A thorough analysis of the [intertitle], unfortunately, needs at least a chapter to itself. Rather than give undue proportion to a comparatively unimportant feature of the motion picture we will restrict ourselves to a few general observations."[50] Throughout the twentieth century, intertitles were given short shrift. Charles Musser's 1984 account of the verbal strategies employed to make early films intelligible does not even give intertitles a subheading, though he bestows this distinction on less common filmic verbal practices, like live lecturers and actors and mechanically synchronized sound.[51]

When intertitles are addressed, they are chiefly disparaged. James Card dubs intertitles "an aesthetic weakness of the medium."[52] As we have seen, film historians consider intertitles to be indicators of silent film's narrative immaturity and inadequacy. But Card's phrasing projects early film's inadequacy onto the intertitles themselves: it is they, not film's dependence on them, that constitute the "aesthetic weakness of the medium."

Nevertheless, intertitles were a constant reminder of the failure of filmic visuals to be the universal language they claimed to be, particularly when intertitles had to be translated for international distribution. Their very detachability was then used to argue their dispensability and essentially "uncinematic" nature, in spite of the fact they were always replaced with other intertitles.[53] Film could not do without intertitles, but it would not allow them to be integral. In this regard, intertitles and novel illustrations share a common fate, their detachability allowing them to be perceived as other than "film" or than "novel."

Purists from the earliest days of film to the present have exalted the pinnacle of filmic representation as one entirely free from verbal language. Card rhapsodizes over "silent films so eloquent in their pantomime that they needed no intertitles whatsoever – no dialogue, no explanatory titles, just pure, uninterrupted images. What a boon to international distribution – no language barrier anywhere!"[54] In fact, few filmmakers after 1906 and before synchronized sound appeared in 1927 made films without intertitles. Silent film historian Kevin Brownlow attests that "Eliminating titles . . . could be done . . . it *was* done; but the results were invariably grossly overlength. Tortuously explanatory visual passages were needed to dispense with one simple title."[55] In 1926, D. W. Griffith averred: "Many important feet of film are saved by the simple expedient of using a few printed words. Every foot of film is precious."[56] Here Griffith, celebrated for his filmic rides to the rescue, casts words as rescuers of "precious" and "important feet of film," heroes economizing for the treasury of film. This rhetoric reverses the old adage, "A picture is worth a thousand words": here, it appears, an intertitle is worth a thousand feet of film.

Although the ideal may have been aesthetic purism, the practice and criticism of early films is marked by verbal/visual hybridity. Film reviews and criticism consider filmed scenes as language, stripping verbal terminology and functions from the intertitles, just as novel criticism had done with prose and illustrations. To cite only a few among countless examples: one silent film reviewer celebrated wordless "scenes [that] speak to you"; another declared: "This picture is not a picture drama, it is an argument, an editorial, an essay . . . No orator, no editorial writer, no essayist could so strongly and effectively present the thoughts that are conveyed in this picture."[57] "Moving objects, not moving lips," asserts silent film theorist Vachel Lindsay, "make the words of the photoplay."[58] Again, verbal language is stripped of verbal terminology bestowed by analogy on film images.

Similarities to nineteenth-century novel criticism and silent film criticism continue. Like those critics who redeemed book illustrations through verbal counteranalogies, the few scholars who value intertitles do so on the basis of cinematic counteranalogies. In 1911, they are "a drop curtain to separate the scenes," not narratively or semantically resonant themselves.[59] In 1924, they are punctuation rather than words for the scenes: "the [intertitle] is first of all a rest for the eye, a punctuation mark for the mind.... Isn't advertising a film as having no [intertitles] like praising Mallarmé's poems because they do not have punctuation?"[60] In both accounts, intertitles are breaks from the film narrative rather than narrative themselves.

Intertitles were also described with counteranalogies that made them "a form of SCENE."[61] But, as in illustration criticism, such counteranalogies did little to raise intertitles in critical esteem, for intertitular "scenes" would always appear scenically inferior to actual scenes. Thus, in both novel and film criticism, the subjected mode (illustrations in novels and words in films) is unable to marshal counteranalogies effectively against the dominant mode (prose in novels and cinematography in film). Indeed, counteranalogies only reinforce their subjection.

As with evaluations of novel illustrations, the analogies used to value intertitles have changed little over the past century. André Gaudreault echoed the 1924 reviewer in 1991, stating that intertitles "punctuate the filmic narrative."[62] Bohdan Y. Nebesio updated the 1911 drop-curtain metaphor from a theatrical to a filmic sectioning in 1996 when he designated intertitles "a function of montage." Like the critics who value Thackeray's illustrations only for their analogical verbal functions, and like James, who insists that photographic illustrations "always [confess] themselves mere optical symbols or echoes, expressions of no particular thing in the text, but only of the type or idea of this or that thing,"[63] Nebesio values intertitles only for functions "beyond their literary semantic role," as when they create "meaningless ... merely phatic ... visual patterns" that establish "the required rhythm and tempo of a film." Only apart from their verbal functions can they be declared cinematic: "For the creative ... [intertitles] served as cinematographic material," he concludes, and putting words to nonverbal uses freed silent film from its "compromise with literature."[64]

But in another sense Nebesio's and other counteranalogical arguments serve to undermine the film language analogy. If intertitles constitute an important and neglected feature of film montage, then words impinge on film language's holy of holies: its claim to language on the basis of montage. In the case studies that follow, I argue that aspects of montage developed from the words of intertitles rather than in opposition to them. Cuts between intertitles and filmed scenes constitute one of the earliest forms of montage, the very word "intertitle" gesturing to intercutting. This kind of editing has been overlooked, I believe, not simply because of the low status of film words, but also because some silent film editing, far from freeing film from its dependence on verbal language, is based in it, and threatens to undermine mainstream film histories and aesthetic theories.

Cinematizing Titles: Intertitles and Montage Theory

Standard accounts of early film hold that film was not born as a language, but rather became a visual language through developments in montage or editing. The aesthetic task of early film was to shake off its dependence on verbal language to tell its stories and replace it with an analogical visual "language" running along a syntax of editing. As early as 1913, Adolph Zukor, president of Famous Players, informed audiences: "We are trying to let the story tell itself as far as possible. To do this we are introducing more scenes and connecting links."[65] Gaudreault is typical of film historians: "until the narrative faculties of *editing* had been further developed – [a] narrator would carry out the work of narration through the use of words, of articulated language, either in written form (intertitles) or oral form (speaker)."[66] The evidence, however, does not support the argument. While a few silent films, like Dziga Vertov's *The Man with the Movie Camera: A Film without Intertitles*, did without intertitles, the dominant pattern of dramatic Anglo-American films indicates a temporary reduction in the length of intertitles between the early silent period (before 1908) and the middle silent period (1908–17), followed by an enormous increase both in the frequency and prolixity of intertitles during the late silent period (1918–26), when the celebrated visual language of editing was firmly established.[67]

Three films of *Vanity Fair* (1911, 1915, and 1922) exemplify the general pattern. The latest film exhibits the most advanced editing – the greatest number of cuts and the most varied shot sizes, camera angles, and points of view. It also contains the longest and the most frequent intertitles. Excluding opening and final titles and reel change cards, the 45-minute 1911 Vitagraph film of *Vanity Fair* contains 37 intertitles – slightly fewer than one per minute; the 1915 102-minute Edison film contains 152 intertitles – about one and a half per minute;[68] while the 18-minute 1922 film uses 31 cards – approximately two cards per minute. The far greater length of the 1922 cards means, however, that they occupy an even greater percentage of screen time.[69]

The cards introducing Rawdon Crawley in each film illustrate this growth in prolixity. The 1911 film announces "Rawdon Crawley, the younger son." The 1915 film includes more characterizing information and an actor credit: "Lord Crawley's younger son is the black sheep of the family. Captain Rawdon Crawley . . . Bigelow Cooper." But the 1922 card waxes most loquacious: "Colonel Rawdon Crawley C. B. . . . the distinguished Waterloo officer . . . . who, in marrying Becky Sharp, the little governess . . . . committed at once the most honest act . . . . and the crowning folly of his life" (the ellipses are printed here as they appear on the intertitle; actor names have been introduced previously on a cast list).[70] Intertitles describing narrative events also grow in length from middle to late silent periods. An intertitle announcing, "The first stain of the revolution" in Vitagraph's 1911 adaptation of *A Tale of Two Cities* expands in a 1926 adaptation on an intertitle introducing the same scene to: "And whilst St. Antoine danced the Carmagnole, never did the moon rise with a milder radiance on a quiet corner in Soho."[71]

Clearly, something is not quite right in standard critical and historical accounts of silent film "language's" relationship to silent film's verbal language. Intriguingly, no film historian contests that intertitles grew longer and more frequent during the late silent period: historians simply do not recognize the problems such prolixity poses for the standard argument and focus instead on ways in which filmmakers eased transitions between scenes and intertitles, or else single out rare titleless films as anomalous evidence of the standard montage argument.

So let us reconsider the evidence here. The very earliest films were single scenes sufficiently explained by the film's title. Film titles in programs from London's Palace Theatre of Varieties, for example, introduce a "Blizzard at Boston," "Hiram Maxim and his Quick-Firing Gun," and the "Emperor of Germany and Staff on the way to the Launch."[72] As films grew longer, included multiple scenes, and aspired to sustained narrative and subplots, reviewers began to call for "headings" to introduce and explain the scenes. A 1906 film reviewer reports that "A subject recently seen was very good photographically, and the plot also seemed to be good, but could not be understood by the audience. If there were a number of headings on the film it would have made the story more tangible."[73] Such headings quickly became the norm.

Cecil Hepworth's 1903 *Alice in Wonderland* illustrates some of the earliest intertitling practices. A card reading, "Alice, now very small, has gained access to the Garden where she meets a Dog and tries to make him play with her" is followed by a scene in which Alice meets a dog in a garden and tries to make him play with her. Despite claims of film as a universal language, early intertitles like these indicate that for audiences, film was a foreign language needing translation into their own. The duplication of words and images here further implies that words and scenes are translatable at the level of character and plot. However, my verbal summary of the scene exaggerates the redundancy of word and image: the intertitle contains information that the scene does not; it names Alice, the dog, and the garden, and offers Alice's point of view. Concomitantly, the scene represents elements absent from the intertitle: it depicts the appearance of players and locale, specifies how the dog and Alice play, and presents a theatrical point of view.

Nevertheless, narrative redundancies remain. Reviewers complained of such redundancies – of the same story told twice in different "languages" – in much the same way that illustration historian Laurence Housman complained in 1896 of being told "twice what [we] need only be told once" by a novel's prose and by its illustrations.[74] They recommended that words only represent what filmed scenes could not, leading to a sharper division of narrative labor between intertitles and scenes in the middle silent period, with the latter doing most of the work. In the 1911 *Vanity Fair*, for instance, a narrative intertitle reading "Bashful Joseph, Amelia's wealthy brother" is followed by a lengthy scene of bumbling greeting, clumsy flirting, inane grinning, and embarrassed fire-poking as Joseph (John Bunny) meets Becky (Helen Gardner) for the first time. Similarly, there is a great deal more mute dialogue mouthed in the scenes than appears on the intertitles ("God forgive me, Mr. Sedley, but you are no better than a coward!"; "Tell father – to – take – care – of – Amelia"), which function as excerpts of fuller mouthed speeches.[75]

For the most part, mid-silent narrative intertitles are curt and factual, leaving the scenes to carry both the bulk of the narrative and to express most of the (melo)dramatic emotion.[76] Between two intertitles in the 1915 *Vanity Fair* that read, "In the hope of catching a glimpse of her son" and "Osborne leaves his entire fortune to Amelia and his grandson," lie shots of anguished waiting, passionate embracing, bitter remorse, resolute repentance, and emotional and financial restitution. From Amelia's tentative approach to the house where her son resides with his remorseless grandfather, to her ecstatic embracing of the boy outdoors, to the grandfather's remorse as he witnesses this embrace from a window, to his fatal heart attack and last-minute will rewrite, to the establishment of the triumphant Amelia in his home after his death, the scenes swell with emotion. The effect is somewhat bipolar: the frugal, predominantly factual intertitles contrast sharply with the lavish emotion and exaggerated facial expressions and bodily gestures of the scenes.

As a result, new complaints regarding the jolting transitions between intertitles and filmed scenes arose. Not only did audiences object to shifting between cognitive processes of reading and viewing, but the emotional bipolarity between intertitles and scenes was emotively jarring as well. Consequently, in the late silent period, filmmakers sought to ease transitions by mixing words and images on the intertitles and in the scenes: they illustrated intertitles, often with pictures that echoed filmed objects, they built a verbally based pictorial symbolism, they increased the use of legible texts within the scenes and the ratio of dialogue to narrative intertitles, so that more words appeared to arise directly from and return to the scenes.[77] Again, the *Vanity Fair* films offer representative examples of this last trend. Of the 37 intertitles in the 1911 film of *Vanity Fair*, only one contains dialogue.[78] By contrast, 77 of the 152 intertitles in the 1915 film are dialogue cards, a ratio of about 1:2, while 20 of the 31 cards in the 1922 film contain dialogue, a ratio of about 2:3. Beyond these examples, a *New York Times* critic notes in 1921 "a move toward the elimination of what are known as 'narrative' sub-titles – those deadly inserts which read, 'Little Mary comes home and tells father that mother has gone away forever,' thereby ruining all the action which follows."[79]

But a more relevant effort to ease transitions between intertitles and scenes for this discussion – one that has not been hitherto identified – lies in the transition from curt, didactic mid-silent intertitles to the more fluid and loquacious prose of later silent intertitles. With these intertitles, new editing patterns emerged, patterns that wove intertitles and filmed scenes into hybrid verbal–visual "sentences." These sentences were governed by verbal syntax, not by visual editing rhythms. It is here that the most substantial challenge to film "language" and to editing as a purely visual cinematic language arises.

If word and image dichotomies broke down in Thackeray's pictorial initials at the lower categorical level of grapheme and graphic lines, in late silent films, these dichotomies collapse at the higher level of filmic sentences, where verbal and pictorial narratives combine and neither is complete without the other. A primitive form of this practice emerges in the 1915 film of *Vanity Fair*. An intertitle announces: "Miss Crawley becomes suspicious – " its dash of punctuation leading into a scene that shows her spying on a scheming, flirtatious Becky and a lumpish, amorous Rawdon. An intertitle concludes the filmic sentence: "And decides to look into Becky's past." While the two intertitles form a complete grammatical sentence without the scenic "clause," the intervening scene does more than illustrate the words: it completes the narrative as if it said: "when she discovers Becky flirting with her enamored nephew."

By the late silent period, however, intertitles frequently do not form complete sentences, but are rather fragments and dependent clauses of hybrid sentences in which filmed scenes function as the main clauses.

The last two cards of Nordisk's 1924 *Little Dorrit* illustrate: "Beyond the sombre shadow of the Marshalsea..." and "And that was one hundred years ago." Between these fragments, the scene of Little Dorrit's wedding to Arthur Clennam forms the main clause of the narrative sentence.[80] Far from begrudged necessities, as critics so often construct intertitles to be, narratively speaking, these intertitles are completely dispensable. But they provide rhetorical and rhythmic effects, closure and enclosure for filmed scenes within a verbal structure. Such practices were widespread in this period. In the 1920 *Bleak House*, for example, of the 49 narrative intertitles that do not constitute introductory descriptions of characters, 33 begin with conjunctions or dependent clauses or are incomplete sentences.[81]

Editing between intertitles and scenes in the late silent period is frequently constructed according to verbal syntax and speech rhythms, rather than to the syntax of image narrative that traditional film histories tout as a purely imagistic affair. The intertitles of the 1922 *Vanity Fair* are punctuated (as are many late silent film intertitles) with ellipses that can only suggest declamatory pauses.[82] One such card reads:

> The seeming ease with which Becky obtained her entree into the exclusive society of 'Gaunt House' .... rather alarmed her husband ... but he had no suspicions........ It was natural that she should shine in society .... she was made to shine there...... Was there any woman like her?

Some later silent films replace titular ellipses with scene shots. In *The Only Way* (a 1926 adaptation of *A Tale of Two Cities*), as Carton waxes earnest in his courtroom defense of Darnay, his speech is punctuated with shots of him and his auditors rather than with ellipses:

> England hated Evrémonde as much as he loves France! [*shot*] All that a man can do for France, that man has done. [*shot*] He renounced his name, title, wealth, estate – he flung them to the wind [*shot*] and went to earn his living in a strange land. [*shot*] That was like a man – a real man, [*shot*] a man who loved his country much, but liberty and manhood more! [*shot*] You, Builders of a New World, will you not forgive that man? [*shot*] His fault is a Name – his atonement a Life. [*shot*] This man who we all know, the Prisoner of the Bastille, [*shot*] DOCTOR MANETTE!!! [*shot*] He has given him his gentle daughter, Lucy [*sic*].[83]

The shots here do more than identify speaker and auditors since they repeatedly show the same speaker and auditors. They function rhetorically, shaping the rhythms of editing to the rhythms and pauses of speech. Contrary to those critics who suggest that intertitles function as punctuation for visual film "language," here scene shots function as punctuation for intertitles.

Such rhetorically based editing is not limited to dialogue cards: it extends to narrative intertitles as well. Another sequence in this film runs:

> *Intertitle*: Then, sixteen years . . .
> *Long shot: Marquis and guests feasting*
> *Intertitle*: . . . Years that to Evrémonde recorded only the passing of Time
> *Midshot: Marquis and guests*
> *Intertitle*: Years that so changed another, that even, freed from the Bastille, the twilight of his mind held him prisoner
> *Midshot: Manette holds a shoe, stares vacantly at the camera, then lowers his eyes.*
> *Long shot: a concerned Defarge, Lorry, and Lucie standing near Manette*
> *Intertitle*: Years that burned the hatred of a decadent aristocracy into one having reason to hate
> *Midshot: Defarge speaks.*[84]

I have transcribed the punctuation on these cards accurately: the absence of punctuation at the end of each intertitle, in a period when almost all intertitles are end-stopped, positions the shots more pointedly as punctuation for the words. The semantic and syntactic relationships of the sequence are established by the run-on verbal sentence of the intertitles, rather than by visual syntactic relationships between scene shots (between looker and recipient of the look, actor and reactor, actor and object, and so on). The intervening shots perform both visual and aural functions, doubling as illustrations of, and as rhetorical spacers between, the words.

Closely related to this practice, late silent films put pressure on the theory that close-ups are always part of an image narrative or syntax. While the 1915 *Vanity Fair* chiefly cuts to close-ups of visual details that do advance an image narrative (a close shot of George's portrait follows a scene in which Amelia refuses Dobbin's proposal to indicate her reason; a close-up of a ring Becky seizes from Sir Pitt attests their illicit liaison and its mercenary dimensions), the majority of close-ups in the 1922 film indicate a speaker before and after dialogue cards. Editing here again follows verbal leads; both intertitle and shots are placed in the service of speech and follow the rhythms of speech.[85]

The speech in these sequences runs between intertitles and scenes when words are read first as graphemes on the intertitles and then seen (rather than heard) as phonemes on the moving lips of muted actors. (This harks back to the vignette of Miss Swartz in Chapter 2.) They are visual phonemes – phonemes we "hear" with our eyes, infusing pictorial images with aural properties, just as scene shots between intertitles take on the aural properties of speech spacers. In the final analysis, though Stephenson and Debrix reflect the predominant opinion that "In silent cinema, the written captions were always an alien element and never combined with the visuals into an artistic whole," the evidence reveals decidedly otherwise, pointing to a far more complex nexus of what is aural, what is graphic, what is language, and what is punctuation in intertitles and scenes.[86] Far from freeing film from words, these forms of montage are based in them.

Book Illustration as Film

For all the discussions of the cinematic Victorian novel, few scholars have credited its illustrations with shaping film art, and those who do identify only the pictorial inheritances that specific film adaptations of these novels have borrowed in their casting, costuming, acting, framing, and set design. Certainly, all three extant silent films of *Vanity Fair* reveal such influences of Thackeray's illustrations, particularly the 1922 British production. The scene of Rawdon's arrest in this film, for example, is costumed, set, and posed almost exactly like the book plate that depicts the event, "Colonel Crawley Wanted." The 1915 Edison film approximates Chapter 4's endpiece of George and Amelia at the piano, and Vitagraph's 1911 film loosely adapts the plate, "Mr. Joseph Entangled" – though in this moving picture, Becky reels him in with the wool, blending the angling pictorial initial that opens the chapter with the plate in a parody of flip book animation.

Beyond the silent era, publicity for MGM's 1935 *David Copperfield* juxtaposes stills of the film's main characters to life-sized enlargements of Phiz's illustrations, casting, costuming, and positioning them like *tableaux vivants* of the drawings.[87] In 1948, David Lean justified his ultra-racist caricature of Fagin (played by Alec Guinness) by insisting that he was only following George Cruikshank's illustrations for *Oliver Twist*. Alice Waley, granddaughter of Dickens, for example, remarked regarding the 1951 adaptation of *A Christmas Carol*, "it seemed as if Leech's original and lovely illustrations had come to life before my eyes."[88] As recently as 1999, Marc Munden, director of a BBC televization of *Vanity Fair*, describes the production as "gritty . . . like a caricature by the cartoonists of the time, men like Cruikshank and Rowlandson."[89]

But what scholars have not yet noted is that book illustrations in Victorian novels are visible pictorial precursors of film montage. Such findings further deconstruct theories of montage in film and the novel.

The standard version of film history notes that the earliest films were shot with static cameras framing the action in long shot to show entire bodies in motion. As film developed, the story goes, the camera began moving in for closer shots, panning, tilting, and finally presenting scenes from many angles and in many shot sizes as well as cutting back and forth between different scenes. As we will see in more detail in Chapter 4, filmmakers like D. W. Griffith claimed he learned such techniques from Victorian prose writers like Charles Dickens. Neither Griffith nor his contemporaries credited the illustrations of these novels. However, these illustrations offer clear precursors of film editing.

The illustrations to *Vanity Fair* offer succinct and convincing evidence of these practices. The pictorial initial that opens Chapter 1, for example, depicts a carriage waiting outside Miss Pinkerton's academy (Figure 19, cited earlier). A page turn produces a reverse angle and an interior of a character looking out of the window at the carriage and speaking to another character in the room (Figure 24). This mode of visual presentation – an establishing shot of a building exterior followed by an interior shot of characters engaged in action and dialogue inside this building – has for decades been a standard technique of film and television. Subsequent illustrations in the chapter present additional angles and perspectives of the same objects and characters in much the same way that standard Hollywood editing practices represent aspects of scenes in various sizes and at various angles. The chapter's plate – of Becky throwing the hallowed dictionary – provides a larger, closer "shot" of the carriage and coachmen than does the pictorial initial (Figure 25); the endpiece changes the angle and reduces the size of the carriage, showing its back as it drives from the school and out of the chapter – a technique that evokes endings of Western films (in both senses of the word "western"), of horse-accelerated heroes riding off into the sunset (Figure 26). Such presentations of a scene from multiple angles at various ranges constitute what traditional film historians argue as uniquely filmic. Although, as I noted in Chapter 1, montage is no longer deemed as film's personal prerogative, the illustrations of Victorian novels have not yet had their share in the crediting. A reviewer of Edison's 1915 *Vanity Fair* attests that its characters "might have stepped from between the pages of [Thackeray's] 'Vanity Fair'"; critics have so far failed to see that aspects of film's montage might have stepped from its illustrations.[90] That both the literal words and the literal pictures of Victorian novels feed so visibly into film's "language" of editing suggests that a more tangible history of influence should replace the current figurative, mythological, and analogical one.

"Say a bouquet, sister Jemima, 'tis more genteel."

"Well, a booky as big almost as a hay-stack; I have put up two bottles of the gillyflower-water for Mrs. Sedley, and the receipt for making it, in Amelia's box."

"And I trust, Miss Jemima, you have made a copy of Miss Sedley's

account. This is it, is it? Very good—ninety-three pounds, four shillings. Be kind enough to address it to John Sedley, Esquire, and to seal this billet which I have written to his lady."

In Miss Jemima's eyes an autograph letter of her sister, Miss Pinkerton, was an object of as deep veneration, as would have been a letter from a sovereign. Only when her pupils quitted the establishment, or when they were about to be married, and once, when poor Miss Birch died of the scarlet fever, was Miss Pinkerton known to write personally to the parents of her pupils; and it was Jemima's opinion that if anything *could* console Mrs. Birch for her daughter's loss, it would be that pious and eloquent composition in which Miss Pinkerton announced the event.

In the present instance Miss Pinkerton's "billet" was to the following effect :—

The Mall, Chiswick, June 15, 18—.

"MADAM,—After her six years' residence at the Mall, I have the honour and happiness of presenting Miss Amelia Sedley to her parents,

24. William Makepeace Thackeray, *Vanity Fair* (New York: Heritage, 1940). Chapter 1's vignette of the Pinkerton sisters.

25. William Makepeace Thackeray's plate, "Rebecca's Farewell," in Chapter 1 of *Vanity Fair* (New York: Heritage, 1940).

Textual Scenes of All Sorts[91]

Just as intertitles form hybrid sentences with silent filmed scenes, silent filmed scenes feature legible texts. Verbal texts – letters, wills, bills, calling cards, newspapers, books, and more – double as pictorial and textual objects inside filmed scenes. The 1901 *Scrooge, Or Marley's Ghost* emblematizes this pictorial framing of texts when it hangs character speech from Dickens's novella in picture frames on the walls of sets. Tiny Tim's "GOD BLESS US EVERYONE" is a huge sign in the Cratchit parlor; Fred's "A MERRY XMAS" is a framed picture in his living room. Here, speech is framed as picture. Just as alphabetic and drawn fictional characters in Thackeray's pictorial initials engage in a variety of relations and shifting hierarchies, so too alphabetic characters on letters, signs, bills, wills, notes, of Miss Swartz, the parlour-boarder, from her room, as no pen can depict, and as the tender heart would fain pass over. The embracing was over; they parted—that is, Miss Sedley parted from her friends. Miss Sharp had demurely entered the carriage some minutes before. Nobody cried for leaving *her*.

Sambo of the bandy-legs slammed the carriage-door on his young weeping mistress. He sprang up behind the carriage. "Stop!" cried Miss Jemima, rushing to the gate with a parcel.

"It's some sandwiches, my dear," said she to Amelia. "You may be hungry, you know; and Becky, Becky Sharp, here's a book for you that my sister—that is, I,—Johnson's Dixonary, you know; you mustn't leave us without that. Good by. Drive on, coachman. God bless you!"

And the kind creature retreated into the garden, overcome with emotions.

But, lo! and just as the coach drove off, Miss Sharp put her pale face out of the window, and actually flung the book back into the garden.

This almost caused Jemima to faint with terror. "Well, I never,"—said she—"what an audacious"—Emotion prevented her from completing either sentence. The carriage rolled away; the great gates were closed; the bell rang for the dancing lesson. The world is before the two young ladies; and so, farewell to Chiswick Mall.

26. William Makepeace Thackeray's endpiece, in Chapter 1 of *Vanity Fair* (London: Bradbury & Evans, 1848). Courtesy of the Bancroft Library, University of California, Berkeley.

invitations, paper money, family Bibles, newspapers, and posters in the 1911 Vitagraph and 1915 Edison films of *Vanity Fair* interact with dramatic characters in multiple ways. Filmed texts (in the form of letters, invitations, and warrants) possess power to move characters from one scene to another and thereby to structure narrative. They determine lives and fates, disinheriting, evicting, and sending characters into battle, to prison, or to balls. Recalling Thackeray's puppet metaphor, verbal texts operate like (in)visible strings pulling filmic characters through their scenes.

Yet the texts of these silent film scenes can just as readily be dominated by actor-characters: produced, stolen, vandalized, possessed, hidden, or waved triumphantly. Varying shot sizes and other cinematic techniques construct a panoply of relationships between alphabetic characters and dramatic characters. At times, texts are arrested in legible close-up, filling the screen and commanding attention; at others, they are reduced to the status of small objects in long shot, discarded, held, or torn to shreds by dramatic characters. Texts thus alternatively wield power over dramatic characters and are overpowered by them.

By way of preface to the following readings, it is essential to note that most of the texts dramatized in films of *Vanity Fair* derive from texts represented by the novel's prose and illustrations.[92] However, in the novel, these texts float in a sea of words, occasionally bobbing up as pictorial objects in the illustrations, but quickly swept away again in the more dominant tide of prose. In the film scenes, the word always appears as a cultural object, emphasizing the constructedness of language and its role in constructing social interactions. These representations denaturalize the word as a mode of representation and, at the same time, distract attention from film's own constructedness and, more importantly for this discussion, from film's construction of relationships between its pictures and its words.

The power of the word, though potent in Thackeray's novel, is hugely accentuated in the silent films that adapt it, as muted victims are tossed, torn, ruined, and exiled by tyrannical written texts, their protesting and lamenting speeches mouthed, but unheard and largely unspecified. Their very muteness in the face of these tyrannical texts accentuates the power of the written word over speech; dialogue cards in the 1911 film are at a minimum (only one of 37 records direct speech) and are limited in the 1915 film. Silenced characters are at the mercy of written texts: of letters, invitations, warrants, newspapers, wills, bills, and calling cards, which set bodies moving through space, often against their wills. Bankrupt stocks and notes of debt force characters from their homes; bank notes make characters act against their own wishes according to the wishes of those who hold the money; characters who defy their parents are disinherited by wills; newspaper announcements and letters lead characters to rage, weep, and exult.

The power of texts over persons permeates both 1911 Vitagraph and 1915 Edison films. In the 1911 film, Becky is one moment enraged by a letter of rejection from Jos and is the next in ecstasies over a letter of invitation from Sir Pitt.[93] Rawdon's arrest, imprisonment, release, and discovery of Becky's intrigue with the Marquis of Steyne unfolds as a drama of documents: there is very little action in this sequence apart from the production of and response to texts. Rawdon's note of debt passes from Steyne to the man who arrests him; Rawdon writes an appeal to Becky; Becky pens her refusal. Subsequently, Rawdon writes a plea to his brother, Pitt; Pitt is both emotionally and geographically moved by the letter to visit Rawdon in prison and aid his release. Rawdon's letter to Pitt further forms a textual bridge between the scenes: Pitt is still clutching the letter as he enters the prison – as if it had physically led him there. (This, incidentally, constitutes another form of textually based montage.) In the debtors' prison, the scene develops primarily through character reactions to documents rather than through character reactions to other characters. Rawdon shows Pitt Becky's letter; Pitt reacts to it with shock and disbelief. Pitt hands papers to Rawdon; Rawdon thanks him vigorously and hands the documents to an official, who signs his release. Rawdon rips up the note of debt, throws it in the air, and waves the release triumphantly. Here the dramatic emphasis is on the victory of one piece of paper over another, the cancellation of one form of textual power by another. Only when this drama of documents is complete can Rawdon leave the prison.

Becky and Steyne's romantic intrigue in this sequence is also far more textual than sexual. Laughter at Rawdon's letter of appeal and the gleeful composition of a mocking reply displaces any sexual dalliance. Rawdon's cuckolding, then, is a textual one, as the climactic confrontation scene makes even more evident. Although Rawdon's beating of Steyne and his violent stripping of Becky's adulterously gained jewels constitute more traditional melodramatic actions of a betrayed husband (Figure 27), the final confrontation and rejection of Becky revolves around a new triangle, in which a text appears as the third party, to be trounced and destroyed. As Steyne lies unconscious on the floor, Rawdon discovers the bank note Steyne gave to Becky – a note that could have effected Rawdon's release from prison. It is this note that should have been sent in response to his written plea to Becky, not her mocking lie. Rawdon realizes that this note, not Steyne, is his chief rival for Becky's affections. (Accentuating this

27. Vitagraph's *Vanity Fair,* 1911. Courtesy of the Academy of Motion Pictures Arts and Sciences.

displacement, the Steyne of this film is far more decrepit than the Steyne of Thackeray's illustrations.) Rawdon tears the note to shreds and casts it on the unconscious Steyne. Both rivals trounced, he then leaves the house. This dramatization departs significantly from the novel. In Thackeray's version, it is Steyne who storms out of the house, denouncing Becky, and Rawdon later returns the note to Steyne. Unlike the novel, the film makes the violent destruction of a text the final climactic confrontation of the sequence.

Elsewhere in the 1911 film, the battle between dramatic and textual characters vies somewhat cacophonously with other significatory modes: with character movement, gestures, and facial expressions; with shot composition, sets, and props. In some scenes, a choreography of character movements carries the bulk of the narration, as in the dance-like sequences that unite George and Amelia and Becky and Jos in wooing couples, leaving a solitary Dobbin holding the coats, or in those that separate George from Amelia and pair him with Becky out walking. Others rely on narrative compositions derived from painting and photography, as in those deep focus shots that pull some characters forward to prominence and push others, quite literally, into the background. More theatrically impelled modes of signing escalate in some scenes into a histrionic frenzy of character gestures – raised eyes and arms, pointed fingers, clenched fists, clutching arms, and stamping feet. In other scenes, a dramatic and narrative use of objects prevails – love tokens seized, cherished portraits worshipped, bank notes torn. The didactic words of legible texts in the filmed scenes, as well as on the intertitles, bubble up amidst all these significatory modes as eruptions in a near frenzy of signing, as this early film, drawing on so many arts, tries to signify with all of them at once.[94]

By the time of the 1915 film, the clamoring significatory cacophony has subsided. The main battle for representational dominance wages between textual and pictorial modes within a tightly codified melodramatic narrative structure. Characters fight and scheme to possess texts, particularly those with financial value, but also those with emotional power over other characters. Even more than the earlier film, the power of the texts over characters is enormous.

Throughout this film, texts spell more than their didactic letters: "Sedley . . . reads the news which spells his ruin." Although the next scene shows a newspaper explicating his failed business venture, the ruin is spelled further in the dramatization. Sedley (Charles Sutton) thrusts the paper at his wife (Mrs. Austin Brown), gestures wildly, raises his arms to heaven and clenches his fists, as if the paper had strings to pull him, puppet-like, into frenzied agitation. The film then dramatizes what the text spelled out, as though the newspaper had been a screenplay: Sedley is evicted from his home and loses social status and allies, along with his earlier equanimity and bonhomie. In this sequence I glimpse film's reaction against the tyranny of its founding texts – the scenarios and screenplays that dictate its character movements, actions, and reactions.

The film's distillation of textual events from the novel and addition of new textual episodes make the dynamics all the more marked, especially given the excision of so many other episodes in the novel. George's (Richard Tucker) temporary romantic defection to Miss Swartz (Lena Davril), for example, is couched as a verbal offense in Dobbin's (Frank McGlynn, Sr.) accusation: "So this is the woman for whom you are breaking your word – and Amelia's heart!"

Thackeray's subtitle makes *Vanity Fair* "A Novel without a Hero." One could argue, concomitantly, that it is also a novel without a villain. By contrast, the 1915 film of *Vanity Fair* abounds in villains. And all the villains are textual ones – Sedley, Steyne, Sir Pitt (the elder), Osborne, and Becky. All but Becky are patriarchal textual villains. Sedley tyrannizes out of textual impotence: his textual and financial ruin leads him in turn to ruin his daughter's happiness and to destroy her contract to marry George. Steyne's (George A. Wright) patriarchal power over his wife (Helen Strickland) is represented as a primarily textual one, most evident when he forces her to produce a text that does not express her wishes, but rather his:

> *Intertitle*: Lady Steyne sends out invitations to a reception at Gaunt House.
>
> *Scene: Lady Steyne sits at a writing table, dictating to a servant. Steyne enters and gestures for the list, which she hands to him. He reads it and speaks.*
>
> *Intertitle*: "You will invite Mr. and Mrs. Rawdon Crawley."
>
> *Scene: Lady Steyne shakes her head, no. Steyne gestures angrily. She speaks.*
>
> *Intertitle*: "Must I have – that woman?"
>
> *Scene: His arm points rigidly and tyrannically at the list. She sinks in her chair and dictates resignedly.*

Children are hugely victimized by patriarchal texts, particularly wills. Rawdon (Bigelow Cooper) and George are disinherited, as in the novel, but the film accentuates the textual aspects of these villainies, as we will see.

In the 1915 film, it is Osborne (Robert Brower) rather than Steyne or Sir Pitt who emerges as the archvillain. Sedley, Steyne, and Sir Pitt (Frank A. Lyon) enjoy only a few scenes of textual villainy each; Osborne revels in multitudes. He is rarely seen without a text in hand. Early in the film, he refuses to lend money to his old friend Sedley (he withholds bank notes), and he schemes to marry George to a wealthy heiress via correspondence:

> *Intertitle*: A letter from Miss Swartz's father.
>
> *Scene: Osborne reading and smiling*
>
> *Shot of letter*: . . . meets with my entire approval. I shall be only too glad to furnish my daughter with a dowry of £20,000 on the day of her marriage to your son, George.
>
> Aaron Swartz[95]
>
> *Scene: A joyous Osborne speaks [his words unrepresented by an intertitle] and pounds the table.*

After Osborne learns of George's marriage to Amelia, however, he erupts into textual vandalism, ripping up his will and a childhood letter from George and crossing out George's name in the family Bible. (In the novel, he simply locks George's textual memorabilia in a box. The violence to the texts is far more extensive and accentuated in the film.)

As the film progresses, the central battle Osborne wages is less one of patriarchal tyrant against disobedient son (George dies soon after his disinheritance) than one of textual villain against picturesque victim and heroine, George's wife, Amelia (Helen Fulton). It is here that this silent film melodrama most fully reveals its pitting of pictures against words. Amelia is by far the most picturesque character in the film, and quite surprisingly filmed much more beautifully and picturesquely than the reputedly more beautiful Becky. Becky (Mrs. Fiske) is seldom shown at close range; her beauty is more theatrically rendered through coquettish mannerisms than through picturesque portraiture. A *Variety* review of the film notes: "Profiting by the mistake of several years ago when Mrs. Fiske was picturized in 'Tess of the D'Urbervilles' and showed the 'ravages of time,' there are no close-ups."[96] Amelia, on the other hand, is constantly posed as if for a painting, shown in pretty cameo pining for George in her cottage garden, in dramatic *tableaux vivants* praying in a virginal white nightgown, and cast in sentimental maternal portraits with her young son. In most of these shots, she barely moves; she looks straight at the camera, as if sitting for a painter. The intertitles that introduce these shots read like the titles of Victorian paintings: "The young wife" precedes a shot of Amelia quietly sewing in a simple domestic setting; "The widowed mother" prefaces a pose with the infant George in which Amelia is garbed like a continental black-veiled madonna.

The film unfolds a melodrama in which a pictorial victim, Amelia, gradually wins out over a textual villain, her father-in-law, Osborne. Shortly after Osborne's greatest textual villainies (his multiple textual deletions of George), an intertitle brings "News from the front." The ensuing shot depicts Osborne reading a newspaper, a characteristic prop and activity for this film's most textual of characters. A close-up specifies what he is reading: the name of his son, "Lieutenant George Sedley Osborne," on a list of "Dead and Missing." Osborne's finger underscores his son's name in a distressing visual echo of his earlier strikethrough of George's name in the family Bible. The writing hand is now the reading hand: the first indication of Osborne's impending textual disempowerment. Paradoxically, however, this first teetering of Osborne's textual power actualizes his figurative textual act. In one sense, this fulfillment portrays him as textually potent – his textual acts have been made flesh. But his powerlessness against the public and descriptive text of the newspaper also unfolds here. His earlier symbolic gesture – the deletion of George's name and date of birth in the family Bible as if he'd never been born – consigned his son to nonexistence. But the still legible name beneath the strikethrough belied the act. The newspaper line now simultaneously undoes and fulfills Osborne's symbolic textual act. Printing George's name without the strikethrough asserts the existence Osborne had denied with his pen at the same time it announces the end of it. Here, Osborne encounters the power of a greater text, one that records rather than symbolizes, one that decrees the nonexistence that his pen could not effect. Osborne's verbal impotence increases as the scene progresses. The camera cuts from the newspaper's revelation to an ashen Osborne silently and repeatedly mouthing George's name until he crumples in despair. Osborne's attempt to aurally reinscribe the deleted written name emerges all the more muted in this context and no intertitle prints his words. The uttered name is powerless to call George home or back into the film frame.

But the film does not simply mark a loss of Osborne's textual and figurative power in the face of more powerful texts or of documentary representation. A melodrama unfolds in which the picturesque eventually conquers the textual. If words cannot recall George, his portrait, cherished by Amelia, appears regularly throughout the film with power to restore his presence. Portraits have power over textual characters. Osborne first begins to soften toward his disowned relatives when he sees a portrait of George's and Amelia's son, also named George (Maurice Stewart). Osborne's initial response to the picture, however, is a textual one. He finds the boy and gives him a £10 note, then writes a letter to the destitute Amelia, offering financial support in exchange for physical custody of the boy. For a time, textual power overwhelms pictorial power. Osborne's letter has enormous emotional power over Amelia: she hovers over the bed of her sleeping son, alternately sobbing and steeling herself to renounce him, torn between attachment to his pictured body and the power of the text to shape the boy's destiny. Embracing the boy and bowing her head in prayer, Amelia yields to the text. An intertitle reads: "For the boy's sake." The next morning, she sends the boy to Osborne with lavish caressing and dressing and histrionic farewells.

Called by Osborne's monetary and epistolary texts from the picturesque world of mother–son portraiture, the boy brings the picturesque with him into Osborne's stronghold of textual tyranny. When we next see Osborne, he is posed in a sentimental armchair portrait with the boy, his dramatic actions resembling Amelia's as he caresses, dresses, and bids the boy farewell in much the same way. More importantly, this scene marks the first time Osborne is shown without a text in hand, though the coin he gives the lad as he departs represents a vestige of his textual power. But the coin bears a face (heads) as well as words (tails), and as such represents a hybrid of the pictorial and verbal, marking a shift in the balance of verbal and pictorial power.

In the next sequence, "heads" wins the toss: textual power capitulates to the picturesque. Moving to the window, Osborne spies Amelia embracing the boy in the street. The sight so moves him that he clutches his heart.

At first the gesture seems to betoken an emotional response to the scene: characters in silent film frequently clutch their hearts to represent strong emotion. The attack on his heart by the picturesque leads Osborne to have a change of heart and to repent of his textual villainies. To make textual amends, he seizes an aging gray paper (presumably his will) and rips it to shreds. Taking a fresh blank piece of paper, he writes a new will. Thus, his change of heart leads to a change of will. As he reads over what he has written, he clutches his heart again and – shockingly – falls dead.

As with George's nominal deletion, another seemingly symbolic gesture is literalized and proves fatal in the film. The sentimental attack on Osborne's heart by the picturesque leads to a fatal physical heart attack. But there is a difference between the two literalizations, one that points to a crucial difference between textual and pictorial power in the film. As we have seen, textual power forces dramatic bodies to move against their desires like puppets: to marry where they do not love, to go to prison, to leave their homes, to send their children away, and to make the young and beautiful dally with old and decrepit bodies. Pictorial power, by contrast, impels bodies to move through their own desires or to change their desires. The seeming weakness of the picturesque in this film (deserted romantic heroines, bereaved and oppressed mothers and children) is deceptive, for it has power to trigger fatal heart attacks. George's literal death in the wake of Osborne's symbolic deletion of him comes across as a bad joke, a bitter irony, a trumping by life of a figurative act. But the sight of Amelia and her son has power to slay textual dragons and to win textual prizes. Indeed, the next scene displays the textual triumph of Amelia, established by the new will in the very house from which she has hitherto been barred – endowed with the Osborne fortune, occupying Osborne's screen space; while Osborne is never seen or mentioned again in the film – not even commemorated in portraiture.

This melodrama is a peculiarly filmic one and differs considerably from Osborne's relenting in the novel. In Thackeray's account, Osborne changes his view of Amelia purely on the basis of Dobbin's verbal account of her. Although he intends to see her, he never does, dying before he has the chance, and he changes his will "off stage," as it were. The novel tells us only that he dies from "a fit"; all rhetoric regarding palpitating or softening hearts belongs to Amelia rather than to Osborne: "Amelia's heart began to beat at the notion of the awful meeting with George's father"; "When Amelia heard that her father-in-law was reconciled to her, her heart melted" (673–75). Clearly, the Edison film has made an original melodrama in which pictures war with texts to explore filmic relationships between words and pictures.

Amelia's pictorial triumph over Osborne is, however, complicated by a later scene in which the textual seems to triumph over the pictorial. Becky routs Amelia's picture-worship of George with a text, an adulterous love note that George had sent to Becky when he was married to Amelia. George's textual representation overcomes his pictorial one and, in the novel and both 1911 and 1915 films, Amelia responds by giving up her worship of George's portrait and marrying Dobbin.[97] It would appear then that in the end the text wins a final victory over the film's picturesque heroine and that the word proves truer and more authoritative than the picture. But in the 1915 film, this is not exactly the case. Throughout the film, Dobbin's primary role has been as a ferrier of words between characters. He carries the returned engagement ring from Amelia to George with her words of regret; he scolds George away from Miss Swartz's portrait to keep his word to Amelia; he pleads with Sedley to forgive George and reinstate the engagement contract; he brings Osborne the news of his son's marriage and later of his son's death. He even brings George's last words to Osborne. An intertitle reads: "I thought you might care to know what your son's last words were, sir."[98] When Dobbin receives Amelia's hand at the end of the film, however, words drop away entirely as he is cast for the first time into the bliss of the picturesque world she has inhabited throughout the film. Becky shows Amelia the note indoors; but Amelia and Dobbin agree to marry outdoors in a beautiful garden filled with flowers, posed as though for an engagement portrait, muted and all but stilled. Dobbin's happily-ever-after is thus as much a translation from the verbal into the pictorial realm as it is from bachelorhood to marriage. Saint George may have fallen from his hallowed portrait, but Dobbin has taken his place and entered Amelia's pictorial realm. Following his transferal to Amelia's pictorial realm, Dobbin remains silent for the rest of the film: the next and last time we see him, he passes with Amelia silently by Becky, seen but not seeing, out of the film.

So far we have considered only the film's male textual villains. Indeed, the genderings so far are perfectly in accord with most gendered word and image studies, which gender the word male and the image female. However, in the case of this film, such a delineation is both inaccurate and simplistic. Indeed, it would not serve filmic attempts to elevate the pictorial above the textual, since a purely female gendering of the image would be culturally and socially disempowering. Becky is also a textual villain, though her mode of villainy differs from that of patriarchal textual tyrants. Against their tyrannous hold on texts, Becky undertakes an appropriation of texts akin to stealthy thieving or overt vandalism. From the flinging of the hallowed dictionary as she leaves Miss Pinkerton's school, to the secreting of George's illicit love note and of Steyne's adulterous bank note, to the lying letter she sends to Rawdon in prison, most of her evident crimes in the novel and film are textual.

Becky is aided in her textual villainy by her visual and theatrical powers (her beauty and her charming ways) – powers that stun and weaken her prey, causing them to yield texts to her or to excuse her villainous textual acts. Although Steyne's title and bank notes give him power over Becky, his body, more decrepit in this film than in Thackeray's illustrations, lacks visual and theatrical power. And, though Rawdon is both strikingly handsome and theatrically compelling in the film, and though, like Amelia, he too is portrayed in picturesque sentimental scenes with his young son, he lacks textual power. Disinherited by father and aunt, a victim of Becky's lying letter and hidden bank note, he is cast primarily not as picturesque victim but as a textually impotent one. His impotence is repeatedly dramatized in the film, which threads his character through a series of textual failures – his losses at cards, his failure to produce bank notes, his unpaid bills and notes of hand, his subjection to arrest warrants and military orders, and his inability to solicit the desired response from Becky with his letter. Unlike Amelia, whose victory lies in her picturesque power alone, Rawdon keeps resorting to textual strategies that fail to move Becky and is, in the end, defeated by her. The film adds a scene of Rawdon's final textual failure that appears nowhere in the novel. In the novel, we hear simply that Rawdon has died. But near the end of the film Becky receives a letter:

> Madam,
> His Excellency Rawdon Crawley [. . .] Governor of Coventry Island, died April 14th last. At the time of his death, the enclosed note was found in his hand . . .

The note, written in barely legible scrawl, reads: "Becky, I am dying ~~I hate you~~. God forgive me I love you still Raw–," the incomplete signature trailing down the page like a failed erection, signaling not only his physical death but his final textual impotence, his failed last words. In contrast to Osborne, Becky does not clutch her heart at this graphically rendered pathos, but instead calmly folds the note, then crosses her arms to indicate her barricaded and unmoved heart – quite literally arm-ored (and arm o'erd).

But Becky, resilient in the face of patriarchal textual villains and unmoved by textual pathos, is defeated in the end by the pictorial – by her own pictorial failures. As we have seen, both her theatrical and textual powers depend in large part upon her beauty. Once this fades, she becomes theatrically and textually impotent. The endpiece of the novel depicts the puppet Becky topped and crushed by a narrator puppet, cleverly pictorializing her final defeat by the prose narration. But in both 1911 and 1915 films, Becky's downfall is primarily a visual and scopic one, asserting the supreme power of the picture over all textual villains. In the earlier film, the last intertitle announces "Becky's Retribution." The following shot depicts Becky gazing at her reflection in an oval mirror. A look of horror spreads over her face – and the film ends. Her final punishment, her sentence, is thus a pictorial one. When she sees the decline of her visual power in the mirror, it signals the end of her narrative and "The End" of the film.[99]

The scopic revenge of the 1915 Edison film is more subtle. The final shot reveals Becky sitting happily in her Vanity Fair booth, selling her wares. But when Dobbin and Amelia pass without observing her, she slumps over, dejected and defeated. A final intertitle reads: "Who is happy in this world . . . ?" The overthrow of her visual magnetism here is quieter but more devastating, in that she does not even possess power to inspire horrified looking, whether her own or that of another, but has become so nondescript as to be overlooked entirely. Becky is no longer visible, even to those who know her best. The film ends because there is nothing left worth looking at.

This episode differs markedly from the novel's account. In the novel, the sight of Becky retains power, albeit negative power, and she holds a retaliatory power of withholding her look.[100] The book plate that represents this event, "Virtue Rewarded: A Booth in Vanity Fair," shows Amelia, Dobbin, and Georgy looking directly at Becky, who does not return their look (Figure 3.5). The prose notes: "She cast down her eyes demurely and smiled as they started away from her" (759). Like other films of *Vanity Fair*, the Edison film shows that Becky's textual and theatrical power cannot exist in the absence of her pictorial power, while pictorial power alone is sufficient for both Amelia's economic and amatory triumph. The filmic moral of the story is that pictorial power reigns and that theatrical and textual power must bow to it.

In the final analysis, while various characters display moments of heroism in both novel and films – Amelia sacrifices, Rawdon trounces Steyne, Dobbin is undyingly loyal, and even Becky abets the Dobbin/Amelia union – no character is consistently heroic or powerful. But while the novel may be truly said to be "A Novel without a Hero," the 1915 film makes the picture itself the hero, with power to slay and defeat textual dragons. In these films, as well as in the critical discourse on film, film images wage war with film words. Far from being redundant and uncinematic, words are grist for the melodramatic mill, necessary mythological dragons, significant others by which to establish the superiority of the moving picture. Critical myth has it that cinema must fight off the contamination of and dependence on literature, on the word; the reality is that film is fighting its own words, its own language as other and creating dramatic cinematic material in so doing.

4 Cinematic Novels/Literary Cinema

From the intra-art analogies of prose pictures and film language, we turn now to the interart analogies of the "cinematic novel" and "literary cinema." No literary form has been declared "cinematic" more frequently than the novel, regardless of what form the novel has taken and regardless of what form the film has taken. Novels have been pronounced "cinematic" whatever decade or style in which they were written. Nineteenth-century novelists Charles Dickens and Thomas Hardy have been dubbed cinematic,[1] but so have twentieth-century authors James Joyce, F. Scott Fitzgerald, and a host of more recent novelists.[2] Novels have been termed "cinematic" whether they are empirical and mimetically realist (they have a "camera eye")[3] or introspective and psychological (they engage in "fragmented vision," "cross-cutting," and "multiple viewpoints").[4] Novels were decreed cinematic when film was silent and when it learned to talk; they were dubbed cinematic when film was black-and-white and when it bloomed into Technicolor®. And novels have been designated cinematic regardless of the adapting film's genre, nationality, technology, or style.

Studies of the cinematic novel fall into two main camps: those that address cotemporaneous cross-fertilizations between novels and films in the twentieth and twenty-first centuries and those that discover a cinematic novel before the birth of cinema and press it into an anachronistic argument of historical influence. The analogy is less problematic when novelists have viewed films and written for films.[5] Keith Cohen, Claude-Edmonde Magny, and Seymour Chatman all argue compellingly that twentieth-century novelists adopt cinematic techniques, like ellipsis, temporal discontinuity, fragmented vision, cross-cutting, and multiple viewpoints.[6] However, to accord cinematic properties to the novel before cinema even existed forges a problematic and mythological anachronistic aesthetic history.

There is certainly evidence that the nineteenth-century novel influenced film. But the far more (chrono)logically cogent analogy for an argument of influence would be "novelistic cinema." This analogy, however, is all but absent from the discourse. Christian Metz is one of very few scholars to describe films as "*romanesque*" or "novelistic," but he does so by redefining these terms as larger categories containing both novel and film: the "*novelistic* as a whole, with its cinematic extensions."[7] "Novelistic" in Metz's account expresses nothing peculiar to the novel: indeed, he uses the term interchangeably with "narrative" and "fiction."

One wonders why the more rational analogy, novelistic cinema, has not been promoted as a counteranalogy to the cinematic novel and why, in the rare instances it is invoked, scholars strip it of anything specifically novelistic. It turns out that the cinematic novel analogy has served literary interests so well that literary scholars have championed it as much as film scholars. From a literary point of view, to nominate the nineteenth-century novel "cinematic" is to lay claim to filmic territory in two ways. First, it bestows on novels and novelists seminal, prophetic, and prescient powers, rendering them not only precursors and progenitors of cinema, but also mystical and atemporal ones. Second, it permits literary scholars to encroach on cinematic territory, positioning literary scholars as established experts with solid credentials to discuss film. As Chapter 1 notes, film has been regularly subjected to scholarly methods derived from literature and linguistics. Not only do such methods tend to occlude the nonlinguistic elements of film and to shackle "meaning" to linguistic models, but such methods are also all but guaranteed to conclude that novels represent "better" than films.

If the analogy of a cinematic nineteenth-century novel has served literary interests, it has also served filmic interests. The anachronism of the cinematic novel makes film the glorious fulfillment of what is only a seed of promise in the novel, a superior art in a march of aesthetic progress, rather than the feeble novelistic offspring of a more potent novel parent.[8] It fosters a hierarchy in which any film trumps any novel, for all films are more "cinematic" than even the most cinematic of novels. More importantly, the analogy has played a crucial role in establishing and maintaining film as the "seventh" art – that is, as an art in its own right alongside classical arts, rather than as a compilation of arts or, worse still, as a mere technological recording device for other arts.[9]

Many early critics perceived film to be an impressive combination of art forms. A 1926 reviewer is representative:

Visual storytelling is so much an art that it might well be the greatest of arts. It is certainly the most complicated. It involves a manipulation of character and acting and stage as in legitimate drama; it involves a manipulation of visual composition as in painting (. . . moving . . . and therefore much more complex); it involves a manipulation of tempo as in music; it involves a manipulation of visual suggestion and visual metaphor as in poetry. Beyond all that, it involves a manipulation of such effects as are peculiar to itself [like cinematography and editing].[10]

But many others declared film derivative precisely because it drew on other arts, insisting moreover on its inferiority to the arts on which it drew. A 1923 reviewer deduced: it "seems improbable" that the moving picture will ever arrive at "true art."

At best it will always be a bastard art. Pictorially it has no significance in its own right; it may . . . serve to reproduce the designs of plastic arts . . . [but] its literary merit is negligible. It remains . . . to be seen whether the film can convert pantomime into genuine drama . . . So long as the debasement of literary and artistic ideas continues to fill the theatres, just so long will the moving picture remain at its low and insufferable stage of vulgarity.[11]

Responding to such attacks, filmmakers strove to outdo other arts while film critics strove to separate film from other arts. Film had no problem surmounting still photography: as early as 1905, film was decreed "the highest branch of photographic art."[12] With its capacity to record movement, film was hailed victor over other static visual arts under the realist aesthetic that dominated much early film criticism. However, film had a more difficult time outdoing and separating itself from theater. It was frequently perceived as a reduced form of theater – theater's color, sound, and live three-dimensional performance reduced to silent black-and-white two-dimensional celluloid and three-hour performances re-duced, particularly in the early days, to elliptic minutes. Theater was film's primary obstacle to becoming the seventh art, for it always made film look like a bad recording of itself.

The preface to a 1917 film adaptation of Tom Taylor's and Charles Reade's play *Masks and Faces* (1852) offers a rare glimpse into percep-tions of film's relationship to theater during film's formative years. The film's subtitle forges a relationship between theater and film: *Masks and Faces* is an "Ideal Picture Play."[13] In the preface, an assemblage of distin-guished dramatists, actors, and theater patrons, including James Barrie and George Bernard Shaw, appear as themselves, deep in discussion, their dialogue printed on intertitles:

Sir Squire Bancroft: We must clear off the debt.
[Narrative intertitle:] What Sir James Barrie knows.
Sir James Barrie: Why not an All-star film – say 'MASKS AND FACES'?[14]
Sir Arthur Pinero: A most excellent suggestion, too. The 'Pictures' owe
  much to the stage. It shall repay.

Film here owes a primary aesthetic debt to theater for techniques, talent,
and narrative. The conference continues:

Sir John Hare: There shall be no caste prejudice. The film is the sister of
  the stage. Film-acting is a useful experience for all – old and young.

While film is acknowledged as theater's sister, she belongs to a different
"caste." Film is ranked as a useful rather than fine art, a training ground
for superannuated or uninitiated actors. Sir George Alexander remarks:
"Such a film would be a worthy memory of the English stage of today."
Here lies theater's greatest threat to film's claim to an independent art:
the resemblances between theater and film are so great that film is perceived as a mere technological recording device for theater, a memori-
alization of theatrical achievement rather than as an achievement in its
own right.

The assembled group of celebrities mouths in unison, some pounding
the table as they cry for an authoritative final word on the subject from a
theatrical luminary:

All: Shaw! Shaw!

The group stills as Shaw rises.

Sir George Bernard Shaw: I'm all for the proposal . . . there's money in it.
  After all, what monument more enduring than brass?[15]

Here, Shaw eviscerates film's role even as a recording device, reducing it
to a purely monetary monument – and to the basest of monetary metals
at that.

Film scholarship's attitude to theater has been every bit as eviscerating
of theater as this filmic preface is of film. While film histories uphold
many of the assertions made in this preface, from them they forge a narrative of rebellion and liberation that politicizes the development of film
art as a movement away from theater. Film histories argue that film freed
itself from its resemblance to theater in the 1910s and 1920s by breaking
up static single-shot scenes with editing. The account of synchronized
sound in the late 1920s and early 1930s views film's chief developmental
task as freeing itself from the new resemblance to theater introduced

by recorded sound dialogue. In the 1980s and 1990s, accounts of computer graphics were similarly hailed as freeing film from the limitations of theatrical production methods.

Although a few historians point to film's origins in vaudeville, optical devices, comic strips, short stories, and fairground entertainments rather than in the classical arts or in the novel,[16] they have done nothing to restore an account of film's many debts to theater. A recent surveyor of the film origins debate notes: "Theatre is probably less considered, whether as a positive or a negative influence on the cinema, by film historians today than at any other time."[17] Even Gilles Deleuze, who otherwise significantly challenges traditional definitions of film art, continues to sound the "not theater" note repeatedly in his (re)definition of film.[18] Attempts to define film against theater resemble attempts to define film against its own words. What emerges from both is a limiting, masochistic, self-mutilating, synecdochal definition of film.

The analogy of the cinematic novel has played a central role in film's antidefinition of itself. Like those early filmic rides to the rescue, interart analogy arrives in aid of interart categorization: the cinematic novel arrives to rescue ingénue film from dastardly theater, just as prose writers once allied with photographers to oust novel illustration and declare it "not the novel."

The adjective "dramatic" applied to film, theater, and the novel offers a far more tenable, less problematic rubric than the "cinematic" novel. Yet it holds no more sway in aesthetic theory than does the novelistic cinema. André Bazin observes: "Drama is the soul of the theater but this soul sometimes inhabits other bodies . . . the cinema is the least likely of arts to escape this influence . . . half of literature and three quarters of the existing films are branches of theater." Yet he continues: "It is equally true that this is not the way to state the problem."[19] Instead, scholars use the cinematic novel analogy first to insist that film resembles the novel more closely than theater, and then to divorce film from the novel and proclaim a virgin birth for the "seventh art" by declaring the words of the novel "uncinematic." In 1999, Timothy Corrigan summed up the general consensus:

Although theatrical structures seemed originally most suited to the stationary camera of early cinema, the development of editing techniques and camera movements pointed the cinema more and more toward the mobile points of view found in the novel and especially in those nineteenth-century prototypes.[20]

In 2000, James Monaco concurred: "The narrative potential of film is so marked that it has developed its strongest bond not with painting, nor even with drama, but with the novel."[21] The cinematic novel frees film from theater by presciently tossing cinema its own differentiating weapons – cinematic techniques. The words of the novel are subsequently declared "uncinematic," like all words. And, since the novel has purged itself of its illustrations, film scholars can decree a virgin birth for film – a birth so virginal that it evaporates the virgin as well as the father. Film, scholars tell us, was born from the cinematic Victorian novel, but not from its words and not from its illustrations. Such a claim requires some probing.

Exposing the Cinematic Victorian Novel

In 1944, Sergei Eisenstein forged a widely adopted argument that "from Dickens, from the Victorian novel, stem the first shoots of American film esthetic."[22] Citing Dickens's attention to visual details, empirical psychology, atmospheric close-ups, his alternation of omniscient and character viewpoints and shifts from one group of characters to another, his sentimental tone, moral values, melodramatic plots, and gallery of eccentric, melodramatic characters, Eisenstein delineated a formal and a cultural heritage for film from the Victorian novel. After Eisenstein "discovered" the cinematic novel, critics ran riot with the analogy, tracing cinematic techniques in literature all the way back to Homer and Virgil.[23]

Numerous critics have supported Eisenstein's claim that filmmaker D. W. Griffith, the so-called father of Western cinema, derived his most seminal film techniques from novelist Charles Dickens. The claim was first propounded by Griffith himself, recorded in 1922 by A. B. Walkley of the London *Times*:

> Mr. Griffith found the idea to which he clung thus heroically in Dickens ... he might have found the same idea almost anywhere ... Newton deduced the law of gravitation from the fall of an apple; but a pear or a plum would have done just as well. The idea is merely that of a break in the narrative, a shifting of the story from one group of characters to another group. You will meet with it in Thackeray, George Eliot, Trollope, Meredith, Hardy, and, I suppose, every other Victorian novelist.[24]

Walkley punctures Griffith's claim to a single prestigious literary ancestor and opens the influence to nineteenth-century novelists in general (he later adds Tolstoy, Balzac, Dumas, and Turgeniev to the list).

Griffith's claim to Dickensian inspiration participates in a long tradition of emulative aspiration between verbal and visual artists. In fact, it echoes an identical interart bid for prestige by Dickens himself. In his preface to *Oliver Twist*'s second edition, Dickens sought to set himself apart from literary peers and predecessors by analogy to the famous popular painter, William Hogarth: "I had *read* of thieves by the score ... But I had never *met* (except in Hogarth) with the miserable reality. It appeared to me that to *draw* a knot of such associates ... to *paint* them in all their deformity ... would be a service to society."[25] The interart emulation does not stop here. Hogarth wrote of his painting by analogy to theater: "my Picture was my Stage, and men and women my actors who were by Means of certain Actions and expression to Exhibit a dumb show."[26] Charles Lamb adjusted the analogy to emphasize the verbal rather than the performative elements of theater: "[Hogarth's] graphic representations are indeed books: they have the teeming, fruitful, suggestive meaning of *words*. Other pictures we look at, – his prints we read."[27]

From here, one can trace an analogical hopscotch between verbal to visual arts all the way back to ancient Greece: Milton, Shakespeare, Spenser, and Chaucer have all been praised as painters, as have Ariosto, Tasso, Virgil, Theocritus, and Homer. Painters too have for centuries been dubbed poets and their paintings hailed as poetry.[28] Sir Joshua Reynolds instanced Michelangelo as the prime witness to "the poetical part of our art" of painting.[29] Indeed, the analogy was so widespread in the eighteenth century that it drove William Hazlitt to complain of "artists or connoisseurs who talk on stilts about the poetry of painting."[30] Hazlitt's protest, however, did little to diminish such analogies, which proliferated throughout the nineteenth century.

But the analogy of a precinematic cinematic novel goes beyond participation in an ancient tradition of interart analogical bids to raise artist prestige, to differentiate artists from their predecessors and contemporaries, and to assert stylistic affinities between verbal and visual arts. The cinematic nineteenth-century novel is most often and problematically invoked in an argument of origins in which film births itself from the cinematic aspects of the novel, while discarding the words of the novel as uncinematic. The following discussion examines film nomenclature, production practices, consumption, and formal and stylistic elements to demonstrate that film shares far more affinities with the theater than with the novel and to contest the claim that nineteenth-century novels are cinematic, while their words are not.

From film's earliest days to the present, film nomenclature offers no evidence that the novel was film's most influential aesthetic predecessor:

indeed, the novel figures as one of the least influential forms. In film's early years, a host of names gesturing to various arts and technologies circulated from which a few emerged dominant. The closest early film names come to referencing the novel is in labels like "narrative animatography" and "narrative sculpture." These are, however, rare and idiosyncratic titles that make "narrative" the modifying adjective and accord the more substantial and definitive noun to a visual art. Moreover, "narrative" is not unique to the novel, but a category which contains it or, conversely, a subcategory of the novel, and "narrative animatography" can be traced to animated narrative optical devices like the animatograph that fed into film quite apart from the novel.[31]

The most common names for emerging film privilege visual and dramatic arts and film's technological properties. Names like "animated pictures," "animated photographs," "living pictures," "living photographs," "lightning photography," and "animated portraits" indicate film's perceived affinities with the visual arts. Titles like "silent drama," "screen drama," "photoplay," "screen play," and "theatrograph" gesture to film's perceived connections with theater. From these two strains, theater emerged dominant. In 1915, film theorist Vachel Lindsay affirmed that film and theater "are still roughly classed together by the public."[32] Well into the 1930s, films continued to be called "photoplays" and "moving picture plays." The more enduring term "movies" is an abbreviation of the latter term. While names like "moving pictures" suggest a blend of visual and theatrical arts, in the early eighteenth century, the term referred to theater alone, pressing film's nominal affinities with theater all the more strongly over its association with purely pictorial arts.[33]

In spite of doomsday critics who feared that film would replace the novel (an argument that implies their interchangeability),[34] the evidence indicates that if film replaced any aesthetic form to the point of extinction, it was *tableaux vivants* in which live actors held poses after famous paintings. Programs from the Palace Theatre of Varieties dating from March 1896 to January 1900 indicate that "The American Biograph" gradually took the place of *tableaux vivants*. Before the films arrived, *tableaux vivants* received prime billing in large typeface, and were afforded more performance time than other acts. Subsequently, the larger typeface and longer amount of time went to "The American Biograph." At first, *tableaux vivants* shrank in the program – both in performance length and typeface size – subsequently, they disappeared altogether. Other acts – songs, juggling and tumbling displays, skits, one-act plays, comedy routines, impersonations, performing animals, dances, and magical illusions – continued as before. The sense that this displacement derived from a perception that early films and *tableaux vivants* were similar forms strengthens when one notes the reassignment of Alfred Plumpton from composing music for the *tableaux vivants* to composing music for the Biograph films.

Although we still refer to the "motion picture industry" and to the "Academy of Motion Picture Arts and Sciences," today the most common English labels, "film" and "cinema," divorce themselves from the arts altogether, privileging only film's technological aspects. Indeed, these may be film's only real claims to aesthetic uniqueness. In Chapter 3, we witnessed scholarship's reduction of one filmic whole (Screen Play) to a part (screenplay) and the expansion of a part (cinematography) to another filmic whole (Cinema). While Chapter 3 focused on the verbal aspects of this displacement, the terminological shift also served to eradicate film's nominative affinities with theater.

Beyond nomenclature, practices of filmic consumption further undermine claims that film's closest aesthetic relative is the novel and again place its primary affinities with theater. While a few early critics propounded terms like "motion picture art gallery" to indicate the location where films are viewed, the dominant term then and now remains "theater."[35] Currently, yellow pages directories throughout the United States list the location where both live plays and films are viewed alike as "theaters."[36] The affinities here extend beyond terminology to architecture and viewing practices: movie theaters resemble live theaters and patrons of both consume performances in highly similar ways. In 1907, a writer perceived that "The nickelodeon . . . is merely the theatre democratized."[37] Little has changed since then in this regard.

Film production practices further challenge assertions that film's primary aesthetic affinity lies with the novel and again place it with theater. A glance at any screenwriting manual immediately reveals the Aristotelian principles of drama that structure most Hollywood and independent feature films.[38] Books addressing other aspects of production – direction, writing, acting, costuming, makeup, music, and set design – regularly group theater, television, and film, with no mention of the novel. *The Training of Directors for Theatre, Film and Television, On Writing for Theatre, Film and Television, Actors on Acting: Performing in Theatre & Film Today,* and *Wigs and Make-Up for Theatre, Television, and Film* all exemplify that theater, film, and television engage in interrelated, even interchangeable production practices.[39]

Beyond production practices, aesthetic criticism – indices of reviews and scholarship, artist biographies, and research resources – also groups theater, film, and television together, as the following titles attest: *Reference Guide to Reviews: A Checklist of Sources for Film, Television, and Theatre*

Reviews, Theatre, Film and Television Biographies Master Index, and *Sourcebook for the Performing Arts: A Directory of Collections, Resources, Scholars, and Critics in Theatre, Film, and Television.*[40] Scholarly and philosophical works regularly link theater, film, and television under a performance rubric: for example, *Performance and Politics in Popular Drama: Aspects of Popular Entertainment in Theatre, Film, and Television, 1800–1976* and *Congressional Theatre: Dramatizing McCarthyism on Stage, Film, and Television.*[41] Viewed through these lenses, theater emerges overwhelmingly as the older art with which film shares the most affinities, not only in its formative years, but today as well.

Why then, do scholars insist that the novel is film's closest relation? Formally speaking, the myth of a cinematic nineteenth-century novel rests on two claims. The first maintains that the novel shares with film a realist, empirical, visual representational style. Leon Edel claims that "Wherever we turn in the nineteenth century we can see the novelist cultivating the camera-eye and the camera movement."[42] The second insists that novel and film alone share a practice of shifting back and forth between groups of characters and of cutting between various points of view within a scene – a practice of montage or editing that is, paradoxically, also film's uniquely defining aesthetic attribute.

Let us examine the evidence for these claims. The assertion that film derived its visuality primarily from nineteenth-century novels is at best dubious. It is highly unlikely that film, with its more tangible visual roots in nineteenth-century photography, magic lanterns shows, public spectacles, theater, painting, *tableaux vivants,* and optical toys, required such an ancestor to discover visuality.[43] While novel and film scholars protest that the novel engaged in a peculiar type of visuality unique to itself and to film, art historians have demonstrated repeatedly that any such "cinematic" propensities in Victorian novels can be more (chrono)logically traced to visual and dramatic media prior to and contemporaneous with these novels.[44] Rhoda Flaxman concludes her study of ekphrasis in Victorian novels with a statement that the practice "often yields an effect we moderns call cinematic."[45] But her book demonstrates that ekphrasis was rooted in Victorian visual arts from which film would later draw as well. Historical evidence joins formal analysis against claims that film gleaned its visuality primarily from the nineteenth-century novel. Early cinematographers, including Griffith's camera man, Billy Bitzer, attest that they turned to Victorian paintings for compositional techniques. Such documentation seriously challenges Griffith's claim that he gleaned his visuality primarily from Dickens's prose.[46]

Why, then, do historians credit the prose of novels for film's visuality? Quite apart from the prestige and interest early film derived from crediting celebrated popular novelists like Dickens, a debt to the invisible visualities of prose is far easier to cast off than debts to tangible visual arts in a bid to declare film a unique art. And nominating these effects "cinematic" rather than "novelistic" further obscures film's debts to the novel. The implication is that cinema deposited itself in the novel, magically from the future, as in a sperm bank, and had only to unite its own seeds with technology to birth itself in the substantial noun of cinema. Such rhetoric participates in mythological narratives of origins.

Just as there is no compelling reason to trace the visuals of film to the invisible visualities of the Victorian novel, so too, there is no reason to glean invisible theatrics from the novel to account for film's dialogue, its embodied, enacted, costumed characters, its symbolic and realist uses of objects and spaces, or, most importantly for this discussion, for its narrative structure of shifting scenes and points of view. The theater is a far more tangible source for each of these practices in the novel as well as the film. While Griffith claimed to find montage in Dickens's prose, Dickens himself attributed his own discovery of montage to theater:

> It is the custom on the stage, in all good murderous melodramas, to present the tragic and the comic scenes, in as regular alternation, as the layers of red and white in a side of streaky bacon ... sudden shiftings of the scene, and rapid changes of time and place, are not only sanctioned in books by long usage, but are by many considered as the great art of authorship ... [47]

Since Griffith was both playwright and actor, it is highly doubtful that he could have gleaned his montage techniques solely from the Victorian novel without any direct influence from theater.[48] More than this, numerous critics argue that montage is a feature of modernity and postmodernity common to many arts and by no means unique to novel and film.[49] Even within film studies, challenges are regularly mounted to montage as film's most uniquely definitive code.[50]

One could even posit that, far from distancing film from theater, montage brings film closer to theater in an effort to restore the theatrical vivacity that film techniques fail to capture with static cameras and single shot scenes. Intercutting and camera movement can be viewed as efforts to restore the three dimensions, live action, and moving spectator eye that the camera had previously removed from the theatrical experience.

In spite of all this evidence to the contrary, the novel/film/montage trinity reigns supreme in the film history textbooks on which each new generation of film scholars is reared and remains unchallenged in overviews of the novel and film debate. And, tellingly, the arguments supporting this trinity frequently express a tension between claims that montage belongs uniquely to film and that it unites film with the novel against theater. Monaco serves as a representative and influential example of this tension: his *How To Read a Film* is one of the most widely read and frequently reissued textbooks on film. Distinguishing the various codes that film shares with other arts from those that are unique to film, Monaco offers montage as a primary example of the latter. Then he backpedals, qualifying that montage is not "truly unique to cinema," but "has always existed in the novel." In an effort to resolve the contradiction, Monaco reads a sequence from Alfred Hitchcock's *Psycho*, concluding: "it's hard to see how the montage of the sequence could be duplicated in any other art. The rapid cutting of the scene may indeed be a unique cinematic code."[51] Here, ratio and relativity aspire troublingly to absolutes and uniqueness. Nowhere else is Monaco so murky in his argumentation: characteristically lucid and piercingly insightful, here he wrestles with a filmic myth of origins that refuses to clarify.

Once the cinematic novel has obscured film's tangible debts to theater and to other visual arts, the novel must now be itself cast off as a tangible progenitor. Here, the insistence that words are "uncinematic" proves indispensable. And here a central paradox of the novel/film debate emerges. We have seen that the novel is everywhere decreed "cinematic" – in every form, decade, nation, and style of novels and films. But we have seen too that words are unilaterally declared "uncinematic." Now that "the novel" has come to be defined as words, its illustrations excised, what is the novel apart from words? How can the novel be cinematic and its words uncinematic?

The paradox is essential to film's myth of origins. If the novel is cinematic, but words are not, then the paternity of the Victorian novel becomes an entirely mystical affair. Margaret Homans and others argue that the literal and tangible constitute the realm of the mother and the figurative and dislocating comprise the realm of the father.[52] Under this configuration, film's tangible mothers, like visual arts and theater, are first displaced by the invisible visualities and unseen scenes of the paternal novel. Then the novel's words, which conveyed these effects, are exiled as "uncinematic," leaving only a mystical and figurative father. Film's inheritance from the novel is insubstantial: it is one of invisible visualities and of blank spaces between words, paragraphs, and chapters (the novel's montage). The novel's invisible visualities are then born as cinematography (hence film's dominant titles, "film" and "cinema"), and the blank spaces of the novel are born as montage, film's most commonly invoked defining aesthetic technique. Film's heritage from the novel is thus one of absence rather than presence. It is a heritage that allows film to disinherit itself from the novel even as it claims its inheritance from it and to be born spontaneously as the seventh art. This is why the analogy of a cinematic novel rather than of a novelistic cinema dominates the discourse. Were film to acknowledge its debt to literal and visible arts (to paintings, sculpture, architecture, photographs, theater, book illustrations, and more) or its tangible debts to the words of novels, its birth would appear far more mundanely derivative, if it appeared as a birth at all.

I do not take this argument so far as to deny affinities between the novel and the film. But to my mind their strongest connection lies not in a linear argument of historical influence that emphasizes only one or two formal techniques to obscure film's other aesthetic debts, but rather in a parallel and overlapping dynamic in which both novel and film draw on a variety of art forms, including and especially theater. If the novel served as a formal precursor of film, it did so primarily by modeling how to combine many art forms in one medium.

Friedrich von Schlegel once referred to the novel as "a confusion of forms." Irving Babbitt lamented this confusion, complaining that the novel lacks "formal laws and limits" and is "the least purposeful of the literary forms." Intriguingly for this discussion, Babbitt delineated the novel as the art that "admits most readily a photographic realism – that is, an art without selection."[53] To my mind, Babbitt's appropriation of "photographic" offers a more apt analogy through which to yoke novels and films than the anachronistic analogy of the cinematic novel. But in the final analysis, such aesthetic omnivorousness and lack of aesthetic purity is equally true of theater. The evidence to my mind is overwhelming: it is theater rather than the novel that has been the dominant aesthetic influence on film and the art form with which film shares the most affinities.

Cinematizing the Cinematic Novel and/or Literary Cinema

While films adapt all types of literature, "literary cinema" most commonly refers to adaptations of canonical literature. A Website entitled "Literary Cinema" lists only canonical authors, like Sophocles, Thomas Hardy, Charles Dickens, William Shakespeare, George Orwell, Nathaniel Hawthorne, Mark Twain, and Richard Wright.[54] Ken Gelder's essay, "Jane Campion and the Limits of Literary Cinema," also addresses only canonical adaptations.[55] For reasons detailed in the following pages, canonical novels have been the most often filmed and the most regularly discussed form of literary film adaptation. Canonical novels tend to be filmed more than once. Canonical Victorian novels have been filmed most frequently of all: many have been filmed or televised at least 20 times and several over 100 times. Amongst Victorian novelists, Charles Dickens has inspired by far the most adaptations. While *The Strange Case of Dr. Jekyll and Mr. Hyde* and *Dracula* vie with Dickens's *A Christmas Carol* and *Oliver Twist* for the most adaptations of a single work, neither Stevenson nor Stoker come anywhere near Dickens in the total number of adaptations they have inspired.

While other reasons certainly contribute to these proportions, the myth of a cinematic novel in general and of a cinematic Victorian novel in particular and of Dickens as the most cinematic of cinematic novelists even more particularly have been major factors. The introduction to this book and Chapter 1 both posit connections between interart analogy and interart adaptation. However, scholarship has not often developed this connection. Although Irving Babbitt perceives the archenemies of categorical rigor to be interart analogies and interart adaptations, he devotes an entire book to combating interart analogies and dismisses interart adaptations in a single sentence. George Bluestone does the opposite: while a few interart analogies are embedded in his prose, he devotes an entire book to combating interart adaptations and no attention to interart analogy.[56] And Eisenstein, for all his probing of the Dickens–Griffith link and use of interart analogies to connect novels and films, places Griffith's actual adaptation of a Dickens story in parentheses: "(By the way, we shouldn't overlook the fact that one of Griffith's earliest films was based on *The Cricket on the Hearth*!)." He then proceeds to do just that: this parenthetical reference marks his only mention of the adaptation.[57] Likewise, in their influential discussion of interart analogies, René Wellek and Austin Warren dismiss interart adaptation out of hand: "One can, of course, deny the possibility of literal metamorphosis of poetry into sculpture, painting, or music."[58] But this is exactly what adaptation purports to do: to push interart analogy into interart metamorphosis.

L. M. Findlay astutely recognizes that Victorian interart analogies and Victorian interart adaptations were intrinsically linked in aesthetic theory and practice. Belief in the "essential kinship" of the arts expressed in interart analogies, he argues, fostered a related belief in their "intertranslatability" and led to a "quasi-incestuous intertranslation" in aesthetic practice.[59] Incestuous analogical couplings between sister arts, then, produce tangible offspring in interart adaptations.

We have seen that counteranalogies to the "cinematic novel," like "novelistic cinema," are decidedly lacking in the discourse. However, the aesthetic practice that purports to fulfill the analogy of the cinematic novel – to cinematize the cinematic novel – ushers in a counteranalogy of "literary cinema" – that is, of literary film adaptation. Adaptation in the other direction – novelization, which adapts film to novel – raises a further counteranalogy of aesthetic practice, but to date scholars have paid little attention to it. Novelizations are too much books to support filmic vaunts over literature and tend to be grouped with other movie "tie-ins," like CDs and McDonald's Happy Meals. Conversely, they are too much byproducts of film and too poor quality literature to be used by literary scholars to assert the superiority of books over films.

Thus, the more compelling counteranalogy lies in literary cinema. Just as the pictured prose of pictorial initials challenges analogies of prose pictures, so too, cinematizations of cinematic Victorian novels challenge analogies of a cinematic Victorian novel. These cinematizations not only form counteranalogies, they also pose counteranachronisms that invert film's myth of its origins and narrative of its growth as an independent art. For, if the analogy of the cinematic novel allows film to birth itself, then it also allows the cinematic novel to cinematize itself: to birth its adjectival cinematic potential in the concrete noun of cinema. In adaptation to cinema, the cinematic Victorian novel refuses to be left behind as precinema, as a cinematic seed that fell to the ground and died giving birth to cinema. Instead, the Victorian novel seizes on the anachronism that makes it cinematic before cinema, turning precinematic essence into cinematic predestination. It catapults itself into the twentieth century where it vies with "pure" cinema as "literary" cinema. From the Film D'Art movement of the 1910s to the highbrow Merchant Ivory films of the 1990s, literary cinema has been positioned as a high art branch of cinema, constantly reminding film proper that it is "low art." Film scholars, in turn, have retaliated by calling literary cinema "bad" cinema or "uncinematic cinema."

As with the rhetorical analogy of the cinematic novel, the aesthetic practice analogy of literary cinema offers grist for both literary and film mills and a battleground on which to contest representational and cultural superiority. Bluestone's seminal *Novels into Film* deals exclusively with literary film adaptations to establish his theories and categorizations of novels and film more generally. When interart adaptations incarnate interart analogies, disanalogous dimensions are incarnated along with analogous ones, rousing more vociferous categorical protests.

Discussions of literary cinema privilege fidelity issues. The literary camp by and large views adaptation as translation. For a film to be a successful adaptation, then, it must be faithful to the original. Some allowance is made for the exigencies of film's own language, but fidelity is indispensable for adaptations to be deemed "successful." Beneath this seemingly objective translation model a battle for dominance lurks. We have seen that most scholars define novels as "words" and films as "images" and insist that the two cannot translate. Adaptation, therefore, is doomed to failure before it begins. The literary camp twists this belief in the impossibility of translation to a claim that film cannot "live up to" literature qualitatively as well as quantitatively. Surveying adaptation criticism through 1977, Robert B. Ray adduces that the typical essay asks: "How does the film compare with the book?" and concludes: "The book is better."[60] While a number of recent publications challenge the preoccupation with fidelity, the emphasis continues. Every essay in Robert Giddings's and Erica Sheen's edited collection, *The Classic Novel: From Page to Screen* (2000), addresses fidelity.[61] Under most literary lenses, literary cinema represents a falling off from the book, an inferior reproduction of a superior original, a failed translation, an infantile filmic drawing displayed on literary refrigerators, pabulum for mass audiences who cannot digest the meatier text, or a pedagogical hook to lure lackluster students from the rising tide of mass culture to the higher, dryer shores of canonical literature. The editors of *Novels into Film: The Encyclopedia of Movies Adapted from Books* (1999) link the last function to the myth of the cinematic novel:

> One would like to believe that movies might serve as a stimulus to reading – even if viewers ended up reading the likes of Stephen King or Michael Crichton – for they might graduate to more serious and demanding authors, some of whom, like Charles Dickens, anticipated the narrative possibilities of the cinema.[62]

In this account, viewers climb a high art ladder into the literary past and discover cinematic "possibilities" there to reward their lexical labors. Yet when literati insist on the cultural and temporal priority of the novel over the film, either chronologically or in such anachronistic configurations, they consider only one of two equally plausible hypotheses. Why, especially when novels are termed "cinematic" and when novelists often write with an eye to lucrative movie rights, does no literary critic argue the novel's failure to adapt to and rise to the superior level of filmic representation?

Against such one-sided fidelity judgments, the film camp and separatists like Bluestone emphasize the other side of a balanced translation model: film's duty to be faithful to its own semiotic system – to cinematic signs, conventions, audiences, and genres. Bluestone's *Novels into Film* was written largely to challenge the belief "that the novel is a norm and the film deviates at its peril."[63] In the mid-1970s, film scholar Morris Beja conducted a searching interrogation of fidelity, attesting to the impossibilities and unreasonableness of the imperative.[64] Around the same time, Geoffrey Wagner valued and ranked his three models of adaptation according to their degree of *in*fidelity to the original.[65] In the 1980s, scholars like J. Dudley Andrew argued for a balanced translation model in which fidelity to the novel and to film conventions is honored equally.[66] This period of moderation, however, was short-lived. In the 1990s into the 2000s, the fidelity imperative has emerged as the arch-villain of adaptation studies, both because of its association with right-wing politics and high art and because of its subjective impressionism.[67] In 1993, Peter Reynolds recommended that adaptations undertake a Marxist subversion of canonical literature, expressing dialectic rather than deference.[68] In 2000, Robert Stam advocated resistance to the "elitist prejudices" of fidelity imperatives through Michel Foucault's demystification of the author, Michail Bahktin's notion of dialogic exchange, Jacques Derrida's blasting of the original/copy differential, and Roland Barthes's semiotic leveling of literature and film alike as "texts."[69] In 1996, narratologist Brian McFarlane objected that fidelity's impressionist and subjective dimensions undermine narratological objectivity and categorical rigor.[70]

But the most common objection raised to fidelity maxims argues that literary cinema is an oxymoron – it is uncinematic cinema. The task of adapting literature to film must therefore be one of deliterarizing literature in order to make it cinematic. Screen adaptation handbook author Linda Seger devotes several chapters to the "uncinematic" nature of various literary genres, then several more to demonstrating how this uncinematic literariness must be eradicated in adaptation to film.[71] If an adaptation fails under this model, it is not because film is an inferior medium, but because a literary work has not been adequately purged of its literariness. "Uncinematic" in this context comes to mean more than simply "not cinema." It means "anticinema." If literature is anticinema, the logic goes, then adaptation must counter this by being "antiliterature." Here a hostile and antagonistic model of adaptation emerges.

Such theories find an epitome in those adaptations that begin with a shot of their founding novel. The novel is shown briefly; the film subsequently "wipes," "blacks out," "cuts," or "dissolves" the novel – terminologies as well as techniques that indicate the film's violence against and erasure of its founding texts.[72] For example, the opening of David Lean's *Great Expectations* (1946) begins with a shot of the novel, *Great Expectations*, opened to Chapter 1. John Mills, who plays the adult Pip, reads the opening paragraph in a formal voice-over: "My father's family name being Pirrip, and my Christian name Philip, my infant tongue could make of both names nothing longer or more explicit than Pip. So, I called myself Pip, and came to be called Pip." The monotone recitation, circling self-referentiality, repetition, and clutter of subordinate clauses render the prose tedious and confusing. Words enunciated at the speed of sound in a medium that can operate at the speed of light emerge all the more tiresomely, so that the viewer is relieved when a scouring wind rises and turns the pages rapidly in a parody of flip-book animation – an animation that subsequently gives way to the more sophisticated and dynamic animation of film.[73] The subsequent scene is noticeably and contrastingly wordless: a silhouetted Pip runs pushed by a howling wind along the shoreline to a chiaroscuro, ghoulish graveyard, where he is menaced by waving troll-like trees and creaking branches that grasp at him like arthritic witches' arms. When we next see text from the novel, it lies on the gravestone recording the deaths of Pip's parents. Unlike most films that open with shots of their founding text, Lean's *Great Expectations* does not end with a shot of the novel's closing page: the novel is dead and buried by the middle of the film's first sequence, commemorated on the gravestone along with Pip's parents. This opening simultaneously credits and erases the novel on which the film purports to be based in much the same way that film history credits and erases the novel as a foundation for film more generally.

William Luhr and Peter Lehman insist that any critical attention to literary sources denotes a failure in film art: "if [a film] makes no sense without recourse to a prior text, then it is not aesthetically realized. If it is aesthetically realized, then its use of source material is of historical, not of aesthetic interest."[74] Like those illustrations that need only appear when words fail to represent, here any attention to literary sources implies film's failure to represent independently as well as to eradicate all traces of its literary sources and literary debts. The novel is relegated to film's prehistory in the case of specific films as well as to film's general aesthetic prehistory. At the turn of the twenty-first century, such conceptions continue. Monaco writes: "It almost seems at times as if the popular novel . . . exists only as a first draft trial for the film."[75] This assessment recalls discussions of illustrations as "sketches worthy of being painted," pinned hierarchically below prose's claim to have arrived at painting.

Adaptations surface in film histories in much the same way: as primitive forms representing misguided fumblings after other arts, which must be discarded for film to discover its own "true" form. The Film D'Art movement of the 1900s and 1910s, which adapted highbrow canonical literature to film, is typically opposed to "true" film art rather than regarded as part of film art. Gerald Mast is representative: "The Film D'Art ran the movies headlong back into the theatre . . . stage acting and film acting were incompatible . . . The Film D'Art had nothing to do with film art."[76] After the Film D'Art movement, film histories remain mostly silent on literary film adaptation. Scholars justify this silence by declaring literary adaptations "poor cinema" or "uncinematic cinema" – thus unworthy of scholarly attention on both counts. But this silence represents a manifestly false history. Between 1927 and 2000, 67% of the Academy of Motion Picture Arts and Sciences Awards for Best Picture went to literary adaptations. (In 1995, the figure was 73%.)[77] And if readers protest that these awards do not represent the best of American film, they might want to consider the identical percentage of literary adaptations (67%) on the American Film Institute's top 100 list – a list selected by their self-described "blue-ribbon panel of more than 1,500 leaders of the American movie community," including prestigious film scholars and distinguished filmmakers. The list, though controversial, reflects much of the American film canon and with it, the values of American film academia. It is striking how consistent the statistic is across both "academies," though the films differ considerably. When one adds to this figure films adapting other written sources – biographies, newspaper articles, and histories – as well as original screenplays written by novelists and playwrights, majority turns to landslide. Given that so many canonical films are literary adaptations, the near silence of film scholars on the subject is baffling – unless one understands that rivalry governs interdisciplinary study. The film camp's neglect of the literature underlying so many of its films extends to scholarly negligence when they do address it. A 1990 essay on Hitchcock's *Rear Window*, published in *American Cinematographer*, inaccurately summarizes the ending of the short story on which the film is based, making not one but several errors – and the story is a scant 40 pages in length. The film scholarship manifested in the article is, by contrast, solid and rigorous.[78]

André Bazin represents a nearly lone and largely unattended voice protesting models of literary cinema that dissolve novels into films and find visual equivalents for verbal representation. He favors a model in which the novel itself, rather than the subject matter of the novel, is the subject of the film, one in which the novel is "affirmed by the film and not dissolved into it." Under such models, there is no need for the film to be faithful to the novel because "it *is* the novel": nevertheless, it is a "new aesthetic creation," the novel "multiplied by cinema." While to some extent this version of literary cinema hallows and preserves the novel, it does so by treating the novel as an object, an artifact, a textile, a cluster of cultural symbols in the film, constituting only a part of the culture that a film represents. While Bazin claims that the novel is thereby "multiplied" and delivered to a wider audience and that novel and film engage in a "dialectic" that precludes film from substituting for the novel or from sharing its identity, the process reduces the novel to a piece of the world that film represents.[79] Like the texts written, waved, torn, burned, and hallowed by silent film characters, this model of literary cinema emphasizes the constructedness of the novel and its status as a cultural artifact while implying the broader, more naturalistic, encompassing, omniscient representational powers of the film. The next chapter probes various ways in which theories, rhetoric, and practices of literary film adaptation consider novels and films as the content of each other or otherwise split form from content to further representational rivalries between them.

5 Literary Cinema and the Form/Content Debate

Recent scholars conclude that adaptation studies lag deplorably behind the critical times. Formal scholars lament their lack of critical rigor and unruly subjective impressionism; cultural studies scholars charge that they promote outmoded theories like high art humanism and New Criticism and foster a retrograde entrenchment of the literary canon against the rising tide of popular culture.[1] But surveying the criticism over the whole of the twentieth century into the twenty-first, one finds that adaptation studies have always been excoriated as outmoded and lagging behind the critical times – by New Critics, as well as by their high art humanist predecessors. Babbitt, as we have seen, lambasted adaptation as a nineteenth-century "confusion of the arts" in 1910; Wellek and Warren dismissed adaptation as a theoretical impossibility in 1942.[2] Film scholar Béla Balázs decreed all adaptations inartistic in 1952 and Bluestone adduced in 1957 that film would not "discover its central principles" until "the current vogue of adaptation ... has run its course."[3]

Adaptation has been the bad boy of interart criticism and decreed inartistic art for over a century now, not only because it blurs categorizations of the arts, muddying their virginal purity in the first half of the twentieth century and precluding their independence in the second half, but also because it commits two central heresies against mainstream twentieth-century aesthetic and semiotic theories. First, it suggests that words and images may be translatable after all. When most scholars assert that words and images do not translate, what remains to transfer between a novel and a film in adaptation? In the answer most commonly posed to this question lies adaptation's second heresy: that form separates from content – that the characters, plots, themes, and rhetoric of a novel distill to content apart from form and transfer into the form of film.

From Walter Pater,[4] to Ferdinand Saussure,[5] to New Critics and structuralists, scholars remain adamant that form does not and cannot separate from content. The dogma remains constant, despite many other changes in semiotic theory. And while poststructuralist semiotics have exploded form/content binarisms, they have done so by debunking and ghosting content altogether, rendering claims that content passes between forms in adaptation even more heretical than in prior theories. Indeed, poststructuralist semiotics have fused form and content in such a way that content evaporates altogether in favor of pure form.

Word/image and form/content dogmas thus conspire to render adaptation a theoretical impossibility. But if adaptation is theoretically impossible, it is culturally ubiquitous. The prevalence of adaptation affronts semiotic and aesthetic theory at every turn. It challenges New Criticism's denial of a paraphrasable core when screenwriting handbooks declare paraphrase the first stage of adaptation.[6] It troubles the inviolable bond of structuralism's signifier and signified when words and images are decreed untranslatable as whole signs, leaving only some part of a novel's signs available for transfer in adaptation. It raises for poststructuralism the untenable specter of an original signified, to say nothing of the more localized signifieds to which both novels and films claim to refer.

Scholars thus find themselves at odds with filmmakers and audiences. They are pinned between concluding that adaptation has not occurred – only an illusion of it – or ascribing to the semiotic heresy that content can have a life apart from form. Novelist and (significantly for this discussion) semiotician Umberto Eco contends that adaptation does not and cannot occur: that it is merely a collective cultural hallucination. He insists that there is no relationship at all between his book, *The Name of the Rose*, and Jean-Jacques Annaud's film of it: they simply happen to share the same name.[7] Yet Annaud and the public perceive the film to be an adaptation of Eco's novel, and Eco was handsomely paid for the film rights to this theoretical impossibility. Eco is in the minority: indeed, if every scholar shared his view, there would be no adaptation studies (sneering dismissals do not amount to "studies"). No scholar, however, has gone so far as to argue that older theories of form and content should be restored (or if one has, she or he remains unpublished). Most have sought to ameliorate or to sidestep the heresy, yet all slip into it in one way or another, generally through a rhetoric that runs counter to theoretical correctness. This tension between theoretical adherence and rhetorical heresy is to my mind a principal reason why adaptation studies appear always to lag behind the critical times. This chapter probes six mostly unofficial concepts of adaptation that split form from content in various ways to account for the process of adaptation. These concepts, gleaned from critical theory and rhetoric, from filmmaker accounts of their work, and from interpretations of adaptations themselves, foster interdisciplinary rivalries and put pressure on the form/content dogma itself. They overlap as frequently as they conflict and are by no means presented here as ideal, prescriptive, or even empirically "true," but rather as concepts operative in practice and criticism, where novel/film rivalries bristle in the cracks and splits forced, forged, and reformed between form and content, as novels and films invade and occupy the splits in each other's signs. In some of these configurations, one medium is considered the content of the other; in others, both media gesture to a shared outer signified; in yet others, filmic and literary form and content merge to create a composite sign. Whether the novel is viewed as a monolithic signified to be faithfully represented by servile filmic signifiers, or as an incomplete sign requiring fuller representation by filmic signs, or whether novel and film vie to better represent a shared outer signified, interdisciplinary rivalry rages more furiously in adaptation than in any other branch of the novel/film debate. Because they have taken so many shapes in discourse, form and content must be understood variably in this discussion, ranging from whole art forms and their "themes" (contents) to pieces of signs (signifiers and signifieds).

Because of its preoccupation with that anthropomorphic version of form and content, the relationship between body and soul, *Wuthering Heights* provides an ideal case study for this discussion. Semioticians and aestheticians have for centuries drawn on body and soul analogies to explicate aesthetic and semiotic theories of form and content.[8] Walter Pater, for example, discussing Flaubert's theory of expression in relationship to Blake, wrote:

> One seems to detect the influence of a philosophic idea there, the idea of a natural economy, of some pre-existent adaptation, between a relative, somewhere in the world of thought, and its correlative, somewhere in the world of language – both alike, rather, somewhere in the mind of the artist, desiderative, expectant, inventive – meeting each other with the readiness of "soul and body reunited," in Blake's rapturous design.[9]

From assertions regarding the shared soul of two bodies (Cathy cries: "Whatever our souls are made of, [Heathcliff's] and mine are the same"), to perplexities of how the dead inhere in the living (Heathcliff's "I *cannot* live without my soul!" leads to ghost chasing alternating with necrophilia), to the perception that Cathy's spirit looks out through the embodied eyes of her relatives, perplexities regarding body/soul relations permeate

Wuthering Heights, offering not only fictive epitomes but also conceptual paradigms for the form/content issues of adaptation.[10] The various ways in which Heathcliff tries to connect with Cathy after her death provide templates for the various ways in which films seek to connect with novels in adaptation in terms of form and content.

The Psychic Concept of Adaptation

The persistent critical ghosting of content in the twentieth century is largely responsible for a psychic concept of adaptation that understands what passes from book to film as "the spirit of the text." This concept is everywhere in adaptation rhetoric – academic, practitioner, and lay. Screenwriting handbook author Linda Seger replaces the form/content dichotomy with a form/spirit one: "The adapter looks for the balance between preserving the spirit of the original and creating a new form."[11] Interdisciplinary scholar Christopher Orr adduces: "A good adaptation must be faithful to the spirit of its literary source."[12] Filmmaker Luis Buñuel claims that his film of *Wuthering Heights, Abismos de Pasion,* "Most importantly... tries to remain true to the *spirit* of Emily Brontë's novel" (his emphasis).[13]

The spirit of a text is commonly equated with the spirit or personality of the author. Pater writes: "There are some to whom nothing has any real interest, or real meaning, except as operative in a given person; and it is they who best appreciate the quality of soul in literary art. They seem to know a person, in a book, and make way by intuition."[14] Algernon Swinburne maintains a fusion of textual and authorial identities, insisting that *Wuthering Heights* "is what it is because the author was what she was; this is the main and central fact to be remembered."[15]

In *Wuthering Heights,* the idea that written words can have a spirit and that this spirit is that of the author unfolds in Lockwood's dream of Cathy. Her graffiti and marginalia evoke her authorial identity didactically in the repeated inscription of her name. Eventually, reading these names produces for Lockwood "an impression which personified itself when I had no longer my imagination under control" and the spirit of Cathy (the author) appears to Lockwood (the reader) (26).

Twentieth-century critics tend to represent this authorial spirit in less mystical ways: the authorial soul or personality becomes authorial intent, imagination, or style. Reviewer Howard Thompson's assessment that a 1951 film of *A Christmas Carol* "may be exactly what Dickens had in mind" is considered by academic critic Lester J. Keyser as synonymous with being true to "the spirit of Dickens."[16] Peter Kosminsky's 1992 film of *Wuthering Heights* opens with Emily Brontë (played by an uncredited Sinéad O'Connor) wandering the moors and beginning to "imagine" her novel:

> First I found the place. I wondered who had lived there; what their lives were like. Something whispered to my mind and I began to write. My pen creates stories of a world that might have been, a world of my imagining. And here is one I'm going to tell. But take care not to smile at any part of it.[17]

In this episode, the last stage in the chain of literary film adaptation – the film – dramatizes the first – pretextual authorial imagination and inspiration. Such a preface touts the film as more comprehensive of the novel's origins than the novel itself and authenticates the film with a dramatized incarnation of the author caught in the very act of inspiration.

Critics in search of more tangible literary manifestations locate the spirit of the text in authorial style.[18] Christopher Orr finds authorial spirit in "the manner in which the narrator communicates to the reader or viewer."[19] But a strain of mystification remains in the concept of authorial style, which always retains an element of *je ne sais quoi*. Pater maintains that although authorial spirit may manifest itself in style, it can never be fully contained or expressed by style: "it is still a characteristic of soul, in this sense of the word, that it does but suggest what can never be uttered, not as being different from, or more obscure than, what actually gets said, but as containing that plenary substance of which there is only one phase or facet in what is there expressed."[20]

The psychic concept of adaptation, however, does not simply advance an infusion of filmic form with authorial literary spirit: it posits a process of psychic connection in which the spirit of a text passes from author to novel to reader-filmmaker to film to viewer. The notion that a text has a spirit to which readers connect psychically finds recent roots in the early nineteenth century, most prominently in the writings of Georg Wilhelm Friedrich Hegel:

> ... art cannot merely work for sensuous perception. It must deliver itself to the inward life, which coalesces with its object simply as though this were none other than itself, in other words, to the intimacy of soul, to the heart, the emotional life, which as the medium of spirit itself essentially strives after freedom, and seeks and possesses its reconciliation only in the inner chamber of the spirit.

In Hegel's account, although the spirit "needs an external vehicle of expression," ultimately, form is "unessential and transient."[21] Similarly, the psychic concept of adaptation figures what transfers from novel to film as spirit and the task of adaptation as capturing that spirit and conveying it through changing mediums and forms to an audience. The term "medium" thus functions in two senses of the word – of persons in touch with spirits and of print and audiovisual mediums. Although the various mediums are indispensable to the operation of the psychic model, they can and must be dispensed with as the spirit passes from one to the other. The form changes; the spirit remains constant. The spirit of the text thus maintains a life beyond form that is neither constrained by nor dependent on form. Indeed, film critic André Bazin highlights a fidelity to "the spirit rather than the letter" that is "compatible with complete independence from the original."[22]

The psychic concept of adaptation can be diagrammed as follows, the parentheses indicating the dispensable and dropped forms that allow for psychic connection:

THE NOVEL'S SPIRIT → (THE NOVEL'S FORM) →
(READER-FILMMAKER RESPONSE) → (FILM) → VIEWER RESPONSE

The spirit of a text originates and ends in formless consciousness as pretextual spirit (generally figured as authorial intent, personality, imagination) and as posttextual response in the film viewer. Orr astutely recognizes that a model beginning with author intent and ending in reader response must elide the two, though they appear at opposite ends of a communications sequence: "The spirit of a verbal or filmic text is a function of both its discourse (the manner in which the narrator communicates to the reader or viewer) and its narrativity (the processes through which the reader/viewer constructs the meaning of the text)" (73).

The authorial spirit appeared frequently in Victorian discussions of paintings of poetry, hovering over and monitoring the adaptation of poem to painting and haunting the audiences of these adaptations. In 1854, John Ruskin fended off criticism that Charles Robert Leslie's painting was unfaithful to Pope's *The Rape of the Lock*, countering that it was, in fact, "admirable as a reading of Pope . . . [so faithful that] it seemed to me as if the spirit of the poet had risen beside the painter as he worked, and guided every touch of the pencil."[23] *The Examiner* review of this painting extended the psychic connection to reader-viewers, asserting that "the more thoroughly a man has entered into the refined *spirit* of Pope's mock-heroic, the more fully will he perceive the tact and skill with which Mr. Leslie has translated it into the painter's language."[24] Here, an authorial spirit lingers in the reader of the poem, preparing the viewer to receive the same spirit incarnate in the painting. In a similar but less approving vein, the ending of the film *Jekyll and Hyde . . . Together Again* (1980) depicts the decaying corpse of Robert Louis Stevenson rolling in his grave, moaning, "Ruined! My book ruined!" Here, the author joins the viewer in condemning the unfaithful adaptation.

Central to literary film rivalries, fidelity to the spirit of a text is typically accompanied by an insistence on the necessity of *in*fidelity to its letter or form. Author Irvine Welsh, whose novel *Trainspotting* was adapted to film in 1996, maintains: "you can't have a faithful interpretation of something; you can maybe have it in spirit, but it's going to change as it moves into a different medium."[25] (Here too, the psychic concept of adaptation finds precursors in the illustration debate. In 1903, Rose D. Sketchley favored an "idea of illustration, as a personal interpretation of the spirit of the text" over a more literal illustration of its words, which she rejected as too "matter-of-fact." In 1971, Jean Mitry cast film adaptations that adhere to the letter of novels as "mere illustrations," preferring those that pursue the novel's spirit as an "inspiration" of their own form.[26])

In *Wuthering Heights*, Heathcliff cannot decide whether to embrace Cathy's corpse, her dead form, or to pursue her elusive spirit. First, he turns to her corpse, vowing, "I'll have her in my arms again!" But as he moves to open her coffin, he senses her spirit in a different location: "I knew no living thing in flesh and blood was by – but . . . I felt that Cathy was there, not under me, but on the earth." He abandons the dead body and pursues the spirit: "Her presence was with me; it remained while I re-filled the grave, and led me home" (289–90). Heathcliff cannot have both body and spirit: he must abandon the body to follow the spirit. Similarly, the psychic concept of adaptation argues, to be true to the spirit of a text, an adaptation must leave behind the literary corpse.

This psychic ghosting of what passes between novel and film in adaptation inevitably allows a host of personal, filmic, and cultural agendas to be projected onto the novel and identified as its spirit. This must be one of the main reasons for the psychic concept's ongoing popularity, even as it is debunked elsewhere. The authority of the literary author is essential to validating these agendas and projections. The author has been slow to die in adaptation criticism and commercial promotions even as she or he lies moldering under other discourses, because she or he represents an "author-ity" on which both novel and film advocates call to assert the priority of their medium. For most of the twentieth century, psychic theories placed adaptation criticism under the auspices of literary rather than film scholarship: literary scholars policed and judged whether a film had captured the authorial spirit. The 1912 *Bioscope* "Special Review [of the Vitagraph *Vanity Fair*] by the Eminent Thackeray Biographer," Lewis

Melville, clearly indicates his role as literary guardian: "An editor of Thackeray's works cannot but be a stickler for the strictly accurate presentment of the great man's masterpiece." The review protests additions and changes to the novel as "inexcusable ... in direct defiance of the text," but offers "pardon under the plea of 'dramatic license' for omissions and condensations." He concludes that "many will disapprove of this tampering with a masterpiece," but adds, "there will be few who will not agree that ... it is a singularly interesting picture."[27] Three rather than two forms come under judgment here: the novel (a "masterpiece"), the adaptation (some parts "inexcusable," others pardoned "under the plea of 'dramatic license'"), and the film ("a singularly interesting picture"). The novel is unilaterally praised; the film, moderately complimented, while adaptation once again emerges as the bad boy, the rake of the interart triad, partly scolded, partly pardoned.

Nelly's speech to Heathcliff regarding his neglect of Bible reading can be extracted almost without modification to voice what many a literary critic has said to many a literary film adapter:

> You must have forgotten the contents of the book, and you may not have space to search it now. Could it be hurtful to send for some one – some minister of any denomination, it does not matter which, to explain it, and show you how very far you have erred from its precepts, and how unfit you will be for its heaven, unless a change takes place ... ? (333)

Substitute "critic of any theoretical school" for "minister of any denomination" and "critical and public favor" for "its heaven" and the rest can remain intact.

Literary critics as well as editors are called on to authorize or condemn adaptations. Indeed, it is difficult to locate an essay on adaptation that does not cite literary critics as authorities on what a novel "means" and then test the adaptation against these interpretations. Brian McFarlane, for instance, summarizes an essay by Q. D. Leavis on *Great Expectations*, concluding: "This seems to me an accurate account of one of the novel's great strengths, and it offers a challenge to the would-be-faithful filmmaker."[28] In this and other accounts, the textual "spirit" is defined and mediated by literary critics.

Less frequently, film reviewers have argued, contrarily, that a film adaptation corrects the errors of literary criticism. A 1939 *New York Times* review of MGM's *Wuthering Heights*, for instance, claims that the film interprets the novel more accurately than Charlotte Brontë: "Charlotte Brontë, in her preface to her sister's novel, said Heathcliff never loved

Cathy . . . But Heathcliff is no demon and he loved Cathy, in the film as in the novel."[29]

In the 1990s a number of film and television makers appropriated the canonical literary author to authorize their adaptations. They did so through a new titling trend that makes the author's name part of the film title, as in *Bram Stoker's Dracula* (1992), *Mary Shelley's Frankenstein* (1994), *Emily Brontë's Wuthering Heights* (used for both 1992 film and 1998 television versions), *William Shakespeare's Hamlet* (1996), *William Shakespeare's Romeo + Juliet* (1996), and *William Shakespeare's A Midsummer Night's Dream* (1999).[30] The expanded titles of promotions, reviews, and posters extend the possessive construction, making directors and production companies the authors' keepers rather than editors and literary critics, as in "Francis Ford Coppola's *Bram Stoker's Dracula*," "Kenneth Branagh's *Mary Shelley's Frankenstein*," "Peter Kosminsky's *Emily Brontë's Wuthering Heights*," and Baz Luhrmann's *William Shakespeare's Romeo + Juliet*." These redoubled possessives assert not only the film's authentication by the literary author, but also the director's or production company's ownership of that authorial authenticating power. The film *auteur* now authors the literary author at the same time s/he is authorized by him/her.

These titles and their accompanying promotions present the films as "the authoritative screen versions" of the texts, just as new editions of novels announce themselves "authoritative texts" in attempts to justify yet another edition. The Norton edition of *Wuthering Heights*, for instance, bears the subtitle "authoritative text, backgrounds, criticism," and its preface proudly announces that it has restored the original 1847 edition, asserting that Charlotte Brontë had "assumed privileges" in editing the 1850 edition "that now seem unwarranted."[31] In a strikingly similar move, Russell Baker, in his introduction to the first U.S. television broadcast of LWT's *Emily Brontë's Wuthering Heights*, confidently asserts that it "finishes the story just as Emily Brontë wrote it," while earlier films had not.[32]

The makers of "authoritative" editions and adaptations frequently invoke authorial spirit to authorize their work. Quite strikingly, Kenneth Branagh claims to understand the spirit of Mary Shelley's *Frankenstein* not only in opposition to earlier filmic interpretations of the novel, but also to the novel's own manifestations of this spirit:

> We have all grown so accustomed to all those screen versions of 'Frankenstein' that we have forgotten that Mary Shelley had something entirely different in mind . . . . Elizabeth is only talked about in the book, and I felt that had to be changed. It seemed ridiculous that she would

not question what he was up to, and I felt we had to have her voice in our story. Considering how times have changed in attitudes toward women's roles in films, it would not seem right to have her in the story just as a love interest. Mary Shelley was a strong woman who I'm sure questioned Percy Shelley, and I'm convinced she intended Elizabeth to be a strong character.[33]

Here, Branagh claims to have fulfilled an authorial intent that the author herself had failed to realize. But in the slippery shift from "times have changed" to "I'm convinced [Mary Shelley] intended," it is clear that "authorial intent" elides with contemporary readings. The film's promotions prove truer than its title: it is indeed "Kenneth Branagh's *Mary Shelley*" more than it is "*Mary Shelley's Frankenstein.*"

Intriguingly, Branagh's film shares an identical title with Harold Bloom's volume of critical essays, *Mary Shelley's Frankenstein*, a volume in which feminist contributions feature prominently.[34] Like these critics, Branagh cuts and pastes episodes from the novel into a feminist binder, adding feminist scenes where literary critics have added feminist critical commentaries. Just as critical articles select and explicate passages to shape a new narrative, so too the London Weekend Television adaptation that claims to be *Emily Brontë's Wuthering Heights* selects, cuts, pastes, and juxtaposes pieces of the novel into a late-twentieth-century feminist critical narrative. It does so, however, wordlessly through editing, sound, and *mise-en-scène*. Shots of a delirious Cathy (Orla Brady) screaming on a bed as she has her hair forcibly cut interpolate with shots of a stunned, mute Isabella (Flora Montgomery), also in bed, as Heathcliff (Robert Cavanah) brutally consummates their marriage. The intercutting begins slowly, so that the episodes appear parallel, rather than integrally connected. Increasingly, however, the image editing grows more rapid, and the sound editing carries the noises of one location into the scenes of the other, until events, locations, and characters intertwine. As Heathcliff approaches Isabella, a piercing scream rings out and the camera cuts to a bed panel. But as the camera rises from the panel to reveal the room, we see that neither the bed nor the scream belong to Isabella at Wuthering Heights, but rather to Cathy screaming in her bed at Thrushcross Grange. The scream does double duty here, figuratively voicing the anguish of the mute Isabella as well Cathy's audible hysteria, conjoining them ideologically as each suffers physical coercion from her husband. Edgar (Crispin Bonham-Carter) holds down a thrashing Cathy as the doctor cuts her hair to fight her fever. The fever, Cathy tells Nelly, has arisen in response to Edgar's insistence on his marital prerogative, so that the cutting is a further attack on her self-assertion. Women's hair is conventionally associated with femininity, sexuality, and soul, connecting through film editing to the forcible rupture of Isabella's single strand of virginity. In both cases, romantic fantasies shatter in the very location where Isabella and television audiences have come to expect a fulfillment of them: the marital bedroom.

Here and elsewhere the psychic concept of adaptation opens up representational spaces in the name of authorial spirit or intent where new spirits or intents enter, just as Cathy's pantheistic spirit allows it to enter many forms for Heathcliff – even those that differ radically from her own bodily form. Indeed, Heathcliff declares that Hareton's "startling likeness to Catherine" – their similar forms – is the least "potent to arrest [his] imagination." Instead, "In every cloud, in every tree – filling the air at night, and caught by glimpses in every object by day, I am surrounded with her image! . . . The entire world is a dreadful collection of memoranda that she did exist, and that I have lost her!" (324). In the same way, the amorphous pantheistic "spirit" of a text allows it to inhabit many forms that do not remotely resemble its own.

The Ventriloquist Concept of Adaptation

The ventriloquist concept of adaptation differs from the psychic concept in that it pays no lip service to authorial spirit: rather, it blatantly empties out the novel's signs and fills them with filmic spirits. If Cathy's and Heathcliff's sense of two bodies sharing a single soul epitomizes the psychic concept, Heathcliff's necrophilia with Cathy's corpse epitomizes the ventriloquist concept of adaptation. It represents what passes from novel to film in adaptation as a dead corpse rather than a living spirit. The adaptation, like a ventriloquist, props up the dead novel, throwing its voice onto the silent corpse. As he digs up her coffin, Heathcliff knows that Cathy's corpse will be cold and unresponsive when he touches it. But he uses deliberate fantasy to offset this reality: "If she be cold, I'll think it is this north wind that chills *me*; and if she be motionless, it is sleep" (289, original emphasis). Here, the ventriloquist concept dovetails as well as contrasts with the psychic concept: when Heathcliff abandons Cathy's corpse to pursue her ghost, the ghost conveniently leads him to his own home – to his own domain, to his own territory and occupations.

Nelly, the chief narrator of Brontë's *Wuthering Heights*, is one who sees "nothing" where others see spirits. She believes them to be "phantoms from thinking" based on responses to local folklore (336–37). Like Nelly, many adaptation critics argue that the spirit of a text is reducible to the sum of its surrounding culture: to semiotic, narrative, and generic conventions; to significations that film brings to its surrounding culture (like the star system); to significations film derives from its surrounding culture (like cultural myths); to industry constraints on the film (like film budget, casting, length constraints); and to cultural constraints on the film industry (like censorship and audience reception).

The ventriloquist process of adaptation resembles Roland Barthes's theory of metalanguage, where what passes between two signifying systems is considered an empty form, subsequently filled with the content of the second system. According to Barthes, in metalanguage, "That which is a sign (namely the associative total of a concept and an image) in the first system, becomes a mere signifier in the second ... When [the passing sign] becomes [pure] form, the meaning leaves its contingency behind; it empties itself, it becomes impoverished, history evaporates, only the letter remains."[35] The ventriloquist adaptation can be diagrammed as two mathematical equations, following Barthes's typography for distinguishing the two systems (the lowercase equation representing the first system, the novel, and the uppercase equation, the second system, the film adaptation):

$$\text{The Novel's Signs} - \text{The Novel's Signifieds} = \text{The Novel's Signifiers}$$

$$\text{THE NOVEL'S SIGNIFIERS} + \text{THE FILM'S SIGNIFIEDS} = \text{THE ADAPTATION'S SIGNS}$$

These equations distinguish "film" from "adaptation": the adaptation here is a composite of novel and film, rather than pure film.

This concept of adaptation produces readings that run contrary to most commentaries on adaptation. Most commentaries lay the blame for an adaptation's semiotic impoverishment at the feet of film, charging it with reducing the novel. These readings focus only on those places where the novel's significations have been emptied out: they rarely attend to significations that the film has added. While film adaptations typically do cut and condense novels, they also add the semiotic richness of moving images, music, props, architecture, costumes, audible dialogue, and more. All of these signs are laden with cultural and symbolic resonances. As in Barthes's account of metalanguage: "The meaning [of the second system] will be for the form [of the first] like an instantaneous reserve of history, a tamed richness."[36] The ventriloquist view, then, points to adaptation's filmic enrichments of the novel. These prove threatening to literary interests. As we saw earlier, eminent biographer Lewis Melville found additions and changes to the novel "inexcusable . . . in direct defiance of the text," while offering "pardon under the plea of 'dramatic license' for omissions and condensations."

In most cases where films empty out content from a novel, they replace it with new content. For example, critics complain that MGM's *Wuthering Heights* reduces Brontë's complex characterological passions to mawkish romantic movie sentiments. MGM unarguably omits most of the novel's more violent and transgressive words and actions, but it replaces them with a mercenary economic process that preys on romantic desire – a scheme closely resembling Heathcliff's preying on romantic illusions (Isabella's and the younger Cathy's) for financial gain.[37] As with many films of this period, the wealth and luxury portrayed on the screen blend with the more tangible luxuries of the motion picture palaces in which the films were consumed to heighten the audience's sense of the movie ticket's value. John Huntley recounts:

> I think it is very difficult really to realize how marvelous it was in the 1930s to enter one of these wonderful Picture Palaces. The home in those days was a pretty bleak place – no central heating, a fire probably just in one room which created more draughts than it actually warmed you up – and suddenly in this luxurious setting of the cinema you were warm and there was a lovely deep carpet and you sank into a very comfortable seat which was such a contrast from the wooden seats you probably had in the kitchen in those days. And everybody was so polite to you, and even when I was 14 I well remember having paid my 6*d*, I was called "Sir" by the staff and escorted to my seat. We used to go in about 12 noon and not come out till 8:00 in the evening and that was a day when you looked forward to not just seeing entertainment on the screen but sheer living luxury in total contrast to what it felt like at home.[38]

Huntley's account describes British motion picture palaces, but the venue was similar in the United States. MGM's *Wuthering Heights* was screened in Britain as well; its British superstar, Laurence Olivier, and largely British-born cast – Crisp, Robson, Fitzgerald, and others – rendering the film a decidedly trans-Atlantic affair.

In MGM's *Wuthering Heights*, the central love story becomes a metaphor for cinematic consumption, channeling viewers' vicarious erotic desires into a desire for cinematic fiction. Cathy's vacillation between the Lintons' pragmatic economic world and the dream world of romance with Heathcliff becomes a prescriptive template for the viewer's alternation between earning in the labor force and spending at the motion picture palace. Cathy (Merle Oberon) and Heathcliff (Laurence Olivier) run back and forth from the "real" world to their dream palace at Penistone

28. William Wyler's *Wuthering Heights*, MGM, 1939. Courtesy of the Academy of Motion Pictures Arts and Sciences.

Crag, where they play at princess and prince (Figure 28). Identifying with this template, film audiences are to earn in the workaday world, then retreat to spend their earnings at the motion picture palaces, where they play vicariously at motion picture palace princesses and princes, caught in an endless cycle of spending to dream and dreaming of spending. The happy ending of MGM's *Wuthering Heights* depicts the lovers' final and eternal return to Penistone Crag, forever filmic in a ghostly half-exposure. This is not the happily-ever-after of marriage, but of eternal cinematic residence.

The Westinghouse live television dramatization of *Wuthering Heights* similarly aligns erotic, narrative, and material desires with Cathy's vacillation between Heathcliff and Edgar to urge consumption, but consumption of a different product by a different audience in a different cultural context.[39] Made in 1950s America, where movie palaces languished and consumer goods flourished, the Westinghouse adaptation of *Wuthering Heights* recasts the relationship between spending and entertainment, aligning the erotics of viewing and consuming fictional romance with the marketing of household products: in some cases, the very medium through which the fiction is consumed – the television set. The commercials interrupting the live dramatization to market Westinghouse products are themselves live performances by an actress who resembles the drama's heroine. The commercials are figured as consultations of a theater program ("And now, let's look at our Westinghouse program"), further eliding the television "program" with the marketing "program" through analogy.

Wuthering Heights is adapted by Westinghouse to foster a tension between desire for what one does not have (Heathcliff, romantic fiction, Westinghouse goods) and the means of attaining it (Edgar, the 1950s husband, and his income). Early in the film, Cathy (Mary Sinclair) rejects the idea of marriage to Heathcliff (Charlton Heston) in original dialogue appearing nowhere in the novel: "It is not the bond to keep us together." In the novel, the only obstacle to union with Heathcliff for Cathy lies in his social degradation and poverty (80–82). This line, however, suggests that marriage destroys romantic love. If marriage could satisfy all desire for romance, housewives would require no romantic fiction and there would be one fewer vehicle through which to sell Westinghouse appliances. Therefore, in this adaptation, Cathy may enjoy extramarital romance with Heathcliff at Penistone Crag, but must return to the duties of marriage and domesticity, to the family home, the space in which domestic appliances are consumed. The drama maintains a constant tension in which Cathy hovers on the brink of adultery, but never commits it. Whereas the Cathy of 1939 flatly rejects adultery or any amatory play, the Cathy of 1950 ardently embraces Heathcliff at Penistone Crag. Ultimately, however, she resists the temptation of full-blown adultery, declaring: "Life is not lived on a point of rock. That green and pleasant valley is my home . . . I do love you, but I fear you as well. If you were to have me, you'd crush me like a sparrow's egg." Heathcliff responds violently, cutting his wrist, demanding Cathy to do the same in order to mingle blood with him, a clear metaphorical invitation to adultery. Frightened, Cathy refuses and runs back to the legitimate embrace of Edgar (Richard Waring).

Quite strikingly, the dialogue of this scene derives from a passage in the novel concerning Isabella and Heathcliff, not Cathy and Heathcliff.[40] Westinghouse's Cathy elides with Brontë's Isabella, running from a mad and violent lover back to the safety of Thrushcross Grange. The flight subliminally legitimates Cathy's liaison with Heathcliff by equating her with Heathcliff's lawful wife, transposing the literary Isabella's flight from her marriage to the television Cathy's flight back to hers. Thus the adaptation arouses adulterous desire, but ultimately sends wives back to their husbands, whose income is required to purchase Westinghouse products.[41]

The commercials are themselves narratives: narratives of appliances that create desire, solve problems, and persuade consumption through echoing narrative threads in the adaptation. Westinghouse spokesmodel Daphne informs viewers that they can trade in their old refrigerator as credit toward a new Westinghouse model. The motif of trading old for new ties to the novel's temptation of trading in old love for new. In the novel, Mr. Earnshaw's new love for Heathcliff displaces his old love for Hindley, Cathy abandons Heathcliff for Edgar, then shifts her loyalties back to Heathcliff again, and her daughter transfers her allegiance from Linton to Hareton. For Westinghouse, however, there is no dilemma: the old model can apply toward the purchase of the new so that the two become one, resolving the tension.

In order to urge consumption, Westinghouse appliances are heavily eroticized in the commercials. Daphne allures buyers with talk of the refrigerator's "famous magic button," which does the work of defrosting at the same time it keeps the freezer's contents desirably "firm" and the housewife labor-free: "You never have to touch that button." A second commercial shows Daphne pulling a decidedly phallic component from a Westinghouse television set (a component so phallic that my students erupt in laughter when they see it, without a word of commentary from me) to prove the technological prowess and dependability of the set. In this commercial, size matters: Daphne urges viewers to purchase a larger screen in order to have a better view of Westinghouse television theater: "Have you a second balcony set?" she asks, "Why don't you get yourself a real front row set?" Commercial and adaptation merge: viewers are aroused by the erotic elements of the fiction to desire a better means of watching that fiction.[42]

Often adaptations engage in mutual projections, mutual hauntings, creating strange ideological combinations. In his discussion of metalanguage, Barthes returns to qualify that the signified is *not* fully emptied in transfer to the second system: "The essential point in all this is that the form does not suppress the meaning, it only impoverishes it, it puts it at a distance, it holds it at one's disposal." He turns to the language of spirits to explicate the process: "One believes that the meaning is going to die, but it is a death with reprieve; the meaning loses its value, but keeps its life, from which the form of the myth will draw its nourishment." Content, he argues, "is not at all an abstract, purified essence; it is a formless, unstable, nebulous condensation ... there is no fixity in concepts: they can come into being, alter, disintegrate, disappear completely ... [they are] ephemeral."[43] In the same way, though the ventriloquist model purports to hold an entirely empty corpse animated by entirely new spirits, this is never quite the case. Two scenes from the LWT *Wuthering Heights* representing the same incident from differing points of view at different temporal moments illustrate. In the first, an adult Heathcliff haunts the child Cathy (Kadie Savage) as a ghost from the future. Startled, she stares at him without recognition, then runs on after the embodied child Heathcliff (Terry Clynes). Toward the end of the film, the scene repeats from Heathcliff's point of view. This time it is he who is embodied and present, while the children are ghosts from the past. This time there is mutual recognition. The child Cathy moves toward the aging Heathcliff with outstretched arms. Cutting on her movement, the sleight of camera replaces the child Cathy with the adult Cathy, who completes the child's movement with an adult's erotic kiss. The uneasy, near pedophilic moment, awkwardly averted by a last-minute adult body double or stand-in, emblematizes confusions and fusions of nineteenth- and twentieth-century ideologies that frequently trouble film and television adaptations of Victorian novels. Nineteenth-century nostalgic yearnings for childhood as the locus of lost innocence merge disturbingly with modern fears of pedophilia. Similarly, nineteenth-century ideals of death as the location of fulfilled desire conspire troublingly with twentieth-century fears of death as a state of nothingness and defeat. The next shot reveals that the kiss demarcated Heathcliff's death: we see Heathcliff stretched out dead on his bed in an allusion to Henry Wallis's 1856 painting, "The Death of [poet Thomas] Chatterton." The allusion renders blatant the implied suicidal elements of Heathcliff's demise in the novel, adding additional discordant notes to the mounting cacophony of conflicting desires. Tragedy and comedy confuse when a consummating Hollywood kiss marks the consummation of death; psyche shatters when erotic union demarcates the rupture of body and soul; nostalgia sickens when romanticized childhood frolics on the borders of pedophilia. Like the icy hand of the ghostly Catherine attaching herself to the warm-blooded hand of the embodied Lockwood, films made under ventriloquist concepts of adaptation often form uneasy alliances of commingled desire and aversion. Such aversive desire represents more broadly conflicting twentieth-century responses to the Victorians when their novels are adapted to film and television.

More broadly, while the ventriloquist concept of adaptation at first appears diametrically opposed to the psychic view, its idea of residual meaning lingering in so-called empty forms does not differ essentially from the idea that a spirit passes from a novel to a film in adaptation. Both concepts of adaptation grapple with the idea that meaning – whether it derives from novel, film, or surrounding culture – is a nebulous spirit that can enter and leave forms. The two concepts thus emerge as inseparable sides of the same coin.

The Genetic Concept of Adaptation

If Cathy's corpse is inanimate and her spirit elusive, she finds a less ghoulish and intangible afterlife in her brother Hindley's genetic resemblance to her – one that evokes and recalls her ("Now that she's dead, I see her in Hindley" – 180). She finds a similar genetic afterlife in her resemblance to her daughter, Cathy ("a second edition of the mother" – 154), and to her nephew, Hareton ("his startling likeness to Catherine connected him fearfully with her" – 324).

The genetic concept of adaptation, though it has not hitherto been so named, is well established in narratological approaches to adaptation. Narratologists figure what transfers between literature and film as an underlying "deep" narrative structure akin to genetic structure, awaiting what Seymour Chatman has called a "manifesting substance" in much the same way that genetic material awaits manifesting substance in the cells and tissues of the body. The most recent book-length narratological study of literary film adaptation by Brian McFarlane defines "narrative" as "a series of events, causally linked, involving a continuing set of characters which influence and are influenced by the course of events." The "cardinal functions" of narrative constitute its "deep structure," and these elements, according to McFarlane, can "transfer" directly from novel to film, although their specific manifestations require what he calls "adaptation proper" – the discovery of filmic signs equivalent to those of the novel. "Novel and film can share the same story, the same 'raw materials'," McFarlane argues, "but are distinguished by means of different plot strategies," like sequencing. In these ways, the narratological approach to adaptation attempts to circumvent the question of form's separation from content. Yet despite official adherence to form/content doctrine at the level of signs, the central terminologies of narratological theory nevertheless articulate a form and content divide at higher categorical levels, whether in Seymour Chatman's *histoire* and *discours*, in McFarlane's application of Benveniste's *l'énoncé* (statement) and *l'énonciation* (utterance), or in David Bordwell's invocation of the Russian formalist terms, *syuzhet* and *fabula*.[44] In each case, the first term represents a notion of content (what is told) and the second, a concept of form (how it is told). Narratological approaches thus allow a separation of form and content at the higher categorical level of narrative, a category that contains both novels and films, while precluding heretical form and content splits at the basic level of categorization, at the level of individual signs.

McFarlane rightly observes that even when signs transfer intact from novel to film (as when lines of dialogue transfer directly), they are "'deformed' by the catalysers that surround them," (as when lines of printed text from the novel are spoken by embodied, costumed, photographed, audible actors).[45] At times, however, changes at the level of manifesting signs go further to deconstruct the deep narrative structure beneath. Paradoxically, both for my own title for this model and for narratological theories of adaptation, genetic resemblances among characters in *Wuthering Heights* dismantle narratological deep "genetic" structure in some of its adaptations to film.

The novel's idea that Cathy and Heathcliff share a soul is most famously articulated in Cathy's ejaculation, "I am Heathcliff!" (82). This notion constitutes a cardinal thematic and ideological point, one that has been included in every film and television adaptation of the novel to date. Although the assertion emerges as a radical statement in any representational form, its expression in the manifesting structure of written words standing alone in an unillustrated novel is less systemically problematic and incongruous than its expression from the lips of an embodied actor in a film. The prose "I am Heathcliff!" engages in no grammatical travesties: the phrase conjugates the conjugal souls correctly; pronoun and proper name agree. Moreover, "I" represents a pronoun in which many names and social identities can and do conjoin as each occupies its subjective stance. In the novel, no other semiotic form appears to contradict the words: no illustration presents a body of Heathcliff that differs from hers and stands apart from hers. The novel may strip the bodies and their associated sociological identities for a fragment of grammatical space and time, but the films do not. In the purely textual expression, yoked pronoun and noun are separated by only the tiniest of bridges, the "am" that presses their identity even as it separates the referents. But in the narrative, Heathcliff has already left Wuthering Heights when Cathy declares their synonymy, so that any visual representation of this speech must belie their asserted union. The lightning, thunder, and violins accompanying the speech in the MGM and Westinghouse versions do not achieve such a merger, despite their association with the supernatural and mythological. Uttered by an actress, the "I" emerges from a specific pair of lips in a female body and fails to equate with or encompass the mute mouth and male body representing Heathcliff. Under conventional western models of proof – the word made flesh or the hypothesis proven by empirical evidence – the visualization of these adaptations appears as empirical evidence refuting Cathy's verbal hypothesis rather than supporting it.

Various adaptations have tried to offset this sense of semiotic contradiction. The 1967 McGraw-Hill "Text Film" of *Wuthering Heights* dilutes the rhetoric, converting radical synonymy to cautious simile: "I am *like* Heathcliff."[46] Other films follow screenwriting handbook suggestions that adapters replace verbal signs with visual equivalents, most commonly forging lip linkages in screen kisses, pushing iconic faces toward identificatory union. Kiju Yoshida's 1988 adaptation, *Arashi ga oka*, is the only adaptation to depict a sexual encounter where whole naked bodies intertwine, so that they appear as two heads on one body.[47] However, their faces continue to differentiate the lovers so that here, as in other versions, heterosexual encounter falls short of homospiritual union.

The Westinghouse adaptation attempts a less erotic, more mystical facial merger through filmic superimpositions and dissolves. As Cathy looks into her mirror, Heathcliff's face appears superimposed over hers and she cries: "Are our two faces one? Are we still two torn halves of each other?" But the effect is one of hybrid rather than half: the reflection's neck and dress remain Cathy's so that Heathcliff appears here as a cross-dressed androgyne. The superimposition of Heathcliff's face combines with a dissolve that eliminates Cathy's, rendering the effect one of displacement rather than union. This displacement is reinforced by dialogue that rejects their synonymy: "No, no!" Cathy cries. "Why is it always your face looking out at me from this glass, never my own?" At her outcry, Heathcliff's face fades and her own returns.[48]

Because filmic attempts at visual synonymy between Heathcliff and Cathy prove either blandly conventional or bizarre, a number of adaptations emphasize instead Cathy's biological resemblance to her relatives. Two filmmakers, Luis Buñuel and Kiju Yoshida, extend genetic physical resemblances to narrative resemblances in ways that deconstruct the deep "genetic" structure of the novel. In the final scenes of Buñuel's *Abismos de Pasion*, Catalina's (Cathy's) physical resemblance to her brother, Roberto (Hindley), is emphasized over any resemblance to Alejandro (Heathcliff), not only in terms of biological genetic structure, but also of narrative structure. At Wuthering Heights, Roberto (Luis Aceves Castañeda) catches a fly and tosses it into a spider's web, smiling sadistically as the spider springs to the center of the web to feed on its trapped, live prey. José (Joseph, played by Francisco Reiguera) reads a nihilistic passage about the final terminus of death, the oblivion of the afterlife, the degradation of devils, and the shortness and tediousness of life. We hear that Alejandro (Jorge Mistral) has gone to Catalina's (Irasema Dilian's) grave. Roberto loads a rifle and goes out. The camera cuts to Alejandro as he approaches the cemetery in the darkness, accompanied by the impassioned strains of Richard Wagner's *Tristran and Isolde*. Finding the vault locked, he struggles unsuccessfully with the chain, then penetrates the padlock with a pointed metal pole. As he throws back the vault's heavy double doors, the camera cuts to an unidentified arm pointing a rifle. A shot rings out. Alejandro clutches his heart. The gun lowers and Alejandro enters the vault. The film cuts to the vault's interior, where Alejandro staggers down the steps toward Catalina's coffin. He throws off the lid, which falls with a loud clang. Catalina lies dressed in bridal white, an opaque veil covering her head and upper torso. Alejandro kneels and takes her hand, but when he tries to pull it toward him, *rigor mortis* forbids. Dropping the unyielding arm, he turns his attention to her face, slowly lifting her veil and kissing her frozen lips. Catalina's echoing voice calls Alejandro's name from somewhere offscreen. Alejandro turns from the corpse toward the camera and the voice. A cut reveals Catalina standing on the vault steps, clad in her bridal-burial gown, smiling, one arm outstretched, beckoning to Alejandro. Suddenly – so suddenly that the viewer jumps – Catalina's shimmering image is replaced by the black-clad Roberto's, pointing a rifle from his similarly outstretched arm. In the superlative horror of Alejandro's necrophilia, the viewer has forgotten the mysterious gunman. A shot rings out, Alejandro falls forward across Catalina's corpse, Roberto slams the door to the vault, and the word "Fin" appears on the screen, seeming to move toward the viewer as it enlarges.

When Catalina's image gives way to Roberto's, the novel-Catherine's "I *am* Heathcliff!" becomes the film-Catalina's "I *am* Roberto!" The manifesting substances of the film here alter the deep structure that identifies Cathy with Heathcliff in the novel, replacing it with an identification between Catalina and Roberto that aligns physical genetic resemblances with structural narrative resemblances. Catalina not only resembles Roberto physically, but also narratively: they engage in similar narrative actions and are placed in similar photographic positions throughout the film. While Roberto closes the film with a rifle shot, sending Alejandro to the death for which he longs, Catalina opens the film with a rifle shot, killing a buzzard to send it to "the liberty of death." In the final sequence, as Alejandro claws, buzzard-like, at Catalina's corpse; she is made visually complicit with Roberto's gunshot, standing in the same pose and spot as her brother, calling him to the death which Roberto brings. Her corpse as well as her ghost colludes with Roberto's deed. Her body, with its gauze veil, resembles the spider in its gauzy web, which minutes before Roberto has fed with a live fly. As Roberto threw the live fly into the spider's web, so too, with his gunshot, he throws Alejandro onto Catalina's gauzy web. Her body thus becomes the bridal lure for the fatal trap, her ghost merging with Roberto's body to throw Alejandro onto hers.

Kiju Yoshida makes little of the Cathy/Hindley resemblance in his *Arashi ga oka* (aka *Onimaru*, 1988); rather, he heightens the genetic resemblance between Kinu (Cathy) and her daughter, young Kinu, who resembles her in face as well as name to such an extent that it is at times hard to differentiate the two. Yoshida introduces a mirror to represent both the elder Kinu's disembodied spiritual connection to Onimaru (Heathcliff) and her physical resemblance to her daughter. But the effects are achieved quite differently and, in the end, stress the affinities between mother and daughter over those between lovers. The mirror connects the elder Kinu (Yuko Tanaka) with Onimaru (Yusaku Matsuda), not through physical resemblance or facial dissolves, but through Kinu's use of its light-reflecting capacities to "touch" Onimaru, even as their bodies remain distanced by class segregation and gender codes. As Onimaru skulks in the shadows of the servants' hut, Kinu catches sunlight with her mirror and throws it across the yard onto his dirty, scowling face. To the light of the sun, she adds smiles and laughter, warming and welcoming him to Higashi no sho (Wuthering Heights). Through the mirror, she touches him without touching him; with the mirror, Yoshida cleverly establishes an intangible yet visible and phenomenologically realist connection between Kinu and Onimaru, avoiding both conventional banality and mystical implausibility.

After Kinu's death, the mirror's refracted light is the film's only attempt at visualizing her spirit. Onimaru is far more obsessed with digging up her dead body than with chasing her ghost, keeping her skeleton in the Forbidden Chamber of his home, where he is said to "embrace it nightly." When Onimaru digs up Kinu's coffin, this normally fearless, ferocious warrior starts in horror as a gleam of light darts and settles on her skull, then on his face, lending a fearful animation to her dry, bleached bones and a ghastly supernatural luster to his features. The film cuts to reveal Kinu's mirror, buried with her, as the natural source of this seemingly supernatural light, given mobility as the wind blows clouds across the sun.

The mirror, effective in such moments, falls flat in the dramatization of Cathy's "I am Heathcliff" speech. When Nelly/Osato (Tokuko Sugiyama) approaches Kinu to inform her of Onimaru's departure, Kinu, gazing at her reflection in the oval mirror, which frames her face with its own shape, replies dreamily: "No. Onimaru has not gone away. He is here." Osato echoes, "Here?" Kinu responds, "Yes. Onimaru is Kinu. [*Shot of her face in the mirror.*] Kinu is Onimaru. Onimaru is myself. [*She looks at the mirror.*]" Yet the viewer sees only her face, its visual representation belying her verbal assertion, so that she or he shares Osato's baffled, "Here?"

However, when young Kinu (Tomoko Takaba) inherits the mirror and prays to her dead mother through it, the physical resemblance between the two women is so striking that, without special effects, we "see" the older Kinu in the younger Kinu's face. As in Buñuel's alignment of Catalina and Roberto, Yoshida supplements this visual resemblance with dramatic and narrative resemblances between mother and daughter. Like her mother, young Kinu regards her face in the mirror and sees a reflection not her own. But it is her mother's, not Onimaru's. Her prayers to her dead mother through the mirror forge a much stronger spiritual connection than any made between her mother and the terrified Onimaru in the graveyard. Young Kinu fulfills her mother's deathbed vow both through her resemblance to her mother and through dramatic action, a vow that, "When I die, so will [Onimaru]. I will take him to the other world with me. I will make sure that we fall in hell. I will not allow him to wreak disaster on you." Kinu the elder has failed to keep her promise and Onimaru torments the second generation. Eventually, young Kinu turns her resemblance to her mother into a taunting, surrogate, embodied haunting of Onimaru that leads to his maiming and overthrow. She also uses the mirror to dazzle and disorient Onimaru with the sun's reflected light, as her mother had done.

To appear as the embodied ghost of her mother, she removes her mother's skeleton from the coffin Onimaru keeps in the Forbidden Chamber and lies in it herself. When Onimaru opens the coffin, her resemblance to her mother is so striking that it utterly terrifies him. When he discovers her deception, fear turns to violent rage. Young Kinu, however, is fearless. She taunts him: "Shall I take off these clothes and show you the body given by my mother? But don't forget, I'm also the daughter of the man you hated. Now, do you love my body? Or do you hate it?" Through a simultaneous taunting of Onimaru and seduction of Hareton/Yoshimaru (Masato Furuoya) with her naked body, young Kinu brings about Onimaru's defeat. She so enrages Onimaru that he strips her and beats her, her nudity and abuse conjoining at last to rouse the reticent Yoshimaru to rebel against Onimaru and maim him. Yoshida has expressed his debt to Buñuel's ending, but he transposes it to the embodied second generation of the novel. Yoshimaru takes his father's role in destroying Onimaru, and the young Kinu becomes the embodied ghost of her mother, luring both men to their final conflict.[49]

Clearly, deep structure cannot always be held intact and inviolate from its manifesting substances. In the same way, narratological applications of the genetic concept, despite their rigorous biologic, are not exempt from contamination by psychic and ventriloquist concepts. For example, in the novel, genetic resemblances between Cathy and her relatives make the latter less human to Heathcliff – ghosts themselves. The resemblance is most marked in the eyes: "Hindley has exactly her eyes"; the eyes of young Cathy and Hareton "are precisely similar, and they are those of Catherine Earnshaw" (180, 322). Literary and cultural convention does not allow eyes to be purely biological affairs: they are proverbially windows of the soul. At times, they prove more windows to Cathy's soul than to the souls of their owners: "When I look for [Hareton's] father in his face," Heathcliff tells Nelly, "I find *her* every day more!" (303, original emphasis). Genetic resemblance, although biologically and empirically grounded, nevertheless jettisons the rational and verifiable through its associations with spirit and thus allows for projections every bit as subjective as those that occur under psychic and ventriloquist concepts of adaptation. In terms of projection, Heathcliff finds not only Cathy's soul in Hareton's aspect, but also his own, a resemblance that serves to dematerialize Hareton further: "Hareton seemed a personification of my youth, not a human being." Finally, Hareton himself becomes a ghost of Heathcliff's youth: "Hareton's aspect was the ghost of my immortal love" (323–24). Conversely, Hareton's body becomes, as in the ventriloquist concept, a site for projection: Hareton "embodies" for Heathcliff a "thousand forms of past associations and ideas." Here, the body is not dropped by the spirit, but rather appropriated by it: Heathcliff and Cathy meet and merge in these perceptions of Hareton; it is in his body that the abstract and transcendental "I *am* Heathcliff!" becomes incarnate flesh. If the novel thus indicates that the rational and biological can be appropriated by the mystical and supernatural, so too, in spite of their goals of a textually and structurally based objectivity, narratological readings involve a considerable degree of subjective selection. McFarlane readily acknowledges "the inevitable degree of subjectivity" in even the most basic task of the narratologist: that of selecting what are a narrative's major cardinal functions.[50] However, it is not so much the impossibility of removing subjectivity that emerges troublingly from McFarlane's recommendations: it is the implication that such a removal is desirable – that it will provide a clearer understanding of adaptation. The next concept of adaptation, based in reader response theory, highlights and celebrates the very subjectivity that narratologists eschew.

The De(Re)composing Concept of Adaptation

One *Wuthering Heights* epitome of the de(re)composing concept of adaptation lies in Heathcliff's desire to be buried beside Cathy and for their corpses to decompose and merge underground. Here, there is no need for a hovering spirit or a thrown voice to infuse life into the adaptation, for dead matter becomes organic life underground. "By the time Linton gets to us," Heathcliff exults, "he'll not know which is which!" (288). Under the de(re)composing concept of adaptation, novel and film decompose, merge, and form a new composition at "underground" levels of reading. The adaptation is a composite of textual and filmic signs merging in audience consciousness together with other cultural narratives and often leads to confusion as to which is novel and which is film.

In *Wuthering Heights*, Cathy's writing appears to Lockwood as "detached sentences" (18). He supplements these detached sentences with his own words and visions of her in his dream. In the same way, in adaptation to film, sentences of novels detach and are infused with reader responses and visual images. Keith Cohen insists that an "adaptation must subvert its original, perform a double and paradoxical job of masking and unveiling its source ... redistribute the formative materials of the original and ... set them askew."[51] This suggests one type of decomposing recomposition: a deconstructive one.

In his theory of cult objects, Umberto Eco suggests another: "In order to transform a work into a cult object one must be able to break, dislocate, unhinge it so that one can remember only parts of it, irrespective of their original relationship with the whole."[52] J. Hillis Miller has written: "each [critic of *Wuthering Heights*] takes some one element in the novel and extrapolates it toward a total explanation."[53] Film adapters have done likewise.

What one discovers is that many so-called "unfaithful" adaptations are operating under a de(re)composing model. They are condemned as unfaithful because critics read only one way – from novel to film – and find that the film has made changes. But if one reads in both directions – from novel to film and then from film back to novel – one often finds the alleged infidelities clearly in the text. These "infidelities" represent rejections of certain parts of the novel in favor of others, not total departures from the novel. For example, a common criticism of the MGM *Wuthering Heights* is that it softens and romanticizes the novel's Heathcliff. However, we find romanticizations of Heathcliff in the novel itself: MGM's Heathcliff is Isabella's romantic ideal. Isabella overlooks Heathcliff's savagery and avarice on the basis of his passion for Cathy: "he has an honourable soul, and a true one, or how could he remember her?" (103). Heathcliff recognizes that Isabella pictures "in me a hero of romance" and scorns her for it (150). Not only filmmakers, but readers more generally have romanticized Heathcliff and clung to Isabella's initial impressions of him. A 1989 survey of reader responses discovered that "Many women remarked on how attractive they found the prospect of a man loving them with such intensity."[54]

MGM's Heathcliff also resembles the Heathcliff that character-narrator Nelly Dean tries to fashion early in the novel:

> Wish and learn to smooth away the surly wrinkles, to raise your lids frankly, and change the fiends [eyes] to confident angels, suspecting and doubting nothing, and always seeing friends where they are not sure of foes – Don't get the expression of a vicious cur that appears to know the kicks it gets are its desert . . . (56)

This is exactly how Laurence Olivier performs the role, which is mostly presented as though Nelly herself had groomed him. The imaginative games of nobility and self-aggrandizement played by MGM's Heathcliff and Cathy at Penistone Crag were also suggested by the Brontë's Nelly: "Were I in your place, I would frame high notions of my birth . . . your father was an Emperor of China, and your mother an Indian queen, each of them able to buy up, with one week's income, Wuthering Heights and Thrushcross Grange together." Nelly concludes that these fictional identifications and narratives can give "courage and dignity to support . . . oppression" (56). The novel's Cathy also detaches a private view of Heathcliff, independent of his actions: "That is not my Heathcliff," she maintains, "I shall love mine yet; and take him with me – he's in my soul" (160).

Such privatizations and idealizations of Heathcliff are not limited to the 1939 film. Robert Fuest's 1970 production presents Heathcliff (Timothy Dalton) as a swashbuckling charmer. In one dizzying sequence, he routs a bevy of male servants, sends a group of female servants screaming with a ferocious roar, smashes a window with a poker, dodges a gunshot, seizes and kisses a gawking Isabella, jumps onto a steaming stallion, and gallops away (Figure 29). Although the Heathcliff of both 1990s adaptations is rougher and more violent, he is nevertheless heavily romanticized as well. Kosminsky casts the beautiful Ralph Fiennes in the role, setting him frolicking with Cathy (Juliette Binoche) in the heather. LWT bathes its hero in a swath of romantic music and displays him engaged in several full-blown romantic kisses that appear nowhere in the novel.

29. Robert Fuest's *Wuthering Heights*, American International Pictures, 1970. Courtesy of the Academy of Motion Pictures Arts and Sciences.

Similarly, the less sympathetic characterization of Cathy in the MGM film, dying from sheer frustration that she cannot have both men, is also Nelly's Cathy: as Cathy enters her final illness, Nelly tells Lockwood that she did not comprehend its severity nor the emotional crisis underlying it, seeing only peevish ill temper, planned fits of passion, and selfishness (117).

Other apparent changes by an adaptation serve to fulfill the disappointed hopes and desires of the novel's characters. A 1966 Bombay adaptation, *Dil Diya Dard Liya* (*Give Your Heart and Receive Anguish*), allows Heathcliff (Shankar) to return in time to prevent Cathy's (Roopa's) marriage to Edgar (Mala).[55] Even Buñuel's famously original ending, celebrated for its surrealistic shock value and betrayal of the canonical reader, realizes a wish expressed by Heathcliff in the novel. As Brontë's Heathcliff stands with the unconscious Cathy in his arms, ready to confront Edgar, he exclaims, "If he shot me so, I'd die with a blessing on my lips" (162). Buñuel's ending spares Heathcliff 18 years of suffering, uniting him body and soul with Cathy immediately after her death. It fulfills other character wishes as well: it allows Hindley's attempt to shoot

Heathcliff, frustrated in the novel, to succeed in the film and realizes the literary Isabella's unheeded invective to Heathcliff: "if I were you, I'd go stretch myself over her grave, and die like a faithful dog" (176). In these ways, fragments of character desire overtake and displace narrator and authorial authority.

At times critics have offered purely cultural and contextual explanations for these effects. Most famously, critics have read the final scene of David Lean's 1946 film of *Great Expectations* as deriving exclusively from social conditions. At the end of the film, Pip (John Mills) returns to Miss Havisham's residence to find Estella, jilted by Drummle, preparing to go the way of Miss Havisham. Pip tears down the curtains and leads her out into the sunlight. Critics rightly associate this revision with the film's cultural context: the men returning after World War II to find women in their peacetime jobs needed to extend military rescue to a myth of domestic rescue, to tear down the blackout curtains, and lead women back out into freedom (though in reality, to put them back into the home).[56] Yet the film's finale is present in the novel as well in one of Pip's fantasies. Pip records his belief that Miss Havisham "reserved it for me to restore the desolate house, admit the sunshine into the dark rooms, set the clocks a going and the cold hearths a blazing, tear down the cobwebs, destroy the vermin – in short, do all the shining deeds of the young Knight of romance, and marry the Princess" (231).

The de(re)composing concept of adaptation allows for other mergers of social context and literary content. Even something as seemingly imposed on the novel as the co-opting of romance to urge economic consumption (as in the MGM and Westinghouse adaptations shown earlier) finds seeds in the novel, where erotics and economics intertwine at the most blatant levels of character motivation and plot. Brontë's Catherine readily admits to marrying Edgar for his money: "he will be rich, and I shall like to be the greatest woman of the neighbourhood" (78). Heathcliff plays mercilessly on Isabella's romantic illusions to gain her inheritance and uses young Catherine's romantic notions to lure her into a forced marriage with his son, bringing him the other half of the Thrushcross fortune.

Intriguingly, however, both MGM and Westinghouse adaptations omit Heathcliff's erotic–economic coercions and displace them with their own. In the MGM film, his financial revenge on Hindley is limited to paying off his gambling debts and legitimately reimbursing himself with Wuthering Heights. The MGM adaptation positions a romanticized, sanitized, socially elevated Heathcliff between the mercenary Cathy and the romantically deluded Isabella as one possessing what both women want: economic affluence and romantic appeal. The Westinghouse version stresses Hindley's vices – his violence toward the young Heathcliff, his alcoholism and gambling – as the bases of Heathcliff's financial ascendancy over him. With the charming Laurence Olivier and the dashing Charlton Heston playing Heathcliff in these productions, the audience sees Isabella's Heathcliff, while the novel's economically coercive Heathcliff is displaced onto cinematic and household marketing. Thus the audience, like Isabella, becomes economic prey to the romanticized Heathcliff. In such adaptations, not only narrators and characters but also audiences and characters decompose and merge at underground levels.

The Incarnational Concept of Adaptation

The incarnational concept of adaptation is, like the psychic concept, a familiar if not a didactically identified one in the rhetoric of adaptation criticism. Predicated on the Christian theology of the word made flesh, wherein the word is only a partial expression of a more total representation that requires incarnation for its fulfillment, it represents adaptation as incarnation. At Wuthering Heights, Lockwood is haunted by the ghosts of words representing Cathy: "a glare of white letters from the dark, as vivid as spectres – the air swarmed with Catherines" (17). These letters are followed by a ghostly incarnation of their referent: an audible, visible, tangible ghost of Catherine. The words that merely hint at sight, sound, touch, taste, and smell tantalize readers into longing for their incarnation in more phenomenological forms. Anthony Burgess notes: "Every best-selling novel has to be turned into a film, the assumption being that the book itself whets an appetite for the true fulfillment – the verbal shadow turned into light, the word made flesh."[57]

A rhetoric of incarnation, materialization, and realization permeates adaptation criticism throughout the twentieth century. The producers of the 1922 *Vanity Fair* adduced that "those who are intimate with the books . . . will be gratified to see the characters so reverently brought to life."[58] The rhetoric suggests that the characters of the novel were not quite alive until their incarnation in film. Eisenstein wrote in the 1940s: "For literature – cinema is an expansion of the strict diction achieved by poetry and prose into a new realm where the desired image is directly materialized in audio-visual perceptions."[59] Lester D. Friedman concluded his 1981 essay on James Whale's adaptation of Mary Shelley's novel, *Frankenstein*: "As this analysis of the film demonstrates, Whale viewed the Frankenstein story much in the same way as did Mary Shelley . . . if Mary Shelley wrote the word, James Whale made it flesh."[60]

Before the rhetoric was applied to literary film adaptation, it had a long run in accounts of earlier forms of adaptation. In his massive and impressive account of Victorian interart exchanges, Martin Meisel documents the pervasive practice of adaptation: poems, novels, plays, paintings, operas, songs, dances, tableaux, and *tableaux vivants* adapted to each other, in every direction and back again. The dominant direction of adaptation, Meisel records, was one of adapting more abstract arts to less abstract arts in a process called "realization." An 1856 review notes, "the desire for realization, which, at the present day, either from a wish for novelty, or from a tendency to idealized materialism, is grown almost a passion with our young artists and poets." Meisel defines realization as

> both literal re-creation and translation into a more real, that is more vivid, visual, physically present medium. To move from mind's eye to body's eye was realization, and to add a third dimension to two was realization, as when words became picture, or when picture became dramatic tableau.[61]

The term "realization" implies both a lack in the original and the greater realism of the adapted art. Yet realism, we know, is a relative and unstable concept. While from a phenomenological point of view, film adaptations may make words more "real," on another continuum, they are regarded as less real. If art draws from real life, then an art adapting another art is one step further away from real life as a representation of a representation. In 1807, painter James Northcote averred: "To paint . . . the passions from the exhibitions of them on the stage . . . is to remove yourself one degree farther from truth."[62] Nevertheless, the incarnational concept of adaptation emphasizes the relative phenomenological realism of the signifiers rather than their proximity to real life signifieds. Cinema is the realist art *par excellence*: deemed so real that films regularly conclude with disclaimers like this one: "The events of this motion picture are purely fictitious. Any resemblance to actual persons or events is purely coincidental."

The incarnational concept of adaptation differs from the psychic view in that it does not posit the novel as a transcendental signified to which the film must attach appropriate signifiers, but rather as a transcendental signif*ier*. In the final quarter of the nineteenth century, Pater countered Lessing's prioritizing of analogues between arts and their referents by restoring the primacy of analogies between the arts. Denying that "every thought and feeling is twin-born with its sensible analogue or symbol," dismissing "widespread" nineteenth-century notions that "poetry, music, and painting – all the various products of art – [are] but translations into different languages of one and the same fixed quantity of imaginative thought," he argued that

> each art may be observed to pass into the condition of some other art, by what German critics term an *Anders-streben* – a partial alienation from its own limitations, by which the arts are able, not indeed to supply the place of each other, but reciprocally to lend each other new forces.

At the heart of this interchange lies art's quest "to get rid of its responsibilities to its subject or material." The partial passing of one art "into the condition of some other art" is no mere figure of speech, but rather a formal interchange:

> Thus some of the most delightful music seems to be always approaching to figure, to pictorial definition . . . Thus, again, sculpture aspires out of the hard limitation of pure form towards colour, or its equivalent; poetry also, in many ways, finding guidance from the other arts, the analogy between a Greek tragedy and a work of Greek sculpture, between a sonnet and a relief, of French poetry generally with the art of engraving, being more than mere figures of speech . . . [63]

In Pater's account, interart analogies press toward adaptation of form rather than of content: the arts do not aspire to re-represent the content of other arts, only their forms.

Pater's assertion that "All art constantly aspires towards the condition of music" positions music as the transcendental signifier in his artistic pantheon. (While Pater does not use the term "transcendental signifier," he does advance the concept.) Music is for Pater the transcendental signifier because its abstract form most successfully resists the signified: it is this transcendence of the signified that renders it a transcendental signifier. When other arts aspire to music, they aspire to transcend signification – to be signifiers without signifieds. [64]

If Pater claimed at the end of the nineteenth century that all the arts aspire to music, Peter Conrad documents that earlier in the century, "all the arts aspire to the condition of literature." [65] The incarnational concept of adaptation represents the novel's signs as transcendental signifiers, wandering ghosts located neither in the heaven of the transcendental signified of the psychic concept nor in the dead corpse of the empty signifier of the ventriloquist concept. In the context of adaptation, the transcendental signifier seeks not a signified, but another signifier that can incarnate it – in Cathy's words, "an existence of yours beyond you . . . What were the use of my creation if I were entirely contained here?" (82). The incarnational concept of adaptation maintains that the word seeks incarnation as ardently as it is sought by incarnating forms. This mutual yearning emerges when we juxtapose Pater's aesthetic theory with the popular Victorian craze for realization that it at first seems to oppose. Although Pater sets himself diametrically against popular realization, pressing the arts instead toward greater abstraction, both formulations emphasize the aspiration and movement of less abstract arts toward more abstract arts. In Pater's aesthetics, the less abstract art presses away from phenomenological realism toward more representationally abstract forms. In Victorian realization, the more abstract art moves away from abstraction toward greater phenomenological realism in less abstract forms. The two processes are thus reciprocally opposed: each side pulls in the opposite direction, but in so doing, meets the other all the more swiftly, as do the poles of magnets.

Adaptation here is not a process of matching signifier with signified, but rather of signifier with signifier. The transcendental signifier does not reach toward a signified, but rather toward other more embodied signifiers, through which it completes its signification. This model heightens the abstraction of the more abstract form and emphasizes the concreteness of the less abstract one, effecting a concomitant perceptual dematerialization of the novel's signs as the films signs appear all the more incarnate. The process is illustrated in the opening of MGM's *Wuthering Heights*, which begins with a shot overcast with thick white letters obscuring Lockwood's shadowy figure as he struggles through a storm:

> On the barren Yorkshire moors in England, a hundred years ago, stood a house as bleak and desolate as the wastes around it. Only a stranger lost in a storm would have dared to knock at the door of Wuthering Heights.

The thick white letters block the viewers' view, making them impatient for the removal of the words, eager to see the film without textual obstruction. As the letters dissolve, the incarnation unfolds: the word "stranger" gives way to a shot of a stranger; the words "Wuthering Heights" dissolve into the film set of the house Wuthering Heights.

* * *

Just as psychic and ventriloquist concepts of adaptation represent two sides of the same coin, so too do genetic and incarnational concepts. If genetic resemblances in *Wuthering Heights* create an embodied haunting, as when Heathcliff "sees" Cathy in Hareton, the incarnational concept fosters a more terrifying form of embodied haunting, as when Cathy appears to Lockwood as a tangible ghost with power to seize and hold him. The genetic concept lies at the more rational and explicable end of the embodied haunting spectrum; the incarnational concept lies at its nightmare end, for the moment when Cathy grabs Lockwood is the moment when "the intense horror of nightmare" descends on him (23). The embodied ghost is far more fearsome than the intangible ghost of the psychic concept of adaptation. Under the psychic concept, readers eagerly seek the authorial spirit. However, under the incarnational concept, they fear and resist it. Lockwood has no fear of the symbolic abstract representations of Cathy, her words. He declares himself "greatly amused" and bristling with "immediate interest," not ceasing to read until he has "examined all." Like a proper literary scholar, he describes the appearance of the books in which she has written, determines her sentence structures, identifies the genre of her prose, characterizes her handwriting, evaluates her drawings, speculates on gaps in the writing sequence, defines her authorial tone, and offers a social and moral criticism of her work (18–20). But when the authorial spirit becomes embodied and seeks to enter his reading space, Lockwood becomes furiously and violently resistant. When her presence becomes audible, he "resolve[s] to silence it," crying, "I must stop it!" When it becomes tangible, he cuts her until she bleeds: "Terror made me cruel." Ironically, he piles the very books in which she has written as a defense against the author, so that what has been a medium for her appearance now becomes a barrier to keep her out. Yet the barrier proves tenuous: as the dream ends, "the pile of books moved as if thrust forward," reopening the space and thrusting the authorial spirit again toward the reader (23–24).

While Lockwood fights to keep Cathy out, however, Heathcliff begs her to "Come in! come in!" (27). Heathcliff yearns for Cathy's embodied ghost because it represents a form in which spirit and body unite, resolving his tensions between necrophilia and ghost chasing as well as the psychological dilemma raised by his hatred of the relatives who genetically resemble her.

A similarly commingled dread and yearning run through the incarnational concept of adaptation. Like Heathcliff, many readers long for a novel's characters and scenes to be made visible, audible, and tangible in adaptation. As film historian Jim Hitt attests: "We long to see the physical reality of a cherished novel or short story, to see the ethereal become solid, touchable."[66] Others, like Lockwood, recoil in horror from such manifestations. Early in the nineteenth century, Charles Lamb evinced that the two responses can coexist in the same person. Reacting to theatrical adaptations of literature, he exclaims:

Never let me be so ungrateful as to forget the very high degree of satisfaction which I received some years back from seeing for the first time a tragedy of Shakespeare performed ... It seemed to embody and realize conceptions which had hitherto assumed no distinct shape.

Yet he notes a greater loss than gain in the incarnation:

But dearly do we pay all our life afterwards for this juvenile pleasure, this sense of distinctness. When the novelty is past, we find to our cost that, instead of realising an idea, we have only materialised and brought down a fine vision to the standard of flesh and blood. We have let go a dream, in quest of an unattainable substance.

How cruelly this operates upon the mind, to have its free conceptions thus cramped and pressed down to the measure of a strait-lacing actuality ... characters in Shakespeare which are within the precincts of nature, have yet something in them which appeals too exclusively to the imagination, to admit of their being made objects to the senses without suffering a change and a diminution.[67]

Lockwood reacts in much the same way: he reads Cathy's words, seeking to ascertain the character of their author, but the moment that character becomes incarnate, he reacts with horror and aversion. Critic Maggie Berg goes further, objecting to graphic realizations of *Wuthering Heights* of any kind – even to those diagrams commonly used to explicate its structure – in a language of incarnation, arguing that such manifestations are "at odds with the spirit of the novel":

What business have we constructing explanatory diagrams for a book which begins and ends with a specter, in which even the distinction between being alive and being dead is uncertain and unclear ... the ghost ... is wholly ignored or repressed by genealogies, charts, and diagrams. In order to listen to what Catherine's ghost is trying to tell us, to read the writing in the margin, we must avoid ... visual aids.[68]

The word made flesh is also the word brought down to the level of flesh. As such, adaptation often appears as sacrilege against the word. Christian mythology claims that for centuries, the Hebrew people longed for the incarnation of their Messiah, for their God made flesh. But when he was thus incarnated, they recoiled, condemning and crucifying him. In much the same way, protesting paintings of Shakespeare's plays, Lamb writes:

I am jealous of the combination of the sister arts. Let them sparkle apart. What injury (short of the theaters) did not Boydell's Shakespeare do me with Shakespeare? ... instead of my, and everybody's Shakespeare [t]o be tied down to an authentic face of Juliet! To have Imogen's portrait! To confine the illimitable! ... 'out upon this half-faced fellowship.'[69]

Lamb, on the one hand, complains of the full-faced "authentic" Juliet of the paintings, but calls the association between theater and painting in adaptation "half-faced." Something has been effaced for Lamb in the authentication. That something is the loss of language's lack, a lack that promised illimitability and universality, but which the specificities of realization have, it seems, exposed as illusive and empty. Indeed, such overt protests that incarnation reduces language mask the real threat that incarnation and visualization present to the word. Incarnation reveals the limitations of language. Indeed, incarnational adaptation may appear too real because it exposes language as unreal. Lamb attests: "Contrary to the old saying, that 'seeing is believing,' the sight actually destroys the faith." Realization disrupts the partly revealing, partly concealing limbo of language – what Lamb has called "all that beautiful compromise which we make in reading" which "the actual sight of the thing [outweighs]."[70]

But Lamb does not pursue the possibility that the lost faith in language was a misplaced one. That realization exposes the lack and emptiness of language is supported by the fact that Lamb and others find it impossible to return to the illusions of the word after seeing a realization of it. Once one recognizes that the Emperor has no clothes, one cannot reconstruct the clothing. Lamb attests: "I confess myself utterly unable to appreciate that celebrated soliloquy in 'Hamlet,' beginning, 'to be or not to be,' or to tell whether it be good, bad, or indifferent, it has been so handled and pawed about by declamatory boys and men."[71] In 1807, Sir George Beaumont too complained of "the perverted representations of the theatres, which have made such impressions on most people early in life, that I, for my part, feel it more difficult to form a picture in my mind [while reading] from any scene . . . that I have seen frequently represented [on the stage]."[72] Similarly, those who have seen a film often document that they continue to "see" the film's actors when they turn to read the book. The incarnational process thus reverses the path of adaptation in cognition, so that the novel now "refers" to the film. The bond between transcendental and incarnating signifiers, then, becomes as tight as bonds between signifiers and signifieds.

Rather than pursue the disruptions and critique that the incarnational concept of adaptation presents to language, however, most critics prefer to castigate realization as carnalization, a sordid, morally reprehensible corruption of spiritual and transcendental signification and of a romanticized "divine" imagination. Spike Milligan's 1994 prose parody of *Wuthering Heights* epitomizes the carnalizing motif when the shepherd boy at the end reports that he has seen the ghost of "Heathcliff, and a woman yonder . . . and they're doing it."[73]

Lamb's account displaces concerns regarding the violence done to language in the incarnational adaptation onto concerns over the dramatization of textual violence. The realization of horrors in the written account, then, masks the horrors of realizing language. In his diatribe against performed Shakespeare, Lamb objects most strenuously to the dramatization of Shakespearean villains:

> ... while we are reading any of his great criminal characters, – Macbeth, Richard, even Iago, – we think not so much of the crimes which they commit, as of the ambition, the aspiring spirit, the intellectual activity which prompts them to overleap those moral fences ... not an atom of all which is made perceivable in Mr. C[ibber]'s way of acting [Richard III] ... we feel ... disgust ... at that butcher-like representation that passes for him on the stage.[74]

For Lamb, reading keeps the focus on the subjectivity of the violent person; dramatization emphasizes its effects on others. Incarnation calls the bluff of subjective linguistic mitigations of objective enacted social actions. By showing the violent subject objectively engaged in violent deeds rather than absorbed in lofty rationalizations and poetic psychologizings of them, incarnation reveals not only the objective horrors of violent deeds that language masks, but also the ethical horror that language can so deftly mitigate egregious social actions.

Returning to *Wuthering Heights*, critics have responded with similar aversion to those adaptations that dramatize Heathcliff's violence. Indeed, it seems that no adaptation can please: those that soften his violence are attacked for diluting the novel and failing to understand its darker psychological dimensions; those that dramatize the violence are accused of turning a transcendental romantic hero into a boorish domestic abuser. Defending MGM's decision to soften the novel's violence, Bluestone explains: "Raw brutality, literally transposed, loses the cushioning effect of language" and "would seem absurd on screen."[75] Quite apart from adaptation, critics of the novel have argued similarly concerning the cushioning effects of the novel's narration, particularly Nelly's commonsensical, homespun, baffled account, which buffers the reader from the violent scenes that she has witnessed directly.[76] Nelly describes one scene of violence as "a strange and fearful picture" (159), but softens the pictorial effect for the reader through mitigating words.

Like Nelly, the first reviewers of *Wuthering Heights* employed an especially heightened pictorial rhetoric when describing scenes of brutality and horror in the novel:

> We know nothing in the whole range of our fictitious literature which presents such shocking pictures of the worst forms of humanity ... The

reality of unreality has never been so aptly illustrated as in the scenes of almost savage life which Ellis Bell has brought so vividly before us.[77]

In a similar vein, George Henry Lewes writes of "strange wild pictures of incult humanity, painted as if by lurid torchlight" and Vere Henry Hobart directly echoes Nelly's phrase: "It is a fearful picture."[78]

Subsequently, a softening critical rhetoric grew up around the novel, mitigating the initial sense of its shockingly graphic representations. As early as the second edition, critics put the novel's vivid and "fearful" pictures into a soft-focus past memory: "one looks back at the whole story as to a world of brilliant figures in an atmosphere of mist; shapes that come out upon the eye, and burn their colours into the brain, and depart into the enveloping fog."[79] While the earliest reviewers complain of the lack of relief in the novel – "The book wants relief. A few glimpses of sunshine";[80] "There are no green spots in it on which the mind can linger with satisfaction"[81] – later critics provide gray misty covers. By 1887, a reviewer fears he is resorting to "truisms or plagiarisms" when he claims that *Wuthering Heights* is "the most beautiful romance of the present century."[82]

The rhetorical soft focus further alters perceptions of the novel's graphically based realism. An *Atlas* reviewer of the first edition adduces that "the *vraisemblance* is so admirably preserved ... when we lay aside the book it is some time before we can persuade ourselves that we have held nothing more than the imaginary intercourse with the ideal creations of the brain." Reviewing the same edition, Lewes discerns that, "although there is a want of air and light in the picture, we cannot deny its truth: sombre, rude, brutal, yet true." And Hobart affirms in 1848: "I fully believe there have been such people ... It is a fearful picture ... drawn with a deep miraculous knowledge of the human heart."[83] But by 1859, the sense of the novel's realism is wavering: "Surely ... there never were such people, at least let us hope not."[84] By 1878, we read: "Here we find a reality more true than the real ... Emily has created people who never were, but are now immortal." One hundred and twenty years later, Russell Baker's introduction to the U.S. broadcast of the LWT production makes an almost identical assertion: "The lives she invented were like no lives ever lived by real people." Echoing Mary Ward's assessment in 1900 regarding "the writer's very ignorance of certain facts and relations of life, combined with the force of imaginative passion which she throws into her conceptions, produces a special poetic effect – a strange and bodiless tragedy – unique in literature," he adduces: "Her book often feels like the work of a lonely young woman, mingling daydreams with nightmares."[85]

Nevertheless, under incarnational concepts of adaptation, late-twentieth-century film and television adaptations, including the one Baker introduces, restored original perceptions of the novel's graphic brutality and hyper-realism in the wake of literary critical mists. LWT's Heathcliff beats and kicks those who dare to share his screen space. When he takes possession of Thrushcross Grange, he smashes its ornaments and furnishings (a particularly distressing dramatization for that large segment of viewers who value Victorian adaptations primarily for their ephemera and antiques). Kosminsky's film, though lushly romantic in its music and cinematography, dramatizes so many of the novel's more brutal episodes that a reviewer of the film protests:

> To admire any part of the truculence is to admire the pain of child-birth... None of it makes any sense. Why is Heathcliff so driven from human decency? Why couldn't his horrendous personality at least partially let up long after he had already destroyed the family? I have no doubt that people like this really exist, but I'm more sure that those type of people had something to do with making this movie.[86]

This reviewer echoes an 1848 reviewer of the novel who attributes the brutality to its author. He sees in the Brontës' works "a sense of... depravity... peculiarly [the Brontës'] own... a last desperate attempt to corrupt the virtue of the sturdy descendants of the Puritans," concluding, "This is especially the case with... the author of *Wuthering Heights*."[87]

While readers and viewers alike express hopes that *Wuthering Heights*'s brutality does not reflect a local social reality, audiences have accepted it when transported to other cultural contexts. In these transpositions, defamiliarized cultures offer contextual rather than semiotic cushionings of the novel's violence. In 1975, Wagner pondered, "How to make a film of [*Wuthering Heights*]? You would have to be Japanese to dare to try."[88] In 1988, Japanese filmmaker Kiju Yoshida did just that. Yoshida cast his Earnshaw family as medieval Yamabe priests on the misty volcanic slopes of Mount Fuji. Thirty-five years earlier, surrealist filmmaker Luis Buñuel set his adaptation of *Wuthering Heights* in a desert of nineteenth-century Mexico, its witchcraft-tinged, pagan, superstitious Catholicism restoring a sense of the novel's elusive and savage mysticism (Figure 30). In these historically, geographically, and culturally defamiliarized contexts, audiences have tolerated augmentations of the novel's violence, as both films add originally scripted scenes of violence. Buñuel's film begins with Catalina shooting a vulture and ends with the murder of Alejandro described earlier. Isabella's and Alejandro's first kiss follows immediately after the painfully drawn-out slaughter of a wildly squealing

30. Luis Buñuel's *Abismos de Pasion*, Plexus Films 1953. Courtesy of BFI stills.

pig. Roberto nearly rapes Isabella when she first arrives at Wuthering Heights. Throughout the film, her brother Eduardo pins writhing flies to cards with the distressing dispassion of the collector who sees specimens rather than suffering. In Yoshida's film, characters whose novel counterparts die from illness meet violent ends. Mr. Earnshaw (Hidemaru, played by Nagare Hagiwara) is shot by soldiers, the arrow splashing the white canvas of his robe a garish red. Frances Earnshaw (Shino, played by Keiko Itoh) does not die in childbirth, but is robbed, stripped, raped, and murdered by a gang of thieves, her body splayed like litter on the unsympathetic landscape. Edgar (Mitsuhiko, played by Tatsuo Nakaka) is attacked by bandits, pierced with multiple spears, and left for dead. Seeking to end his pain and shame, he slits his own throat, dying with a horrifying gurgle and gush of blood. Isabella (Tae, played by Eri Ishida) hangs herself in a slow, ritual suicide after Onimaru sodomizes her and refuses to marry her. Even Brontë's horrific hints of necrophilia are rendered far more ghastly in Yoshida's film. When Onimaru digs up Kinu, maggots range through her open and bleeding corpse.

But it is not only cultural defamiliarization that makes critics more receptive to these adaptations than to those Anglo-American adaptations that dramatize the novel's violence. Buñuel's and Yoshida's films also employ formal methods of mitigating graphic violence. Buñuel's camera functions similarly to the "cool spectator" Nelly nominates herself in the novel (159). Primarily static, avoiding close-ups of people, it also resembles Eduardo's surveillance of his insects, its cool, distant, objective eye fixed on pinned, writhing, suffering creatures hovering between life and death. Yoshida mitigates his scenes of horrific graphic violence by alternating them with scenes of astonishing softness and lyrical visual and aural beauty. Gauzy mists float over the starkly beautiful volcanic landscape, whose slopes are punctuated by script-like architectural erections and tiny human figures (Figure 31). Indoors, firelight and candles illuminate haunted and beautiful faces in close-up and walls glow gold. The film alternates slow, graceful, ceremonial movements with the wild runnings of torch-bearing priests, the ferocious stabbings of Samurai warriors, and the groveling scrambling of greedy, violent villagers, as they scratch in the dirt for stones to kill or coins to spend. Aurally, the film shifts back and forth between haunting music and the soothing strains of female voices to the roars, grunts, and growls of males dominating, threatening, fighting, cursing, killing, and being killed. The tension between Eastern and Western representations of the human figure – tiny dots on immense landscapes, after conventions of Japanese art, alternating with intense facial close-ups, hallmarks of Western film – intensifies the sense of alternating attraction and repulsion, as characters shift between a lyrical distance from and a startling proximity to the camera. When incarnation makes realization too real, or language appear too unreal, narrators, critics, and filmmakers alike resort to distancing strategies, casting verbal, contextual, and visual mists and veils to keep the distance between representation and audience.

31. Kiju Yoshida's *Arashi ga oka*, Seiyô Films, 1988. Courtesy of BFI stills.

The Trumping Concept of Adaptation

etween Lockwood's reading of Catherine's diary and his nightmare of her lies another dream of a battle with an incarnated author, the Reverend Jabes Branderham, whose sermon title lulls Lockwood to sleep even before Lockwood has embarked on the sermon. But there is no escape from the sermon in sleep: Lockwood dreams of both sermon and preacher and, as in his dream of Cathy, violently opposes the author. But in this instance, Lockwood opposes both text and author, faulting Branderham's "private manner of interpreting," the oddness of his ideas, and the weariness and length of the address. As in the dream of Cathy, a violent battle ensues between author and reader. Lockwood condemns Branderham and his sermon, calling the assembled congregation to "Drag him down, and crush him to atoms, that the place which knows him may know him no more!" Branderham in turn condemns Lockwood as a bad auditor, calling on textual authority and on the congregation to "execute upon him the judgment written." The congregation turns on Lockwood rather than Branderham, on reader rather than author.

The transition from read text to performed text in the dream approximates the process of literary film adaptation. Indeed, many critics have noted a connection between filming and dreaming.[89] Like Lockwood, adapters often declare literary texts too idiosyncratic, odd, dull, and long for audience consumption in the dramatic medium of film. And, like Branderham, literati typically retaliate, condemning mass culture's mainstreaming and cutting of literary texts to make film adaptations. As in Lockwood's dream, the public more often turns on the film adaptation than on the literary author.

The trumping concept of adaptation shares these concerns in that it addresses which medium represents better. Although it can take either side, the majority of adaptation criticism favors the novel over the film. To offset this imbalance, my discussion emphasizes instances in which films claim to trump the novels they adapt. Instead of asking, what's wrong with the adaptation? as so much adaptation criticism does, this side of the trumping coin asks, What's wrong with the original? Lockwood's suggestion that Catherine's writing is "not altogether legitimate" (18) epitomizes such readings for, in much the same way that Lockwood represents Cathy's writing as immature, antiquated, not readily legible, and misappropriating other texts, so too, adaptations frequently condemn novels of prior centuries as representationally immature, their values antiquated, irrelevant, and inexplicable to contemporary audiences, and their accounts of history, psychology, and politics inaccurate. Like Cathy's marginalia, deemed "not altogether legitimate" in the margins of printed texts, the trumping concept of adaptation tests the novel's representations against other texts deemed more authoritative – against written and artifactual history, psychoanalytic theories, and contemporary politics – and finds the novel not altogether legitimate.

Under the trumping concept of adaptation, the novel's signs lose representational authority in the name of a signified that the novel "meant to" or "tried to" or "should have" represented. The adapting film claims to have represented that signified better. At their last meeting, Heathcliff accuses Catherine of being "false" to and betraying her own heart (161). The trumping model of adaptation splits the novel's form from its content to assert that the one has betrayed the other: that the novel's signifiers have been false to and have betrayed their own signifieds, their own heart.

The few critical accounts that posit film adaptation as criticism rather than translation take one of two approaches: they either engage in appreciative criticism or derogatory criticism of the adapted novel. In both, adaptations serve as can(n)on fodder for interdisciplinary and theoretical wars. Neil Sinyard's "Adaptation as Criticism" exemplifies the appreciative approach: "the best adaptations of books for film can often

best be approached as an activity of literary criticism, not a pictoriali-
sation of the complete novel, but a critical essay which stresses what it
sees as the main theme."[90] Peter Reynolds's Marxist dialectic model of
adaptation illustrates the second approach, where adaptation constitutes
"a forum in which [to] debate and contest social and moral issues."[91]
Keith Cohen's deconstructive model, however, lies closer to the trumping concept of adaptation, in that the film critiques the novel's claim to
representational prowess while asserting its own: "Adaptation is a truly
artistic feat only when the new version carries with it a hidden criticism of
its model, or at least renders implicit (through a process we should call
'deconstruction') certain key contradictions implanted or glossed over
in the original."[92]

But the trumping concept of adaptation is not limited to deconstructive
applications: it finds a more general application in aesthetic practice
that emerges in reviews. A *New York Times* review of MGM's *Wuthering
Heights*, for example, declares that the film "is Goldwyn at his best, and
better still, Emily Brontë at hers... poetically written as the novel not
always was, sinister and wild as it was meant to be, far more compact
dramatically than Miss Brontë had made it." It claims that "the sheltered"
Emily "only dimly sensed the potent force she was wielding," a force
the film has realized, drawing "dramatic fire from the savage flints of
scene and character hidden" in the novel.[93] This account primitivizes
the novel aesthetically and makes the film an archaeological dig of the
novel's buried elements and of its maker's potential.

Another reviewer of the MGM film perceives the film to have toned
down rather than fired up the novel, correcting Brontë's faulty narrative
structure and authorial excesses:

> In some respects the film play even improves upon the novel by concen-
> trating upon the central drama in the lives of the possessed lovers and
> dispensing with some of the Gothic hugger-mugger and exaggerations
> of the book that was born in the fevered brain of a brilliant recluse.[94]

Sixty years later, Russell Baker presented the LWT *Wuthering Heights* with
a similarly patronizing criticism: "it's a novel verging on poetry and, as
with poetry, everything in it's just a little bit more fantastic, a little bit
more bizarre than real life ... *Wuthering Heights* was the work of a relatively
young woman with a raging poetic imagination."

If these film adaptations purport to civilize and rationalize the novel,
another form of trumping, growing out of the incarnational concept of
adaptation, claims to realize it correctly. As an adaptation seeks to realize
a novel's words, its historical research into material culture often finds

fault with the novel's representations and "corrects" them. An interview
with Hugo Ballin, director of a now lost 1923 film of *Vanity Fair*, illustrates.
At the end of *Vanity Fair*'s Chapter 6, Thackeray explains his decision to
costume his characters in the styles of the 1840s rather than in those of
the Napoleonic period in which the novel is set:

> When I remember the appearance of those people in those days, and
> that an officer and lady were actually habited like this – [*vignette*] – I have
> not the heart to disfigure my heroes and heroines by costumes so hideous
> and have, on the contrary, engaged a model of rank dressed according
> to the present fashion.[95]

The excision of Thackeray's illustrations in later editions conspires
with the trumping view of adaptation to "correct" Thackeray's anachronistic costumes in the name of historical authenticity.[96] The title of
the published interview, "Hugo Ballin Edits 'Vanity Fair,' Cutting the
Anachronisms," refers not to the film's editing of its own footage but to
its editing of the novel: to its reedition of the novel's visual representations, both in the illustrations and in verbal descriptions. Ballin explains:

> The costumes in the picture are more correct than those described in
> the book . . . [Thackeray] had whiskers on his soldiers [when] there was
> at that time a rule in the British army against any growth of hair on the
> face . . . The novelist also describes men smoking cigars in the presence
> of ladies. This was decidedly "not done" at the time of the Battle of
> Waterloo . . . He speaks of the use of envelopes for letters; the historical
> fact is that envelopes were not used until 1839 . . . in the picture we strove
> to get all these details as nearly right as humanly possible, as a matter of
> course.[97]

Ballin represents such changes "as a matter of course," much as textual
editors might correct an author's spelling and punctuation. He assumes
that both novel and film signs point to an authoritative outer signified –
in this case, material history – which the film must represent correctly
and faithfully, even if it means being unfaithful to the novel. Hyperfidelity
to the text's context here mandates infidelity to the text itself. The film
thus exploits concepts of splits between signifier and signified to correct
rather than to incarnate the novel.

In the process, filmmakers have frequently called on outside authorities to validate their corrections of the novel. While the first title
card of a 1925 adaptation – "HENRY KING'S production of 'ROMOLA'
Adapted from the novel by GEORGE ELIOT" – invokes its founding

novel, the second invokes an outside historical authority: "Historical authenticity of this production is attested by DR. GUIDO BLAGI, Director of the Laurentian Library, FLORENCE, ITALY."[98] Similarly, MGM's 1935 *A Tale of Two Cities* contains in its credits a "bibliography," including Thomas Carlyle's *The French Revolution* and Clery's *Journal of the Temple*.[99]

However, the line between correcting a novel's material history and its ideology has proven a fine one. Peter Bogandovich's *Daisy Miller* (1974) adds a scene of mixed nude bathing. Defending criticisms of this scene, Bogandovich asserts: "The mixed bathing is authentically of the period." McFarlane astutely counters: "Authentically of the period, perhaps, but not so of Henry James."[100] Implicit in this historically authentic embellishment lies a criticism of James's sexual reticence. Similarly, Patricia Rozema's *Mansfield Park* (1999) contains a superadded feminist postcolonial critique of slavery that adapts late-twentieth-century literary criticism of the novel beyond the novel itself. These historical additions extend to a correction of the author's psychology and ideology.

Indeed, film adapters build on a hypercorrect historical material realism to usher in a host of anachronistic ideological "corrections" of novels. Quite inconsistently, while adaptations pursue a hyperfidelity to nineteenth-century material culture, they reject and correct Victorian psychology, ethics, and politics. When filmmakers set modern politically correct views against historically correct backdrops, the effect is to authorize these modern ideologies as historically authentic.

Frequently such corrections have been expressed as revealing what Victorians "really" thought and felt, against their own representations. Defending his *Daisy Miller*, Bogandovitch quipped: "What James meant to say with the story [*Daisy Miller*] doesn't really concern me .... I think all that stuff is based on some other kind of repression anyway."[101] Bogandovitch implies that his film does a work of psychoanalysis for the novel, its author, and culture.

In a similar vein, Robert Fuest's *Wuthering Heights* (1970), released just after censorship codes relaxed in 1969, celebrates not only a release from stringent film censorship, but also from Victorian sexual repression. The film "corrects" any fastidiousness that the novel's characters might have had engaging in illicit sexuality, or Nelly in narrating it, or Brontë in authoring it. Cathy (Anna Calder Marshall), her long hair loose and decked with flowers, dallies amorously with Heathcliff (Timothy Dalton) like a 1960s free love flower child. Joseph (Aubrey Woods) smirks that Edgar is "waiting to see the color of [Cathy's baby's] eyes."[102] Heathcliff is a rambunctious, swashbuckling sexual rogue, expressing the actor's relief at the release from film censorship as much as his Victorian character's release from sexual repression:

ISABELLA: Let me go! You're hurting me.
HEATHCLIFF: You love it. [*She struggles.*] Do you fancy a tumble, then?
ISABELLA: What's that?
HEATHCLIFF: Do you want it here or in bed?
ISABELLA: You beast! [*She slaps him.*][103]

Less in the flower-child tradition, the 1998 LWT *Wuthering Heights* accentuates the violence of Heathcliff's sexuality over its bawdiness. In addition to graphically representing his brutal topping of Isabella on their wedding night, the televization includes a scene in which he crudely gropes Cathy's breast, asking: "Is this what you want?" (She doesn't.) The characters in both adaptations remain partly clothed during their sexual encounters, but here the Victorian costumes serve to heighten the titillations of sexualizing repressed Victorians and, at the same time, to keep the adaptations' sexual emendations clothed in material historical accuracy.

However, twentieth-century ideology only partially accounts for such emendations. Michel Foucault has persuasively countered the notion that the Victorians were sexually repressed.[104] But quite apart from his arguments, nineteenth-century visual artists and dramatists regularly increase the sexuality of literary texts, pointing to a transhistorical dynamic between verbal and visual representations that may be more formal and cognitive than cultural and psychoanalytic. A reviewer of William Etty's 1832 painting of nymphs from Milton's *Comus* urged the painter to "study more attentively the dignified sobriety of style which characterizes Milton: the old Puritan bard has none of those startling unsober postures, in all his works."[105] In 1887, Robert Louis Stevenson complained that a theatrical adaptation of his *The Strange Case of Dr. Jekyll and Mr. Hyde* depicted Hyde as a "mere voluptuary," adducing that "people are so full of folly and inverted lust, they can think of nothing but sexuality."[106] This effect must derive in part from the greater phenomenology of pictorial and theatrical signs. Adaptation thus creates an effect of literary striptease.

More often, formal and contextual factors meet and combine to create trumping effects. In some adaptations, twentieth-century psychoanalytic master narratives intersect with nineteenth-century melodramatic structures to invert the designations of hero and villain. In the first reviews of *Wuthering Heights*, there is no question that Heathcliff is the novel's villain. He is set in sharp contrast to Edgar, who is cast as the novel's gentle hero. An 1848 *Britannia* review depicts Heathcliff as "brutal in his language and sentiments, and cruel in his conduct," offering "Edgar Linton, in all respects [as] a contrast to Heathcliff. He is very fair and handsome, and naturally of a gentle temper."[107] *The Examiner* too represents Heathcliff as "an incarnation of evil qualities" and Edgar as "a kind-hearted, effeminate boy."[108] By the 1850 edition, however, Heathcliff has begun to be "fascinating" and his love for Catherine admirable: George Henry Lewes delineates him as a "devil... with a dusky splendour which fascinates," adducing that "we feel the truth of his burning and impassioned love." Nevertheless, he remains in contrast to "the kind, weak, elegant Edgar... [who] appeals to [Catherine's] love of refinement, and goodness, and culture... the man who alone is fit to call her wife."[109] Through these designations of hero and villain, Lewes presses a dualistic psychological moral:

> The fierce ungoverned instincts of powerful organizations, bred up amidst violence, revolt, and moral apathy, are here seen in operation; such brutes we should all be, or the most of us, were our lives as insubordinate to law; were our affections and sympathies as little cultivated, our imaginations as undirected. And herein lies the moral of the book...[110]

Lewes and twentieth-century psychoanalytic critics of the novel agree that Heathcliff represents a "brute" or "id" (psychoanalytic critic Thomas Moser, for example, writes that "the primary traits Freud ascribed to the *id* apply perfectly to Heathcliff... selfish, asocial, impulsive"[111]), but they disagree in their assignation of culpability. Sigmund Freud's triadic model of superego, ego, and id contrasts with Victorian dualistic models expressed by an 1848 reviewer of *Wuthering Heights* as a battle between "brutal instinct and divine reason."[112]

Freud's idea that an overwrought superego is as destructive to a balanced psyche as an unbridled id finds popular expression in several twentieth-century adaptations of *Wuthering Heights*. In these adaptations, the "kind, weak, elegant Edgar" of the Victorian novel becomes a tyrannical superego and the arch-villain of the film, while Heathcliff, the id, is tamed into a Harlequin romance figure. Buñuel's Edgar (Eduardo) is a cold, heartless, calculating entomologist, whose primary occupation is pinning live, writhing insects to index cards. By the 1960s, the superego has come to be identified with oppressive government and the very social structures that Lewes believed essential to taming the human brute. These structures are represented as more violent and violating than the countercultural ones they combat, which are dramatized as harmlessly libidinal sorts. Fuest's Heathcliff is a roguish swashbuckler reveling in the wake of the 1960s liberation, while Edgar is a spiteful, peevish, controlling

representative of the establishment. Both *The Piano* (1993), which Jane
Campion has nominated her "tribute" to *Wuthering Heights*,[113] and a
1980 *Fantasy Island* television episode, "Wuthering Heights/House of
Dolls,"[114] go further to invert the roles of Heathcliff and Edgar according to the belief that it is repression, not an unbridled id, that destroys
sanity and social bonds. In both adaptations, Edgar behaves as violently
as the most untamed id, while Heathcliff becomes a softened romantic
hero almost as gentle as the Victorian Edgar.

In Campion's film, it is the civilized, decorous Edgar-equivalent Stewart
(Sam Neill), who nearly rapes and does dismember Ada (Holly Hunter),
not her unkempt, libidinous, less civilized lover Baines (Harvey Keitel),
whose partially completed Maori tattoo and long hair marks him as deliciously inter- and countercultural. Baines is gradually tamed from a sexually and economically coercive opportunist into a romance novel fantasy
figure displaying nothing but erotic tenderness and domestic support.

The *Fantasy Island* television episode, "Wuthering Heights/House of
Dolls," also makes Edgar a rapacious villain and Heathcliff a tender lover.
The beautiful Clarissa (Britt Eckland) is a social worker unable to fall in
love with real men because she has been obsessed with Brontë's Heathcliff
since the onset of puberty. Her fantasy is to meet Heathcliff. On Fantasy
Island, she is magically coifed in historical ringlets, clad in a cleavage-
enhancing red dress, and transported to the moors and domiciles of
Wuthering Heights, where she appears to Edgar (Richard Anderson) and
Heathcliff (Hugh O'Brian) as Cathy returned from the dead. As the men
fight over her, it is Edgar, not Heathcliff, who emerges as violent and economically and sexually vengeful. He orders a savage beating of Heathcliff
and plots to have him certified as insane, so that he can claim his estate.
He ties Clarissa to the marital bed in preparation for raping her, hissing
through his teeth, "If you fight me, I shall have to break you." This being television, the 1970s, and *Fantasy Island*, Clarissa is rescued from the
brink of rape and Edgar's plots to incarcerate Heathcliff are thwarted.

Heathcliff in this production is, by contrast, a harmless smooth-talking
Harlequin romancer with a touch of the second-rate Shakespearean actor ("I'll go tell Nelly to prepare a worthy feast for us"; "Heaven could not
be so cruel as to take you away a second time"; "Good night! Good night,
sweet love!"). At the end, as a raving Edgar is led away and a tranquil
Heathcliff stands by, the local magistrate (Wilfrid Hyde-White) sums up
the transposition: "Perhaps the wrong gentleman was considered for the
asylum."[115] Similarly, when critics fault adaptations for departing from
the original, viewing adaptation as translation rather than as criticism,
perhaps the wrong medium is considered the aesthetic failure. These

readings, illustrative rather than exhaustive, indicate that many adaptations faulted as faithless are, in fact, engaging in trumping activities – in outrepresenting rather than in misrepresenting the novels they adapt.

Conclusion

learly, to dismiss the splits forged between form and content by adaptation theory, rhetoric, and practice is to miss a great deal that transpires between novels and films. We learn more from adaptation's heresies than we do from attempts to conform adaptation to semiotic dogma and rigid categorical models. But beyond this, to dismiss these dynamics as inadmissible heresies unworthy of scholarly attention is to miss the illumination they bring to current polarities between formal and contextual approaches to adaptation and to humanities criticism more generally.

While oppositions between formal and contextual approaches are manifest in many areas of scholarship, they have been particularly marked in adaptation studies. Cultural studies scholars of adaptation have, since 1996, mounted a strong challenge to formal dominance of the field. They claim that, at best, formalist approaches offer only a partial account of adaptation and, at worst, that they deliberately obscure vital cultural issues in the interests of a reactionary political and cultural conservatism. An increasing number of voices declare formal approaches to adaptation overdone, needing no more doing (indeed, needing some undoing), formal scholarship outmoded and requiring updating (Mikhail Bahktin, Jacques Derrida, and Roland Barthes are the most commonly suggested upgrades), and formal studies politically reprehensible, supporting hierarchical, logocentric, white, patriarchal, capitalist, Western values that mandate exposure and correction by cultural studies, deconstruction, multiculturalism, feminism, Marxism, and Althusserian psychoanalysis. *Pulping Fictions* (1996) is the most outspoken volume in this regard. The editors delineate their aim to "destablize" the "high/lowbrow divide" and "to scrutinise some continuing tensions in literary and film analyses, which betray an abiding hostility to mass culture and a reluctance to engage with a wider postmodern field of cultural production." They choose adaptation of canonical fiction for their subject matter because they regard it as a last bastion, a holdout of such attitudes: "This cultural elitism is nowhere more apparent than in the adaptation of classic literature into commercial film."[116]

There are certainly substantial grounds for associations between formalism and high art. When Bluestone pressed for a separation of novels and films in 1957, he did so chiefly through arguing that high art can only be achieved by respecting Lessing's formal differentiations of the arts.[117] High or "good" art under formalist aesthetics is, as we have seen, predicated on maintaining the congruity between form and content: thus, verbal arts are designated temporal and ordered to represent temporal things; visual arts are designated spatial and static and ordered to represent spatial and static things. "Good" art is thus well-behaved art, dutifully following formalist rules – above all, the rule governing content's subjugation to formal rules and concerns. Formalism's propositions create a closed circuit. Only by subjugating content to form can "good" or "high" art emerge. And since only good art is worthy of study under formal principles, only art that serves formalist doctrines can enter that discourse.

What is striking for this discussion is that contextual scholars have not yet dared to challenge formalism in its holy of holies, in its insistence on subjugating content to form under a mandate of their union. Content vanishes just as surely as women did in marriage laws that made two one; form dominates and triumphs just as surely as men did under the same equation. Instead, scholars now pick up concerns that were formerly discussed under "content" ("themes," "meaning," "ideology," and so on) on the margins of representation as cultural "context." While context figures as an afterthought or footnote (if at all) in formalist criticism – extrinsic and supplementary rather than intrinsic and central to its concerns – in cultural studies, context in the form of cultural ideology is accorded power to determine not only the content of forms, but the forms themselves. Context is considered the new universal, always operative everywhere, constructing forms while remaining in excess of form just as much as any Judeo-Christian God, original signified, neoclassical Ideal, Romantic Imagination, or authorial spirit ever did. In the battle between formalist and cultural studies approaches, aspects of the older debate between form and content that had seemed to be resolved by structuralism and silenced by poststructuralism continue.

If adaptation has served as a last bastion for formalism against the rising tide of cultural studies, it has done so chiefly by remaining a forum for formalist dogmas that content be subject to form. Concerns about form and content have precluded a ready acceptance of poststructuralist tenets, not necessarily because of political agendas, but because poststructuralism does not offer a satisfactory answer as to how adaptation occurs. Culturally speaking, it is not enough to dismiss adaptation as a mass cultural hallucination simply because it does not follow semiotic dogma concerning form and content.

The heretical constructions of form and content forged by these six models of adaptation challenge formalist dominance in their heresies regarding the form/content union and poststructuralist ghostings of content. The psychic model stresses cognitive linguistic processes; the incarnational model introduces the concept of a transcendental signifier. These and other heretical formulations of form and content further tramp across the field's sharply drawn formal and contextual lines. Ventriloquist, de(re)composing, genetic, and trumping concepts of adaptation all represent content seeping into form from context in multifarious ways, confusing categories of form, content, and context, blurring narratological lines between surface and deep structure. Further study is needed to probe the philosophical and semiotic issues in the depth and detail they warrant. The chief purpose of this chapter has been to show that the form/content heresies of adaptation rhetoric and practice so marginalized in the novel and film debate are central to its dynamics rather than peripheral and that they present difficult, challenging, and rich points from which to explore formal, contentual, and contextual elements of representation further in theoretically invigorating ways.

6 Adaptation and Analogy

In response to critical partitions that make novels "words" and films "images" and the two untranslatable, and to the insistence that content does not exist apart from form (if it exists at all), a structural analogical model of adaptation has been favored throughout the twentieth century into the twenty-first.[1] In 1926, Russian formalist Boris M. Eikhenbaum assessed that "To translate a literary work into the language of film means to find in film language analogues for the stylistic principles of that literary work."[2] At the other end of the twentieth century, Martin C. Battestin insisted in 1998 that analogy is necessary for adaptation because "the two media, visual and verbal, [are] in every essential respect disparate."[3] Between these dates, analogy remains the preferred model. In 1957, George Bluestone probed "cinematic equivalents... which function on... analogical levels" to the novels they adapt.[4] In 1975, Geoffrey Wagner propounded "analogy" as the best model for adaptation, not only on grounds of semiotic necessity, but also in the service of aesthetic quality.[5] In 1985, Joy Gould Boyum affirmed that "The rhetoric of fiction is simply not the rhetoric of film, and it's in finding analogous strategies whereby the one achieves the effects of the other that the greatest challenge of adaptation lies."[6] The analogical model dominates most screenwriting guides to adaptation, influencing aesthetic practice as well as academic theory and criticism.[7]

Officially, analogy maneuvers between the two problematic semiotic dogmas with which this book is concerned – the unbridgeable divide between words and images and the unbreakable bond between form and content – but unofficially, it serves a number of other agendas. For Wagner and others, analogy brings an ameliorating diplomacy to the fidelity wars while maintaining separate representational spheres: "For our purpose here analogy must represent a fairly considerable departure for the sake of making *another* work of art... [it] cannot be indicted as a violation of a literary original since the director has not attempted (or has only minimally attempted) to reproduce the original." Yet fealty is not entirely abandoned: analogies must be "worthy of the original" or at least take "hints from their sources."[8] Analogy further navigates between the success of an adaptation as a work of art and its success as a translation of the novel. Wagner concurs with Battestin's 1966 assessment that "To judge whether or not a film is a successful adaptation of a novel is to evaluate the skill of its makers in striking analogous attitudes and in finding analogous rhetorical techniques."[9]

But the structural analogical model is only the most favored among several analogical models explaining and prescribing literary film adaptation. This chapter outlines them and propounds a new (yet also old) model of analogy that offers a way out of the gaps and binds of word/ image and form/content dogmas. The first two models of analogy – the literalized analogy and the structural analogy – are well-established in adaptation criticism, though they have not been thus named. The third lurks implicitly in psychoanalytic theories of film and forms an essential bridge to the fourth. This last model is "my own invention" only in Lewis Carroll's White Knight's sense of the phrase. Gleaned from centuries-old interart analogies and wedded to recent cognitive studies, it yokes the pictorial and the verbal in cognition without erasing all differentiations between them and opens a space between form and content that nevertheless maintains their bond.[10] Recently, cognitive linguistics has mounted significant challenges to both structural objective linguistic and psychoanalytic approaches to film.[11] My discussion examines and to some extent integrates these three approaches, but finds that a cognitive linguistic approach offers the best available solution to the novel and film debate's problematic dogmas. However, structural, deconstructive, and psychoanalytic approaches offer vital and indispensable steps on the way to the cognitive linguistic conclusion/solution, which, one discovers, lurks implicitly in reciprocal interart analogies dating back to classical times.

While almost any case study material could serve for this discussion, I selected Lewis Carroll's *Alice's Adventures in Wonderland* (1865) and *Through the Looking Glass* (1871) and their film adaptations because they are self-consciously concerned with the representational capacities of verbal and pictorial signs, with dynamics between the aural and visual aspects inside individual signs, and with splits between form and content.[12] Since these issues are well established in Carrollian criticism, I highlight only a few illustrative examples here by way of introduction.

Carroll's *Alice* books are manifestly concerned with the referentiality of signs, particularly of words. In *Through the Looking Glass*, Humpty Dumpty takes words and redefines them eccentrically, arbitrarily, and dogmatically:

> "When I use a word," Humpty Dumpty said in a rather scornful tone, "it means just what I choose it to mean – neither more nor less."
> "The question is," said Alice, "whether you can make words mean so many different things." (LG 274–75)

Whether or not words can mean so many different things, Carroll's words have given rise to many different film adaptations: I have located nearly 50 and, given the erratic nature of film and television records, my list cannot be exhaustive. Adaptations range from all-star casts (Paramount's 1933 film, Warner Brothers' 1985 two-part television series, and NBC's 1999 three-hour television special), to Lou Bunin's puppet extravaganza (1948), to a social satire (Jonathan Miller casts Victorian eccentrics in place of Carroll's animals in his 1966 adaptation), to a murder mystery (Jerry Gruza's in 1980), to a biographical adaptation (Gavin Miller's 1985 *Dream Child*), to numerous animated versions (including Disney's in 1951, Jan Švankmajer's surrealist animation in 1988, and the "Sugar & Spice Special Stories for Little Girls" cartoon of 1991), to a late-1990s modernized syndicated television series, *Adventures in Wonderland*, complete with roller-blading White Rabbit, rap, hip hop, and rock, to Playboy's pornographic *Alice's Adventures in Wonderland: The World's Greatest Bedtime Story* (1976).

In the *Alice* books, sometimes words are empty, disappointingly dislocated from their referents. A jar labeled "ORANGE MARMALADE" contains no marmalade: the label denotes the absence of content – perhaps a past presence – but ultimately the "promise" of language proves empty.[13] Some words appear to have no referents at all. When the Mouse monotones that historical dignitaries "found it advisable" to take a particular course of action, the Duck interrupts to demand the referent of "it," insisting: "when I find a thing ... it's generally a frog or worm." The Mouse cannot comply with this demand for concretism, nor can the dry history he reads dry the creatures from the sea of tears (AW 44). Elsewhere, verbal meaning is destabilized by context to such an extent that antonyms and synonyms, like "important" and "unimportant," become interchangeable, with no bearing on the final word, on the verdict of the trial in which they appear as evidence (AW 152). At other points, degrees of comparison turn words into their own antonyms: "I've seen gardens, compared with which this would be a wilderness ... I could show you hills, in comparison with which you'd call that a valley... I've heard nonsense, compared with which that would be as sensible as a dictionary!" (LG 213). Negations like unbirthdays prove weightier than affirmations, and Nobody is personified and much talked about (LG 273, 286). Syntactic inversions radically changing meaning are declared immaterial ("as she couldn't answer either question [Do cats eat bats? Do bats eat cats?] it didn't much matter which way she put it"–AW 26), while inversions with little semantic effect are strenuously protested (the tea party guests object vociferously to Alice's assertion that "I mean what I say" is the same thing as "I say what I mean"–AW 94).

Relationships between words and actions also prove highly unstable in the *Alice* books. Some words resound authoritatively, but are impotent to effect action. The Queen constantly orders heads off, but the Gryphon tells Alice: "It's all her fancy, that: they never executes nobody," the double negative here adding a delicious note of uncertainty (AW 123). By contrast, words that appear feeble and fictional, like nursery rhymes, possess prophetic power, becoming deterministic scripts for fated and fatal actions and events. Tweedle Dee and Dum and Humpty Dumpty enact the lines of the rhymes Alice recites concerning them against their will to their danger and destruction (LG Chapters 4 and 6). Conversely and ironically given his scripted fate, Humpty Dumpty boasts of his power over words, personifying them as characters who work for him: "They've a temper some of them – particularly the verbs... however, I can manage the whole lot of them" (LG 275).

I also selected the *Alice* books because they address sensory–cognitive semiotic aspects fundamental to signification and to the final model of analogy outlined in this chapter. Carroll plays on distinctions between "sense" as semantic meaning and "sense" as sensory perception, placing them in conflict with each other. This tension comes to bear on form and content questions most evidently in his buoyant, dislocating homonymic puns – puns that gleefully subvert the Duchess's admonition, "Take care of the sense, and the sounds will take care of themselves" (AW 119), as pairings between sounds confuse and subvert pairings between signifiers and signifieds. If linguistic signification is predicated, as so many have argued, on phonetic difference, homonymic puns prove particularly unsettling figures. "Axis" and "axes" sound nearly identical, but refer to vastly different concepts; trees that bark and say "Bough-wough" or ground flour that confuses with the ground in which flowers grow place semantic difference in phonetic similitude and require other cognitive processes to reach signification (AW 83; LG 208, 324). These processes typically place the auditory discrimination of phonemes at odds with the visual discrimination of graphemes. "Axis" and "axes" sound nearly identical, but look different. These near homonymic puns heighten dissonances between graphic and phonic elements of language, an effect that brings the two problematic dogmas of this book closer together, as splits between verbal and visual aspects of signs coalesce with attempts to match signifiers with signifieds.

Carroll's *Alice* books, written ostensibly for children, have grappled more profoundly with issues of language, cognition, and signification than most books written for adults. Besides their application to linguistics, they have been studied and invoked by logicians, mathematicians, psychoanalysts, philosophers, theologians, and historians. Beyond this, they have been used to explain scientific theories: for example, the Cheshire Cat phenomenon in quantum physics and the Red Queen theory in evolutionary biology. In a similar vein, animated adaptations of the *Alice* books prove more illuminating for my investigation into adaptation theories than live-action films. Just as Carroll's child's play with language highlights problems and features common to all linguistic expression, so too, animated films highlight problems and features common to all films, since all films operate according to principles and technologies of animation.

Adaptation and the Literalized Analogy

Analogical models of adaptation claim to reconcile demands that the arts be categorized as different species with the claim that they are related sister arts. As we have seen, adaptation frequently literalizes inter-art analogies, including their repressed differentials, raising categorical hackles all the more highly. And because the play between figurative and literal dimensions is essential to analogy, such literalizations tend to destroy the analogy even as they seem to realize it. For example, stage adaptations of *Vanity Fair* typically literalize the theatrical analogies of the novel's preface, "The Author: Before the Curtain," which likens the novel to a performance, its characters to puppets, the page turn to a rising curtain, the narrator to a stage manager, and the illustrations to candles lighting the stage. In stage adaptations, an actor stands before a literal stage curtain and delivers the preface verbatim, announcing "scenes of all sorts . . . the whole accompanied by appropriate scenery, and brilliantly illuminated with the Author's own candles." The adapting literalization realizes parts of the analogy, but effaces others. The narrator becomes a stage manager and the page turn a real curtain rising, but the analogy of book illustrations to stage candles evaporates. Thackeray's analogy already literalizes the etymology of "to illustrate," which means "to throw light on."[14] When the theatrical adaptation reliteralizes it – when "candles" become literal stage lights – the book illustrations are entirely lost. The reference to the "Author's own candles" must either be interpreted literally (the stage candles belong to the author) or abstractly (the spirit of the author hovers over and illumines the play), or be read as a new analogy (for example, lines from the novel illuminate the play's dialogue). The overly literal, the overly abstract, and the digressively new all characterize adaptation under a model of literalized analogy.

While there are many forms of literalized interart analogies, this discussion focuses on the analogy of literary film adaptation as filmed literature in performance. A long tradition of performed literature – dramatic readings of literature, stage adaptations, and radio dramas – precedes, informs, and feeds into film and television adaptations of literature. This model of interart adaptation emphasizes the dramatic performance of literary words. Thus characters typically engage in ceaseless conversation and the adaptation unfolds primarily through dialogue rather than visual display. The cinematography and videography of such adaptations favor shots of talking heads, with occasional long shots to showcase sets, grounds, artifacts, and costumes, particularly in historical adaptations. Building on earlier radio dramas, BBC literary adaptations before the mid-1990s offer prototypical examples of the filmed literature in performance model of adaptation.[15]

The literalized analogy of filmed literature in performance reduces each mode of representation – literary, theatrical, and filmic. It reduces the words of the novel to dialogue[16]; it flattens, shrinks, and cans three-dimensional, life-size, live theatrical performance to two-dimensional, screen-size, pre-recorded drama; and it relegates cinematography, videography, and sound to mere recording devices for performance. While critics tend to fault such adaptations only with reducing the novel, it is crucial to note that they reduce theatrical and filmic expression as well.

"You Know Very Well You're Not Real": Alice in Literaland

In Carroll's *Alice's Adventures in Wonderland*, Alice experiences the dangers and disappointments of literalized figures of speech: she nearly expires in a literalization of the proverb that leaves crying children drowning in their own tears and subsequently experiences the disappointing failure of another figure to literalize: of dry history to dry her off from that sea of tears (AW 44 ff.). Alice later wonders why growing larger fails to make her a "grownup." As she swells to an enormous size, filling the White Rabbit's house to capacity, she exclaims: "There ought to be a book written about

me, that there ought! And when I grow up, I'll write one – but I'm grown
up now... at least there's no room to grow up any more *here*" (AW 55,
original emphasis).

Adaptations under the literalized analogy of literature in performance
render Alice the book as confined and gauche on film and television
as Alice the character in the White Rabbit's house. NBC's 1999 *Alice in
Wonderland* epitomizes this model when theatrical sets open from pop-up
books and characters step from book illustration plates.[17] Most critics
conclude that this sense of confinement derives from the inherently inferior representational capacities of the adapting media. I argue that such
ungainly adaptations derive not from anything inherently inferior in the
adapting media, but rather from the model of adaptation itself. Such
adaptations are arrested aesthetic developments, caught between literature, theater, and film, and frozen at the midpoints of the interart analogy
that makes adaptation a performed filmed reading.

The effects are readily apparent when one examines what happens to
Carroll's devastating and witty critique of linguistic representation under literalized analogical models of adaptation. Critics have shown that
Carroll's *Alice* books point to the instability of language and reveal how
the arbitrary rules of language foster an unjust, predatory, and abusive
society. But natural–realist film techniques and the layered artifice of
theatrical performance both undermine this sense of linguistic disruption. Carroll's nonsensical words emerge from congruous bodies moving
according to biological and physical laws in coherent filmic space, shot
at rational camera angles, and edited according to logical spatial transitions. Theatrical television and film adaptations of the *Alice* books typically
package Carroll's linguistic and social critique as stand-up comedy, dramatic recitation, song, and dance, presented by congruous performing
bodies on highly theatrical, artificial sets that place any critique of language in fantasy and artificiality. Most adapters fail to recognize the te-
dium of such performances, although Carroll's Alice should have alerted
them to it, for she often sighs over the performances of jokes, poems,
and songs in Wonderland and through the looking glass.[18] In musical
versions, the harmonic tunes and symmetrically choreographed dance
sequences soothe, harmonize, and regularize any sense of linguistic disruption or incongruity. And when realist camera techniques record theatrical artifice, Carroll's dislocated dream worlds appear artificial rather
than surreal. Instead of quasi-nightmarish, quasi-comical apparitions, we
see adult actors dressed as animals frolicking amidst paper and plastic
flowers in cardboard houses with plastic dinnerware. Such theatrical layering displaces Carroll's effects of wonder and illogic, for beneath the

32. Norman Z. McLeod's *Alice in Wonderland,* Paramount, 1933. Courtesy of the Academy of Motion Pictures Arts and Sciences.

artificial theatrical layers lies a puncturing realism that never allows fantasy, nonsense, or dream to take flight. Animal characters are clearly human actors layered over with fictional names, costumes, and makeup. This effect is most marked in the all-star productions of *Alice*, where filmmakers are anxious to showcase famous actors beneath their roles.[19] In Harry Harris's 1985 version, for example, Telly Savalas's signature baldness was deemed so essential to his recognition in his role as the Cheshire Cat that he is covered with fur – including his face – *except* for his bald head.[20] In the 1985 version, Sammy Davis Jr. must shed his Caterpillar costume in order to tap dance; in the 1999 NBC production, Whoopi Goldberg as the Cheshire Cat performs her trademark stand-up comedy and the Mad Hatter (Martin Short) and March Hare (Francis Wright) receive canned applause at the conclusion of their vaudeville song.

Performance becomes the central narrative theme as well as the dominant presentational mode of the 1999 NBC televization. Alice (Tina Majorino) goes to Wonderland principally to overcome performance anxiety – she must sing for guests at home, but dreads doing so. In this production, the mixed up words of Carroll's poetic parodies are not dislocations from linguistic convention and grammatical sense, but rather failed rehearsals in which Alice "gets things wrong" and must try again until she gets them right. The Wonderland cure not only turns Alice into a competent performer, it also "corrects" Carroll's "errors" by restoring the conventional originals he parodied.

Infusions of rationalism, morality, and psychology further conventionalize Carroll's linguistic exposures and disruptions in adaptations operating under a model of literalized analogy. In the 1985 televization, magical events are explained in terms of cause and effect, with Alice's soliloquies serving as captioning for the narratively impaired ("It was the fan that was making me shrink"; "These are my tears from when I was nine feet tall"). When offered wine, Alice primly invokes the legal drinking age ("I'm not supposed to drink wine – I'm too young"). Song lyrics are more like the moralistic rhymes Carroll parodies than his parodies, as when Alice sings to the Fawn:

> Why do people act as if they're crazy?
> Why can't they be kind to one another?
> And see the beauty of the golden rule?
> Will there come a day when we'll all know how to say,
> "I love you"?

Other lyrics run directly counter to Carroll's central point that the arbitrary rules of English grammar prepare young children to accept unjust and irrational social structures, codes, and practices in opposition to their own more rational cognitive linguistic structures. Cultural icon Ringo Starr, clad in a most unflattering pair of salmon tights for his role as the Mock Turtle, spouts lyrics that argue the direct opposite of Carroll's point. He sings that the world needs *more* nonsense as relief from the sober, rational, and sensible operations of society: "There's far too much accurate communication/And if it continues, I fear for the nation . . . / 'Tis nonsense will save the blooming human race." The song thus becomes a sales pitch for the entertainment industry.

Since the case studies that support and illustrate my preferred models of analogy in the following are both animated films, it is important to stress here that the literalized analogical model encompasses some animated adaptations. Franco Cristofani's animated *Alice in Wonderland* (1988) mimics the logical camera angles and coherent editing conventions of realist live-action films.[21] It too is infused with rational and moral overlays that run directly counter to Carroll's linguistic and social critique. The White Rabbit sees Alice as a consistent creation, never mistaking her for Mary Ann or for a giant in his house, and the Duchess and Cook throw plates as the result of a debate over pepper, rather than as acts of random violence. The adaptation disintegrates into a child's confessional, as a very non-Carrollian Alice ties up all her moral loose ends through ardent apologies to the resentful creatures she has injured – to the animals nearly drowned in her tears, to the White Rabbit whose house was burned, and to Bill the Lizard, still smarting from her kick up the chimney. She even confesses to stealing the tarts – a complete departure from the book, where the Knave of Hearts is the guilty party. In this adaptation, sense arrives to tame nonsense, and morality and manners enter to mitigate the aggressive and violent undertones of Carroll's books – undertones rumbling beneath Alice's seemingly innocent boasts to mice and birds of her cat's predatory skills, in the final word of the Mouse's Tail/Tale ("death"), in the Queen of Hearts's beheading commands, in the Jabberwocky poem, and in the predatory food chains running between characters.

One live-action theatrical adaptation, however, augments the predatory aspects of *Alice's Adventures in Wonderland* and shapes them into a sexist fable and immorality tale.[22] Playboy's *Alice's Adventures in Wonderland: The World's Greatest Bedtime Story* (1976) participates in a well-established tradition of pornographic parody. But it also participates (albeit inadvertently) in the strain of literary and biographical criticism surrounding Carroll's relationships with young girls.[23] Any live-action production that does not use special effects turns the animal–child ratio of Tenniel's illustrations into a more sinister adult–child ratio, one that renders Alice more vulnerable physically to the animals.[24] These adaptations simultaneously mitigate and sexualize the physical threat of the adult animals by casting buxom young teenagers in the role of Alice, rather than the seven-year-old of the books.[25] The Playboy adaptation makes the implicit sexualization explicit. Alice (Kristine de Bell) is a virginal ingenue, a mousy librarian who cannot respond sexually to men in the "real" world and so must go to Wonderland to learn to "grow up all over again." Playboy defines growing up as a reconditioning of this sexually appetizing but sexually latent girl through an apprenticeship to various Wonderland "animals" (in both senses of the word), amongst whom paunchy middle-aged men feature prominently. Alice sups the Mad Hatter rather than tea, helps an impotent Humpty Dumpty to rise, and learns to flee an aggressively lesbian Queen of Hearts, whose screaming mantra is "Give me some head!" All of this occurs in the name of self-actualization, of growing up, and of freeing herself from repressive moral codes. Her rewards at the end of the film – her first experience of heterosexual intercourse, marriage, children, a puppy, and a suburban house with a white picket fence – however, clearly position her in a male-dominated social order where her own wishes and desires are subject to theirs.[26]

Quite strikingly, this XXX film differs little from the socializing processes of the G-rated 1985 and 1999 all-star televizations. Performance in each has socially adaptive as well as formally adaptive functions: adapting Alice (the book and the character) to a dramatic medium makes performance an analogy for socialization as well as for literary film adaptation. In each case, Wonderland serves as a training ground where Alice learns to perform in more socially acceptable ways. In the Harris version, Alice returns from Wonderland to find she is old enough to have tea with grownups. At the end of the NBC production, she sings confidently before guests at her home, cured of her earlier reluctance to render parental command performances. The Playboy Alice too learns to act for and on grown, growing, and groaning men – actions she has hitherto been reluctant to perform in order to enter mainstream social structures at the end of the film. By contrast, Carroll's Alice repeatedly fails to perform correctly, whether in her mis-recitations of poetry, or in her failure to follow instructions or to please Wonderland and looking glass characters.

We see, then, that the literalized analogical model of adaptation can function formally, reducing literary, theatrical, and filmic representation in an interart merger, or culturally, conforming innate instincts and cognitive structures to conscribed social performance and coerced social role playing. In both cases, the model distorts and erodes Carroll's linguistic and social critique. Formally, the model freezes literature, theater, and film at the midpoints of their interart analogies, so that these adaptations are neither satisfying reading, nor engaging performance, nor compelling film or television. Stranded between book, theater, and film/television, these literalized analogies are half wraps: taxidermied live action, artificial realism, conventional fantasy, moralistic deviants. Culturally, the model subjects linguistic and social protest to the drama school of social conformity. Adaptation allows a deviant literary Alice to be resocialized by a new medium for a new, but always older, generation.

The literalized analogical model of adaptation is responsible for all of these effects, yet instead of faulting the model, critics fault the adapting media, claiming the essentialist formal inferiority of film and television to literature. The second analogical model of adaptation has led to similarly misguided conclusions about the nature of these media and the assertions of their essentialist nonrelationship to literature.

Adaptation and the Structural Analogy

Chapter 1 established that twentieth-century academic discourse has approved only a structurally constrained model of interart analogy, one that maintains structural consistency, relational focus, and systematicity;

allows no extraneous associations or mixed analogies; insists that analogy is not causation; and claims no essential affinities between the arts. Thus the structural analogy upholds categorizations of novels as words and films as images and the inviolable bond of signifier and signified. The model perceives adaptation as locating visual equivalents for verbal expression without admitting any inherence between words and images or any separation of form and content. As we saw earlier, for Battestin and many others, categorical differentiations that make novels and films untranslatable and irreducible as "words" and "images" mandate just such a structural analogical model of adaptation. Since direct translation between them is decreed impossible, critics argue that adapters can at best only locate stylistic and structural analogies across the two systems. Scholars of adaptation also reject any notion that signifieds can separate from their signifiers and move from novel into film, there joining with new signifiers. Bluestone, for example, quips that literary characters are inseparable from the medium that constructs them and "cannot be liberated in order to make a personal appearance in another medium."[27] Adapters, he protests, can only find filmic equivalents for literary characters.

Quite apart from the word–image mix in both novels and films and from the words that transfer directly from novel to film as dialogue, title cards, or voice-over, this model is more problematic than its advocates have acknowledged. Adapters working under a verbal-to-visual model of adaptation typically seek visual symbols to approximate words. However, given the cliched and monosyllabic nature of most visual symbols, this model of adaptation feeds perceptions that film and television are crude and reductive modes of representation far inferior to verbal representation. In her 1926 diatribe against literary film adaptation, Virginia Woolf complained: "we lurch and lumber through the most famous novels of the world . . . we spell them out in words of one syllable . . . A kiss is love. A broken cup is jealousy. A grin is happiness. Death is a hearse."[28] Monty Python's *Semaphore Version of Wuthering Heights* (1970) also parodies adaptation as crude sign language. As Heathcliff and Catherine wave flags to each other, subtitles indicate the reduction of their literary speeches: "Oh, Catherine!"; "Oh, Heathcliff!" Baby Hareton flags, "Waaah!", Nelly waves, "Ssssh!", and Joseph's flag sputters, "Zzzz." Finally, Edgar arrives with an enormous flag "loudly" proclaiming his marital prerogative, ending the film with supersized monogamous monosyllables.[29]

Again, it is the model rather than the adapting medium that is responsible for such reductions. From a purely objective standpoint, cinema and television are semiotically richer than novels, for they employ spoken and written words and bodily gestures, facial expression, music, images, dance, theater, artifacts, architecture, sound and computer effects, and more. Condensations of lengthy novels to two-hour films have also fed essentialist judgments that film and television reduce literature.

However, the model is not solely responsible for such perceptions. The order in which words and images appear combines with philosophies about words and images to further advance such impressions. Both Judeo-Christian theologies of truth and scientific empirical models of proof place images in the service of words, affirming and confirming verbal dogmas and hypotheses. Under such models, when images follow and replicate words, words appear to possess power over those images, creating, shaping, and defining them before and after their appearance. When the Talking Doorknob of Disney's *Alice in Wonderland* suggests, "Why don't you try the bottle on the table?" neither bottle nor table is present. But at the moment he utters the words, bottle and table appear, as if the words had magical power to conjure them. Images following words in this way appear secondary, derivative, dependent, and redundant. However, when words follow images, they appear equally uninspired and derivative. In Disney's *Alice*, a stuttering Dodo bird ponders how to get Alice out of the White Rabbit's house: "What we need is . . . " – then he stops, stymied. Glancing down the road, he spots a lizard with a ladder. He exclaims, as if inspired, " – a lizard with a ladder!" When words follow images in this way, they appear as derivative afterthoughts and their speaker mentally impaired. Moreover, coming after the vibrant, detailed, colorful, mobile, dramatic audiovisual representation of the lizard with the ladder, here words appear semiotically reductive and lacking.

Since sequencing influences perceptions of each medium's representational capacities, the prevalence of adaptations from novel to film over novelizations of films and the preponderance of critical attention given to literary film adaptation have tended to propound ideas of film as reductive of literature and as a more primitive mode of representation. Western philosophical traditions that insist on the primacy of the word over phenomenological signification (Christ the Word as primary revelation over nature as secondary revelation, the scientific hypothesis as truth merely supported by empirical evidence) have very likely predisposed scholars and audiences to such emphases, as well as to the preoccupation with fidelity that has so dominated and skewed adaptation studies.

"As Large as Life and Twice as Natural": Alice in Verbal-to-Visualand

In spite of the semiotic inaccuracies and crudities of the verbal-to-visual structural model of adaptation, it has served some adaptations well.

Jan Švankmajer's *Alice* (1988) is one such film. Švankmajer rejects both the model that figures adaptation as literature in performance and the conventional monosyllabic visual symbolism that so reduces literature in adaptation. In his *Jabberwocky* (1971), a short film that adapts a poem from *Through the Looking Glass*, written papers seep from a school satchel to form paper airplanes, boats, and horses that fly, sail, and gallop amok. The word here metamorphoses from its flat, static position on two-dimensional paper rectangles to decorate three-dimensional, animated, interactive playthings. These animated filmic papers appear far more semiotically resonant than the satchel-ensconced, illegible pages from whence they came.

Švankmajer adamantly rejects the "filmed literature in performance" model of adaptation:

> [The author] succeeds in describing the most intimate reactions of the human soul . . . Transforming these "descriptions" into a dramatic form of dialogue, with the miming and gestures of actors etc. is always inadequate, superficial, because [the author's] "descriptions" are impossible to translate into conventional dramatic language.

In keeping with this, Švankmajer's *Alice* eschews dramatic dialogue. Its speech is more exclamatory than conversational: "Please sir!"; "I'm late!"; "Ow!"; "Wait for me, sir!"; "Mind the step, Bill!"; "She'll have my head!"; and "Off with their heads!" When there is dialogue, since Alice does all the voices (her mouth shown in extreme close-up shaping each word, lest there be any doubt), the effect is more one of schizophrenic soliloquy than of dramatic dialogue.

In place of the filmed literature in performance model, Švankmajer adheres to a structural visual-to-verbal analogical model of adaptation:

> In the end I decided to take the same path as [the author] took in writing the story. With the help of visual "descriptions" (as opposed to [the author's] verbal "descriptions") I tried to evoke the appropriate feelings at the level of analogy. To get those corresponding feelings I took the path of "objectively descriptive" visual analogy.[30]

As in Wagner's account, analogy allows the filmmaker both to "take the same path as [the author]" and, simultaneously and paradoxically, to be "opposed to" the author. Of Carroll, Švankmajer has said: "mentally we're on the same side of the river . . . my subjective interpretations of . . . Carroll swim in the same subterranean waters."[31] Nevertheless, he insists on his aesthetic independence: "I do not follow the objectives of the author, but I follow my own. I am not interested in 'what the author wanted to say by this' but purely in how a particular motif relates to my own experiences."[32] Švankmajer thus stakes his model of adaptation on traditional accounts that figure words and images as opposed but novels and films as analogical kin to strike an "opposed affinity" to/with the author.

This model of subterranean similitude in overt semiotic opposition produces physical, objective, visual, and aural equivalents for Carroll's disruptive linguistic representations in ways that both resemble and depart from his representations. In short, Švankmajer's *Alice* disrupts the laws of biology and physics just as Carroll's *Alice* disrupts the laws of logic and language. But the laws of language are not the same as physical laws, as his adaptation makes manifestly clear. The structural analogical model may emphasize affinities, but it stresses differences as well.

Švankmajer attends closely to the simulacra of the verbal-to-visual analogy, playing on the formal and cognitive properties of film to disrupt physical laws in the same way that Carroll plays on the formal and cognitive properties of language to disrupt linguistic laws. Just as Carroll manipulates conventional language to confuse cognition and signification, so too Švankmajer manipulates conventional naturalist-realist audiovisual film techniques to confuse cognition and signification. He lacerates auditor-viewer attempts to perceive a cogent cinematic phenomenological world with sudden, dreamlike editing shifts. Sounds occur more loudly than they do in life, dislocating normative sound–distance relationships. Sounds and images frequently form incongruous combinations, as when chickens neigh like horses, pitting visual against aural cognition, just as Carroll's puns pit visual perception of graphemes against aural discrimination of phonemes.

As Carroll uses intrinsic linguistic features to disrupt linguistic sense, so too Švankmajer uses intrinsic filmic properties, like the projection of 24 slightly variant still photographic frames per second, to disrupt perceptual sense. His hallmark combination of live-action photography with stop-action animation renders organic beings and inanimate objects equally "alive." Organic beings "move" in exactly the same way as inanimate objects do: through a sequence of rapidly projected still frames that does not actually represent movement, but only gives an illusion of it through critical flicker fusion interacting with persistence of vision. Although his actors have moved before a camera, their images reside on celluloid as still photographs; although his objects have been moved by animators between takes, they too remain only as still celluloid photographs minus these movements. Carroll's own Wonderland croquet scene prefigures the effects of such pan-animation when an exasperated Alice, wrestling with a live flamingo mallet and live hedgehog ball, exclaims,

"You've no idea how confusing it is all the things being alive" (AW 112). Švankmajer transforms Carroll's "all the things being alive" into a pervasive aesthetic principle. In his *Alice*, everything is alive via animation – not only croquet mallets and balls (these are, less magically, represented by live chickens and hedgehogs), but also toys, games, food, furniture, glass eyes, bones, nails, and clothing.

Švankmajer's *Alice* opens, however, in a natural, realist, outdoor world. A sulky, bored Alice throws rocks into a brook as her older sister reads beside her. Alice's impatient hand flips through the pages of the book looking for pictures, only to receive a sharp slap for attempting to animate literature flip-book fashion. The next scene locates Alice in a dingy cluttered interior surrounded by faded toys and old objects, still sulky and bored, now throwing rocks into cups of black tea. The scene withholds an image of the live Alice: we only hear the rocks she tosses splashing and clinking into cups of tea while the camera darts from object to object, like a watchful, suspicious eye looking for any sign of movement in the lifeless objects. The sequence appears like a series of still photographs bursting at the editing seams to become animated moving images. Like a ticking time bomb, the scene is ready to explode into movement at any moment. A bare light bulb sizzles, and the first inanimate object comes to life. (Švankmajer's own definition of animation is "to make objects alive.") The White Rabbit, a taxidermied specimen nailed inside a glass case, rips his paws free from the nails, dons a jacket, dapper hat, lace cuffs, and buttoned gloves, and hastens away, sawdust leaking from his parodic stigmata in paradoxical defiance of the process of taxidermy (Figure 33). Here, the substance that rendered him inanimate after organic death leaks from him like life blood. Švankmajer frees his rabbit and other objects from eternal inanimate existence into an afterlife of vivid animation.

From this point, film frames burst with inanimate objects animated. These objects do not, however, act according to physical laws. Instead, they participate in what Švankmajer has called "the concrete irrational," which corresponds analogically and structurally to Carroll's verbal irrational. Just as Carroll dislocates words from conventional contexts and combines them with other words to dislocate conventional comprehension ("flamingoes and mustard both bite" – AW 119), so too, Švankmajer dismembers objects and recombines them to create grotesque and fantastical things. A fish skeleton houses two hen's eggs in its fragile rib cage and sports a dapper red hat; a headless toy crib flies on feathered wings and lands on bird feet. Thus, far from monosyllabic reductions of words, Švankmajer adapts Carroll's play between linguistic relations to play between physical relations.

33. Jan Švankmajer's *Alice.* Condor Films, 1988. Courtesy of BFI stills.

Both Carroll and Švankmajer disrupt their respective representational systems to distress and confuse conventional categories, definitions, and identities. Some of Carroll's dislocating puns replace one part of speech with another, disrupting grammatical categories as well as semantics, as when the Gnat renders Alice a noun-Miss who may verb-miss her lessons (LG 229) or when Alice and the White Queen confuse verb-ground flour with the noun-ground in which flowers grow (LG 324). Such puns dislocate and elide essence, action, and modification. In the same way, Švankmajer's animation of everything dislocates and elides categorizations of what is alive and what is not. His Alice is alternately a live actress and an animated plastic doll. In one scene, his live actress is herself rendered inanimate, encased in a plaster cast doll shell, her live eyes peering out through holes in the plaster, her eyelashes and eyebrows supplanted by painted ones. His Caterpillar is made of a sock, sawdust, glass eyes, and false teeth, but a close-up shot reveals a beating heart pulsing inside the sock. The taxidermied White Rabbit similarly stores a ticking watch in the sawdust cavity where a live rabbit's heart once beat.

Such confusions and displacements carry social and political implications, as do Carroll's verbal confusions and displacements. For example, in certain scenes of violence and mutilation, the confusion as to what is an actor and what is a prop extends to questions regarding what is an act of murder and what is merely an act of vandalism. When the White

Rabbit beheads two dueling Jacks, has he killed two characters or has he simply vandalized a deck of cards? Švankmajer described *Alice* to Communist censors as "an audio-visual demonstration of the demystification of space and time." Sensing the film's subversion of established laws, the government moved to ban the film as "ideologically confused," but the government relented when faced with losing Swiss dollars from the film's backers.[33] If the film is a demystification, it is a mystifying one in the same way that Carroll's exposé of language intensifies rather than unravels its confusions. Both author and filmmaker maintain their illogic logically, their irrationality rationally, and unravel their systems systematically. In Carroll's *Wonderland*, the Dormouse's tale of three sisters in a treacle well demonstrates how confusing syntax and semantics can be maintained according to the strictest grammatical laws and the most exact dictionary definitions. The process unfolds largely through homonymic puns, in which semantics diverge from aurally consonant springboards. The Dormouse tells of three sisters living in a treacle well, learning to draw. Alice, thinking of conventional education, assumes that the sisters were learning graphic drawing. But the Dormouse insists on a definition derived from the word's more immediate verbal context: the girls were learning to draw treacle from the well. Although Alice can make grammatical and semantic sense of this redefinition, it represents a physical and narrative impossibility: "But they were *in* the well," she objects, assuming that one cannot draw something out of a well which one is in oneself. Once again, however, the Dormouse privileges signification based on immediate textual context, both affirming and denying Alice's protest: "Of course they were ... – well in" (100–1, original emphasis). Moreover, by grammatically inverting her question, he appears, after syntactic conventions ("What is a well?"; "A well is a ... "), to have answered it. However, the Dormouse has done nothing to answer her question in any substantial or referential sense. Instead, he has sidestepped Alice's protest by deftly shifting a substantial noun (well) to an elusive modifying adverb. Here and throughout the *Alice* books, Carroll uses the rules and conventions designed to render language coherent to mystify linguistic comprehension.

In much the same way, Švankmajer derives his surreal and irrational animated actions from actions associated naturally, conventionally, or rationally with the objects that he animates. As Michael O'Pray notes, "Švankmajer uses the characteristic properties of objects as the basis for the animated life he gives them ... Thus many of the fantasies expressed in Svankmajer's films operate not at the level of content: in the pure surrealist manner, they are simply extensions of the intrinsic nature of things – a material one always."[34] In drawing on unconventional but intrinsic properties of objects, Švankmajer creates an effect he has called "objective humor." This humor, he attests, "does not deny the rationality and logic of meaning: it engulfs them. If both are based on a conventional definition, then the principle of objective humour develops logic and rational links which overstep the limit set by the dominant convention."[35] Carroll's Gnat builds on a conventional insect taxonomy – Horse-fly, Dragon-fly, and Butterfly – to create linguistically logical but fantastical insects found nowhere in nature – a Rocking-horse-fly, Snap-Dragon-fly, and Bread-and-Butterfly (LG 226–28). In the same way, Švankmajer assembles fantastical species from disparate objects – from clothing, toys, food, feathers, glass eyes, bones, and other household objects. A sock, glass eye, and false teeth form a Caterpillar, who sits, appropriately, on a darning mushroom. Švankmajer even incorporates the quotidian use of the darning mushroom when the Caterpillar sews his eye shut on it to fall asleep.

Both Švankmajer and Carroll intensify their logic in illogic by encasing it in repetitive sensory patterns that both create an illusion of systematicity and work hypnotically to lull readers and viewers into a trance from which shocks and surprises explode all the more forcefully. Carroll situates much of his linguistic nonsense in poems maintaining regular rhymes and rhythms, so that no matter how nonsensical the semantics, readers can rely on a predictable sensory order. Thus, no matter how confusing the semantics of "Jabberwocky," readers pulse down recognizable syntactic structures at regular rhythms to predictable rhymes, their semantic confusion blanketed in aural and structural patterning. In a similar vein, Švankmajer situates his dislocations of physical laws amidst repetitive visual and aural patterns. The same objects reappear repeatedly in the same contexts – rocks are thrown into liquid, scissors snap shut, nails sprout from loaves, drawer knobs pop off, sawdust leaks out – and the same sounds recur throughout the film – water drips, rocks splash, watches tick, doors creak, knobs pop.[36] Repetition is essential to the establishment and maintenance of laws, whether linguistic, political, or scientific. But in Švankmajer's highly patterned anarchy, repetition is, disturbingly, enlisted in the breaking of laws, pressing sensory repetition toward empirical insanity, suggesting new laws that consist entirely of broken ones. Just as Carroll's use of language to violate linguistic laws leaves no independent context or system from which to tame or contain his disruptions, so too, Švankmajer's use of sensory repetition and patterning to violate physical laws leaves no independent context or system from which to tame or contain his dislocations.

It is readily apparent from this account that a structural verbal-to-visual analogical model of adaptation can result in a dynamic film consonant with its adapted book. However, the model has limitations. Though there are parallels, the laws of language are not the same as the laws of physics. Carroll's disruption of linguistic laws emerges much more gleefully and comically than Švankmajer's disruption of physical laws. Objects that refuse to conform to the laws of biology and physics are, like Catherine's ghost seizing Lockwood with her icy hand, far more nightmarish than verbal games, like Catherine's whimsical play with her varying surnames, which only amuses Lockwood. Unlike Carroll's marmalade jar, which is disappointingly empty, Švankmajer's marmalade jar is filled to the brim with marmalade and contains a lethal surplus content: in a sinister parody of the nursery rhyme boy who put in his thumb and pulled out a plum, Alice puts in her finger and pulls out a thumbtack. Carroll's linguistic play frequently functions like a conjuring trick – a puff of smoke, and referents vanish into thin air as new ones appear. Švankmajer's animated play, on the other hand, brings incongruous and grotesque objects to animated life and menaces characters and viewers with them. While sinister subtexts lurk in Carroll's *Alice* books, Carroll keeps the lid on them. "Death," the final word of the Mouse's Tail, is almost illegible; Alice sweetly sugarcoats and politely detracts her repeated terrorizing of Wonderland mice and birds with her cat, Dinah ("She is such a dear quiet thing . . . and she is such a nice soft thing to nurse – and she's such a capital one for catching mice – oh, I beg your pardon!" – AW 40–41); and, though the Queen cries "Off with his/her/their head(s)!" repeatedly, the Gryphon reveals "Its all her fancy, that: they never executes nobody, you know" (AW 123). But in Švankmajer's adaptation, the violent and lethal subtexts lurking below the comic surface of Carroll's text burst through the film's surfaces: loaves of bread sprout nails, live beetles explode from cans of "sardines," and bird skulls hatch from eggs – death and decay from places of birth. Švankmajer's verbal-to-visual model of adaptation leads him to replace Carroll's verbal banter with physical menace and violence. Instead of ordering Alice about and contradicting her, Švankmajer's creatures attack Alice physically. The Mouse cooks a meal on her head, drives a stake into her skull, and starts a fire in her hair. The White Rabbit throws plates and kitchenware at her, slams her hand in a door, tries to saw her arm off, and threatens to cut off her head with a huge pair of scissors. Like the banter of the book, the film's violence is retaliatory. Alice smirks when she sees the Mouse caught in a trap and echoes the violence of the White Rabbit against her, flinging blocks from his house at him, slamming his hand in a door, knocking him off a ladder from a second-story window, and threatening to decapitate him with the same pair of scissors.

But these more physically menacing transpositions leave little space for laughter, replacing verbal impossibilities and absurdities with physical threats and bodily horror. Švankmajer perceives that, in his *Alice*, "Children's games with imagery and infantile dreams gain an 'objectively' real dimension which freezes the patronizing smile on the lips of all those who consider themselves too grown-up and wise."[37] But his verbal-to-visual translation not only freezes patronizing smiles, it kills Carrollian laughter and audience release and relief. For Švankmajer, humor is a "weapon," not an acknowledgment of absurdity.[38] Švankmajer's *Alice* is an endless gasp of inhalation without exhalation in laughter. If his film refuses comedy (except perhaps for the uneasy laughter of squirming discomfort, leagues away from the exuberant glee accompanying Carroll's jokes), his relentless animation precludes even the cathartic relief offered by tragedy – the relief of physical death. Nothing is allowed to die in his film, no matter how many injuries and dismemberments it sustains.[39] Two sock-caterpillars crushed by Alice are blown up and reanimated in a grim parody of CPR; decapitated Jacks continue fencing without any reduction of vivacity or aggression; a beheaded March Hare and Mad Hatter calmly grope for, pick up, and don each other's heads and continue their card game as before. The film thus unfolds as a horrific, endless night of the living animated dead, leaving the audience blinking, its alternately shuttered and open eyes trying to accommodate to the lens of the camera-shuttered animation.

Nor does Švankmajer's filmic nightmare allow release in waking, as Carroll's *Alice* books do. At its conclusion, Alice appears to waken where she appeared to fall asleep. All the animated objects are once again still – only the live Alice moves. The pieces that assembled to form grotesque creatures – bones, glass eyes, toys, clothing, and food – are disassembled, as before. But the White Rabbit who began the animation of the taxidermied dead remains missing from his case. When Alice sees this, she seizes the scissors and says vehemently, "I think I'll cut *his* head off," positioning herself at a point of vengeful continuation of the dream rather than of innocent or relieved awakening. The dream has not ended; it is simply ready to reinaugurate *da capo* with intensified violence, its original sense of curiosity, wonder, and adventure entirely dissipated. This is a far cry from Carroll's sentimental dream frames and the even more sentimental poetry with which he frames both *Alice* books. Such effects, however, do not derive purely or simply from filmmaker philosophy, but from the structural verbal-to-visual analogical model of adaptation, which, while it forges many dynamic connections between book and film, also forces divergences between them. These limitations are not inherent to all adaptations – only those operating under a model that derives from erroneous assumptions that make books words and films images and adaptation a matter of finding visual equivalents for verbal expression.

Adaptation and Psychoanalytic Analogy

Given the extensive and frequent connections of film and dream, the visual-to-verbal translation involved in Freudian dream interpretation, and the central role of Lacanian psychoanalysis in recent academic film criticism, it is surprising that no psychoanalytic critic has yet proposed a theory of adaptation.[40] Certain psychoanalytic tenets – particularly developmental divisions into scopic and verbal stages – seem ready-made for interdisciplinary dogmas that make novels "words" and films "images." Such tenets might fuel theories that regard film viewing as more developmentally regressive than reading, harking back to the visual preoccupations of infancy and early childhood, to eye gazing at the mother's breast and to the mirror stage of development. These tenets might well support associations of books and reading with Oedipal and post-Oedipal stages of development, when the law of the father and of language intrude on, separate, and disrupt the visual engagements of infant and (m)other. A psychoanalytic theory of literary film adaptation would, then, likely support beliefs that films reduce or regress novels in adaptation. Adaptation might represent both a desire to regress from a post-Oedipal stage of development to a pre-Oedipal stage and a desire to see language and the law of the father regressed and subjected to the scopic maternal realm (and the *seeing* of it would heighten the scopic triumph). Such a psychoanalytic theory of adaption would support recent poststructuralist, cultural studies, and feminist approaches that figure canonical literature as a patriarchal structure to be deconstructed, overthrown, or subverted by the very things (low culture, the feminine, and so forth) it represses and subjugates. Under such models, formalist complaints that films "reduce," "violate," or "betray" a book would express desires that films should and must do these things to books.

Such theories, however, would do little to redress the division of novels and films into word and image camps or the privileging of words as more representationally mature than images. Freud presented dream images as deceptive manifest content whose deeper, truer latent content can only be accessed through talk therapy; Lacan referred to latent content as "the words of the soul," again configuring the deepest psychic structures in terms of language.[41] These assumptions have fed and been fed by cultural beliefs that words are more complex, deeper, truer modes of representation than images, which are, by contrast, seen as primitive, superficial, and deceptive.

Psychoanalytic theories that make film viewing a more regressive psychological process than book reading also feed critical favorings of word over image, particularly perceptions that film viewing paradoxically fosters both infantile passivity and libidinal violence. On 9 May 2001, Judge Martin Sheehan of Covington, Kentucky's Kenton District Court ordered four teenagers to read and write book reports on 12 literary classics over a six-month period as punishment for the "incredibly dangerous" stunt of jumping over a moving car – a stunt allegedly inspired by a television show. The boys were forbidden to watch any television other than the nightly news for six months. Failure to comply with these terms, the judge warned, could result in prosecution on felony charges of wanton endangerment, punishable in adult court by up to five years in prison.[42] The judge's decision reflects wider cultural beliefs that viewing television is socially dangerous and that reading literary classics is restorative of normative social behavior. Such a view is not limited to the Anglo-American West. For years, communist authorities forbade Švankmajer to make films; subsequently, he was allowed only to film adaptations of literary classics, the clear implication being that such work would prove less subversive. Such cultural proclivities do not differ essentially from psychoanalytic clinical methods that press patients from visual to verbal expression in order to heal psychological disturbances and effect a more socially acceptable integration of libidinal drives. (We are all too prone to forget that similar claims about the dangers and corruptions of novel reading ran rife in the eighteenth and nineteenth centuries.)

These preliminary comments by no means substitute for a more rigorous and detailed psychoanalytic theory of adaptation. This is not, however, the purpose of this chapter. My concern here is to probe how psychoanalytic concepts of analogy may contribute to resolving the word and image divide and the form and content union that have so troubled novel and film studies.

"I Don't Like Belonging to Another Person's Dream":
Alice in Latentland

Although no academic psychoanalytic theory of adaptation has yet been formulated, Švankmajer has applied psychoanalytic concepts of latent content and of analogy to his aesthetics of adaptation. At the beginning of his *Alice*, Alice cautions the audience, "You must close your eyes, otherwise you won't see *anything*" (her vocal emphasis). Under a straightforward verbal-to-visual model of adaptation, such a caution is baffling, for visual analogies must be seen and not heard. Švankmajer's psychoanalytic concepts of analogy, however, serve to clarify the admonition. Despite his commitment to a verbal-to-visual model of adaptation, Švankmajer rejects conventional and literal analogies aiming at direct semantic identity in favor of less apparent psychoanalytic analogy:

> Our rationalistic civilisation is founded on the conceptual principle of identity. [By contrast] analogy is natural to primitive cultures and, of course, to young children, because by means of analogy they broaden the horizons of their knowledge.... By means of analogy a child adds other objects and things that resemble each other in some aspect of their existence to what it knows (and can name).... Such understanding does not, of course, disappear with the rationalism of older age, it is only suppressed into the unconscious from whence it continues to function by means of symbols or poetic images.[43]

For Švankmajer, the process of interpretation is an individual one predicated on analogical associations: "The audience may decipher the latent content of the imaginative work only by means of his [sic] own associations, analogies anchored in his own mental morphology."[44]

Adaptation under psychoanalytic theories of manifest and latent content is a process of encoding and mystification rather than of visualizing or objectifying verbally referenced objects. One of the reasons why Švankmajer's *Alice* does not fall into the crude visual symbolism of which Virginia Woolf complained is that his visual analogies are not transparent, literal, dictionary equivalents of Carroll's words, but rather analogies predicated on psychoanalytic theories of manifest and latent content. In his *Interpretation of Dreams* (1900), Freud defines latent content as the condensation and displacement of unconscious drives by the dreaming subject, who encodes them as cryptic dream images, narratives, and words. A broken cup is not necessarily jealousy, even though culturally and conventionally the cup symbolizes truth and love, and a broken cup, the violation of that truth and love. Under psychoanalytic analogies, a broken cup can represent loss of virginity, fertility, or potency, loss of control, domestic discord, divorce, relational rupture, schizoid tendencies, and a host of more privatized meanings. All of these bear a tangential, associative, condensed, or displaced relation to the symbolism of the cup.

Concepts of manifest and latent content not only complicate visual and verbal analogies, they also confuse conventional concepts of form and content. Although both manifest and latent content are referenced as "content," manifest content lies closer to concepts of form, to a signifier connected to and distanced from a ghosted latent content or signified. Švankmajer connects manifest and latent content to older ideas of content as spirit in his psychic theory of adaptation – "I believe in the spiritual affinity of my Alice with Carroll's Alice"[45] – and in his psychospiritual theory of animation: "I can characterize animation shortly as magic . . . I'm not trying to just make inanimate objects alive . . . I try to make objects alive in the real sense of the word . . . In that sense you can compare an animator to a shaman."[46] For this reason, Švankmajer objects strenuously "to computer [and drawn] animation . . . because the objects are created artificially [they] have no content or soul as new objects."[47] The soul or content of his animated objects, however, is a psychological rather than a mystical one:

> People were touching the objects and things [I use in my films] in certain situations in life, while experiencing various tensions or moods and they have deposited their own feelings and emotions in them through their touch. The more an object has been touched, the richer its content. I have always tried in my films to "excavate" this content from objects, to listen to them, and then illustrate their story.

Here, the collector's passion for possessing objects (to which Švankmajer confesses) yields to a spirit possession of those objects through film animation. Švankmajer's inanimate objects carry within themselves the psyches of animate beings, which possess (in the spiritual sense of the term) the objects they have possessed (owned). But this latent content does not require talk therapy in order to manifest. Rather, it reveals itself in analogical, wordless language: "In my opinion, this should be the purpose of any animation: to let objects speak for themselves. This creates a meaningful relationship between man and things, founded on a dialogue."[48] The dialogue here is not a literal but an analogical one.

   Although earlier I represented the ending of Švankmajer's *Alice* as a refusal to awaken, more accurately, it represents a partial awakening, one that fuses dream and waking. At the end of *Through the Looking Glass*, Carroll asks, "Life, what is it but a dream?" Švankmajer inverts the syntax looking glass fashion when he answers, "Dream is life, which added to the rest of our life creates that which we call human existence. Dreams gradually merge into our waking and it is impossible to say where one begins and the other ends."[49] At the end of his film, Alice awakens where she fell asleep. All is as before, except for the White Rabbit. The dream has transformed waking reality, so that it cannot return to what it was before Alice fell asleep. Švankmajer's refusal to allow a full awakening here expresses his commitment to surrealism, where waking reality and dreaming unreality combine to create surreality, where the imaginary is real and the real imaginary. Waking for Švankmajer is thus not a didactic verbal decoding of dream images, but rather a synthesis of waking and dreaming, in which each carries the other as its inherent antithesis. In his refusal to awaken from dream or to provide actual words for his "speaking" objects, Švankmajer departs from traditional psychoanalytic approaches to manifest and latent content, in that his does not require either a waking state or translation into verbal language.

Importantly for the deadlocks of the novel/film debate, psychoanalytic concepts of analogy suggest that words and images are indeed translatable, but not at the level of conventional semantics and dictionary definitions. This is why viewers must close their eyes to "see": they must close their eyes not only in an approximation of dreaming, but also in an approximation of the therapeutic process that looks past the visible manifest content to the invisible latent content. In these psychoanalytic tenets, where visual-to-verbal translation complicates connections between form and content, the gaps between the novel and film debate's two problematic dogmas begin to close. Surrealism's concept of inherent otherness (the waking inhering in the dreaming, the latent in the manifest content) and the cognitive and semiotic excesses such a concept raises pave the way to the final analogical model of this chapter, one that moves a step closer toward resolving the novel/film debate's word/image and form/content dilemmas.

Adaptation and Looking Glass Analogies

How oft our slowly-growing works impart
While images reflect from art to art.
Alexander Pope, Epistle to [Painter] George Jervas, 1716

In Carroll's *Through the Looking Glass*, there is some confusion as to who is doing the dreaming. Tweedle Dee and Dum startle Alice when they insist she is a character in the Red King's dream: "If he wakes up, you'd be nowhere . . . you'd go out – bang! – just like a candle" (LG 244). Alice had assumed that she was the one dreaming. Upon waking, this is the question that most perplexes her: "let's consider who it was that dreamed it all . . . it *must* have been either me or the Red King. He was part of my dream, of course – but then I was part of his dream too!" (LG 346, original emphasis). If Alice is in the Red King's dream and he in hers, their reciprocal dreaming functions like two facing looking glasses, in which each is contained by the other, constructing a mutual containment that refracts into countless reflected containments: Alice dreaming of the Red King dreaming of Alice dreaming of the Red King dreaming of Alice dreaming of the Red King – and so on, into infinity. The endlessly inverting mutual containment of facing mirrors epitomizes the blend of opposition and inherence propounded by looking glass interart analogies.

Reciprocal looking glass analogies have for centuries fostered the sister arts tradition, for their rhetorical mirroring creates an effect of family resemblance. Chapter 1 cited Sir Richard Blakemore's extended analogy of painting and poetry: "The painter is a poet to the eye, and a poet a painter to the ear. One gives us pleasure by silent eloquence, the other by vocal imagery."[50] This analogy sets up reciprocal looking glass effects in several ways. First, grammar and sentence structure mirror each other. But they do not express an identical resemblance. As in a looking glass, which seems to present an exact reflection but in fact reverses left and right fields of vision, so too, in this looking glass analogy, grammatical structure and sequence invert left and right fields. Artists exchange subject and nominative predicate positions, and words that describe one art primarily and literally describe the other secondarily and figuratively. They do this reciprocally, however, rather than hierarchically: each is the secondary and figurative modifier of the other. Arts and artists also interchange primary and secondary bodily senses: the painter retains the actual eye and the poet keeps the literal ear, but the analogy gives the painter a figurative power of speech and the poet a figurative power of imaging. These figures are more than rhetorical ornaments: they point to a cognitive process in which the painter's images arouse linguistic processes in the viewer and the poet's words evoke mental images in the auditor. Though a painting lacks actual words, it evokes verbalizing and narrative effects in cognition so that it seems to possess a silent eloquence. Though a poem lacks illustrations, its words arouse mental images, so that it seems to possess vocal powers of painting.

Ellen J. Esrock has written extensively on mental imaging as reader response.[51] This discussion attends to the other side of the reciprocal interart analogy, addressing mental verbalizing as viewer response. The painter's power of speech, directed to the eye rather than the ear, is oxymoronically "silent" and "eloquent," while the poet splashes the ear with the lines, shadings, and colors of "vocal imagery." The painter's speech is carried mutely through the eyes to the inner ear, while the poet's images are borne blindly through the ears to the inner eye. In this and other analogies like it, verbal and visual signs interweave in cognition, each producing the other as a secondary cognitive effect. Indeed, one of the main arguments for eliminating novel illustrations has been that the words evoke their own images and that illustrations present rivals to those images. Similarly, as we have seen, a central argument against words in film complains of their competition with the "language" of film images.[52]

As Blakemore's analogy so clearly illustrates, verbal/visual looking glass analogies are predicated on the reciprocal power of words to evoke mental images and of pictures to evoke verbal figures in cognition. In Disney's *Alice in Wonderland*, Alice hears flowers speaking, but counters her perception: "That's nonsense: flowers can't talk." A flower promptly rejoins: "But of course we can talk." Critics have paid far more attention to words that picture than to pictures that "talk." As the subsequent case study shows, Wonderland flowers not only sp(r)out dialogue, but their pictorial lines also "speak," quite apart from their voiced words, in filmic figures. Finding terminology to refer to the verbal effects aroused by pictures proves highly problematic since so few scholars have discussed this side of the looking glass and since most terms have been conscripted to describe verbal pictorial effects. Language monopolizes "pictorial words," "verbal pictures," "figures of speech," and "verbal figures." One counterpart to "mental images" is "mental words," but the phrase conjures internal monologues more than the verbalizing effects raised by pictures, and once again carries one confusingly back to literary territory. Thus I have chosen "mental verbalization" and "mental verbalizing" to signal the quasi-linguistic cognitive effects aroused by pictures.

Though poetry and painting have monopolized interart discourse, reciprocal looking glass analogies also appear in discussions of novel illustration and in novel and film discourse. Aubrey Beardsley wrote in 1894 of "story painters and picture writers," a terse reciprocal analogy that accords book illustrators narrative functions and prose writers pictorial ones.[53] Again, the analogy inverts left and right fields of grammar and syntax; again, painters and writers lend their primary aesthetic functions to each other in a secondary sense. The predominance of nouns in this reciprocal analogy reflects nineteenth-century convictions that the arts bear a literal and essential relationship to one another.

Reciprocal interart analogies continue in twentieth- and twenty-first-century discussions of novels and films. In 2000, for example, Milena Michalski wrote of "Cinematic Literature and Literary Cinema."[54] In this analogy, syntax and sequencing invert as before, but the parts of speech differ from previous examples, indicating differing underlying concepts. Gone is Beardsley's redoubled noun reciprocity gesturing to a substantial shared essence. This analogy makes each art the modifying adjective of the other, a grammatical construction that aptly highlights the dynamics outlined in this book, in which critical rhetoric and artistic practice situate novels and films as wrangling modifiers of each other, wresting cultural and representational power from each other and defining themselves against each other.

However, reciprocal interart analogies differ from the usurping and rivalrous analogies addressed in the middle chapters of this book, for their reciprocity creates a mutual and inherent rather than a hierarchical and averse dynamic. The reciprocity of looking glass analogies ensures an endless series of inversions and reversals rather than a one-sided usurpation. As with the many configurations of form and content outlined in Chapter 5, these topsy-turvy dynamics are most clearly manifested in adaptation practice and in discussions of adaptation.

Reciprocal looking glass analogies do not eradicate categorical differentiation. Rather, they make the otherness of categorical differentiation (word/image, visual/verbal, eye/ear, etc.) an integral part of aesthetic and semiotic identity. Looking glass analogies maintain oppositions between the arts, but integrate these oppositions as an inextricable secondary identity. Two arts contain and invert the otherness of each other reciprocally, inversely, and inherently, rather than being divided from the other by their otherness. Thus difference is as much a part of identity as resemblance. Moreover, it is an identical difference, for each art differs from and inheres in the other *in exactly the same way*. It is the same difference. In looking glass analogies, each art takes exactly the same grammatical, conceptual, and sensory position in the rhetoric of the other.

The opening of Disney's 1951 *Alice in Wonderland* introduces a rhetoric in which inherent difference functions as identity. Alice declares: "In my world, everything would be nonsense. Nothing would be what it is, because everything would be what it isn't. And contrariwise, what it is, it wouldn't be. And what it wouldn't be, it would."[55] When nothing is itself and everything is what it is not, negation doubles as identity. Stated separately, the two phrases conform to deconstructive ideas of difference/*différance*; juxtaposed, they engage in looking glass rhetoric, becoming mirrored inversions of each other that make negation a substantial affirmation rather than a vaporous absence. In "Nothing (would be what it) is" and "Everything (would be what it) isn't," the middle words remain identical: only left and right fields invert, as in a mirror reflection. And, in keeping with conventional grammatical and mathematical rules that make two negatives a positive, the two mirrored antonyms form a synonym, turning negation into affirmation and difference/*différance* into inherent identity. Reciprocal looking glass analogies differ further from deconstructive *différance* in that their definitive otherness is inherent, reciprocal, and contingent rather than random, associative, jettisoned, and arbitrary. As in negative and positive views of a photograph, if one expresses a lack in the other, it is a lack that the other has already filled, even as it exposes it. Any absence, therefore, is always already inverse inherent presence.

Carroll's and Tenniel's Mock Turtle illustrates the looking glass analogy's difference from *différance*. The Queen of Hearts asks Alice:

> "Have you seen the Mock Turtle yet?"
> "No," said Alice, "I don't even know what a Mock Turtle is."
> "It's the thing Mock Turtle Soup is made from," said the Queen.
> "I never saw one, or heard of one," said Alice.
> "Come on, then," said the Queen, "and he shall tell you his history."
> (AW 122)

The Mock Turtle can certainly be marched into deconstructive readings. As soup ingredient, he should be all calf (or at least those parts of calf used to make mock turtle soup). Yet as soup title, he should be all turtle, even though the species of turtle to which he is assigned, "Mock," negates him as "not real" turtle.[56] If the title denies calf and the soup denies turtle, the two terms not only cancel each other out, but also evaporate any sense of a viable signified. What remains is only the linguistic trace of another recipe for real turtle soup.

The Mock Turtle seeks to compensate for his economic and linguistic fallings off in a nostalgic song celebrating former times when he was "a real Turtle" (AW 124). He does so by expanding linguistic sounds, as though to compensate for its referential lack. In "Beautiful Soup," he extends each sound, multiplying and capitalizing graphemes, adding heavy exclamatory seasoning and expansive punctuation to soup up the non-ingredient words – the words of a nonentity's nostalgia for nonexistent times:

> Beau-ootiful Soo-oop!
> Beau-ootiful Soo-oop!
> Soo-oop of the e-e-evening,
>   Beautiful, beauti-FUL SOUP! (AW 138)

Further off still lies another lost and nonexistent origin: the real turtle preceding the mock turtle. This musical nostalgia over a lost origin and name is utterly fraudulent. Real turtles can appear in other contexts, while the sole purpose of a mock turtle is to appear in soup. And, at the moment the mock turtle makes such an appearance, it is substantiated as calf, as turtle substitute, therefore not turtle. Indeed, when Alice awakens at the end of *Wonderland*, the sobs of the mock turtle turn out to be nothing but the lowing of cattle.

Beyond this mode of negation, throughout his song, the Mock Turtle is perversely in love with his own death, with his conversion into soup. But it is a death that doubles as lost origin, for it is only in conversion to soup that he can become Mock Turtle. At that moment, however, he is both revealed as sham and ceases to exist – he dies and all traces of him are consumed.

When one juxtaposes Carroll's verbal Mock Turtle to Tenniel's illustrations of him, however, another reading emerges, one that demonstrates how visual – verbal looking glass analogies differ from deconstructive *différance*. Carroll provides no verbal description of the Mock Turtle, but Tenniel's illustrations of him undo his verbal emaciation, creating a plump, cacophonous semiotic surplus (Figure 34, AW 125). Rather

34. John Tenniel: The Mock Turtle from Lewis Carroll's *Alice in Wonderland*, Chapter 9.

than calf and turtle as terms that negate each other, fading from trace to trace until they (nearly) cancel each other out, Tenniel's Mock Turtle is a cluttered hybrid – hooves, shell, tail, ears, and flippers – a both/and rather than a neither/nor figure. The illustrations capture perfectly the *idea* of mock turtle soup: of calf aspiring to turtle and never quite attaining to it; of turtle reduced to calf and never quite admitting it. In this hybrid representation, "Mock Turtle" becomes at once a blatantly admitted, deftly obscured falsehood – one that simultaneously showcases and denies the presence of calf, and that concurrently pretends to and embodies the presence of turtle. In these illustrations of nonce words, neither calf nor turtle, neither nonce words nor pictures cancel each other out. Absence and presence, negation and affirmation coexist in the jointures of linguistic and pictorial representation. In the same way, looking glass analogies turn negation and absence into a surplus presence: poetry and painting, words and images, aural and graphic elements of words, and pictorial and symbolic elements of pictures are both/and figures rather than the either/or of categorical differentiation or the neither/nor or deconstructive *différance*. Like the Mock Turtle, adaptation under looking glass analogies is excess rather than reduction, as the following case studies demonstrate. But first, a few words on figuration are in order.

From Word and Image to Figure and Image

We have seen that interart analogies point to links between figuration and cognition: that the figurative positioning of one art as another or inside another gestures to the process by which one art raises the cognitive effects of another. We have seen too that adaptation purports to realize or literalize interart analogies when it makes poetry or novels into paintings and paintings or illustrations or film images into verbal narrative. Putting the two concepts together, adaptation inverts the primary and secondary cognition of visual and verbal signs. For example, a painting of a poem incarnates the poem's mental images while ghosting the poem's words; a film of a novel reduces the novel's words and realizes its implied images; a novelization of a film turns perceptual and auditory images into verbal signs. In this way, adaptation inverts verbal and visual hierarchies and suggests the incompleteness of both forms of representation.

In navigating between objectivist structural analyses and subjective reader-viewer responses, figuration offers a middle ground. While one can analyze figures somewhat substantially, many figures highlight, even necessitate, special cognitive operations. Figures like literary metaphors and similes frequently require the creation of mental pictorial images in order to process them. Figures like homonymic puns typically require discrimination between their graphic and aural aspects for signification. In film, visual symbols (and other figures I establish later) depend on processes of mental verbalizing or narration for their comprehension. As we will see in the following, cognitive studies have shown that mental images engage both linguistic and perceptual areas of the brain, combining aspects of linguistic cognition, like prior adaptation into parts and properties, with aspects of visual perception, like optical images. The mutual and reciprocal process of verbal and pictorial figuration moves us toward a resolution of the novel/film debate's categorical and analogical tensions, of its word and image impasses, and of its form and content binds.

If "word" and "image" fail to adequately explicate relations between novels and films, "figure" and "image" prove more elucidating. The terms permeate literary and filmic discourse independently of each other: we read of figures of speech, screen figures, literary images, celluloid images, star images, and more. Frequently, "figure" and "image" carry both pictorial and symbolic resonances. According to the *OED*, a "figure" is the form of anything as determined by its outline: this would be the outline of a drawing in the visual arts and the shape of a letter in the verbal arts.[57] Cognitive psychologist Nicholas Wade observes that

> the written form of language and graphics have more in common than is often supposed. That is, the processes in the visual system that recognize the objects in the environment and pictorial images operate in a similar manner to recognize the diverse written symbols we produce ... Written words form graphical images that are rarely acknowledged as such because their significance is defined almost entirely at the mental image level.[58]

The phonological basis of Western languages accentuates graphic sublimation, as readers convert graphemes into phonemes and then into mental images – mental images that generally bear no physical resemblance to the original graphemes.

Having moved from earlier linguistic forms combining phonological with pictorial symbols, Western language now depends on figurative expression, as well as other devices like ekphrasis, to infuse the symbolic with the pictorial. A "figure of speech" points to the graphic visualizations a word or phrase raises; the *OED* definition of an "image" as "a vivid or graphic description in speech or writing" gestures to the mental pictures language conjures. Less prominent in the discourse or dictionary, but prevalent in aesthetic practice, certain pictures inspire verbal thinking and, I argue in the following, do so in ways inversely comparable to words that inspire mental images.

Figuration not only bridges word and image divides, it also opens a space between form and content bonds. Visualizing a figure of speech pulls a reader/auditor out of binary semantic matchings of signifiers and signifieds into a third space that is neither signifier nor signified at the same time that it is both.[59] From one angle, mental pictures and mental verbalizations are the signifieds of signifiers: the word evokes the mental picture as referent; the picture evokes the mental verbalization as referent. Yet mental pictures and mental verbalizations are also signifiers, pointing to signifieds beyond themselves. They are thus both secondary signifiers and preliminary signifieds.

Yet despite the prevalence of the terms "figure" and "image" in both literary and film arts and their promise for resolving central dilemmas of interdisciplinary discourse, they have inspired few interdisciplinary musings. The omission is by no means a matter of oversight, for nowhere are critics more agreed than in a conviction that film is incapable of effective figurative expression.[60] Roy Paul Madsen is typical: "The novel, moreover, makes use of such literary devices as tropes, which have no counterpart in the experience of film."[61] Christian Metz insists that "Pure metaphor, with no metonymic complications, occurs only with extra-diegetic images or sounds . . . it is a highly marked operation, actually quite rare even in avant-garde productions."[62] By contrast, literary critics, regardless of their theoretical position, have been unanimous in proclaiming figurative language, particularly metaphor, central to literary studies and, in some cases, definitive of language itself. Over the twentieth century, metaphor evolved from a term found primarily in dusty grammar and rhetoric books to become a primary indicator of literary merit, a hallmark of "high" literature and "fine" writing, and a tool through which critics unpack the hidden meanings of a text (whether New Critical ironies, psychoanalytic latent content, hidden political agendas, or deconstructive unravelings). In some versions of deconstruction, metaphor becomes the epitome of language itself, and in Lacanian theory it is synonymous with deep psychological structures.[63] Metaphor joins analogy in cognitive linguistics as a mental principle: "metaphor is more than a literary device. It is fundamental to our capacity to give meaning to and to deal with the complex world around us. Metaphor gives us new insights into one idea or concept by comparing it with another."[64] In "Why Many Concepts are Metaphorical," Raymond W. Gibbs, Jr., states that "metaphor is not merely a figure of speech, but is a specific mental mapping that influences a good deal of how people think, reason, and imagine everyday life."[65] Pamela Fry cites

M. Friquenon's aphoristic assessment: "To know is to use metaphor."[66] Thus to deny metaphor and, more broadly, figuration to film is more than a mere formal or semiotic distinction: it is to deny film access to vital aspects of human cognition.

It should come as no surprise at this point to learn that such categorical caveats find their recent roots in eighteenth-century poetry and painting discourse. Hildebrand Jacobs was one of many to argue that "there are almost innumerable Images in Poetry, which Painting is not capable of forming, and which are often the greatest Ornaments in Poetry."[67] It is striking, however, that studies of symbol, metaphor, and other figures abound in discussions of painting on its own. Juxtaposed to poetry, however, painting is suddenly incapable of all these effects, or else does them badly and crudely by comparison to poetry. In the same way, film studies abound in essays on visual symbolism, but such assertions shrink or vanish entirely in comparisons of literature and film.

The literary camp is not solely responsible for the imbalance. Film scholars and filmmakers have been reluctant to claim figuration for film largely because of their celebration of film's naturalist–realist aspects and their use of realism to trump verbal representation. Metz is both typical and eloquent on the subject:

> In the cinema, aesthetic expressiveness is grafted onto natural expressiveness – that of the landscape or face the film shows. In the verbal arts, it is grafted, not onto any genuine prior expressiveness, but onto a conventional *signification* – that of language – which is generally inexpressive . . . . Literature – especially poetry – is a so much more improbable art! How can that insane craft ever succeed?[68]

Filmmakers regard verbal imagery as unnecessary beside film's perceptual images and scorn it as a type of braille for visually impaired readers. Film, they argue, restores sight to narrative so that verbal imagery can be discarded. Terry Ramsaye writes: "Allusion, simile and metaphor can succeed in the printed and spoken word as an aid to the dim pictorial quality of the word expression. The motion picture has no use for them because it itself is the event. It is too specific and final to accept such aids."[69] Metz concurs and expands: "The cinema is the 'phenomenological' art *par excellence*, the signifier is coextensive with the whole of the significate, the spectacle is its own signification, thus short-circuiting the sign itself."[70]

N. Roy Clifton, the lone champion of filmic figuration, has done little to remedy these impressions largely because he seeks to establish filmic tropes under literary definitions. Clifton's failure to convince other critics amidst many compelling examples and painstaking research suggests the impossibility of establishing film figuration according to literary templates. Metz observes:

> you do not find the same figures in film, but rather the same distinctions; to look for the same figures, in such a completely different language, would be a hopeless task as well as a completely artificial attempt to apply the rules of one system to another; but the underlying principles remain, since their scope is by definition general, and it is these which will eventually enable us to find our way around filmic figurations.

Subsequently, however, Metz's psychoanalytic stance led him to subjugate filmic figures to linguistic structures: "will it even be possible to find completely isolable metaphors and metonymies in the cinema? Should we not rather try to identify the textual traces of the metaphorical process and the metonymic process?"[71]

Looking glass analogies, however, point to a theory of filmic figuration bearing "textual traces" – a theory not based in literary figuration, but rather bearing an inverse relationship to it. In 1957, George Bluestone proposed a widely adopted, oft-cited distinction between novels and films: "Between the *percept* of the visual image and the *concept* of the mental image lies the root difference between the two media."[72] This distinction replaces Blakemore's sensory eye/ear distinction in verbal and visual arts with a more philosophically loaded, hierarchical eye/mind dichotomy that favors words as mental sense over images as bodily sense. The dichotomy by no means originates with Bluestone. While Blakemore assessed in 1713 that "The painter is a poet to the eye, and the poet is a painter to the ear," John Dryden declared in 1745 that "The chief end of Painting is to please the Eyes; and 'tis one great End of Poetry to please the Mind."[73] The rise of a pictorial aesthetic for verbal as well as visual and theatrical arts, as well as the far greater size and sophistication of the human visual cortex over the auditory cortex means that the ear held a far-off second place. Acutely aware of this, William Wordsworth, often proclaimed the Romantic poet of the eye, complained bitterly in 1846 of book illustration: "Must eyes be all in all, the tongue and ear/Nothing?"[74] An eye/mind dichotomy accords words a resounding triumph over images as mind over sensation, spirit over flesh, divine reason over animal instinct – depending on the operative terminology and philosophy.

Dryden's eye/mind dichotomy of poetry and painting differs little from Virginia Woolf's assessment of novels and films. Discussing a 1926 film adaptation of *Anna Karenina*, she objected that "the alliance [of novel and film] is unnatural . . . the brain knows [the literary] Anna almost entirely by the inside of her mind ... all the emphasis is laid by the cinema on her teeth, her pearls, her velvet."[75] The novel claims the brain and human psychology for words and leaves film the eyes, the body, and the inanimate material world. (It is perplexing, unless one understands the skewing influence of interart rivalry, that Woolf should claim such an alliance between mind and eye "unnatural," when elsewhere she celebrates "great writers" who "make us exclaim that now at last writers have begun to use their eyes.")[76] Closely related to this critique, in the 1940s, F. Scott Fitzgerald echoed poetry/painting critic James Harris's 1744 assertion that mind and psyche find their best expression in verbal expression divorced from pictorial signs:

> I saw that the novel, which at my maturity was the strongest and supplest medium for conveying thought and emotion from one human being to another, was becoming subordinate to a mechanical and communal art that, whether in the hands of Hollywood merchants or Russian ideal-ists, was capable of reflecting only the tritest thought, the most obvious emotion.[77]

Despite occasional rebuttals to the eye/brain dichotomy, (Jonathan Trapp in the eighteenth century and Hugh Kenner in the twentieth, for example), it remains entrenched in novel and film discourse.[78]

Reserving the mind and emotions for words not only places images on a lower hierarchical rung philosophically, it also limits them to one particular sense, while words are given access to all the senses through the brain. In consequence, image arts are often presented as sensorially disabled by comparison to words, which are represented as sensorially enhanced. Indeed, the most frequently cited poetry/painting analogy by Simonides of Ceos – "Painting is mute poetry and poetry is a speaking picture" – disables painting as mute while lending poetry additional sensory powers. Similar hobblings of visual art pervade interdisciplinary discourse. Richard D. Altick concludes that the decline of Victorian literary painting at the end of the nineteenth century was due to the "inherent disability of the visual medium." Paintings, he maintains,

> could deal only with surfaces: with appearances, situations, and actions (but with only an instant of an action). They could not fathom or rep-resent the true depth and complexity of a literary work or even of a moment from that work ... They could not represent the special effects of language, formal structure, developing characterization, ongoing nar-rative. They could not reproduce dialogue. They could not represent ideas, except those that could be simplified and conveyed by a single image or set of images.[79]

In the same vein, despite film's multiple channels of representation – photography, music, text, textiles, architecture, performing arts, sound, lighting, special effects, computer graphics, experimental additions of touch and smell, and more – the list of things film "cannot do" compared with the novel flourishes in interdisciplinary criticism.[80] A partial list of film's impairments includes pronouncements that "Film necessarily leaves behind tropes, dreams, memories,"[81] lacks a thought process mechanism,[82] cannot effectively convey first-person point of view,[83] has no tense other than the present tense,[84] and cannot convey abstractions.[85] While newer theories of film counter some of these claims, they continue to be advanced whenever the novel and the film are juxtaposed.

I want to modify Bluestone's famous maxim to argue that between the concept evoked by the picture and the percept evoked by the word lies a root connection between novels and films and, more generally, between visual and verbal expression. I am not returning to a simple designation of novels as words and films as images here, but rather locating ways to navigate between the visual and the verbal within as well as between signs and arts, down to the visual–aural and signifier–signified splits running within signs themselves. Under looking glass principles, if a verbal metaphor raises mental imaging, then conversely and inversely, a pictorial metaphor raises mental verbalizing. Returning to *OED* definitions of figure and image, we see not only terms like "a figure of speech," which infuse verbal symbols with mental images, but also terms like "public image" and "figure-head," which infuse perceptual images with symbolic significance.

These processes find support from cognitive linguistics and neuropsychology, which have largely eroded the categorical differences between mental and perceptual images prevalent in Bluestone's day. Refuting earlier categorical assignations of verbal cognition to the left brain and spatial cognition to the right brain, current neuropsychological studies find "no sharp border between the anatomical locations of verbal and visual knowledge."[86] Mental imaging, once thought to be a purely visual operation, has been shown to engage both linguistic and perceptual areas of the brain. Neuropsychologist Robert G. Kunzendorf has demonstrated that "retinal structures are centrifugally innervated during visually imaged sensations."[87] J. T. E. Richardson has shown that the most crucial parts of the brain for mental imaging are the occipital lobes and an area close to the posterior language centers of the left hemisphere.[88] The "mind's eye," another study affirms, is "a processor that interprets quasi-pictorial representations . . . in terms of conceptual categories" akin to those used in linguistic cognition "such as fleetness, degradation and prior adaptation into parts and properties."[89] From the other side of the looking glass, Edward Branigan cites studies demonstrating that visual perception combines sensory input with higher cognition, including mental operations that draw on linguistic areas of the brain. Human perception is a "top-down" cognitive function, in which acquired knowledge and schemas are applied to and shape perception.[90] Indeed, without higher cognitive input, humans would see upside down, with left/right fields reversed, and in only two dimensions, because this is the image our retinas provide.[91]

Verbalizing and visualizing thus prove to be connected rather than opposed cognitive processes. But they are not simply "connected": rather, they inhere looking glass fashion. The cognition of mental images and of perceptual images has been shown to be a directly inverse process: "the [mental] image is first represented as *sensationless qualities* and later represented as *sensory qualities*, whereas the percept is first represented as *sensory qualities* and later represented as *sensationless qualities*."[92] The mental image begins in the central nervous system and travels to the peripheral nervous system; the perceptual image originates in the peripheral nervous system and courses to the central nervous system. A decade before these studies were published, Dudley Andrew expressed just such an idea in his astutely intuitive contrast of how we read books and view films:

> Generally film is found to work from perception towards signification, from external facts to interior motivations and consequences, from the givenness of a world to the meaning of a story cut out of that world. Literary fiction works oppositely. It begins with signs (graphemes and words) building to propositions which attempt to develop perception. As a product of human language it naturally treats human motivation and values, seeking to throw them out onto the external world, elaborating a world out of a story.[93]

Reciprocal looking glass analogies, Andrew's hypothesis, and the cognitive studies that bear both out give the reader an eye and the viewer a brain, undoing the entrenched eye/mind dichotomy that has clouded discussions of verbal and visual arts for so long.[94] The two case studies that follow expand on these premises to demonstrate how an inversely inherent looking glass model of literary and filmic figuration provides a bridge between novels and films in adaptation and, by extension, between the verbal and the visual more generally.

"Why Is a Raven (Film) Like a Writing Desk (Novel)?": Alice Through the Looking Glass

Švankmajer believes that "Disney is one of the great liquidators of Western culture. It destroys children's souls."[95] Yet Švankmajer has been likened to Disney, most famously in Milos Forman's equation, "Buñuel + Disney = Švankmajer," which currently emblazons the English language videocassette box for his *Alice*. The formula implies, in aptly Carrollian mathematical form, that the sum of Švankmajer's film is greater than Disney's. Mine is an unpopular thesis – particularly among that overrepresented portion of the academic population that favors countercultural, iconoclastic, avant-garde, non-Anglo-American films and eschews Disney as mainstream, mindless, and machinating – but it is my contention that the Disney *Alice* rather than the Švankmajer *Alice* offers the more conceptually and aesthetically versatile model for literary film adaptation. Rather than substituting visual for verbal expression or placing them in manifest/latent relation to one another, it offers a fluid path between verbal and visual modes and posits each as the content of the other. Rather than displacing Carroll's violation of linguistic laws with Švankmajer's of physical laws, Disney's half-cup of tea, sliced in half yet still miraculously holding tea, encompasses both: it violates both linguistic conventions and physical laws.

Disney's Alice becomes lost in the Tulgey Woods, surrounded, menaced, and then abandoned by strange creatures. Hope revives when a path appears and Alice exults: "A path! Oh, thank goodness! I just knew I'd find one sooner or later." But a moment later, a dog erases the path, leaving Alice stranded on a rectangular remnant going nowhere. Eventually she is rescued by the Cheshire Cat, who opens a door in a tree leading to the royal garden. As he shows her the way out, he quips: "Some go this way, some go that way, but as for me myself personally, I prefer the short cut." I found one way out of novel and film discourse's Tulgey Woods after word and image and form and content "dog-mas" had left me similarly stranded: the shortcut of verbal–visual figuration. Andrew has said: "Figures are . . . more than shortcuts by way of association and substitutes; they have the power to disrupt the relation of context to sign and to reorient not only the discursive event but the system itself."[96] Figuration has potential to reorganize literary and filmic systems in relationship to each other and, beyond that, to reorient word and image and form and content dogmas.

Figurative language has shaped many evolutions in linguistic systems: it can also guide the journey from verbal to visual. In a discussion of the

35. Alice and the Caterpillar, Walt Disney's *Alice in Wonderland,* 1951. © Disney Enterprises, Inc.

figure's role in linguistic evolution, Metz proposes that "the rhetorical tradition should have prepared us to think of figurations as kinds of turning movements, with a fifty-fifty chance, so to speak, of surmounting the barrier of the word; should have taught us to *dissociate the figural from the lexical.*"[97] The Disney filmmakers manage to do just this, charting a continuum from purely verbal figures through hybrid visual–verbal figures to purely visual figures, illustrating the fluid journey from verbal to visual that is possible through figuration (Figure 35).

Disney's Caterpillar scene provides a perfect entry point into this discussion, for it mocks verbal language along graphic–phonetic lines, challenges the ability of words and pictures to represent each other, and tests models of literary film adaptation when it creates a miniature film adaptation of a Carrollian poem. Alice discovers the hookah-smoking Caterpillar exhaling smoke in the shape of alphabetic letters, simultaneously singing and signing "A, E, I, O, U" to a hypnotic Eastern melody. The letters the Caterpillar exhales mock the relationship between graphemes and phonemes. Rather than the conventional order of language apprehension, in which letters precede and symbolize speech sounds, here the mouth shapes and the breath emits phonemes and graphemes simultaneously. As the Caterpillar sings the phoneme "a," the blue smoke he exudes shapes the letter "A," as if phoneme and grapheme inhered in each other and formed naturally from the biological function of breath. But when Alice approaches, their implied inherence turns to rupture and mockery. When the Caterpillar asks Alice, "Who are you?" his respiratory smoke forms the letters: "O – R – U?" In doing away with six of the nine letters that would spell the question, the smoke-speak exposes the arbitrary relationship between phonemes and graphemes, as well as the phonetic redundancy of much written language.

The Caterpillar's mockery of the relationship between graphic and phonetic aspects of letters extends subsequently to a mockery of the relationship between words and illustrative pictures when his smoke-art attempts to illustrate a word. As he scathingly exhales, "I do *not* see" (his vocal emphasis), a smoke rope ties itself into a knot.[98] The Caterpillar has produced a perfect phonetic match, displaying, as Carroll does throughout the *Alice* books, the puns that so confuse semantics and fragment signification. There is no discrepancy between the sounds "n" and "kn" here, but graphemes and signifieds differ considerably. The mockery extends from language to the representational capacities of pictures: how would one illustrate the word "not," unless with another letter, an "X" that would turn it back to linguistic symbol?[99]

The failure of words and pictures to represent reliably and consistently or to represent each other coherently expands to a critique of relations between verbal narration and animated film adaptation when the Caterpillar recites Carroll's "How doth the little crocodile" and illustrates it with a colored smoke animation. The poem goes:

> How doth the little crocodile
> Improve his shining tail,
> And pour the waters of the Nile
> On every golden scale!
>
> How cheerfully he seems to grin,
> How neatly spread his claws,
> And welcome little fishes in
> With gently smiling jaws!   (AW 37)

The accompanying animation conjures a crocodile with a sparkling tail and represents the golden scales as a line of golden musical notes ascending in a scale, rather than as scales on the crocodile's body. This mistranslation by no means derives from necessity – crocodile scales can be drawn – it is rather a choice, one that simultaneously subverts and extends the referents. Eventually, however, the Caterpillar tames his straying smoke-art into a dutiful, mimetic adaptation of the poem: colored smoke-fish swim blithely into smoke-crocodile jaws, helped along by wispy smoke-crocodile claws, the pictures faithfully illustrating, following, and supporting the words of the rhyme. Throughout the recitation, the smoke images dissolve as the sounds fade, their existence dependent on the same breath that produced the words, with little persistence beyond the words.

Much of Carroll's mockery of language occurs through forging ruptures between semantic sense and sensory sense and, within sensory sense, between auditory and visual senses. This tension is most apparent in his homonymic puns. Homonymic puns are particularly elucidating figures through which to probe and connect verbal–visual and form–content issues, for they run along the eye/ear discrepancies used to differentiate verbal and visual arts as well as between words and images more generally, yet they do so inside signs, pitting their phonic against their graphic elements to disrupt signifier–signified bonds. Here eye and ear join to confuse the mind rather than lying in hierarchical subordination to it.

In some cases, the eye acts as arbiter of ear and mind, of visual sense and semantic sense. When the Gnat suggests to Alice that she "might make a joke on . . . 'horse' and 'hoarse'," one must see the spelling to differentiate the two meanings, for they are phonetically identical (LG 222). The eye/ear/mind significatory triad is not limited to homonymic puns. The necessity of "seeing a word done" to understand it extends to dramatic enactments of words, with implications for literary film adaptation. During the trial scene of *Alice's Adventures in Wonderland*,

> . . . one of the guinea-pigs cheered, and was immediately suppressed by the officers of the court. (As that is rather a hard word, I will just explain to you how it was done. They had a large canvas bag, which tied up at the mouth with strings: into this they slipped the guinea-pig, head first, and then sat upon it.)
>
> "I'm glad I've seen that done," thought Alice. "I've so often read in the newspapers, at the end of trials, 'There was some attempt at applause, which was immediately suppressed by the officers of the court,' and I never understood what it meant till now." (AW 147)

Here, seeing is not only believing, it is also understanding, meaning, signification. Beyond the incarnational model of adaptation, which positions dramatization as the realization and completion of the word, here dramatic enactment is essential to understanding the word. Yet Alice's comprehension of the phrase is specific to the point of inaccuracy. For Alice, to "suppress" now means "to put something in a bag and sit on it." Returning to Lamb's complaints about the dramatic performance of literature, here we see that it is simultaneously essential to and reductive of verbal comprehension. Without it, the words make no sense; with it, the words make limited sense.

Through a graded journey from purely verbal through hybrid verbal–visual to purely visual puns, the Disney *Alice* forges a contiguous bridge for adaptation, both in terms of visual–verbal and form-content dynamics. At a purely verbal level, the Disney screenwriters match Carroll's word play with their own. A talking doorknob (the voice of Joseph Kearns) bombards Alice with one witty pun after another ("You did give me quite a turn... One good turn deserves another") and with dizzying word play ("Read the directions and directly you'll be directed in the right direction"). When Disney's Mad Hatter asks Alice, "Why is a raven like a writing desk?" Disney's March Hare cries, "Don't ask her; she's stark ravin' mad!"

Midway between the purely verbal and the purely visual pun lies the hybrid verbal–visual pun, a pun in which the picture *makes* the pun happen, rather than merely illustrating it. Carroll's Mouse's Tale/Tail is one such hybrid pun. The words (the tale) make a picture (the tail) and the picture (the tail) makes the words (the tale) (Figure 36; AW 49). Paradoxically, the hybrid pun moves from fragmentation of sound and sight toward their inherence. In the verbal horse/hoarse pun, a single sound shoots off in two different graphic forms toward two different referents, splitting the binarism of signifier and signified into an uneasy trio. In the pun on the Mouse's Tail/Tale, however, the tail *is* a tale and the tale *is* a tail, pressing the two toward union. The words are the picture and the picture is the words. In a parody of the dogma that makes form and content indivisible, the tail as form is one with the tale as content. However, the tail as form holds the tale as content even as the tale forms the tail, so that one cannot confidently determine which is the form and which is the content in the union. As in facing looking glasses, the tale forms the tail which forms the tail which forms the tale endlessly, turning form and content relations topsy-turvy, *ad infinitum.*

Disney expands on this and on other word and illustration dynamics in the *Alice* books to create mobile audiovisual puns that play between word and image. Tenniel illustrates some of Carroll's word play, like the looking glass insects (LG 226, 228). The Disney film faithfully creates animated versions of Tenniel's Rocking-horse-fly and Bread-and-Butterfly. But it goes beyond merely illustrating verbal word play to create hybrid puns in which a mobile audiovisual representation *makes* the pun happen. The smoke rope that ties itself in a knot makes the not/knot pun happen: the picture pulls the signification from its contextual, conventional, and abstract referent ("not") to an untextual, unconventional, concrete signification ("knot"). Disney's DandeLION and TIGER Lily (hybrids of lion, tiger, and flowers) also represent hybrid puns based on the longstanding visual association of dandelion petals with lion manes and tiger lily petals with tiger skins. Here Disney is doing what Freud claims dreams do and what linguists claim figuration does: restoring pictorial significance to verbal language.

"Fury said to
    a mouse, That
        he met in the
            house, 'Let
                us both go
                to law: I
                    will prose-
                    cute *you.* –
                Come, I'll
                take no de-
            nial: We
        must have
    the trial;
    For really
    this morn-
ing I've
nothing
to do.'
    Said the
        mouse to
            the cur,
                'Such a
                    trial, dear
                        sir, With
                            no jury
                                or judge,
                                would
                                    be wast-
                                    ing our
                                    breath.'
                        'I'll be
                        judge,
                        I'll be
                        jury,'
                    said
                    cun-
                        ning
                        old
                            Fury:
                            'I'll
                        try
                            the
                                whole
                                cause,
                                and
                                con-
                                demn
                            you to
            death'."

36. Lewis Carroll's The Mouse's Tail/Tale from his *Alice in Wonderland*, Chapter 3.

Other hybrid verbal–visual puns in the film are comically nonsensical. The words "half a cup of tea" are pictorially illustrated by a cup of tea sliced in half, rather than the conventional half-full cup; Disney's Cheshire Cat follows his question, "Can you stand on your head?" by standing on top of his disembodied head and dramatizes his assertion, "I'm not all there," by vanishing through a skeletal dismemberment of his stripes.

Since it is a perceptual visual image, the pictorial articulation of a hybrid verbal–visual pun can have a trumping effect on the fainter conceptual mental image associated with the conventional referent. Margaret J. Intons-Peterson, Mark A. McDaniel, and others have demonstrated that perceptual pictures interfere with mental images and tend to override them.[100] Metz too attests that: "The image impresses itself on us, blocking everything that is not itself."[101]

At the far end of Disney's punning journey lie purely visual puns that have blocked out everything not themselves: they do not derive from language at all. Like all puns, they maintain a double articulation, but in this case, both articulations are pictorial ones. One half of a baby oyster shell forms a bonnet for a personified oyster, but it never ceases to be a shell. Plant leaves of all shapes and sizes double as arms, feet, skirts, collars, blouses, screens, seats, pillows, blankets, beds, a bread board, and a boat – yet they remain leaves. These purely visual puns play on the shared lines of two visual images without any need for verbal mediation at all. Cone-shaped flower trumpets, harp-string stamens, unblown dandelion drums, leaf chairs, arm stems, and cobweb hammocks constitute two things at once based on their shapes and uses rather than on their names. There is no verbal pun on flower and trumpet, on stamen and harp-string, on dandelion and drum, on leaf and chair, on arm and stem, or on cobweb and hammock. These puns can, of course, be described by language, as I do here, but they do not depend on language for their manifestation or comprehension, only on shared pictorial lines.

This continuum of figurative expression, of figures and images running across and between verbal and pictorial signs, provides an incremental bridge along which words can transform to images and through which words and images can inhere in each other. More than this, looking glass figures point to a reciprocally transformative model of adaptation, in which the film is not translation or copy, but rather metamorphoses the novel and is, in turn, metamorphosed by it. Adaptation under such a model is neither translation nor interpretation, neither incarnation nor deconstruction: rather it is mutual and reciprocal inverse transformation that nevertheless restores neither to its original place.

Looking glass figuration is by no means limited to puns, but extends to other verbal–visual figures, like metaphor. Scholars have suggested links between metaphor and metamorphosis that prove highly suggestive for this discussion. Cognitive linguists Cathy Dent-Read and Agnes Szokolszky propose that

Metaphor [be] defined as a species of perceptually guided, adaptive action that involves the detection and use of structural or dynamic properties that remain invariant across kinds. Metaphor, in addition, involves an active, partial transformation of one kind of thing (the tenor) under the guidance of another kind of thing (the vehicle). This definition rejects views stating that metaphor is a deceptive language use, or a form of special purpose classification, and extends the scope of metaphor to action as well as visual displays.[102]

This concept of metaphor emerges as an ideal model for literary film adaptation. It allows the original book (the tenor) to be transformed by its film adaptation (the vehicle). It renders adaptation metamorphosis rather than a crude or reductive literalization of interart analogies.

Under looking glass analogical models, metaphor presses further toward a less linear, more cyclical, less binary, more multiplicative process of metamorphosis. In Carroll's *Through the Looking Glass*, a wool-shawled White Queen metamorphoses into a knitting woolly sheep (LG 258–59). In the process, humanesque character regresses to personified animal and wool shawl reverts to sheep wool. But the metamorphosis is not a straight, linear regression, for the sheep is knitting – perhaps the very shawl that the White Queen has worn/will wear. The metamorphosis thus creates a temporal inversion, expressed in my two verb tenses and in the Queen's description of "living backwards," where fingers bleed before they are pricked and where villains are punished before they commit their crimes. Living backwards is not a linear process either: the Queen attests that "memory works both ways." Knowing that a suddenly bleeding finger means imminent pricking, or that punishment signals an impending crime, one remembers what has not yet happened (LG 253–54). When memory works both ways, forwards and backwards, time inheres looking glass fashion: one moves forwards backwards and backwards forwards in an endless rupture of linear progress and binary opposition. Like the memory that works both ways, the facing mirrors of novel and film under a looking glass analogical model of adaptation reflect both ways, distorting sequences of origin and copy. Looking glass analogies reverberate in an endless return to origins and a transformation of those origins through the act of returning, a return that is always original.

For Švankmajer, dream and film are both places of metamorphosis: "in the film, as in a dream...objects metamorphose."[103] At the end of his *Alice*, the toys and objects that have moved and joined together to form grotesque combinations return to their predream states, motionless and disassembled. But although the start and end of the film/dream appear identical, we can no longer regard these objects as we did at first, having witnessed their metamorphoses in the dream/film world. Švankmajer's *Alice* attests that there can be no real return to origins, whether to a predream waking world or to the prefilmic words of an adapted novel. Rather, origins are transformed by the film/dream journey, which acts as a figuratively transformative vehicle for the novel's tenor. If figures change the meanings of words and shape other branches of knowledge, then a figurative model of literary film adaptation changes the books films adapt.

This broader process is epitomized and illustrated in animated processes that carry metaphor into metamorphosis. Frequently, animated metaphors press toward metamorphoses – metamorphoses that are predicated on those metaphors. The central metamorphosis of Carroll's *Alice's Adventures in Wonderland* is the one in which the baby boy becomes a pig (AW 86). From one point of view, the metamorphosis is verbally scripted: the baby is named "Pig" before it metamorphoses into one. But the baby is also named other things into which it does not metamorphose: a star-fish and a steam engine. The metamorphosis is primarily based on the visual and aural resemblances of baby boys and pigs: that is to say, on visual metaphor. Through the incremental changes associated with metamorphic processes and with animation, these resemblances lead gradually to a change in identity, in which the tenor *becomes* the vehicle. At first the baby is more baby than pig. But gradually, sneezes and sobbing give way to grunting (at a middle point, they are indistinguishable); the "precious nose" becomes a "*very* turn-up nose" and then "a snout"; the eyes grow "extremely small for a baby," until they are decreed "just the right size" for a pig. Finally, "This time there could be no mistake about it: it was neither more nor less than a pig" (AW 85–86, Carroll's emphasis). In metaphoric metamorphosis, the double articulation of the metaphor vanishes as one articulation displaces the other.

In Carroll's and Tenniel's move from "Shaking" to "Waking" at the end of *Through the Looking Glass*, a flip-book animation page turn metamorphoses, somewhat crudely and suddenly, Red Queen into black kitten (LG 340, 343). At 24 frames per second, however, film animation can create more subtle and radical metamorphoses. It was not until I attempted to take still photographs of Disney's *Alice* that I became fully aware of the vital role movement and sound play in filmic figurative expression. Tenniel's bread and butterfly, a single winged crust, is mobilized and multiplied in the swarm of Disney butterflies that fly together to form a loaf. Temporal sound combines with animated movement to achieve the figure of Disney's owl concertina: when the owl flies, its neck opens out into a concertina; when it lands, it reverts to neck, a concertina sound accompanying the movement. Movement and sound are further indispensable to the punning connections that Disney makes between playing cards and soldiers, shuffling, cutting, and fanning the deck into the most polished military maneuvers. Similarly, when Alice falls down the rabbit hole and her skirt doubles as a parachute, the double articulation depends on sound and movement as well as shared visual lines: when the skirt functions as parachute, there is a clothy snap, the skirt pops out in parachute shape, and Alice falls slowly; when parachute reverts to skirt, the garment flies over her head, and she falls quickly. Film animation has the power to make objects quite unlike each other metamorphose into each other over a brief period of time. In Švankmajer's trial scene, as Alice shakes her head in denial of the charges against her, it metamorphoses into other heads quite unlike her own through the "magic" of stop-action animation.

However, images, whether verbally or pictorially evoked, do not have a monopoly on such metamorphoses. Carroll's doublet game, in which words turn one letter at a time into other words, offers a purely verbal version of this cellular, frame-by-frame metamorphosis. "I call the two given words 'a Doublet', the interposed words 'Links', and the entire series 'a chain'."[104] Carroll changes LOVE to HATE in three miniscule steps: LOVE–LAVE–LATE–HATE. As in film animation, tiny graphic changes produce a semantic shift so great that a word turns into its own antonym. In the same way, looking glass analogies suggest a far more subtle and nuanced interchange between aural and verbal expression than the structural model that mandates leaps from words to images crudely based on shared referents. Rather than huge leaps, tiny steps along figurative bridges effect, paradoxically, radical changes that transform both novel and film through their own inversely inherent resemblances.

Animated films provide a perfectly solid base from which to forge such theories and stake such claims, since all films are based on animation techniques. Just as Carroll's play with language heightens certain features and dynamics of linguistic expression more generally through its iconoclastic comedy, so too film animation allows for a greater degree of subversive and comical manipulation of filmic signs. The question inevitably arises as to how such figurative theories of adaptation apply to live-action, natural-realist, dramatic, serious (even tragic) film. To answer this question, I offer a case study of Roman Polanski's *Tess* (1979), which adapts Thomas Hardy's *Tess of the D'Urbervilles* (1891).[105] In this case study, the frenzied, even manic dynamics of reciprocal looking glass analogies give way to a more multifaceted figurative prism, as filmic figures run multifariously and complexly through the multiple channels of filmic signification (acting, costumes, props, sets, music, sound, dialogue, cinematography, editing, and more), creating figurative resonances every bit as dense as (one can even argue more dense than) literary figuration because of the many and varied sign systems film engages.

Live-Action Figures: Thomas Hardy's Tess of the D'Urbervilles (1897) and Roman Polanski's Tess (1979)

Novelist and critic David Lodge invokes a cinematic analogy to pay tribute to Hardy's prose: "Hardy uses verbal description as a film director uses the lens of his camera – to select, highlight, distort and enhance, creating a visualised world that is both recognisably 'real' and yet more vivid, intense and dramatically charged than our ordinary perception of the real world." Having enhanced Hardy's prose by a cinematic analogy, Lodge precludes a counteranalogy:

> It is difficult for film adaptation to do justice to Hardy's novels precisely because effects that are unusual in written description are commonplace in film . . . Subtract all the description . . . from the novel, and you would be left with a rather confused melodrama of unhappy love, relieved by some amusing comic dialogue from the rustics.[106]

Lodge implies that any film adaptation must represent just such a subtraction, placing all the value of Hardy's writing in his figurative effects while denying figurative power to filmic images.

In a similar vein, interdisciplinary scholar William V. Constanzo cites the failure of film to represent "figurative truths" as the root cause of his dissatisfaction with Polanski's adaptation of *Tess*: "That proverbial advantage of photography over print, its capacity to condense a thousand words into a single picture, is counterbalanced by its literal-mindedness, which makes it a clumsy instrument for representing figurative truth." Extolling the "almost metaphysical" effect of Hardy's metaphors, "a violent yoking of images perceived by the eye and the imagination," he proclaims the novel vastly superior to the "literal-minded," clumsy film. Yet intriguingly for this discussion, he acknowledges – albeit in an aside – that Polanski's "images . . . speak more eloquently than the characters themselves."[107] Unintentionally given Constanzo's thesis, the aside raises the other side of the looking glass: a filmic figuration that functions inversely to literary figuration. Just as Hardy's literary figures fuse eye and image(-ination) for Constanzo, Polanski's filmic figures fuse eye and eloquence. Constanzo here forges an interart looking glass analogy in which words evoke optical cognitive effects and images evoke verbal cognitive effects.

Constanzo is not the only critic to use *Tess* as a proof text against the figurative capacity of pictures. Jonathan Miller invokes Hardy's description of Tess's "mobile peony mouth" (Hardy 20) as central evidence for his claim that "It is only in language that one can state an explicit comparison between one thing and another – between lips and peonies . . . there are no communicative resources within the pictorial format for making such implications explicit."[108] Miller reiterates the objection of earlier critics that realist film has no way to signal which is the figurative part of a metaphor or simile and which is the literal part. Paul Roy Madsen argues that because of this, filmic figures must be comical: "Similes and metaphors may enrich the pages of the novel . . . yet they cannot be practicably rendered on film without becoming laughable" (255). Whereas the reader of "peony mouth" understands which half of the metaphor is nonliteral and nondiegetic based on context and on training in literary conventions and grammatical relationships, film has established few comparable conventions. Madsen and Miller would thus argue that Tess Durbeyfield's "mobile peony mouth" can only be a pair of lips on screen. A superimposition of a peony over Tess's lips would appear ludicrous or confusing to a film viewer (is she kissing it, wearing it, eating it, or dreaming of it?) and, since editing conventions tend to be syntactical rather than figurative, a cut from her lips to a shot of a peony would be more likely to imply a narrative relationship between Tess and the peony (is she looking at it, about to pick it, or desiring it?).

Unlike Carroll's and Disney's iconoclastic puns, serious figuration in literature or film requires a hierarchical relationship and clear signaling of which is the figure's literal and which is the figure's figurative part. It demands a resolute subordination of vehicle to tenor, of connotative to denotative element, to avoid comedy or confusion.

Critics have tended to see metaphor from a literary perspective – as two visual images, one literal, the other figurative – and have been stymied as to how to derealize the realist filmic image in order to create a filmic metaphor. But filmmakers have been making filmic metaphors for decades: we simply have not recognized them as such. The hierarchy of literal and figurative elements for serious figuration is achieved and maintained through the hierarchies of film's various representational layers and channels. The film image dominates, providing the denotative or literal aspect of the figure. The connotative dimensions of filmic figures are found in elements of the image (acting, costume, sets, and props) as opposed to the whole image, in ways of presenting the image (lighting, framing, camera angle, and camera movement), in juxtapositions of images (the rhythms, dissociations, and connections of editing), and in accompaniments to the image (music and sound).

In fact, Polanski creates a highly effective adaptation of Tess's "peony lips" in a filmic metaphor on "lips" and "strawberries" (Hardy 44–45). In the film, a strawberry enhances and modifies Tess's lips visually in much the same way that "peony" does in Hardy's text. As Tess (Natassia Kinski) opens her mouth to receive a strawberry from Alec (Leigh Lawson), lips and strawberry are similarly colored and shaped, so that the strawberry visibly enhances and modifies Tess's lips just as the word "peony" enhances and modifies the word "lips" in the novel. The tenor (mouth) is briefly juxtaposed to and enhanced by the vehicle (strawberry) before the vehicle vanishes. Tess's open mouth creates a strawberry-shaped space into which the fruit is set briefly before she closes her lips over it and swallows it, just as the figurative verbal peony fades, while the literal lips remain in the novel's scene. The strawberry–lip metaphor avoids confusion because the strawberry is a diegetic part of the scene, with realist and narrative as well as metaphorical significance. Indeed, it takes on a further symbolic significance by prefiguring other scenes in which Alec will penetrate Tess against her will and gestures to his broader role as Tess's tempter-provider.

This figure is a purely visual one, based on the visual resemblances (color, shape, and texture) of lips and strawberries. However, just as some puns in the Disney *Alice* are hybrids of verbal and visual representation, so too are a number of figures in Polanski's *Tess*. Acting constitutes an element of the film image, not the whole, and can carry figurative resonances that blend verbal figures with dramatic audiovisual signs. Characters can fall in rank, into disrepute, into despair, and into sin as well as to the ground. So, when the drunken Durbeyfield exclaims, "I'm the head of the noblest branch around, and I've got my pride to think of," then promptly collapses, the fall carries both figurative and literal resonances. Figuratively it points to his economic and social fallen state, as well as to the degeneration and demise of his ancestors and points forward to the many forced lyings down of his daughter later in the film. But the action has a literal and realist function as well as a figurative one. Drunken men do fall down. For figures to be effective in realist film, the connotative, nonliteral element of the figure must also hold its own in the realist filmic world.

Sets and lit objects also carry figurative and symbolic expressions. The living light of the Durbeyfields' tent pitched beside the darkened tombs of their dead ancestors points figuratively to their impending extinction. Light functions figuratively when Retty (Caroline Embling), Izz (Susanna Hamilton), and Marian (Carolyn Pickles) gaze longingly and hopelessly at Angel Clare (Peter Firth) through their bedroom window and the window frame casts the shadow of a cross on their faces, symbolizing their suffering for love. In Hardy's account, there is no mention of such a shadow (139–40). Like other effective filmic figures, the symbolic shadow has a realist, quotidian source in the intersecting bars of the window. But light splits the connotative shadow from its denotative object, lending it the double articulation of figuration.

All of these figures draw some of their effect from cultural symbolism and from other art forms. But film also undertakes figurations that are unique to itself. For example, camera angle and movement create figurative effects, separating connotative from denotative aspects of a figure by exploiting the tensions between film's actual two-dimensional presentation and its implied three-dimensional representation. As Tess whistles to Mrs. d'Urberville's birds, the camera shoots both Tess and birds through cage bars. The birds are literally and actually in the cages; Tess is only figuratively and visually so. Yet in film's two dimensions, she appears as much behind the bars as they. Actor and camera movement extend the figuration: as Tess walks slowly along the row of cages, she appears alternately in and out of the cages, an alternation that not only figuratively represents her ambiguous state between servitude and freedom in the d'Urberville household, but also pulls the viewer back and forth between the literal and the figurative dimensions of the Tess-in-the-cages metaphor.

Frame composition, perspective, and camera focus further exploit tensions between implied three-dimensional filmic space and actual two-dimensional celluloid space to figurative effect. As the newly married Tess confesses her past to Angel, her face fills the left half of the frame in a glowing, fire-lit close-up, her natural beauty enhanced by her sparkling wedding jewels. Angel occupies the right half of the frame, but stands at a distance in mid-shot, stiff and out of focus. If his stance indicates his moral rigidity, his unfocused image expresses more figuratively his uncertainty. As the nature of her confession becomes clear, Angel moves still further from Tess, sitting apart in an armchair.[109] When Tess finishes speaking, he rises slowly and, taking a sharp poker, methodically and ominously stirs the fire until sparks fly, expressing a rage that he smothers in his curt announcement: "I'm going out." His growing emotional distance unfolds in an interminable exit shot as he walks zombie-like through the back of the frame, a lingering but resolute journey through two adjoining rooms until he is only a tiny, dark, completely unfocused figure in the film frame. While his exit is a realist, diegetic dramatization of a narrative event, his diminution, darkening, and blurring effected by the camera create figurative effects, as he disappears as much through shrinkage as through the door.

The film's figurative expression carries political and ideological resonances as well as formal and narrative ones. Kaja Silverman has argued that "figuration is associated with a terrifying coercion of people and events–with deterioration rather than amelioration, constraint rather than liberation" and to prove this point, she reads the figuration in Hardy's *Tess*, showing its complicity in Tess's oppression by men, including the male narrator. Silverman shows that the narrator's own coercive desire emerges in his figures and places readers in a similar position, aligning us with Tess's abuse.[110] Polanski undertakes similar figurative effects. As Hardy's Alec leads Tess into the Chase, the narrator increasingly obscures the event with fog and darkness: "a faint luminous fog, which had hung in the hollows all the evening, became general, and enveloped them" (73). Against the darkness, he places Tess's virginal muslin: "The obscurity was now so great that he could see absolutely nothing but a pale nebulousness at his feet, which represented the white muslin figure he had left upon the dead leaves" (76). In the darkness, Tess and her costume merge metaphorically: "this beautiful feminine tissue, sensitive as gossamer, and practically blank as snow as yet" (77). In Polanski's film, as Alec struggles with and conquers Tess, a mist washes over the film frame, rendering Tess invisible, obscuring the sexual conquest of Tess, just as Hardy does ("Tess became invisible"–76, Figure 37). Polanski extends this obscuring into subsequent scenes, emphasizing the economic benefits to Tess from her sexual oppression. Through a filmic dissolve, the mist

37. The Chase, Roman Polanski's *Tess*, Renn Productions, 1979. Courtesy of the Academy of Motion Pictures Arts and Sciences.

38. The Aftermath, Roman Polanski's *Tess*, Renn Productions, 1979. Courtesy of BFI stills.

of the Chase metamorphoses to white tissue paper enveloping a lavish hat Alec offers to Tess. The hat belongs to a higher social class than Tess's. Tess, still wearing her demure servant's Quaker cap, lifts the hat from the box. A musical bridge carries the viewer into the next scene, where Tess sits languidly wearing the new hat and costume as Alec rows her over a lake (Figure 38). This figure implicates Tess in her own coercion and complicates Silverman's feminist critique.

When Alec reenters Tess's life later in the film after her abandonment by Angel, the mist metaphor returns. Elaine Scarry has observed a connection between Alec and the engine-man who tends the threshing machine (both "in the agricultural world but not of it").[111] In Polanski's film, the engine-man is merely one of many extras. Instead, Polanski aligns Alec and the threshing machine itself through a mobile visual metaphor of smoke. As Alec sits in the dark waiting for Tess, a billow of smoke from the threshing machine crosses the frame, answered by a puff of smoke from Alec's glowing cigar. If the cigar is phallic, then its smoke represents a sinister seminal emanation – part breath, part combustion. On film, smoke is figuratively threatening to Tess as filmic sign on more than one occasion when it covers and obscures her image. In this scene, Tess emerges from the dissipating smoke of the machine exactly as Alec exhales cigar smoke in her direction. The misting of the Chase and tissued gifts align with these obscuring emissions. Tess's movement from the smoke of the machine into the smoke of Alec's cigar intimates her impending transition from economic dependence on farm labor to economic dependence on Alec. Although her dialogue in the scene adamantly resists Alec's overtures, the moving belt of the machine behind their heads joins their bodies visually and metaphorically, pulling Tess toward Alec as he urges, "Come away with me." Again the effect is metaphorical: Tess and Alec are not literally inside the machine, but only figuratively in the film's two-dimensional presentation.[112] Here images belie words and visual metaphors carry stronger narrative resonances than didactic verbal assertions.

Not all filmic figurations, however, are visual: there are auditory figures as well. Music and sound in *Tess* form an invisible, aural, figurative, connotative layer in conjunction with denotative images. In the novel, when Alec teaches Tess to whistle, denotative significance lies in the unspoken words of the tune he whistles, "Take O take those lips away" – lyrics that are lost on Tess and many readers, for Hardy does not print them (63). And if the musical notes function metaphorically, they are not represented in the novel. But in the film, music works with images to create figurative effects. Alec's offscreen whistle overlays aurally the image of Tess's soundlessly blowing lips – puckered lips that gesture back to the scene where he placed strawberries in her mouth. This time Alec is putting his breath and his tune rather than fruit into her mouth. In the next scene, representing a later time, Tess whistles Alec's tune to the birds fluidly without his prompting. His off-screen presence, invasive in the previous scene, has been internalized and is now represented as her own expression.

Extradiegetic orchestral music also functions figuratively in Polanski's film. As Alec presses an increasingly resistant Tess to the ground in the Chase, a series of orchestral notes plays: two identical notes followed by a much lower and longer note, at an atonal rather than a harmonic interval. The triad of notes repeats at the same interval in varying keys throughout their struggle, the two higher notes pressing the single note heavily downward. The downward direction of the notes represents acoustically not only the pressing of Tess to the ground in this instance, but her more general downward spiral in the narrative.[113] Yet after Tess kills Alec at the Sandbourne boarding house, the same three notes play, then invert, with the lower note sounding twice first and the higher note subsequently and only once, indicating as didactically as music can Tess's rising from her downtrodden status to enact a final revenge against Alec through the overturning of the musical pattern. The music here functions connotatively and extradiegetically, while the images present the events denotatively and diegetically.

Nonmusical sound too produces figurative effects in the film. The kissing sound Alec makes to his horse immediately after he kisses Tess creates an aural simile that links animal with girl, later expressed more didactically in his assertion: "I was your master once and will be again," as he thrashes his riding crop in Tess's direction. The snipping shears of the gardener outside the Sandbourne lodging house – initially a random, incidental sound – take on an increasingly ominous significance after Tess kills Alec, alluding to the mythological shears that snip the thread of life. When the landlady reaches up to touch Alec's blood dripping through the ceiling, her own scream is usurped by the shrill scream of a train whistle, personifying the train at the same time it depersonalizes the landlady, cutting her off from the image and soundtrack. The screaming locomotive figuratively conjoins discovery with flight, as Tess escapes on the shrieking train.

These represent only some of the many figurations in Polanski's film. But without piling up further examples, they demonstrate amply that, far from being incapable of figurative expression, film possesses figurative capacities that can operate simultaneously on multiple channels, achieving subliminally and simultaneously what writing must accomplish didactically and sequentially. Polanski's figurative presentation of photographic images through props, costume, acting, set design, lighting, music, sound, cinematography, and editing is so striking that, despite poor casting, mediocre acting, and an uninspired script, *Tess* has been internationally admired and awarded. But although Polanski's *Tess* garnered Academy Awards for Best Art Direction, Best Set Decoration, Best Cinematography, and Best Costume Design and nominations for Best Director, Best Picture, and Best Original Score, Césars for Best Director and Best Film, the Golden Globe Award for Best Foreign Film (1981), the Los Angeles Film Critics Association Award for Best Director, and was listed among the National Board of Review's Ten Best Films of the Year, it did not muster a single writing or acting award from professional critics or film artists.[114] One is reminded here of Lodge's assessment of the novel cited earlier: "Subtract all the description . . . from the novel, and you would be left with a rather confused melodrama of unhappy love, relieved by some amusing comic dialogue from the rustics." It appears that Polanski's adaptation received a similar critical verdict.

Here we see that the layering that failed in theatrical adaptations of the *Alice* books is essential to realist, live-action figuration, which depends on hierarchies of denotative and connotative elements. In the final analysis, realist filmic figuration departs from the frenzied reciprocal looking glass model to reveal a more versatile layered potential, carrying figuration beyond visual and verbal oppositions and inherences into pieces of images, modes of image presentation, and interactions between images and nonverbal sounds–carrying us away from the verbal/visual dyad into other elements of filmic representation. Such figures also carry adaptation beyond binaristic semantic translation models preoccupied with form and content to multiplicative, layered significatory effects–effects that need to be explored in greater detail in future studies.

Prefatory Conclusions/Concluding Prefaces

Pressed by scores of readers for an answer to his riddle, "Why is a raven like a writing desk?" Carroll at last ventured one: "Because they can both produce a few notes, tho [*sic*] they are very flat; and it is nevar [*sic*] put with the wrong end in front." Carroll added: "This, however, is merely an afterthought; the Riddle, as originally invented, had no answer at all."[115] Similarly, while some critics have concluded that there is no answer at all to the question, "Why is a novel like a film?" many more have propounded answers. Carroll's answer to his riddle connects raven and writing desk in two ways: the first, figurative, the second, categorical. The figurative connection links them through a pun on flat notes; the categorical bond places them under a mammoth overarching category– "they are nevar [*sic*] put with the wrong end in front"–a category that includes most physical objects and says little about their specific relationship to one another. Carroll's answer epitomizes the two branches, analogical and categorical, of the novel/film debate that seek to answer the interdisciplinary question, Why is a film like a novel? This book has endeavored to show that analogical answers offer a much more substantial account of interdisciplinary relations and criticism than has hitherto been acknowledged and that categorical yokings at such high levels of categorization as "representations" or "narrative" prove too broad for any real understanding of interdisciplinary engagements, conscripting them instead without much differentiation into the service of larger formal, contextual, and ideological concerns. This book has also indicated that categories like "word" and "image" are both too crude and too inaccurate to account for formal relations between novels and films. Instead, it recommends that scholars pay attention to the whole word and image spectrum within as well as between these arts, all the way to verbal–visual splits inside signs and to verbal and visual aspects of cognition. If categorization divides the visual from the verbal, and many analogies support such divisions, looking glass analogies place them inside each other, as each other's formal content.

However, my own conclusion cannot reasonably or persistently maintain a categorical stance in which analogies are favored over categories, for we have also seen that analogy and category frequently collapse into each other and confuse with each other. It turns out that the second part of Carroll's "answer" to his riddle is not such a clumsy categorical clunker after all. Carroll deliberately (mis)spelled "never" "nevar" – "raven" backwards – and in so doing, contradicted the overt claim of the clause in which it appears. The clause asserts that raven is never put with the wrong end in front, but "nevar" is "raven" spelled with the wrong end in front. Humorously (or sadly, depending on one's purview), the editor of the next edition, believing he had discovered a typographical error, "corrected" the spelling, which was "nevar" restored to subsequent editions. It is this editorial "correction" of looking glass spelling that turns the second half of Carroll's answer into the moronic, doltish übercategory under which ravens and writing desks are numbly subsumed along with most other objects, eradicating any sense of dynamic interrelationship. In a similar vein, my research indicates that concerns with categorical correctness and doctrinaire dogmas have done a great deal more to obscure than to elucidate interdisciplinary engagements, which are much more lively, unstable, agenda driven, and topsy-turvy than categorical lenses have revealed.

Quite appropriately for a section that aspires to final words, Carroll's answer to his raven/writing desk riddle has by no means been accepted as the final word but, in keeping with the looking glass play that "nevar" allows one side to dominate for long or to have the last word, a host of other answers to the riddle has been propounded. As with comparisons of novels and films, they range from the prosaically literal and empirically observable ("Because they both have legs"), to the sequentially and pragmatically functional ("Because the raven's feathers become quills used for writing at the desk"), to the playfully figurative ("Because they both have inky quills"). The vast majority of the propounded answers have, intriguingly, taken a looking glass form, as in the following examples:

> Because one has flapping fits and the other has fitting flaps.
> Because a writing desk is a rest for pens and a raven is a pest for wrens.
> Because one is good for writing books and the other is better for biting rooks.

While the sound exchange is even, mutual, and equal, the semantic sense shift is radical to the point of diametric opposition. For instance, "flapping fits" are unexpected and out of control: "fitting flaps" are preplanned, ordered, and in place. Carroll epitomizes such tensions between congruous sounds and incongruous senses when he parodies the thrifty maxim: "Take care of the pence and the pounds will take care of themselves" thus: "Take care of the sense and the sounds will take care of themselves" (AW 119). Each proverb – original and adapted parody – offers a moral for further interdisciplinary study: the first for word and image issues and the second for form and content questions. (As the Duchess quips, "Everything's got a moral, if only you can find it" – AW 118.) The original proverb avers that if one attends to the smaller units, the pence, then the larger units, the pounds, will take care of themselves. Likewise, this book concludes that if interdisciplinary scholars and interart adapters attend to the more minute divisions inside phonetic-graphic signs, the relations between the larger units – between words and images and between novels and films – will take care of themselves.

The parody offers a second moral. In admonishing the listener to take care of the sense rather than the sound, it inverts the moral of the original proverb, for to care for linguistic sense is to care for a larger unit than sound: after all, monemes (the smallest units of sense) are typically larger than phonemes (the smallest units of sound). Yet the parody inverts again, looking glass fashion, when it pays more attention to parodying the phonemes of the original (pence/sense, pounds/sounds) than its monemes and flatly contradicts the sense of the original in so doing. But this is not the final inversion: in contradicting the sense of the original, it contradicts its own sense as well, for in taking care to echo the original's sounds rather than its sense, it contradicts its own admonition to care for the sense and ignore the sounds. The parody ends up inverting its own form and content, its own sound and sense. In so doing, it epitomizes the way in which cultural practice unravels and opposes critical dogmas. Thus looking glass analogies and adaptations rupture and confuse theoretical fusions of form and content as heretically as they leap across the lines of the word and image divide.

The two proverbs together – original and parody – provide one final moral. Often the cultural practice that purports to apply and prove interart theories ends by unraveling the theories and parodying its application of them. As adaptation purports to bear out interart analogies, it ends up belying them. In readings of cultural practice, we find a system of checks and balances for our dogmas every bit as effective as the checks and balances that reciprocal inverse interart analogies offer to interdisciplinary theory and practice. Cultural practice runs ahead of interart theory: today, words and images mix almost as fluidly as they did in the nineteenth century – in print and television advertising, on the Internet and in computer graphics, as well as in dramatic films and television.[116] Theories must run to catch up.

I observed in the course of my research that interart theories tend to follow dominant contemporaneous scientific models. Lessing applied Linnaean classifications to the arts; later nineteenth-century analogies reflected Darwinian notions that competition is most intense between similar species. Now, at the turn of the twenty-first century, the sciences are increasingly crossing disciplinary lines, as the creation of so many hyphenated scientific fields attests. It may be time for interart discourse once again to heed scientific example. But if so, the humanities must also take heed of the new occlusions and obfuscations that such modeling will inevitably generate.

This book represents only a beginning toward the establishment of new critical models for the novel/film debate. It takes one step away from categorical models that divide the verbal from the pictorial, focusing instead on critical rhetoric and aesthetic practices that place the verbal and pictorial inside each other: on hybrid word and image arts, on verbal–pictorial analogies, and on literary film adaptation. It has of necessity been devoted to historicizing problematic threads of the novel/film debate and to clearing a preliminary metacritical path through outworn, agenda-driven, and inadequate dogmas. These clearings will doubtless require further clarification, especially given that looking glass aesthetics and looking glass criticism have a pernicious tendency to invert and twist endlessly. Nevertheless, looking glass analogies and practices establish places where interdisciplinary paradoxes are both reconciled and maintained, points where categorical differentiation and analogical affinity, verbal and visual representations, and form and content inhere inversely in each other. Breaking free both from older binarisms and indissoluble unions, going beyond newer theories that figure the verbal and pictorial only in hierarchical, oppressive-resistant, dialectical, or parasitic relationships to one another, or erasing one-half of form/content binarisms entirely, looking glass principles contain a system of checks and balances with potential to redress some of the larger imbalances in theories of words and images, as well as of form and content more generally.

Notes

Introduction

1 J. Dudley Andrew, *Concepts in Film Theory* (Oxford: Oxford University Press, 1984) 103. The chapter in which he makes this comment, "Film Adaptation," is reprinted in James Naremore's *Film Adaptation* (New Brunswick, NJ: Rutgers University Press, 2000) and in Timothy Corrigan, *Literature and Film: An Introduction and a Reader* (New York: Prentice Hall, 1999).

2 For example, Keith Cohen, *Film and Fiction: The Dynamics of Exchange* (New Haven: Yale University Press, 1979); Claude-Edmonde Magny, *The Age of the American Novel: The Film Aesthetic of Fiction between the Two Wars* (New York: Frederick Ungar, 1972; originally published 1948); and Seymour Chatman, *Story and Discourse: Narrative Structure in Fiction and Film* (Ithaca, NY: Cornell University Press, 1978).

3 Sergei Eisenstein, *Film Form: Essays in Film Theory*, ed. and trans. Jay Leyda (New York: Harcourt, Brace & World, 1949) 195.

4 Christian Metz, *The Imaginary Signifier: Psychoanalysis and the Cinema*, trans. Celia Britton, Annwyl Williams, Ben Brewster, and Alfred Guzzetti (Bloomington: Indiana University Press, 1977) 110.

5 J. S. Mill, "What Is Poetry?" *The Broadview Anthology of Victorian Poetry and Poetic Theory*, eds. Thomas J. Collins and Vivienne J. Rundle (Peterborough, Ontario, Canada: Broadview, 1999) 1214.

6 Robert B. Ray, "The Field of 'Literature and Film'," *Film Adaptation*, ed. James Naremore (New Brunswick, NJ: Rutgers University Press, 2000) 44; Brian McFarlane, *Novel to Film: An Introduction to the Theory of Adaptation* (Oxford: Clarendon, 1996) 1.

7 See, for example, Deborah Cartmell, I. Q. Hunter, Heidi Kaye, and Imelda Whelehan, eds., *Pulping Fictions: Consuming Culture Across the Literature/Media Divide* (London: Pluto, 1996); Deborah Cartmell and Imelda Whelehan, eds., *Adaptations: From Text to Screen, Screen to Text* (New York: Routledge, 1999); and Naremore's *Film Adaptation*, cited above.

8 See, for example, the introduction to Cartmell's and Whelehan's *Adaptations*.

Chapter 1. Analogy and Category

1 Sir Richard Blakemore, *Lay-Monastery* 31 (25 Jan. 1713), reprinted in *The Gleaner: A Series of Periodical Essays*, ed. Nathan Drake (London: Suttaby, Evance, & Co., 1811) 1: 33.

2 Cited in Nathan Drake's notes to Blakemore's essay, *Gleaner* 36. He further notes: "The version of Fresnoy by Mason is one of the very few translations which can boast of excelling the original" (37).

3 Gotthold Ephraim Lessing, *Laocoön: An Essay upon the Limits of Painting and Poetry* (Indianapolis: Bobbs-Merrill, 1962; originally published 1766).

4 Irving Babbitt, *The New Laocoön: An Essay on the Confusion of the Arts* (Boston: Houghton Mifflin, 1910) ix.

5 John Ruskin, *Modern Painters, The Works of John Ruskin*, vol. V (London: George Allen, 1909) 328; "Of General Principles," *The Works of John Ruskin*, vol. III (London: George Allen, 1909) 88; Walter Pater, "Style," *Appreciations* (London: Macmillan, 1890) 20; "Notre-Dame d'Amiens," *Miscellaneous Studies* (London: Macmillan, 1913) 114.

6 John Ruskin, "The Study of Art," *The Works of John Ruskin*, vol. XVI ((London: George Allen, 1909) 458; Pater, "Style" 13.

7 Martin Meisel, *Realizations: Narrative, Pictorial, and Theatrical Arts in Nineteenth-Century England* (Princeton: Princeton University Press, 1983) 3.

8 Babbitt uses this phrase throughout his *Laocoön*.

9 René Wellek and Austin Warren, *Theory of Literature* (New York: Harcourt, 1942) 128.

10 W. J. T. Mitchell, *Iconology: Image, Text, Ideology* (Chicago: University of Chicago Press, 1986) 49.

11 Mary Jacobus, *Romanticism, Writing, and Sexual Difference* (Oxford: Clarendon, 1989) 266.

12 This taxonomy builds on the more expanded set of poetry and painting differentiations developed since Lessing. George Bluestone, *Novels into Film* (Berkeley: University of California Press, 1957) vi–vii; 61.

13 Bluestone 218; 1–64.

14 Samuel Johnson, *The History of Rasselas: Prince of Abisinnia* [sic], eds. Geoffrey Tillotson and Brian Jenkins (London: Oxford University Press, 1971; originally published 1759) 28; James Monaco, *How to Read a Film: The Art, Technology, Language, History, and Theory of Film and Media*, 1st ed. (New York: Oxford University Press, 1977) 30.

15 Béla Balázs, *Theory of Film: Character and Growth of a New Art*, trans. Edith Bone (New York: Dover, 1970; originally trans., 1952) 258.

16 Truffaut and Burgess cited in Morris Beja, *Film and Literature* (New York: Longman, 1976) 85. Burgess's article, "On the Hopelessness of Turning Good Books into Films," was published in the *New York Times*, 20 April 1975.

17 Ira Konigsberg, *The Complete Film Dictionary* (New York: New American Library, 1987) 6. I am indebted to James Griffith for alerting me to this entry. See also Joy Gould Boyum, *Double Exposure: Fiction into Film* (New York: Plume, 1985), which also states the opinion as fact: "lesser novels often make for fine movies while fine novels often make for lesser movies" (65).

18 E. H. Gombrich, for example, contests the naturalness of the visual sign and advances the temporality of painting, Murray Krieger propounds the spatiality of literary representation, while Mitchell has brought the space-time continuum to bear on the temporal/spatial dichotomy. See E. H. Gombrich, "Moment and Movement in Art," *Journal of Warburg and Courtauld Institutes* 27 (1964) and "Meditations on a Hobby Horse," *Meditations on a Hobby Horse and Other Essays on the Theory of Art* (London: Phaidon, 1963); Murray Krieger, "The Ekphrastic Principle and the Still Movement of Poetry; or *Laokoon* Revisited," *The Play and Place of Criticism* (Baltimore: Johns Hopkins University Press, 1976); W. J. T. Mitchell, "Spatial Form in Literature: Toward a General Theory," *Critical Inquiry* 6 (Spring 1980); 539–67. More recently, an issue of *Eighteenth-Century Fiction* was devoted to spatiality in literature (vol. 10.4, July 1998).

19 Christian Metz, for example, applies the natural/symbolic dichotomy to his semiotics of film and literature in "The Cinema: Language or Language System?", *Film Language: A Semiotics of the Cinema*, trans. Michael Taylor (Oxford: Oxford University Press, 1991) 77. Richard L. Stromgren and Martin F. Norden popularize the discursive/presentational opposition in pithier terminology: the novel "represents"; the film "presents." (*Movies: A Language in Light*, Englewood Cliffs, NJ: Prentice-Hall, 1984).

20 Robert Scholes, "Narration and Narrativity in Film," *Quarterly Review of Film Studies* 1.111 (August 1976): 290.

21 Cohen, *Film and Fiction* 4. See also Keith Cohen, "Eisenstein's Subversive Adaptation," *The Classic American Novel and the Movies*, eds. G. Peary and R. Shatzkin (New York: Ungar, 1977) 255.

22 Andrew 103.

23 McFarlane, *Novel to Film* 26-8. An earlier book by McFarlane is entitled *Words and Images: Australian Novels into Film* (Melbourne: Heinemann, 1983).

24 Metz, *Film Language* 58.

25 Mitchell, *Iconology* 43.

26 Bluestone 2.

27 He does refer briefly to a few nineteenth-century Continental critics, but they are all categorical critics. Henryk Markiewicz, "Ut Pictura Poesis...A History of the Topos and the Problem," *New Literary History* 18.3 (Spring 1987): 535–59.

28 W. J. T. Mitchell, "Going Too Far with the Sister Arts," *Space, Time, Image, Sign: Essays on Literature and the Visual Arts*, ed. James A. W. Heffernan (New York: Peter Lang, 1987) 2; his *Iconology* cited above.

29 Meisel 3–5.

30 Elizabeth Abel, "Redefining the Sister Arts: Baudelaire's Response to the Art of Delacroix," *Critical Inquiry* 6.3 (1980): 369.

31 Dedre Gentner and Kenneth D. Forbus, "Analogy, Mental Models, and Conceptual Change," project in process. Cited from project summary http://www.qrg.nwu.edu/projects/ONR-SM/analogy.htm.

32 Dedre Gentner and Michael Jeziorski, "The Shift from Metaphor to Analogy in Western Science," *Metaphor and Thought*, 2nd ed., ed. Andrew Ortony (Cambridge University Press, 1993) 447–80.

33 Babbitt 244.

34 *David Copperfield,* dir. Thomas Bentley, prod. Cecil Hepworth, Hepworth Films, UK, 1913. Young David is played by Eric Desmond; the actress who plays his mother is uncredited.

35 Donald Hannah, "'The Author's Own Candles': The Significance of the Illustrations to *Vanity Fair,*" *Renaissance and Modern Essays,* ed. G. R. Hibbard (New York: Barnes & Noble, 1966) 119.

36 Edward Hodnett, *Image and Text: Studies in the Illustration of English Literature* (London: Scolar, 1982) 12.

37 A. R. Kennedy, cited in David Bordwell, Janet Staiger, and Kristin Thompson, *The Hollywood Classical Cinema: Film Style and Mode of Production to 1960* (London: Routledge and Kegan Paul, 1985) 185.

38 Matthew Josephson, "Masters of the Motion Pictures," *Motion Picture Classic* 23.6 (August 1926): 25.

39 Until 1820, Meisel tells us, "illustration" referred primarily to verbal annotation (30). However, the *OED* documents that, from the seventeenth century, it also referred to illuminated initials. *The Oxford English Dictionary,* eds. J. A. Simpson and E. S. C. Weiner, 2nd ed. (Oxford: Clarendon, 1989) VII: 662.

40 Uncredited film located at the National Film Archive in London.

41 Maxim Gorky, review of the Lumière program at the Nizhni–Novgorod Fair, trans. Leda Swan, cited in Jay Leyda, *Kino: A History of the Russian and Soviet Film* (London: Allen & Unwin, 1960) 408.

42 William Makepeace Thackeray, *Vanity Fair: A Novel without a Hero,* 1st ed. (London: Bradbury & Evans, 1848).

43 See, for example, Bluestone and Monaco. In 1980, Joan Dagle convincingly trounced the claim that film has only a present tense, arguing that the act of reading also takes place in the present tense, that all narrative is sequential and temporally contextual, that tense signifiers exist in film, and that film dialogue contains various verb tenses. Joan Dagle, "Narrative Discourse in Film and Fiction: The Question of the Present Tense," *Narrative Strategies: Original Essays in Film and Prose Fiction,* eds. Syndy M. Conger and Janet R. Welsch (Western Illinois University Press, 1980): 47–59. Marie-Claire Ropars-Wuilleumier also challenges this temporal issue, although in less detail. See her *De la littérature au cinéma: genèse d'un écriture* (Paris: Armand Colin, 1970).

44 William Makepeace Thackeray, *Vanity Fair* (New York: Heritage, 1940) 7–8.

45 Mitchell, "Going Too Far with the Sister Arts" 2.

46 *OED* 1: 432.

47 Monaco 157, my emphasis.

48 Metz, *Film Language* 60.

49 David Bordwell, *Narration in the Fiction Film* (Madison: University of Wisconsin Press, 1985) 17.

50 Roland Barthes, "Myth Today," *Mythologies,* trans. Annette Lavers (New York: Hill and Wang, 1984) 110–11; 111.

51 Cohen, *Film and Fiction* 92.

52 Calvin Pryluck, "The Film Metaphor: The Use of Language-Based Models in Film Study," *Literature/Film Quarterly* 3 (1975): 123.

53 W. J. T. Mitchell, *Picture Theory* (Chicago: University of Chicago Press, 1994) 9.

54 Eleanor Rosch has published many essays explaining her theory, most notably "Principles of Categorization," *Cognition and Categorization,* eds. Eleanor Rosch

and Barbara B. Lloyd (Hillsdale, NJ: Lawrence Erlbaum, 1978). I am indebted to Mark Turner, "Categories and Analogies," *Analogical Reasoning: Perspectives of Artificial Intelligence, Cognitive Science, and Philosophy*, ed. David H. Helman (Boston: Kluwer, 1988), for alerting me to Rosch's work.

Chapter 2. Prose Pictures

1   Richard D. Altick, *Paintings from Books: Art and Literature in Britain, 1760–1900* (Columbus: Ohio State University Press, 1985) 37, 200.

2   Discussions of illustration tend to ally poetry and prose as verbal arts against illustration as a visual art, minimizing contrasts between poetry and prose. Changes in poetic form also served to diminish distinctions between types of writing and to heighten oppositions between pictorial and verbal arts by the end of the century. As Celeste Langan has noted, the dominance of blank verse in the nineteenth century served to weaken many prior differentiations between poetry and prose. Celeste Langan, "Understanding Media in 1805: Audiovisual Hallucination in The Lay of the Last Minstrel," *Studies in Romanticism* 40 (Spring 2001): 49–70. Moreover, changes in aesthetic theory and rhetoric led to the increasingly common use of "poetical" to refer to artistic writing of any sort – to prose as well as to poetry – further eroding distinctions between prose and poetry. P. G. Hammerton's 1888 dramatic dialogue on illustration pits a generic Poet against a generic Artist. Hammerton notes in his introduction that "The Poet represents imaginative literature generally." P. G. Hammerton, "Book Illustration," *Portfolio Papers* (Boston: Roberts, 1889) 293; originally published in *The Portfolio* 19 (1888): 17–21.

3   Charles Dickens, *Oliver Twist*, preface to the second edition (London: Penguin, 1966; originally published 1836–37) 34–35.

4   Edward Bulwer-Lytton, *The Last of the Barons* (Boston: Estes and Lauriat, 1892) preface. Cited in Richard Stang, *The Theory of the Novel in England, 1850–1879* (New York: Columbia University Press, 1959) 12.

5   Joseph Conrad, preface to *The Nigger of the "Narcissus"* (London: Penguin, 1987) xlix. Although Conrad defers to the aesthetic movement's claim that music is "the art of arts," his emphasis on vision renders his painterly aspirations more central. Music appears nowhere in his conclusion that "the aim of art [is] to arrest, for the space of a breath, the hands busy about the work of the earth, and compel men entranced by the sight of distant goals to glance for a moment at the surrounding vision of form and colour, of sunshine and shadows; to make them pause for a look, for a sigh, for a smile – such is the aim, difficult and evanescent, and reserved only for a very few to achieve" (li).

6   Mario Praz, *The Hero in Eclipse in Victorian Fiction*, trans. Angus Davidson (London: Oxford University Press, 1956) 29.

7   See, for example, Rhoda L. Flaxman, *Victorian Word-Painting and Narrative: Toward the Blending of Genres* (Ann Arbor, MI: University Microfilms International Research Press, 1987).

8   John Harthan's *The History of the Illustrated Book: The Western Tradition* (London: Thames & Hudson, 1981) provides a succinct overview. J. R. Harvey's *Victorian Novelists and Their Illustrators* (London: Sidgwick & Jackson, 1970) traces Victorian author–illustrator relations in terms of these factors. The suicide to

which I refer is that of illustrator Robert Seymour, which some scholars have attributed to Dickens's ascendancy over him in the publication of *The Pickwick Papers.* Thackeray was one of the rejected applicants to replace Seymour.

9 Hammerton 302, 301.

10 *The Spectator* (26 Dec. 1836): 1234.

11 See Harvey 31.

12 T. H. Lister, *The Edinburgh Review* 68.137 (1838): 77. Cited in Harvey 51.

13 Gerard Curtis, "Shared Lines: Pen and Pencil as Trace," *Victorian Literature and the Victorian Visual Imagination,* eds. Carol T. Christ and John O. Jordan (Berkeley: University of California Press, 1995) 27.

14 End-piece for George Du Maurier, "The Illustrating of Books: From the Serious Artist's Point of View," *The Magazine of Art* XIII (1890): 375. Cited in Sybille Pantazzi, "Author and Illustrator: Images in Confrontation," originally published 1976; reprinted in *A History of Book Illustration: 29 Points of View,* ed. Bill Katz (Metuchen, NJ: Scarecrow, 1994) 585; subsequently discussed in Curtis 54.

15 Richard C. Sha notes the pervasiveness and conventionality of this analogy in the nineteenth century. See his *The Visual and Verbal Sketch in British Romanticism* (Philadelphia: University of Pennsylvania Press, 1998). Although Thackeray was by no means the first to designate written prose a "sketch," an earlier title of his, "Comic Tales and Sketches" (1841) avoids the analogy, indicating that it is by no means a mandatory one.

16 Etymologically, there is no connection between "pen" (from the Latin *penna,* meaning feather or wing, obviously related to the feather quills used to write in ink) and "pencil" (from the Latin *penis,* meaning tail, descending into *pencillus,* "paintbrush," through the use of animal tail bristles to make paintbrushes). The two words have different Indo-European roots: pen/pet-; pencil/pes-. However, the lack of shared etymological roots has not prevented copious wordplay between the two. Moreover the yoking of two unrelated etymologies in this way reflects the yoking of unrelated persons under shared names in marriage. See the entries for "pen" and "pencil" in the *OED,* 2nd ed., vol. XI; Calvert Watkins, ed. *The American Heritage Dictionary of Indo-European Roots* (Boston: Houghton Mifflin, 2000); John Ayto, ed. *Dictionary of Word Origins* (New York: Arcade, 1991).

17 Mitchell's *Iconology* points to ancient traditions that gender text male and image female; Lorraine Janzen Kooistra's *The Artist as Critic: Bitextuality in Fin-de-Siecle Illustrated Books* (Aldershot, England: Scolar, 1995) reads legal and economic relations between authors and illustrators in terms of marriage contracts.

18 Cited in Pantazzi 585.

19 Hammerton 295.

20 George Somes Layard, "Our Graphic Humourists: W. M. Thackeray," *The Magazine of Art* 22 (February 1899): 261.

21 Elizabeth Rigby, *Quarterly Review* 84.167 (December 1848): 162.

22 [George Henry Lewes], "Vanity Fair: A Novel without a Hero," *Athenaeum* (12 August 1848): 795.

23 [Robert Bell], "Vanity Fair," *Fraser's Magazine* 38 (September 1848): 320.

24 *North British Review* 15 (May 1851): 68.

25 *Blackwood's Magazine* 77 (January 1855): 91; *Athenaeum* (12 November 1881): 624; *Athenaeum* (24 September 1898): 418; *Scribner's Magazine* (25 February 1899): 248.

26 Edmund J. Sullivan is one of many to write of illustration as a "form of applied art" in his *The Art of Illustration* (London: Chapman Hall, 1921) v.

27 *Fraser's Magazine* 320–22; 333.

28 Gleeson White, *English Illustration: The Sixties, 1855–1870* (Westminster: A. Constable, 1897) 10.

29 London *Times* review of "Kickleburys on the Rhine," cited in *North British Review* (May 1851) 79.

30 *Fraser's Magazine* 333; *North British Review* (May 1851) 76.

31 Henry Kingsley, *Macmillan's Magazine* 9 (1864): 359–60; John Brown, *North British Review* 40 (1864): 255.

32 Layard 256, 260.

33 The reviewer refers to "Peg of Limavaddy" here. Russell Sturgiss, "Thackeray as Draughtsman," *Scribner's Monthly* 20.2 (June 1880): 261.

34 Sturgiss 256–57; 274.

35 Harvey cites Joseph Pennell in 1895 (161). Not all turn-of-the-century critics were equally enthralled with newer styles. W. C. Brownell in 1899 sees, but does not welcome, the change in aesthetics, noting that the "vigorous filing and sand-papering ... of our critics' and craftsmen's culture-evolution" renders Thackeray artistically vulnerable "as an old practitioner." "William Makepeace Thackeray," *Scribner's Magazine*, 25 February 1899: 236.

36 White 18.

37 Patricia Runk Sweeney, "Thackeray's Best Illustrator,"*Costerus* 2 (1974): 83–111 documents some of the replacement illustrations, which proliferated between 1896 and 1920. See also the Hooder and Stoughton edition, London 1913 (illustrations by Lewis Baumer); Dodd's and Mead's 1924 American edition (illustrations by Charles Crombie).

38 Harvey 77.

39 Layard 260–61. Similarly, Sturgiss suggested in 1880 that "in so far as a literary feeling for character – shall we say a novelist's feeling for character? – is expressible in graphic art, so far as he was able to express himself, though with a tripping pencil which he never fully mastered" (274).

40 John Sloan, "In Praise of Thackeray's Pictures," *Vanity Fair* (New York: Heritage, 1940) xiii.

41 Joan Stevens, "Thackeray's 'Vanity Fair'," *A Review of English Literature*, ed. A. Norman Jeffares, vol. VI (London: Longmans, Green & Co., 1965) 19–38.

42 Christopher Coates, "Thackeray's Editors and the Dual Text of *Vanity Fair*," *Word & Image* 9.1 (1993): 44.

43 Judith Fisher, "Image versus Text in the Illustrated Novels of William Makepeace Thackeray," *Victorian Literature and the Victorian Visual Imagination*, eds. Carol T. Christ and John O. Jordan (Berkeley: University of California Press, 1995) 65.

44 Charles Lamb, "On the Genius and Character of Hogarth, "*The Reflector* 3 (1811): 62, his emphasis.

45 Harvey 82–91; 162; Victor R. Kennedy, "Pictures as Metaphors in Thackeray's Illustrated Novels," *Metaphor and Symbolic Activity* 9.2 (1994): 135–47.

46 Fisher 64; Rigby 161.

47 Meisel 330. See also Lisa Jadwin, "Clytemnestra Rewarded: The Double Conclusion of Vanity Fair," *Famous Last Words: Changes in Gender and Narrative Closure*, ed. Alison Booth (Charlottesville: University of Virginia Press, 1993): 35–61.

48 Teona Tone Gneiting, "The Pencil's Role in Vanity Fair," *Huntington Library Quarterly* 39 (1976): 171–202.

49 Laurence Housman, *Arthur Boyd Houghton: A Selection from His Book in Black and White* (London: Kegan Paul, 1896) 20. I am indebted to Kooistra for this reference.

50 Harvey 166. See also Kooistra 43.

51 Coates 44.

52 Here, I cite both Harthan's view on the decline of adult novel illustration and his list, with a few later twentieth-century additions, of places where illustration continued to flourish (278–79). It is intriguing but beyond the scope of this discussion that the more famous collaborations between writers and artists in twentieth-century illustration occur in *avant-garde* poetry and art and then most prevalently in Europe.

53 Babbitt, *The New Laocoön*, cited earlier.

54 Altick 245 ff.; William Morris, *The Ideal Book: Essays and Selections on the Arts of the Book*, ed. William S. Peterson (Berkeley: University of California Press, 1982) 26.

55 Hammerton 296–97.

56 Henry Blackburn, *The Art of Illustration* (London: W. H. Allen, 1896) 3, 19, 23–24.

57 Hammerton 301.

58 Henry James, "The Art of Fiction," *Partial Portraits* (New York: Haskell House, 1968; originally published 1884 in *Longman's Magazine*) 378. He continues: "Their inspiration is the same, their process (allowing for the different quality of the vehicle) is the same, their success is the same. They may learn from each other, they may explain and sustain each other. Their cause is the same, and the honour of one is the honour of another."

59 Henry James, preface to *The Golden Bowl, The Art of the Novel*, ed. R. P. Blackmur (New York: Scribner's, 1947, originally published 1909) ix. Examples of other articles on the subject include Charles T. Congdon, "Over-Illustration," *North American Review* 139 (1884): 480–91; Sidney Fairfield, "The Tyranny of the Pictorial," *Lippincott's Monthly Magazine* 55 (1895): 861–64.

60 Cited in Ralph Bogardus, ed., *Pictures and Texts: Henry James, A. L. Coburn, and New Ways of Seeing in Literary Culture* (Ann Arbor, MI: University Microfilms International Research Press, 1984) 60. In a similar vein, Hammerton's Poet says, "if illustrations are appreciated for high artistic reasons, they are the more dangerous as rivals and we who write have the stronger reasons for keeping them out" (302).

61 James, *The Golden Bowl*, preface x–xi.

62 Any search of a library database quickly reveals these trends.

63 London: Smith Elder; New York: Harper Bros.

64 Sketch by Basil Davenport (New York: Dodd, Mead & Co., 1943).

65 London: Bradbury, 1847.

66 Oxford University Press, 1931.

67 New York: New American Library, 1962.

68 Boston: Houghton Mifflin, 1963.

69 New York: Norton, 1994. This edition restores Thackeray's illustrations, but includes verbal annotations and commentaries as well.

70 New York: Garland, 1989.
71 These words appear in the subtitles of the Norton and Garland editions.
72 James, *The Golden Bowl*, preface x–xi, his emphasis.
73 Cited in Curtis 36. See also Harthan: "modern novels and poetry are rarely illustrated, the gift book is defunct, its place taken by the numerous compilations and popular summaries of art, travel and science made glamorous by the resources of colour photography" 279.
74 James Thorpe, *English Illustration: The Nineties* (London: Faber, 1935) 252.
75 Stephane Mallarmé, "Sur le livre illustré," *Oeuvres complètes*, eds. Henri Mondor and G. Jean-Aubrey (Paris: Gallimard, 1945) 878. Cited in J. Hillis Miller, "The 'Grafted' Image: James on Illustration," *Henry James's New York Edition: The Construction of Authorship*, ed. David McWhirter (Stanford: Stanford University Press, 1995) 138.
76 "Exceptional Photoplays: *Secrets of the Soul*," *National Board of Review Magazine* 1.5 (Sept.–Oct. 1926): 7–8.
77 *Boston Transcript*, 11 Jan. 1916, cited in Robert A. Colby, "'Scenes of All Sorts ...': *Vanity Fair* on Stage and Screen," *Dickens Studies Annual* 9 (1981): 178.
78 Cited in William Torbert Leonard, *From Theatre: Stage to Screen to Television* (London: Scarecrow, 1981) vol. 2 (M-Z): 1672.
79 Philip James, *English Book Illustration 1800–1900* (London: King Penguin, 1947) 9. See also Harthan.
80 Review of *Shattered*, "Screen: Pictorial Efficiency," The *New York Times* 11 Dec. 1921, section 6: 3.
81 James, *The Golden Bowl* ix–x, his emphasis.
82 Cited in John Harrington, ed., *Film And/As Literature* (Englewood Cliffs, NJ: Prentice Hall, 1977) 117.
83 Cecile Starr, *Discovering the Movies* (New York: Van Nostrand Reinhold, 1972) 32.
84 Markiewicz notes similar tendencies in the twentieth-century branch of the poetry/painting debate.
85 Bluestone 46.
86 Donald Hannah's 1966 evaluation of *Vanity Fair*'s illustrations, which assesses that "the pen does not really need (and can even be hampered by) the pencil" and attacks illustrations in general as one-dimensional, lacking implication and complexity, distracting the reader, and as too explicit to allow for imagination, is typical (120).
87 Ellen J. Esrock, *The Reader's Eye: Visual Imaging as Reader Response* (Baltimore: Johns Hopkins University Press, 1994) 32.
88 Most critics concur with Bluestone's argument that "Proust and Joyce would seem ... absurd on film" (61). See also Ghislaine Géloin, "The Plight of Film Adaptation in France: Toward Dialogic Process in the *Auteur* Film," *Film and Literature: A Comparative Approach to Adaptation*, eds. Wendell Aycock and Michael Shoenecke (Lubbock: Texas Tech University Press, 1988) 136, on the unfilmability of the high modern novel.
89 Virginia Woolf, "The Cinema," *Collected Essays*, vol. 2 (London: Hogarth, 1966; essay date 1926) 268–72.
90 Virginia Woolf, "Pictures," *The Moment and Other Essays* (London: Harcourt Brace Jovanovich, 1948) 173–78.
91 "Pictures" 176; "The Cinema" 271.

92 William Luhr, "Dickens's Narrative, Hollywood's Vignettes," *The English Novel and the Movies*, eds. Michael Klein and Gillian Parker (New York: Frederick Ungar, 1981) 132–92.

93 Geoffrey Wagner, *The Novel and the Cinema* (London: Tanting, 1975) 223. Wagner's categories of adaptation are addressed further elsewhere in this book.

94 John Orr, "Introduction: Proust, the Movie," *Cinema and Fiction: New Modes of Adapting 1950–1990*, eds. John Orr and Colin Nicholson (Edinburgh: Edinburgh University Press, 1992) 1, 4.

95 Harvey notes that illustrated books in the nineteenth century "were directed partly to 'the thousands who read, but did not purchase the work' and would do, for many readers, in lieu of the text" (10).

96 Bluestone cites other instances of increased circulation following films of *Pride and Prejudice, David Copperfield, The Good Earth, Moby Dick, War and Peace*, and *Lost Horizon* (4). Almost any glance at a best-seller list attests to similar effects around many other films.

97 Robert Giddings, Keith Selby, and Chris Wensley, *Screening the Novel: The Theory and Practice of Literary Dramatization* (London: Macmillan, 1990) 22–23.

98 Penguin "Film and TV tie-in edition," 1998 (to cite copyright page), a co-publication of Penguin and BBC.

99 The promoters of this film, however, insisted that a "completely new scenario has been prepared for the screen version, based upon the book, instead of the play, because of the wide opportunities allowed in motion pictures." Advertisement, *The New York Dramatic Mirror* (30 June 1915): 20.

100 *Saturday Review* critic [n. d.] cited in Curtis 34. We saw in Chapter 1 Meisel's note that the use of the word "illustrations" to represent drawings did not take hold in Britain until about 1820 and that before that time, it referred to verbal annotations (30). However, the *OED* cites the first use of the word "illustrator" in 1689 to describe a "picturer of great letters in books" (*OED* VII: 662). Pictorial initials have many historical roots and contemporaneous connections – hieroglyphics of all sorts, crests and logos, the illuminated letters of medieval manuscripts, Renaissance emblems and historiated initials, even the contemporaneous *Punch* cartoons and pictorial initials that Thackeray was producing at the same time he was writing and drawing *Vanity Fair*.

101 For example, although generally disparaging of Thackeray's draughtsmanship, Harvey praises Thackeray's pictorial initials highly and without qualification (82).

102 I have opted, against convention, to bold the capital letters of pictorial initials, finding quotation marks too cumbersome and graphically distracting for this discussion. My thanks to Joss Marsh for this suggestion.

103 Chapters 6, 10, 18, 19, 20, 27, 31, 37, 40, 49.

104 Chapters 5, 22, 34, 42, 56.

105 The British version of American Chutes and Ladders.

106 On the basis other such drawings in letters as well as elsewhere, the illustration is widely agreed to be a caricatured self-portrait of the author.

107 Cited in Harvey 84.

108 J. Hillis Miller, *Illustration* (Cambridge, MA: Harvard University Press, 1992) 77.

109 Hillis Miller, *Illustration* 95.

110 Roland Barthes, "The Photographic Message," *Image—Music—Text*, ed. and trans. Stephen Heath (New York: Hill & Wang, 1977) 205.

111 "The drawing of the pipe and the text that ought to name it cannot find a place to meet." Michel Foucault, *This Is Not a Pipe*, trans. James Harkness (Berkeley: University of California Press, 1981) 36.

112 Mitchell, "Going Too Far with the Sister Arts," 1, his emphasis.

113 Chapter 8 opens with a vignette, rather than with a pictorial initial.

114 Nicholas Wade, *Visual Allusions: Pictures of Perception* (London: Lawrence Erlbaum Associates, 1992) 1, 4.

115 To recap briefly, the basic level of categorization is the one in a vertical chain of categorization at which category members are recognized most rapidly, the highest level at which category members share perceived shapes and at which an image can stand for the category, the level earliest coded in languages, and the level learned first by children. Thus, in a line extending from everything to physical objects to organisms to vertebrates to mammals to cats to domestic cats to Himalayan cats to my cat Hubert, "cats" would constitute the basic level of categorization. See Chapter 1.

116 Hillis Miller, *Illustration* 66.

117 See, for example, the pictorial initials prefacing Chapters 18 (Napoleon represented), 2 (ancient mythology), 22 (family crests and Roman dress), 7 (Renaissance historical scene and costumes), and 16 (eighteenth-century dress).

118 I expand this concept in Chapter 6.

119 Eve Tavor Bannet, "The Scene of Translation: After Jakobson, Benjamin, de Man, and Derrida," *New Literary History* 24 (1993): 583, her emphasis. Bannet cites page 89 of de Man's "Conclusions: Walter Benjamin's 'The Task of the Translator'."

Chapter 3. Film Language

1 Metz, *Film Language* 64.

2 For example, Rensselaer W. Lee, *Ut Pictura Poesis, The Humanistic Theory of Painting* (New York: Norton, 1967).

3 John Ruskin, "The Theory of Expression," *Modern Painters* (London: Smith, Elder, 1843) 20.

4 Mary Barton cited in Curtis 37.

5 Edmund J. Sullivan, *The Art of Illustration* (London: Chapman Hall, 1921) viii.

6 Metz, *Film language* 46.

7 Sergei Eisenstein, "Film Language," *Film Form: Essays in Film Theory*, ed. and trans. Jay Leyda (New York: Harcourt, Brace & World, 1949) 108–21. Eisenstein extends the literary analogy from practice to criticism. Lamenting that, "in comparison with analyses of [literature] ... my analysis is still quite descriptive and easy," he offers various analogical remedies, noting: "An analysis of the very lenses employed in filming ... with camera angles and lighting ... would serve as an exact analogy to an analysis of the expressiveness of phrases and words ... in a literary work."

8 Eisenstein 108.

9 Ralph Stephenson and J. R. Debrix, *The Cinema as Art* (London: Penguin, 1978; first published 1965) 199, 202, 200. Most of the chapter on film sound deals with music and nonverbal sound; the five pages on film words do not even run continuously.

10 André Bazin is the most famous of these voices, represented by David Bordwell as the chief opposition to "The Standard Version of Stylistic History." Under Bazin's realist film aesthetic, the addition of sound and then color only enhanced film art. André Bazin, *What Is Cinema?* vol. I, trans. Hugh Gray (Berkeley: University of California Press, 1967) 139. David Bordwell, *On the History of Film Style* (Cambridge, MA: Harvard University Press, 1997).

11 Louis Giannetti, *Understanding Movies*, 8th ed. (Upper Saddle River, NJ: Prentice-Hall, 1999) 222–35.

12 Henri Colpi, "Debasement of the Art of Montage," *Film Culture* 22–23 (Summer 1961) 36.

13 Henry Blackburn, *The Art of Illustration* (London: W. H. Allen, 1896) 24.

14 Rouben Mamoulian, *Sound and the Cinema*, ed. Evan William Cameron (New York: Redgrave, 1980) 91.

15 Adolph Zukor, *Photoplay* (June 1921): 42.

16 Rex Beach, "The Author and the Film," *Mentor* 9.6 (July 1921): 31; Gore Vidal, "Who Makes the Movies," *New York Review of Books* (25 Nov. 1976): 8.

17 Cited in David Kipen, "Auteurism's Great Snow Job," *San Francisco Chronicle Magazine*, (22 April 2001): 17.

18 Again, dissenting voices have emerged, most famously Richard Corliss's, but they have had little impact.

19 Roland Barthes also writes of the "rhetoric of the image." See his *Image – Music – Text* and Ropars-Wuilleumier, cited earlier.

20 "Ever since the beginning of film history, theorists have been fond of comparing film with verbal language . . . but it wasn't until a new, larger category of thought developed in the late fifties and early sixties [semiotics] . . . that the *real* study of film as a language could proceed." James Monaco, *How to Read a Film: Movies, Media, Multimedia* (Oxford: Oxford University Press, 2000) 157, my emphasis.

21 Metz's *Film Language* is a prime example.

22 Monaco 125.

23 Gilles Deleuze, *Cinema 2: The Time-Image*, trans. Hugh Tomlinson and Robert Galeta (Minneapolis: University of Minnesota Press, 1989) 241.

24 Geoff Mayer, *Film as Text* (Milton, Queensland, Australia: Jacaranda, 1991); Kevin Jackson, *The Language of Cinema* (Manchester: Carcanet, 1998). See also Jean-Claude Carrière, *The Secret Language of Film*, trans. Jeremy Leggatt (New York: Pantheon Books, 1994) and Inez Hedges, *Breaking the Frame: Film Language and the Experience of Limits* (Bloomington: Indiana University Press, 1991).

25 Deleuze 226, 233, his emphasis.

26 See Bordwell, Staiger, and Thompson, *The Hollywood Classical Cinema*.

27 Eric Elliott, *Anatomy of Motion Picture Art* (Territet, Switzerland: Riant Chateau, 1928) 77, 80.

28 Harrington 102–03; Richard Corliss, "The Hollywood Screenwriter," *Film Theory and Criticism*, eds. Gerald Mast and Marshall Cohen, 2nd ed. (Oxford: Oxford University Press, 1979) 700; Bernard F. Dick, *Anatomy of Film*, 3rd. ed (New York: St. Martin's, 1998) 220: "Still, a serious student of film will always look for the screenwriter's name in the credits."

29 Dick 220.

30 William H. Phillips, *Film: An Introduction* (Boston: Bedford/St. Martin's 1999) 199.

31 Leonid Skrypnyk, *Narysyz teorii mystetstva kino* (Kiev: Derzhavne vyd. Ukraine, 1928) 20. Trans. and cited in Bohdan Y. Nebesio, "A Compromise with Literature? Making Sense of Intertitles in the Silent Films of Alexander Dovzhenko," *Canadian Review of Comparative Literature* 23.2 (Sept. 1996): 679–80.

32 "Lubitsch on Directing," *The New York Times* (16 Dec. 1923), section 9: 5.

33 See Chapter 2.

34 David A. Cook, *A History of Narrative Film* (New York: Norton, 1981) 252.

35 Gerald Mast, *A Short History of the Movies* (Indianapolis: Bobbs-Merrill, 1981) 185.

36 Hammerton, "Book Illustration, 301. Chapter 2 contains a fuller discussion.

37 Arthur Knight, *The Liveliest Art: A Panoramic History of the Movies* (New York: Macmillan, 1957) 142 ff.

38 Sarah Kozloff, *Invisible Storytellers* (Berkeley: University of California Press, 1988) 23.

39 Richard L. Stromgren and Martin F. Norden, *Movies: A Language in Light* (Englewood Cliffs, NJ: Prentice-Hall, 1984) 173.

40 See Chapter 2.

41 Eisenstein, "Film Language," 115, 108.

42 Cited in Kevin Brownlow, *The Parade's Gone By* (New York: Ballantine, 1968) 316.

43 Agnes Smith, *Photoplay* (May 1927): 29.

44 Edmund Wilson, *The Boys in the Back Room* (San Francisco: Colt, 1941) 56.

45 Dick 215.

46 "The Art of the Sub-Title," *The Picturegoer* (May 1921): 21.

47 Both examples cited here are from the British intertitles written to accompany the First National 1922 *Oliver Twist*, dir. Frank Lloyd, USA.

48 Peter Milne, "The Development of the Subtitle." *Photoplay* 28.5 (Oct. 1925): 132.

49 This may soon change. Several recent international conferences have been held to consider intertitles; for example: "Intertitle and Film: History, Theory Restoration," Cinémathèque française, Paris, 26–27 March, 1999.

50 Elliott 80. Although published in 1928 after the initial arrival of synchronized sound, the book addresses silent film art.

51 Charles Musser, "The Nickelodeon Era Begins: Establishing the Frame for Hollywood's Mode of Representation," *Early Cinema: Space, Frame, Narrative*, eds. Thomas Elsaesser and Adam Barker (London: British Film Institute, 1990) 256–73.

52 James Card, *Seductive Cinema: The Art of Silent Film* (New York: Knopf, 1994) 57.

53 Ruth Vasey, *The World According to Hollywood, 1918–1939* (Madison: University of Wisconsin Press, 1997), documents that international adaptation in this period consisted mainly of rewriting intertitles (68).

54 Card 60. Such claims are dubious. Cultures contain many visual objects specific to themselves, requiring translation or explication for other cultures.

55 Brownlow 334–35.

56 Cited in Elliott 74–75.

57 "The Screen: A Movie of the Prairies," The *New York Times* (17 March 1923): 9; review of D. W. Griffith's *A Corner in Wheat*, "Reviews of Licensed Films, "*The New York Dramatic Mirror* 62.1618 (25 Dec. 1909): 15.

58 Vachel Lindsay, *The Art of the Moving Picture* (New York: Macmillan, 1915) 161.

59 Epes Winthrop Sargent, *Moving Picture World* (12 Aug. 1911): 363.

60 Jean Epstein (1924) cited in P. Adams Sitney, *Modernist Montage* (New York: Columbia, 1990) 22.

61 Elliott 82. Chapter 4 discusses the cinematic novel.

62 André Gaudreault, "Showing and Telling: Image and Word in Early Cinema," *Early Cinema: Space, Frame, Narrative*, eds. Thomas Elsaesser and Adam Barker (London: British Film Institute, 1990; essay originally published in 1984) 279.

63 James, *The Golden Bowl*, preface x–xi, his emphasis.

64 Nebesio 694–99.

65 Cited in Bordwell et al. 186.

66 Gaudreault 277, his emphasis.

67 Silent film periods are commonly divided according to the dates I list here. Although intertitular prolixity lessened slightly in the final years of the late silent period, they remained more prolix than those of the mid-silent period.

68 Intertitles have been cut from the seven-reel version I viewed, as have characters advertised in promotions for the film. The card I counted as 152 is numbered 214 by Edison. There is, however, no record of a film longer than seven reels being exhibited, which indicates that these cuts were made before distribution.

69 *Vanity Fair*, dir. Charles Kent, Vitagraph, USA, 1911; *Vanity Fair*, dir. Charles J. Brabin and Eugene Nowland, Edison, USA, 1915; *Vanity Fair*, dir. W. C. Rowden, Tense Moments with Great Authors Series, UK, 1922.

70 While the number of elliptic dots varies, it appears to follow the constraints of justified margins rather than to indicate variable lengths for declamatory pauses.

71 *A Tale of Two Cities*, dir. William Humphrey, Vitagraph, USA, 1911. The 1926 film is *The Only Way*, dir. Herbert Wilcox, Herbert Wilcox Productions, UK.

72 The Palace Theatre of Varieties programs 11 April, 1898 and 2 Jan. 1900.

73 *Views and Films Index*, Sept. 1906. Cited in Musser 261.

74 Housman 20.

75 Brownlow attests to the economic motivation behind the minimalist approach to intertitles in this period: "A motion-picture title writer got about two dollars and twenty cents a word – not for the number of words he wrote so much as for the number he avoided writing – while still managing to tell the story" (334).

76 All these examples are taken from the 1911 and 1915 versions of *Vanity Fair*.

77 This information is well documented in many histories of film. See Mast or Cook, for example.

78 Two cards indicate indirect speech: "Mrs. Osborne requests Captain Dobbin to take her home" and "Becky urges Amelia to marry Major Dobbin." Another intertitle introducing a leave-taking scene reads: "Good night," but does not indicate a speaker or appear in quotation marks.

79 *New York Times*, (4 Sept. 1921), section 6: 3.

80 *Little Dorrit* (*Lille Dorrit*), dir. A. W. Sandberg, Nordisk Films, DN, 1924.

81 *Bleak House*, dir. Maurice Elvey, Ideal Films, UK, 1920.

82 Fragmentation in cubist painting, experimental music, and film montage extend here to verbal expression; the point I am stressing, however, is that the spaces between these pauses are those of speech rhythms rather than of musical or visual rhythms.

83 *The Only Way*.

84 I have omitted actor credits for Manette and Defarge that appear on two of the intertitles.

85 A similar verbally based mode of editing revolves around the production of letters. Typically, a character is shown writing in mid- or long midshot, followed by a close-up of the text, then a shot of the character sealing, folding, powdering, or sending the letter. The editing in such sequences creates a similar hybrid visual–verbal syntax in which the verbal leads.

86 Stephenson and Debrix 207.

87 I am indebted to Guerric DeBona for this data.

88 Cited in Lester J. Keyser, "A Scrooge for All Seasons," *The English Novel and the Movies*, eds. Michael Klein and Gillian Parker (New York: Frederick Ungar, 1981) 123. Keyser notes: "Leech's preliminary sketches actually look like part of the story board for the film."

89 Astonishingly, he does not mention Thackeray's illustrations, which are in the same school. A disclaimer of his literary background elsewhere in the interview implies that he had not studied the novel. Interview on http://www.bbc.co.uk/education/bookcase/bookworm/vanity/vanity5.shtml.

90 Arguments have, however, been made regarding the influence of the comic strip. See, for example, John L. Fell, *Film and the Narrative Tradition* (Norman: University of Oklahoma Press, 1974).

91 The phrase "scenes of all sorts" is taken from Thackeray's preface to *Vanity Fair*.

92 Thackeray's plates and vignettes frequently depict letters, books, invitations, bank notes, and newspapers as illegible objects wielded by characters in various ways, but their text must appear in the prose narrative, if it appears at all. Thackeray frequently deems the content of these texts unworthy of specification. For example, he declares that not even the most sentimental reader could bear to read Amelia's letters to George (128), and the climactic note from George to Becky is only summarized, not spelled out (752). Distinctions between documents as objects and as legible texts also exist within the prose itself: the letter with which George is disinherited is given to Dobbin pages before its text is rendered legible. In the 1940 edition (which I reference as more readily accessible than the first edition), see, for example, the frontispiece of Amelia weeping over George's letter and the plates and vignettes on pages 4, 8, 9, 44, 68, 92, 138, 142, 169, 171, 257, 363, 378, 449, 479, 518, 528, 594, 614, and 647.

93 The Internet Movie Database (http://us.imdb.com) lists other actors in the film, but not the roles they played. They include William V. Ranous (probably Rawdon), Harry Northrup, Alec B. Francis, Leo Delaney, Tefft Johnson, and Kate Price (probably Amelia).

94 Even the widespread denigration of the signing gestures of early films (pointing, shaking fists, raising arms to heaven) is further linked to a general disparagement of the word in film. Metz describes these gestures as "a subconscious attempt to speak without words, and to say without verbal language not only what one would have said with it . . . but *in the same way* it would have been said" (*Film Language* 50, his emphasis). This style of acting is typically nominated "historic," differentiated from a "verisimilar" style, the latter being regarded as preferable. Roberta E. Pearson, for example, argues both that "the historic code more nearly resembles spoken language than does the verisimilar code" and that "with the move to psychological causality the historic code became increasingly inadequate . . . unsuitable for the portrayal of individualized, psychologized characters [while] the verisimilar code contributed to the creation of credibly

psychologized individuals." Roberta E. Pearson, *Eloquent Gestures: The Transformation of Performance Style in the Griffith Biograph Films* (Berkeley: University of California Press, 1992) 55.

95 The novel represents Miss Swartz as a mulatto; her physical appearance and the name of her father in the film clearly cast her as Jewish.

96 "Vanity Fair," *Variety* (29 Oct. 1915): 22.

97 The 1922 film does not dramatize this portion of the novel.

98 Interestingly, the film does not warrant the words themselves worthy of intertitular representation; we see only Dobbin's mouthing.

99 A 1932 film of *Vanity Fair* develops this mirror ending at greater length. Becky (Myrna Loy) picks up a mirror and, seeing at first an illusory reflection that shows her still beautiful, declares with delight that she hasn't changed at all. But after Jos (Billy Bevan) walks out in disgust (he does not die in this film), she picks up the mirror again and sees herself as she is – an aging hag – and crumples in despair. *Vanity Fair*, dir. Chester M. Franklin, RCA, USA, 1932.

100 I am aware that psychoanalytic theories of the gaze construct the look as power; I am not operating under this model here.

Chapter 4. Cinematic Novels/Literary Cinema

1 See, for example, Taylor Stoehr, *Dickens: The Dreamer's Stance* (Ithaca: Cornell University Press, 1965); Frank Magill, ed., *The Novel into Film* (Pasadena: Salem, 1980) 74: "Dickens is, of course, among the easiest novelists to adapt to film. He had a strong visual sense in his writings, creating the totality of scene through pithy, descriptive passages, and exploiting in a precinematic era cinematic devices such as the flashback and parallel editing between stories"; Julian Moynahan, "Seeing the Book: Reading the Movie," *The English Novel and the Movies*, eds. Michael Klein and Gillian Parker (New York: Frederick Ungar, 1981) 143–54; and Jeremy Tambling, "Dickens, Digression, and Montage," *The Yearbook of English Studies: Strategies of Reading*, ed. Andrew Gurr (Leeds, England: Modern Humanities Research Association, 1996) 43–53. On Hardy's cinematic writing, see David Lodge, "Thomas Hardy as a Cinematic Novelist," *Thomas Hardy after Fifty Years*, ed. Lance St. John Butler (New York: Macmillan, 1977) 78–89; Joan Grundy, *Hardy and the Sister Arts* (New York: Macmillan, 1979) 106–33.

2 Keith Williams, "Cinematic Joyce," *James Joyce Broadsheet* 57 (Oct. 2000): 3; Wheeler Winston Dixon, *The Cinematic Vision of F. Scott Fitzgerald, Studies in Modern Literature* 62 (Ann Arbor, MI: University Microfilms International Research Press, 1986); Scott F. Stoddart, "Redirecting Fitzgerald's 'Gaze': Masculine Perception and Cinematic License in *The Great Gatsby*," *F. Scott Fitzgerald: New Perspectives*, eds. Jackson R. Bryer, Alan Margolies, Ruth Prigozy (Athens, GA: University of Georgia Press, 2000) 102–14. See also Earl. G. Ingersoll, "Cinematic Effects in Conrad's The Secret Agent," *Conradiana* 21.1 (1989): 29–36; J. M. Armistead, "Henry James for the Cinematic Mind," *English Record* 26:3 (1975): 27–33; Alan Nadel, "Ambassadors from an Imaginary Elsewhere: Cinematic Convention and the Jamesian Sensibility," *Henry James Review* 19.3 (Fall 1998): 279–85. Among other essays published between 1990 and 2000, Emile Zola, Honore de Balzac, G. W. Pabst, Nathaniel West, Eudora Welty, Thomas Pynchon, Don DeLillo, Salmon Rushdie, and Toni Morrison, as well as more generally "ethnographic

writing," "clerical crime novels," and "Spanish vanguard prose" have all been designated "cinematic" in the titles, to say nothing of the hordes of writers who have been so designated in the bodies of academic essays.

3 Leon Edel writes: "Wherever we turn in the nineteenth century we can see the novelist cultivating the camera-eye and the camera movement." Leon Edel, "Novel and the Cinema," *The Theory of the Novel*, ed. John Halperin (New York: Macmillan, 1977) 177.

4 See, for example, Cohen, Magny, and Chatman, all cited earlier.

5 Richard Fine's *Hollywood and the Profession of Authorship, 1928–1940* (Ann Arbor, MI: University Microfilms International Research Press, 1985) and numerous other accounts document the frequency with which novelists have become screenwriters or written with an eye to movie rights.

6 See note 4.

7 Metz, *The Imaginary Signifier* 104, 106–7, 110, 129, 141.

8 Indeed, Eisenstein infantilizes both Dickens and Griffith in order to allow Soviet cinema to take the "mature" position. Referring to "that spontaneous, childlike skill for story-telling, equally typical for Dickens and for the American cinema, which so surely and delicately plays upon the infantile traits in its audience," he concludes, "As adults, we rarely re-read his novels." Sergei Eisenstein, "Dickens, Griffith, and the Film Today," in *Film Form* 201.

9 Bordwell's *On the History of Film Style* details efforts to distance film from other arts in order to create it as "the seventh art."

10 John Grierson, "Putting Punch in a Picture," *Motion Picture News* 34.22 (27 Nov. 1926): 2025.

11 Thomas Craven, "Salome and the Cinema," *The New Republic* 33.425 (24 Jan. 1923): 226.

12 "Motion Picture Films," *Complete Illustrated Catalog of Moving Picture Machines, Stereopticons, Slides, Films* (Chicago: Kleine Optical Co., 1905) 206.

13 Although "Ideal" designates the production company, the aspiration of film to be a better form of painting and theater emerges in term as well.

14 "Stars" includes literary celebrities: a 65-year-old Weedon Grossmith plays the Fiddler.

15 *Masks and Faces*, dir. Fred Paul, Ideal Film Company, UK, 1917.

16 Fell is one of the earliest to address these roots.

17 Ben Brewster and Lea Jacobs, *Theatre to Cinema: Stage Pictorialism and the Early Feature Film* (Oxford: Oxford University Press, 1997) 5.

18 Deleuze, *Cinema 2* 161, 178, 191 ff., 228, 231, 235, 242–43 – these point to only some of the many places where he seeks for "something specific to cinema which has nothing to do with theatre" (263).

19 Bazin 81–82.

20 Timothy Corrigan, *Film and Literature: An Introduction and a Reader* (New York: Prentice-Hall, 1999) 36.

21 Monaco, *How To Read a Film* (2000 edition) 44.

22 Eisenstein 195.

23 See Bruce Morrissette, *Novel and Film* (Chicago: University of Chicago Press, 1985) 15 for references to Homer, Virgil, and cinema. See also G. W. Turner, "Cinematic Effects in Medieval and Modern Narrative," *Southern Review* 27.2 (June 1994): 196–206 and Steven G. Kellman, "The Cinematic Novel: Tracking a Concept,"

Modern Fiction Studies 33.3 (Autumn 1987): 467–77, although the latter discussion is brief and inconclusive.

24 Cited in Eisenstein 205.

25 Charles Dickens, *Oliver Twist*, preface to the second edition (London: Penguin, 1966; originally published 1838) 34–35, his emphasis on "read" and "met," mine on "paint" and "draw."

26 Cited in Robert E. Moore, *Hogarth's Literary Relationships* (Minneapolis: University of Minnesota Press, 1948) 22. Hogarth forges the connection of his painting to theater pictorially as well as verbally: his self-portrait sets a painting of his atop the works of Shakespeare, Milton, and Swift. See Altick 13.

27 Charles Lamb, "On the Genius and Character of Hogarth," *The Reflector* 3 (1811): 62, his emphasis.

28 Chaucer spoke analogically of his poetry as painting: "With soutil pencel was depeynted this storie." *The Oxford English Dictionary*, 2nd ed., eds. J. A. Simpson and E. S. C. Weiner (Oxford: Clarendon, 1989) XI: 464.

29 Sir Joshua Reynolds, *Discourse* 15, 1790, cited in *The Encyclopedia of Poetry and Poetics*, ed. Alex Preminger (Princeton, NJ: Princeton University Press, 1965) description xxiv, 906 p. 25 cm. I am indebted to Alan Filreis for this reference.

30 Cited in George Landow, "Ruskin's Theories of the Sister Arts," http://landow.stg.brown.edu/victorian/ruskin/atheories/1.4.html.

31 Cited in Marion Howard Brazier, *Stage and Screen* (Boston: Trinity Court, 1920) 87. Other common early names gesture to film's technological roots in Edison's Kinetoscope ("kinematograph" or "cinématographe" or "cinematograph," frequently shortened to "kinema" or "cinema"), in magic lanterns ("cinematographic slides"), and in other optical devices ("animatograph").

32 Lindsay 169.

33 Jonathan Richardson did so (see Altick 212).

34 Most famously F. Scott Fitzgerald, cited in later chapters. See also Elizabeth Bruss, "Autobiography and Film: The Eye/I of the Camera," *Autobiography: Essays Theoretical and Critical*, ed. James Olney (Princeton, NJ: Princeton University Press, 1980) 296–320.

35 Lindsay 163.

36 The 2001 Pacific Bell *Smart Yellow Pages*, for example, indexes "Theatres, Concert Halls & Venues," followed by "Theaters – Movie."

37 Joseph Medill Patterson, "The Nickelodeons: The Poor Man's Elementary Course in the Drama," *The Saturday Evening Post* 180.21 (23 Nov. 1917): 38.

38 One of the best known and most widely circulated is Syd Field's *Screenplay: The Foundations of Screenwriting* (New York: Dell Pub. Co., 1979; reprinted 1982, 1984, 1994).

39 To cite just a few examples: Kenneth Rea, ed., *A Better Direction: A National Enquiry into the Training of Directors for Theatre, Film and Television* (London: Calouste Gulbenkian Foundation, 1989); Peter Ansorge, *From Liverpool to Los Angeles: On Writing for Theatre, Film and Television* (London, Boston: Faber and Faber, 1997); Joanmarie Kalter, *Actors on Acting: Performing in Theatre & Film Today* (New York: Sterling, 1979); Rich Rose, *Drawing Scenery for Theater, Film, and Television* (Cincinnati, Ohio: Betterway Books, 1994); Patsy Baker, *Wigs and Make-Up for Theatre, Television, and Film* (Oxford, Boston: Focal, 1993); Lee Baygan, *Makeup for Theatre, Film & Television* (New York: Drama Book Specialists, 1982).

40 Again, to cite only a few sources, see Jennifer Forbes, *Reference Guide to Reviews: A Checklist of Sources for Film, Television, and Theatre Reviews* (Vancouver: University of British Columbia Library, 1976); Dennis La Beau's *Theatre, Film and Television Biographies Master Index* (Detroit: Gale Research Co., 1979); Anthony Slide, Patricia King Hanson, and Stephen L. Hanson, *Sourcebook for the Performing Arts: A Directory of Collections, Resources, Scholars, and Critics in Theatre, Film, and Television* (New York: Greenwood, 1988).

41 The former, a collection edited by David Bradby, Louis James, and Bernard Sharratt (Cambridge University Press, 1980); the latter, a book by Brenda Murphy, also from Cambridge University Press, 1999.

42 Edel 177.

43 Moreover, scholars like Grahame Smith have traced Dickens's visuality to many of the same roots in popular Victorian visual entertainments. See his "Dickens and Adaptation" in *Novel Images: Literature in Performance*, ed. Peter Reynolds (New York: Routledge, 1993) 49–63.

44 See, for example, Harvey 54.

45 Flaxman 9–10.

46 For example, Tom Gunning, *D. W. Griffith and the Origins of American Narrative Film* (Urbana: University of Illinois Press, 1991) 250. See also Angela Dalle Vacche, *Cinema and Painting: How Art is Used in Film* (Austin: University of Texas Press, 1996) for a more general account.

47 Dickens, *Oliver Twist* 168–69. Charlotte Brontë concurs: volume I, chapter 11 of *Jane Eyre* opens, "A new chapter in a novel is something like a new scene in a play." Charlotte Brontë, *Jane Eyre* (Oxford: Oxford University Press, 1993) 97. Eisenstein cites this passage, but suggests that Dickens was a "connecting link" between stage melodrama and Griffith. However, this argument makes neither logical nor chronological sense.

48 Eisenstein 224, 226.

49 See, for example, *Montage and Modern Life, 1919–1942*, ed. Matthew Teitelbaum (Cambridge, MA: MIT Press, 1992); Winston Smith, *"Act Like Nothing's Wrong": The Montage Art of Winston Smith* (San Francisco: Last Gasp, 1994); Zdenek Horinek, "The Possibilities of Theatrical Montage (Successive and Simultaneous)," trans. Eva Poskocilova and Michael Quinn, *Theater Survey* 36:1 (May 1995): 77–86; Russell A. Berman, "Montage as a Literary Technique: Thomas Mann's *Tristan* and T. S. Eliot's *The Waste Land*," *Selecta* 2 (1981): 20–23; Horst Pritz, *Montage in Theater and Film* (Tubingen: Francke, 1993).

50 David Bordwell's *On the History of Film Style* offers a succinct account of the opposition to the montage theory of film art; however, it identifies Montage theory as "the standard version of stylistic history" (12).

51 Monaco 419, 229, 176–78.

52 Margaret Homans, "The Name of the Mother in *Wuthering Heights*," *Bearing the Word: Language and Female Experience in Nineteenth-Century Women's Writings* (Chicago: University of Chicago Press, 1986).

53 Babbitt 204–05. Schlegel cited in Babbitt.

54 "Literary Cinema," 1995–2002, http://library.thinkquest.org/2847/films.htm.

55 Ken Gelder, "Jane Campion and the Limits of Literary Cinema," *Adaptations: From Text to Screen, Screen to Text*, eds. Deborah Cartmell and Imelda Whelehan (London: Routledge, 1999) 157–71.

56 Babbitt and Bluestone cited earlier.

57 Eisenstein 199. Eisenstein's neglect of the more overt and tangible link between Griffith and Dickens is, however, perfectly congruous with the mystifying uses of analogy, which also place film's more tangible aesthetic debts in formal and historical parentheses. Griffith also adapted George Eliot's *Silas Marner* (1859) in 1909 (titled *A Fair Exchange*), Robert Louis Stevenson's *The Suicide Club* (1882) in 1909, Charles Reade's *The Course of True Love Never Did Run Smooth* (1857) in 1910, and Marie Corelli's *The Sorrows of Satan* (1895) in 1926, the last long after his "discovery" of montage.

58 Wellek and Warren 126.

59 L. M. Findlay, "Aspects of Analogy: The Changing Role of the Sister Arts Tradition in Victorian Criticism," *English Studies in Canada* 3.1 (Spring 1977): 51–52.

60 Robert B. Ray, surveying Jeffrey Egan Welch's *Literature and Film: An Annotated Bibliography, 1909–1977* (New York: Garland, 1981), notes that the majority of the 1,235 entries address adaptation. See his "The Field of 'Literature and Film'," cited earlier, 44. See also James R. Messenger, "I Think I Liked the Book Better: Nineteen Novelists Look at the Film Version of Their Work" *Literature/Film Quarterly* 6.1 (1978): 125–34.

61 Robert Giddings and Erica Sheen, eds., *The Classic Novel: From Page to Screen* (Manchester: Manchester University Press, 2000).

62 John C. Tibbetts and James M. Welsh, *Novels into Film: The Encyclopedia of Movies Adapted from Books* (New York: Checkmark Books, 1999) xix.

63 Bluestone 5. Bluestone told me in 1995 that his book was intended in part as a declaration of independence for film from literature.

64 Beja, *Film and Literature.*

65 Wagner, *The Novel and the Cinema.*

66 J. Dudley Andrew, "The Well-Worn Muse: Adaptation in Film History and Theory," *Narrative Strategies: Original Essays in Film and Prose Fiction*, eds. Syndy M. Conger and Janice R. Welsch (Macomb: Western Illinois University, 1980) 12.

67 The following authors and books all fault the fidelity imperative for the state of adaptation studies: McFarlane, *Novel to Film*, cited earlier; Cartmell, Hunter, Kaye, and Whelehan, eds., *Pulping Fictions*, cited earlier; Deborah Cartmell and Imelda Whelehan, eds., *Adaptation: From Text to Screen, Screen to Text* (New York: Routledge, 1999); and James Naremore, ed., *Film Adaptation* (New Brunswick, NJ: Rutgers University Press, 2000).

68 Peter Reynolds, *Novel Images: Literature in Performance* (New York: Routledge, 1993) 3.

69 Robert Stam, "Beyond Fidelity: The Dialogics of Adaptation," *Film Adaptation*, ed. James Naremore (New Brunswick, NJ: Rutgers University Press, 2000) 58.

70 McFarlane 1996.

71 Seger cited earlier. Many academic critics agree: Moynahan describes what he considers to be the uncinematic aspects of Dickens, as well as the cinematic dimensions. See his "Seeing the Book, Reading the Movie," cited earlier.

72 The 1933 Monogram film of *Oliver Twist* uses a wipe shot; the 1934 Monogram *Jane Eyre* blacks out the text, then cuts away to the first scene; the 1944 Fox film of *Jane Eyre*, which shows legible text purportedly from the novel throughout, changes the novel's diction entirely.

73 The 1935 *A Tale of Two Cities* uses several sets of ellipses to condense the book's opening paragraph.

74 William Luhr and Peter Lehman, *Authorship and Narrative in the Cinema: Issues in Contemporary Aesthetics and Criticism* (New York: Putnam, 1977). Cited in Giddings, Selby, and Wensley 10.

75 Monaco 45.

76 Mast, *A Short History of the Movies* 43.

77 This figure includes theatrical literature as well as prose fiction. Linda Seger estimates that in 1992, 85% of Best Picture awards up to 1992 had gone to adaptations, but she includes adaptations of "true life stories" and film remakes in her estimate. Linda Seger, *The Art of Adaptation: Turning Fact and Fiction into Film* (New York: Henry Holt, 1992).

78 "Eventually the killer attempts to shoot the invalid from across the yard. However, the invalid manages to protect himself at the last minute by grabbing a bust of Beethoven and using it as a shield" (35). In Woolrich's story, the killer shoots at the invalid inside his room and the bust is of Rousseau or Montesquieu; the first-person narrator cannot decide which. David Atkinson, in "Hitchcock's Techniques Tell Rear Window Story," *American Cinematographer* 71.1 (1990): 34–40.

79 Bazin 141–43, original emphasis.

Chapter 5. Literary Cinema and the Form/Content Debate

1 McFarlane is the primary spokesman for formalist complaints; John O. Thompson represents one of several cultural studies protests. See his "Film Adaptation and the Mystery of the Original," *Pulping Fictions: Consuming Culture across the Literature/Media Divide* (London: Pluto, 1996) 12.

2 Babbitt, Wellek, and Warren cited in Chapter 4.

3 Balázs 258–61; Bluestone 216.

4 "As it is impossible to extract from a physical body the qualities which really constitute it – colour, extension, and the like – without reducing it to a hollow abstraction, in a word, without destroying it; just so it is impossible to detach the form from the idea, for the idea only exists by virtue of the form." Walter Pater, "Style," *Appreciations* (London: Macmillan, 1890) 28.

5 "Language can be compared with a sheet of paper: thought is the front and the sound the back; one cannot cut the front without cutting the back at the same time; likewise in language, one can neither divide sound from thought nor thought from sound." Ferdinand de Saussure, "The Nature of the Linguistic Sign," *Critical Theory Since 1965*, eds. Hazard Adams and Leroy Searle (Tallahassee: Florida State University Press, 1986) 649.

6 See, for example, Ben Brady, *The Principles of Adaptation for Film and Television* (Austin: University of Texas Press, 1994) and Linda Seger, *The Art of Adaptation: Turning Fact and Fiction into Film* (New York: Henry Holt, 1992).

7 Cited in Anon., "Adaptations: Novel to Film," Urban Cinefile article published online, http://www.urbancinefile.com.au/home/article_view.asp? Article_ID=3463&Section=Features, April 2000.

8 Hegel uses the body/soul analogy throughout his discussion of form and content in *The Philosophy of Fine Art*; Derrida's rejection of the original signified is predicated on a rejection of the Christian theology of incarnation.

9 Pater, "Style" 27.

10 Emily Brontë, *Wuthering Heights* (Oxford: Oxford University Press, World's Classics, 1995; originally published 1847) 80, 167, original emphasis. Further references follow parenthetically in the text.

11 Seger 9.

12 Christopher Orr, "The Discourse on Adaptation," *Wide Angle* 6.2 (1984): 72.

13 Luis Buñuel, *Abismos de Pasion*, Plexus Films, Mexico, 1953.

14 Pater, "Style" 24.

15 Charles Algernon Swinburne, "Emily Brontë," *Athenaeum* (16 June 1883): 762–63. Swinburne robustly rejects the biographical reading in Mary F. Robinson, *The Life of Emily Brontë* (London: Allen, 1883), although he allows that biography could account for the work of a nongenius, like her sister, Anne.

16 Howard Thompson, *The New York Guide to Movies on Television* (Chicago: Quadrangle, 1970) 47; Lester J. Keyser, "A Scrooge for All Seasons," *The English Novel and the Movies*, eds. Michael Klein and Gillian Parker (New York: Frederick Ungar, 1981) 121–22.

17 *Wuthering Heights*, dir. Peter Kosminsky, Paramount, USA, 1992.

18 For example, Martin C. Battestin, "*Tom Jones* on the Telly: Fielding, the BBC, and the Sister Arts," *Eighteenth-Century Fiction* 10.4 (July 1998): 501–5.

19 Orr 73.

20 Pater, "Style" 24, 33.

21 Hegel 525.

22 Bazin 66–67.

23 Cited in the notes to Altick's books as "John Ruskin, 14:38" (no further information, either in the notes or the bibliography).

24 *The Examiner* (13 May 1854): 294, emphasis added.

25 Cited in John Hodge, *Trainspotting and the Shallow Grave* (London: Faber & Faber, 1996) 118.

26 Rose D. Sketchley, *English Book Illustration To-day* (London: Kegan Paul, 1903) 2–3, 56; Jean Mitry, "Remarks on the Problem of Cinematic Adaptation," trans. Richard Dyer, *The Bulletin of the Midwest Modern Language Association* 4 (1971): 4–5.

27 Lewis Melville, "Vanity Fair," *Bioscope* 14. 279 (15 Feb. 1912): 415, 417.

28 McFarlane 119. See also Wagner, Bluestone, and Morris Beja's discussion of "Twenty-Five Films" in his *Film and Literature* cited earlier, one of many such examples.

29 Frank Nugent, review of MGM's *Wuthering Heights*, *The New York Times* 28 (14 April 1939): 2.

30 These films and televizations were directed by Francis Ford Coppola, Kenneth Branagh, Peter Kosminsky, David Skynner, Kenneth Branagh, Baz Luhrmann, and Michael Hoffman, respectively.

31 *Wuthering Heights*, eds. William M. Sale, Jr. and Richard H. Dunn, preface reprinted in the 3rd ed. (New York: Norton, 1990) xi.

32 *Wuthering Heights*, dir. David Skynner, London Weekend Television, UK/USA, 1998. Baker has evidently not seen Kiju Yoshida's *Arashi ga oka* (1988), which also dramatizes both generations from the novel.

33 Barry Koltnow, "Kenneth Branagh Picks Up the Pieces in Mary Shelley's Monster Classic," *Buffalo News* (5 November 1994): 10.

34 New York : Chelsea House Publishers, 1987.

35 Roland Barthes, "Myth Today," *Mythologies*, trans. Annette Lavers (New York: Hill and Wang, 1984) 114, 117.

36 Barthes, *Mythologies* 118.

37 *Wuthering Heights*, dir. William Wyler, MGM, USA, 1939.

38 Cited in Gavin Weightman, *Bright Lights, Big City: London Entertained 1830–1950* (London: Collins & Brown, 1988) 44.

39 *Wuthering Heights*, dir. Paul Nickell, Westinghouse Television Theater, CBS, USA, 1950.

40 In the novel, Cathy tells the love-struck Isabella, "he'd crush you like a sparrow's egg, Isabella, if he found you a troublesome charge. I know he couldn't love a Linton, and yet he'd be quite capable of marrying your fortunes and expectations" (102).

41 The excision of outdoor scenes is partly a result of the theatrical format, but it also serves to prioritize domestic spaces.

42 Since the video has excised the commercials from the *Wuthering Heights* Westinghouse production, and John Maslansky, Video Yesteryear Director of Licensing and Sales, affirms that the CBS stock footage has also removed the commercials, these examples are taken from the Westinghouse adaptation of *Jane Eyre* (aired August 4, 1952), which targeted a similar audience. The intertextuality of *Jane Eyre* and *Wuthering Heights* (trading in old love for new is a central theme in both) and their shared twentieth-century cultural currency, advanced most notably by Patsy Stoneman, seemed to justify the liberty. Moreover, my extensive research into Westinghouse adaptations reveals that every commercial plays either on resemblances between spokesmodels and leading actresses or on affinities between the text's plot and the sales pitch, so that my broader arguments hold firmly here.

43 Barthes 115, 114, 123, 118, 119–121.

44 Seymour Chatman, *Story and Discourse: Narrative Structure in Fiction and Film* (Ithaca, NY: Cornell University Press, 1978); Bordwell, *Narration in the Fiction Film* 50–57 ff.

45 McFarlane 12, 23, 14.

46 *Wuthering Heights*, McGraw-Hill Text Films, USA, 1967.

47 *Arashi ga oka*, dir. Kiju Yoshida, prod. Kaz Yamaguchi and Francis von Buren, Japan, 1988.

48 In the novel, Cathy catches sight of an unidentified figure in her mirror, which Nelly insists is Cathy herself (123–24).

49 Two other films also play heavily on resemblances between the two Cathys: Juliette Binoche plays both mother and daughter in Kosminsky's film; in the LWT version, the young Cathy discovers and reads her mother's writings at Wuthering Heights.

50 McFarlane 115.

51 Keith Cohen, "Eisenstein's Subversive Adaptation," *The Classic American Novel and the Movies*, eds. G. Peary and R. Shatzkin (New York: Ungar, 1977) 255.

52 Umberto Eco, "Casablanca: Cult Movies and Intertextual Collage," *Modern Criticism and Theory: A Reader*, ed. David Lodge (London/New York: Longman, 1988) 447.

53 J. Hillis Miller, "*Wuthering Heights*: Repetition and the Uncanny," *Fiction and Repetition: Seven English Novels* (Cambridge: Harvard University Press, 1982) 50.

54 Sara Mills, Lynne Pearce, Sue Spaull, and Elaine Millard, eds., *Feminist Break Readings/Feminists Reading* (Charlottesville: University of Virginia Press, 1989) 76.

55 *Dil Diya Dard Liya*, dir. A. R. Kardar, Kary Productions, Bombay, India, 1966.

56 For example, Guerric Debona, "Doing Time; Undoing Time: Plot Mutation in David Lean's *Great Expectations*," *Literature/Film Quarterly* 20.1 (1992): 77–100.

57 Anthony Burgess, "On the Hopelessness of Turning Good Books into Films," *New York Times* 20 (April 1975): 15. I am indebted to McFarlane for this reference.

58 Preview of the 1922 film of *Vanity Fair*, *Bioscope* (26 Jan. 1922): 59.

59 Sergei Eisenstein, "Achievement," *Film Form: Essays in Film Theory*, ed. and trans. Jay Leyda (New York: Harcourt, Brace, & World, 1949) 182.

60 Lester D. Friedman, "The Blasted Tree," *The English Novel and the Movies* 52–66.

61 Meisel 36, 30.

62 James Northcote, essay in *The Artist* (1807), cited in Roy Park, *Hazlitt and the Spirit of the Age* (Oxford: Oxford University Press, 1971) 140 and in Altick 219.

63 Walter Pater, "The School of Giorgione," *The Renaissance: Studies in Art and Poetry* (London: Macmillan, 1900; originally published 1873) 130–38.

64 Many literal-minded Victorian painters missed this point, responding to Pater's call by painting musical instruments and musicians! Christopher Wood, *Victorian Painting* (London: Weidenfeld & Nicholson, 1999) 143.

65 Peter Conrad, *Shandyism* (Oxford: Blackwell, 1978) 152.

66 Jim Hitt, *Words and Shadows: Literature on the Screen* (New York: Citadel, 1992) 2.

67 Charles Lamb, "On the Tragedies of Shakespeare, Considered with Reference to the Fitness for Stage Representation," *The Collected Essays of Charles Lamb* (New York: Dutton, 1929) 166–67; 189.

68 Maggie Berg, "A (Provisional) Conclusion, and a Warning About Visual Aids!" *Wuthering Heights: The Writing in the Margin* (New York: Twayne, 1996) 115, 117.

69 Charles Lamb, letter to Samuel Rogers, n.d. (estimated date December, 1833), *The Letters of Charles Lamb*, ed. (New York: Dutton, 1945) 394.

70 Lamb, "Tragedies" 188, 190.

71 Lamb, "Tragedies" 167–68.

72 Letter to Benjamin Robert Haydon dated March 23, 1807, cited in his *The Autobiography of Benjamin Robert Haydon* (Oxford: Oxford University Press, 1927) 61–62. I am indebted to Altick for alerting me to this letter.

73 Spike Milligan, *Wuthering Heights According to Spike Milligan* (London: Michael Joseph, 1994) 118.

74 Lamb, "Tragedies" 183.

75 Bluestone 108.

76 See, for example, John K. Mathison, "Nelly Dean and the Power of *Wuthering Heights*," *NCF* 11 (Sept. 1956): 106–29.

77 *Atlas* 22 Jan. 1848:59.

78 George Henry Lewes, review of *Wuthering Heights* and *Agnes Grey*, *Leader*, (28 Dec. 1850): 953; Vere Henry Hobart, "Thoughts on Modern English Literature," *Fraser's* 60.355 (July 1859): 103.

79 Sydney Dobell, "Currer Bell," *Palladium* Vol. 1 (Sept. 1850): 161–75.

80 *Atlas* 59.

81 *Britannia* (15 Jan. 1848): 42.

82 J. F. "Wuthering Heights," *Temple Bar* 81 (Dec. 1887): 562.

83 Lewes 953; Hobart 103.

84 Hobart 103.

85 John Hutton Balfour Browne, "Charlotte Brontë," *The Westminster Review* LIII.1 (1 Jan. 1878): 55; Russell Baker, introduction to LWT *Wuthering Heights* for WGBH Boston; Mary Ward, "Introduction," *Wuthering Heights* (London: Smith, Elder & Co., 1900) xi–xli.

86 David Keyes, "Wuthering Heights," http://www.geocities.com/Hollywood/Cinema/4069/reviews/1999/wutheringheights.html, 1999.

87 E. P. Whipple, "Novels of the Season," *North American Review* 67 (Oct. 1848): 357–59.

88 Wagner 236.

89 See Chapter 6 for details of this link.

90 Neil Sinyard, *Filming Literature: The Art of Screen Adaptation* (New York: St. Martin's, 1986) 117.

91 Peter Reynolds, *Novel Images: Literature in Performance* (New York: Routledge, 1993) 3.

92 Cohen 255.

93 Nugent 2.

94 1943 review, cited in Bluestone 111.

95 William Makepeace Thackeray, *Vanity Fair* (New York: Heritage, 1940) 70.

96 This emphasis on material historical accuracy became prevalent in late-eighteenth-century theater and painting and continues today.

97 *New York Tribune* (6 May 1923), VI: 3.

98 *Romola*, prod. Henry King, USA, 1925.

99 The bibliography reads:

> The French Revolution . . . . Thomas Carlyle
> Journal of the Temple . . . . M. Clery
> The Memoire of Mlle Echerelles
> The Memoire of M. Nicholas

In citing Carlyle, it cites a common source: Dickens also drew heavily on this work.

100 McFarlane 9.

101 Cited in Hitt 50.

102 This sexual correction is by no means limited to literary film adaptations, but appears in critical analyses of the novel as well. A few years earlier, in 1962, Thomas Moser's Freudian analysis of *Wuthering Heights* argues that "Heathcliff as the embodiment of sexual energy requires detailed explanation not only because critics have largely ignored this role but also because Emily Brontë apparently tried to disguise the truth from herself." "What Is the Matter with Emily Jane?: Conflicting Impulses in *Wuthering Heights*," *NCF* 17 (June 1962): 5.

103 The dialogue has been edited slightly for concision.

104 Michel Foucault, *The History of Sexuality*, trans. Robert Hurley (New York: Pantheon, 1978).

105 *Athenaeum* (11 Feb. 1832): 98.

106 Harry M. Geduld, *The Definitive Jekyll and Hyde Companion* (New York: Garland, 1983) 115.

107 *Britannia* 42.

108 *The Examiner* (8 Jan. 1848): 21.

109 Lewes 953.
110 Lewes 953.
111 Moser 4.
112 *Britannia* 42.
113 Caryn James, "Australia's Films Display a Distinctive Gothic Darkness," *New York Times* 28.2 (28 November 1993): 13:1 cites Campion: "I feel a kinship between the kind of romance Emily Brontë portrayed in *Wuthering Heights* and this film."
114 The episode aired 9 January 1982 on ABC television.
115 The 1998 LWT/WGBH production also villainizes Edgar far beyond Brontë's rendition, though it does not romanticize Heathcliff. When a grown Cathy and Heathcliff are caught spying on Edgar and Isabella, Edgar sets the dogs on them, even after he has clearly seen their faces at close range.
116 Cartmell and Whelehan, "Introduction," *Pulping Fictions* 2–3.
117 See Chapter 1.

Chapter 6. Adaptation and Analogy

1 Analogical models have been popular in discussing translation more generally. See, for example, Eve Tavor Bannet, "Analogy as Translation: Wittgenstein, Derrida, and the Law of Language," *New Literary History* 28.4 (1997): 655–72.
2 Boris M. Eikhenbaum, "Literature and Cinema," *Russian Formalism*, eds. Stephen Bann and John Bowlt (Edinburgh: Edinburgh University Press, 1973) 122.
3 Martin C. Battestin, "*Tom Jones* on the Telly: Fielding, the BBC, and the Sister Arts," *Eighteenth-Century Fiction* 10.4 (July 1998): 503.
4 Bluestone 80.
5 Wagner 226–31.
6 Boyum 81.
7 See, for example, Ben Brady, *The Principles of Adaptation for Film and Television* (Austin: University of Texas Press, 1994); and Linda Seger, *The Art of Adaptation: Turning Fact and Fiction into Film* (New York: Henry Holt, 1992).
8 Wagner 226–27, 322, 230. Wagner's subsequent discussion of analogy is meditative and unstructured: a filmic analogy he does not like (sexual groping in place of a character's idealism) he labels a "violation with a vengeance"; an analogy he does like (stormy weather for a character's troubled mind) he applauds.
9 Martin C. Battestin, "Osborne's *Tom Jones*: Adapting a Classic," *Virginia Quarterly Review* 42 (1966): 378–93.
10 The White Knight insists that the tune of a song he sings is his own invention, but Alice recognizes it as a familiar popular tune wedded to new words (LG 312–13).
11 See, for example, Warren Buckland, *The Cognitive Semiotics of Film* (Cambridge: Cambridge University Press, 2000).
12 The *Alice* books have spawned a wide array of criticism on their language. Two of the better known publications are Robert D. Sutherland's *Language and Lewis Carroll* (Paris: Mouton, 1970) and Gilles Deleuze's and Josue V. Harari's, "The Schizophrenic and Language: Surface and Depth in Lewis Carroll and Antonin Artaud," *Textual Strategies: Perspectives in Post-Structuralist Criticism*, ed. Josue V. Harari (Ithaca : Cornell University Press, 1979) 277–95.
13 Lewis Carroll, *Alice's Adventures in Wonderland* and *Through the Looking Glass*

(New York: Puffin Books, 1962; originally published 1865 and 1872, respectively) 25. Further references follow parenthetically in the text: *Alice's Adventures in Wonderland* is referenced as "AW"; *Through the Looking Glass* is cited as "LG."

14 Thackeray, preface to *Vanity Fair* xvi.

15 In the 1990s, the BBC considerably revamped its adaptation style, partly in response to competition from LWT and partly due to the infusion of more cinematic styles in television generally. It added extradiegetic music, employed more camera angles and movements, and devised melodramatic back stories. See, for example, the BBC's *Hard Times* (1994), *Our Mutual Friend* (1998), and *Oliver Twist* (2000).

16 The BBC's 1979 adaptation of Jane Austen's *Pride and Prejudice* places its famous opening line, "It is a truth universally acknowledged that a single man in possession of a good fortune must be in want of a wife," in the mouth of Elizabeth Bennett (Elizabeth Garvie). *Pride and Prejudice,* prod. Jonathan Powell, dir. Cyril Coke, scr. Fay Weldon, BBC, UK, 1979. The 1989 Anglo-French adaptation of *A Tale of Two Cities* gives its celebrated opening line, "It was the best of times, it was the worst of times," to Sydney Carton (James Wilby). *A Tale of Two Cities,* dir. Philippe Monnier, Granada, FR/GB, 1989.

17 *Alice in Wonderland,* dir. Nick Willing, NBC, USA, 1999.

18 LG 229 (the Gnat's bad joke); LG 238, 278–79, 311 (Alice is reluctant to hear songs and poetry).

19 Paramount's 1933 film features Gary Cooper as the White Knight, W. C. Fields as Humpty Dumpty, Cary Grant as the Mock Turtle, Baby LeRoy as the Joker, Mae Marsh as the Sheep (Figure 32). The 1985 two-part televization, *Alice's Adventures in Wonderland* and *Through the Looking Glass,* casts Red Buttons as the White Rabbit, Ringo Starr as the Mock Turtle, Sammy Davis, Jr., as the Caterpillar, Roddy McDowall as the March Hare, Telly Savalas as the Cheshire Cat, Shelley Winters as the Dodo Bird, Sid Caesar as the Gryphon, Scott Baio as the Pig, Ernest Borgnine as the Lion, Beau Bridges as the Unicorn, Lloyd Bridges as the White Knight, Jonathan Winters as Humpty Dumpty, and Karl Malden as the Walrus. The 1999 NBC televization (cited earlier) stars Whoopi Goldberg as the Cheshire Cat, Gene Wilder as the Mock Turtle, Ben Kingsley as the Caterpillar, Miranda Richardson as the Queen of Hearts, Peter Ustinov as the Walrus, and a number of British television celebrities (including Joanna Lumley as the Tiger Lily). *Alice in Wonderland,* dir. Norman Z. McLeod, USA, 1933. I have not been able to see this film, only stills of it. *Alice's Adventures in Wonderland* and *Through the Looking Glass,* dir. Harry Harris, Columbia TV, USA, 1985. NBC version cited earlier.

20 By contrast, Cary Grant's costume in the 1933 production renders the actor unrecognizable.

21 For a discussion of this style, see Bordwell, Staiger, and Thompson, *The Hollywood Classical Cinema.*

22 This reduction of complex psychological drives to primitive libidinal ones is common to many twentieth-century interpretations of Victorian narratives. See (or don't see) *Dracula Sucks* (1979), *Love at First Bite* (adapts *Dracula,* 1979), *Dr. Sexual and Mr. Hyde* (1971) with Anthony Brzezinski, and *The Adult Version of Dr. Jekyll and Mr. Hide* [sic] (1972), in which the Jekyll character (Chris Leeder, played by Jack Buddliner) metamorphoses into a murderous, castrating lesbian (played by Jane Tsentas).

23 Anthony Goldschmidt's "Alice in Wonderland Psycho-Analyzed," *New Oxford Outlook*, (May 1933): 68–72 reads Carroll as a latent pedophile. Paul Schilder, William Empson, John Skinner, Martin Grotjan have continued the emphasis, as have numerous biographers, from Florence Becker Lennon in 1945 to Michael Bakewell's and Donald Thomas's 1996 biographies. Jan Švankmajer, whose *Alice* forms my second case study, has said, "Carroll is an illustration of the fact that children are better understood by paedophiliacs than by pedagogues." Jan Švankmajer, "Švankmajer on *Alice*," *Afterimage* 13 (Autumn 1987): 51. Cultural links of the *Alice* books to pedophilia extend beyond academic and filmmaker readings. In 1998, British police cracked an Internet child pornography ring called the Wonderland Club, after Carroll's book. Carroll's work as a child photographer as well as his ingenious encryptings of words and numbers reappears in the practices of this ring. Members had to be in possession of at least 10,000 images of child pornography and used complicated encrypting devices and codes to communicate these images.

24 The NBC production is the only one to adjust some of these ratios with special effects, but it by no means adjusts them all.

25 Nine-year-old Natalie Gregory, who plays Alice in the 1985 televization, is an exception.

26 *Alice's Adventures in Wonderland: The World's Favorite Bedtime Story*, dir. Bud Townsend, Playboy Films, USA, 1976.

27 Bluestone 48.

28 Virginia Woolf, "The Cinema" 270.

29 In the same vein, Monty Python also creates a Morse code adaptation of *Gunfight at the OK Corral* and a smoke signal version of *Gentlemen Prefer Blondes*.

30 Jan Švankmajer in conversation with Vratislav Effenberger regarding his adaptation of Edgar Allen Poe's *The Fall of the House of Usher*, originally published in *Film a Doba* 5 (1982), trans. Gaby Dowdell for *Afterimage* 13 (Autumn 1987). Located online at http://yrol.free.fr/CINEMA/SVANKMAJER/interviews.htm.

31 Geoff Andrew, "Malice in Wonderland," *Time Out*, (19–26 October 1988): 16–17; Hames 108.

32 Hames 113.

33 Anthony Lane, "Kafka's Heir," *The New Yorker* (31 Oct. 1994): 54.

34 Michael O'Pray, "Surrealism, Fantasy and the Grotesque: The Cinema of Jan Švankmajer," *Fantasy and the Cinema*, ed. James Donald (London: BFI, 1989) 262.

35 Švankmajer cites this definition by Vratislav Effenberger in an interview with Peter Hames. Peter Hames, "Interview with Jan Švankmajer," trans. Karolina Vocadlo, *Dark Alchemy: The Films of Jan Švankmajer*, ed. Peter Hames (Westport, CT: Greenwood, 1995) 112.

36 The obsessive repetition extends to the exclamatory dialogue cited earlier.

37 Švankmajer, *Afterimage* 13 (1987): 52.

38 Hames 111.

39 A dead mouse in a trap is a possible exception; however, one expects it to rise at any moment.

40 Bruce Kawin offers a capsule summary of the film/dream analogy: "both [films and dreams] are experienced as predominantly visual hallucinations occurring while the subject is physically passive in a darkened environment. Dreams have been described as films that the dreamer generates and watches in a cerebral

theater, as films have been described as dreams generated by artists or businessmen and rendered sharable through the technology of cinematography and projection." Bruce Kawin, "Right-Hemisphere Processing in Dreams and Films," *Dreamworks* 2.1 (1981): 13. Chapters 6–9 of Christian Metz's *The Imaginary Signifier* also address film and dream, as does Robert T. Eberwein's *Film and the Dream Screen: A Sleep and a Forgetting* (Princeton, NJ: Princeton University Press, 1984), Parker Tyler's *The Three Faces of the Film: The Art, the Dream, the Cult* (South Brunswick, NJ: A. S. Barnes, 1967), and numerous studies of individual filmmakers, such as T. Jefferson Kline's *Bertolucci's Dream Loom: A Psychoanalytic Study of Cinema* (Amherst, MA: University of Massachusetts Press, 1987).

41 Jacques Lacan, "Situation de la psychanalyse en 1956,"*Ecrits: A. Selection*, trans. A. Sheridan (New York: Norton,1977)470.

42 Associated Press, 10 May 2001.

43 Effenberger, "Švankmajer on *The Fall of the House of Usher*" 33.

44 Hames 113, 111.

45 Hames 113.

46 Wendy Hall, "Interview with Jan Švankmajer," *Animato*, July 1997. Reprinted online at http://www.illumin.co.uk/svank/biog/inter/hall.html.

47 Hall, cited earlier.

48 Švankmajer in conversation with Vratislav Effenberger, Website cited earlier.

49 Effenberger, "Švankmajer on *Alice*" 53.

50 Sir Richard Blakemore, *Lay-Monastery* 31 (25 Jan. 1713).

51 Esrock, *The Reader's Eye*.

52 See Henry James on illustration in Chapter 2 and Chapter 3's discussion of words in film.

53 Aubrey Beardsley, letter to Robert Ross, circa 3 Jan. 1894, *The Letters of Aubrey Beardsley*, eds. Henry Maas, J. L. Duncan, and W. G. Good (Rutherford: Fairleigh Dickinson, 1970) 61.

54 Milena Michalski, "Cinematic Literature and Literary Cinema: Olesha, Room and the Search for a New Art Form," *Russian Literature, Modernism and the Visual Arts*, eds. Catriona Kelly and Stephen Lovell (Cambridge: Cambridge University Press, 2000) 220–49.

55 *Alice in Wonderland*, dirs. Clyde Geronimi, Hamilton Luske, Wilfred Jackson, The Walt Disney Company, USA, 1951.

56 At the end of the story, the sobs of the Mock Turtle are shown to have derived from cattle lowing in the waking world.

57 *OED*, 2nd ed., VII: 666.

58 Wade, *Visual Allusions* 1, 4.

59 Not all imaging is visual: we can image sound, taste, smell, and touch. Susanna Miller has shown the evocative imaging of blind subjects in her essay, "Imagery and Blindness," *Imagery: Current Developments*, eds. Peter J. Hampson, David F. Marks, and J. T. E. Richardson (London: Routledge, 1990) 129–49.

60 N. Roy Clifton's *The Figure in Film* (London: Associated University Press, 1983) constitutes a notable exception, but his argument has had little impact largely because it applies verbal paradigms, which rest uneasily on film. I am, however, indebted to Clifton for inspiring my research into animated figures, which are his most convincing examples.

61 Roy Paul Madsen, *The Impact of Film* (New York: Macmillan, 1973) 255.

62 Metz, *Imaginary Signifier* 197.

63 Paul de Man, for example, has argued: "All language is . . . a conceptual, figural, metaphorical metalanguage." *Allegories of Reading* (New Haven: Yale University Press, 1979) 152–53.

64 Liam F. Heaney, "The Essence of Language: Metaphorically Speaking," *Contemporary Review* 266.1553 (1995): 313–19.

65 Raymond W. Gibbs, Jr., "Why Many Concepts Are Metaphorical," *Cognition* 61 (1996): 309.

66 Pamela G. Fry, "Is Reading a Metaphorical Process? A Vichian Approach to Language and Thought," *Reading Psychology* 15 (1994): 279.

67 Hildebrand Jacobs, "Of the Sister Arts; An Essay," (Los Angeles, CA: The Augustan Reprint Society, 1974; essay date 1734) 5.

68 Metz, *Film Language* 45, his emphasis.

69 Terry Ramsaye, *A Million and One Nights: A History of the Motion Picture* (New York: Simon and Schuster, 1926) 1: lxi.

70 Metz, *Film Language* 43.

71 Metz, *Imaginary Signifier* 209, 172.

72 Bluestone 1, emphasis added.

73 John Dryden, "A Parallel betwixt Painting and Poetry," preface to *De Arte Graphica* by C. A. Du Fresnoy (London: J. Hepinstall, 1745) xx.

74 William Wordsworth, "Illustrated Books and Newspapers," *Poetical Works of William Wordsworth,* eds. E. de Selincourt and Helen Darbishire (Oxford: Clarendon, 1947) 75.

75 Virginia Woolf, "The Cinema" 270.

76 Virginia Woolf, "Pictures" 174.

77 James Harris, "Three Treatises. The First Concerning Art. The Second Concerning Music, Painting, and Poetry. The Third Concerning Happiness" (J. H. London, J. Nourse and P. Vaillant, 1744). Harris is one of many to advance this argument. Fitzgerald cited in Harrington 117.

78 Trapp adduced that "Thoughts are the images of things as words are of thoughts" in much the same way that Kenner has advanced that "A word is an image of an idea, and an idea is an image of a thing." Cited in Mitchell, *Iconology* 19, 22.

79 Altick 241–42.

80 Stromgren and Norden describe experiments with adding touch and smell to film viewing and listening in the patented technologies of Emergo™, Smellavision™, and Odorama™ (250).

81 Bluestone vi. Although avant-garde film and psychoanalytic criticism have linked film to dream, there is a strong counterclaim insisting that "the paradoxical experiences of dreaming cannot be reproduced literally in the form of explicit visual images." Jonathan Miller, *Subsequent Performances* (London: Faber, 1986) 240.

82 Stromgren and Norden 173.

83 Bruss 296–320 and Raymond Tallis, "The Realistic Novel versus the Cinema," *Critical Quarterly* 27.2 (1985): 57–65 give examples of this common critique.

84 Bluestone 48.

85 Morris Beja says that film can show us someone in pain, but not pain. Cited in Giddings, Selby, and Wensley 20.

86 Georg Goldenberg, Christa Artner, and Ivo Podreka, "Image Generation and the Territory of the Left Posterior Cerebral Artery," *Mental Images in Human Cognition,*

eds. Robert Logie and Michel Denis (New York: Elsevier Science Publishers, 1991) 393.

87 Robert G. Kunzendorf, "Mind-Brain Identity Theory: A Materialistic Foundation for the Psychophysiology of Mental Imagery," *The Psychophysiology of Mental Imagery: Theory, Research and Applications,* eds. Robert G. Kunzendorf and Anees A. Sheikh (Amityville, NY: Baywood Publishing Co., 1990) 21.

88 J. T. E. Richardson, "Imagery and the Brain," *Imagery and Cognition,* eds. Cesare Cornoldi and Mark A. McDaniel (New York: Springer-Verlag, 1991) 5.

89 Stephen Michael Kosslyn, *Image and Mind* (Cambridge, MA: Harvard University Press, 1980) 7, 18.

90 Edward Branigan, *Narrative Comprehension and Film* (New York: Routledge, 1992) 36.

91 See Branigan 36. For a fuller discussion, see Nicholas J. Wade and Michael Swanston, *Visual Perception: An Introduction* (London: Routledge, 1991).

92 Kunzendorf 25, original emphasis.

93 Andrew 101.

94 See also Esrock on this subject.

95 Lane 52.

96 J. Dudley Andrew, "The Primacy of Figure in Cinematic Signification," *Cinema and Language,* eds. Stephen Heath and Patricia Mellencamp (Frederick, MD: University Publications of America, 1983) 140.

97 Metz, *Imaginary Signifier* 215, original emphasis.

98 This pun derives from Carroll's discussion between Alice and the Mouse (AW 50).

99 Carroll too tackles the problems of visual representation in the Dormouse's story of the three sisters who "were learning to draw ... and they drew all manner of things – everything that begins with an M ... such as mouse-traps, and the moon, and memory, and muchness – you know you say things are 'much of a muchness' – did you ever see such a thing as a drawing of a muchness?" (AW 101–2). Tenniel wisely did not attempt the illustration.

100 Margaret J. Intons-Peterson and Mark A. McDaniel, "Symmetries and Asymmetries Between Imagery and Perception," *Imagery and Cognition,* eds. Cesare Cornoldi and Mark A. McDaniel (New York: Springer-Verlag, 1991) 47–76.

101 Metz, *Film Language* 69.

102 Cathy H. Dent-Read and Agnes Szokolszky, "Where Do Metaphors Come From?" *Metaphor and Symbolic Activity* 8.3 (1993): 227, original emphasis.

103 Michel Ciment and Lorenzo Codelli, "Entretien avec Jan Švankmajer," *Positif* 345 (1989): 45, my translation.

104 Lewis Carroll, *Vanity Fair* 24 (March 1879), cited in Martin Gardner, *The Universe in a Handkerchief: Lewis Carroll's Mathematical Recreations, Games, Puzzles, and Word Plays* (New York: Copernicus, 1996) 98.

105 *Tess,* dir. Roman Polanski, Renn, FR/Columbia, USA, 1979.

106 David Lodge, "Thomas Hardy as a Cinematic Novelist," *Thomas Hardy After 50 Years,* ed. Lance St. John Butler, (New York: Macmillan, 1977) 80, 81, 85.

107 William V. Constanzo, "Polanski in Wessex: Filming *Tess of the d'Urbervilles,*" *Literature/Film Quarterly* 9.2 (1981): 76, 74.

108 Thomas Hardy, *Tess of the D'Urbervilles* (Oxford: Oxford University Press, 1988; originally published 1891) 20; Jonathan Miller, *Subsequent Performances* (London: Faber, 1986) 226.

109 In the video, which is not widescreen, Angel steps out of the frame. In the next shot, the "pan and scan" mode used to adapt widescreen films to video engages in an abrupt pan to locate him in the chair.

110 Kaja Silverman, "History, Figuration, and Female Subjectivity in *Tess of the D'Urbervilles*," *Novel* 18.1 (1984): 15. A central concern is with the way "the assimilation of figure into background means the abolition not just of hierarchy, but of difference, and hence of identity" (27).

111 Elaine Scarry, graduate seminar at Harvard University, Spring 1992. See chapter XLVII of *Tess of the d'Urbervilles*.

112 As Tess listens to Alec's appeal, the workings of her mind are metaphorically represented by the cogitating machine wheel that frames her head.

113 Rescreening the film, one notes that the same musical pattern accompanies Tess's biting of the strawberry, a prefiguring of her later sexual penetration by Alec and that an identical knife to the one Tess uses to kill Alec is represented in this scene as Alec carves meat to feed Tess.

114 Kinski won a Golden Globe audience award for "best newcomer." Reviews and criticism of the film generally deride the acting and screenwriting.

115 Preface to the 1896 edition, original emphasis.

116 Since the 1990s, taboos against voice-over and verbal titles in film and television have been melting, as films like *Babe* and television programs like *Frasier* make clear.

Works Cited

Prose Works Cited

Abel, Elizabeth. "Redefining the Sister Arts: Baudelaire's Response to the Art of Delacroix." *Critical Inquiry* 6.3 (1980): 363–84.

Altick, Richard D. *Paintings from Books: Art and Literature in Britain. 1760–1900.* Columbus: Ohio State Press, 1985.

Andrew, Dudley. *Concepts in Film Theory.* New York: Oxford University Press, 1981.

"The Primacy of Figure in Cinematic Signification." *Cinema and Language.* Eds. Stephen Heath and Patricia Mellencamp. Frederick, MD: University Publications of America, 1983.

"The Well-Worn Muse: Adaptation in Film History and Theory." *Narrative Strategies: Original Essays in Film and Prose Fiction.* Eds. Syndy M. Conger and Janice R. Welsch. Macomb: Western Illinois University Press, 1980.

Andrew, Geoff. "Malice in Wonderland." *Time Out* 19–26 Oct. 1988: 16–17.

Ansorge, Peter. *From Liverpool to Los Angeles: On Writing for Theatre, Film and Television.* Boston: Faber and Faber, 1997.

Armistead, J. M. "Henry James for the Cinematic Mind." *English Record* 26.3 (1975): 27–33.

Atkinson, David. "Hitchcock's Techniques Tell Rear Window Story." *American Cinematographer* 71.1 (1990): 34–40.

Aycock, Wendell, and Michael Shoenecke, eds. *Film and Literature: A Comparative Approach to Adaptation.* Lubbock: Texas Tech University Press, 1988.

Ayto, John, ed. *Dictionary of Word Origins.* New York: Arcade, 1991.

Babbitt, Irving. *The New Laocoön: An Essay on the Confusion of the Arts.* Boston: Houghton Mifflin, 1910.

Baker, Patsy. *Wigs and Make-Up for Theatre, Television, and Film.* Boston: Focal, 1993.

Balázs, Béla. *Theory of Film: Character and Growth of a New Art.* Trans. Edith Bone. New York: Dover, 1970. Originally trans. 1952.

Bann, Stephen, and John Bowlt, eds. *Russian Formalism.* Edinburgh: Edinburgh University Press, 1973.

Bannet, Eve Tavor. "The Scene of Translation: After Jakobson, Benjamin, de Man, and Derrida." *New Literary History* 24 (1993): 577–95.

Barthes, Roland. *Image – Music – Text.* London: Fontana, 1977.

Mythologies. Trans. Annette Lavers. New York: Hill and Wang, 1984.

Battestin, Martin C. "Osborne's *Tom Jones*: Adapting a Classic." *Virginia Quarterly Review* 42 (1966): 378–93.

"*Tom Jones* on the Telly: Fielding, the BBC, and the Sister Arts." *Eighteenth-Century Fiction* 10.4 (July 1998): 501–05.

Baygan, Lee. *Makeup for Theatre, Film & Television.* New York: Drama Book Specialists, 1982.

Bazin, André. *What Is Cinema?* 2 vols. Trans. Hugh Gray. Berkeley: University of California Press, 1967, 1971.

Beach, Rex. "The Author and the Film." *Mentor* 9.6 (July 1921): 31.

Beardsley, Aubrey. Letter to Robert Ross. Circa 3 Jan. 1894. *The Letters of Aubrey Beardsley.* Eds. Henry Maas, J. L. Duncan, and W. G. Good. Rutherford: Fairleigh Dickinson, 1970. 61.

Beja, Morris. *Film and Literature.* New York: Longman, 1976.

Berg, Maggie. "A Provisional Conclusion, and a Warning About Visual Aids!" *Wuthering Heights: The Writing in the Margin.* New York: Twayne, 1996.

Berman, Russell A. "Montage as a Literary Technique: Thomas Mann's *Tristan* and T. S. Eliot's *The Waste Land.*" *Selecta* 2 1981: 20–23.

Blackburn, Henry. *The Art of Illustration.* London: W. H. Allen, 1896.

Blakemore, Sir Richard. *Lay-Monastery* 31 (25 Jan. 1713). Reprinted in *The Gleaner: A Series of Periodical Essays.* Ed. Nathan Drake (London: Suttaby, Evance, & Co., 1811) 1: 30–37.

Bluestone, George. *Novels into Film.* Berkeley: University of California Press, 1957.

Bogardus, Ralph, ed. *Pictures and Texts: Henry James, A. L. Coborn, and New Ways of Seeing in Literary Culture.* Ann Arbor, MI: University of Microfilms International Research Press, 1984.

Bordwell, David. *Narration in the Fiction Film.* Madison: University of Wisconsin Press, 1985.

On the History of Film Style. Cambridge, MA: Harvard University Press, 1997.

Bordwell, David, Janet Staiger, and Kristin Thompson. *The Hollywood Classical Cinema: Film Style and Mode of Production to 1960.* London: Routledge and Kegan Paul, 1985.

Boyum, Joy Gould. *Double Exposure: Fiction into Film.* New York: Plume, 1985.

Brady, Ben. *Principles of Adaptation for Film and Television.* Austin: University of Texas Press, 1994.

Bradby, David, Louis James, and Bernard Sharratt. *Performance and Politics in Popular Drama: Aspects of Popular Entertainment in Theatre, Film, and Television. 1800–1976.* Cambridge University Press, 1980.

Branigan, Edward. *Narrative Comprehension and Film.* New York: Routledge, 1992.

Brazier, Marion Howard. *Stage and Screen.* Boston: Trinity Court, 1920.

Brewster, Ben, and Lea Jacobs. *Theatre to Cinema: Stage Pictorialism and the Early Feature Film.* Oxford: Oxford University Press, 1997.

Brontë, Charlotte. *Jane Eyre.* New York: Oxford University Press, 1975. Originally published 1847.

Brontë, Emily. *Wuthering Heights.* Oxford: Oxford University Press, World's Classics, 1995. Originally published 1847.

Brown, John. *North British Review* 40 (1864): 255.

Browne, John Hutton Balfour. "Charlotte Brontë." *The Westminster Review* LIII.1 (1 Jan. 1878): 55.

Brownell, W. C. "William Makepeace Thackeray." *Scribner's Magazine* 25 (Feb. 1899): 236–49.

Brownlow, Kevin. *The Parade's Gone By.* New York: Knopf, 1968.

Bruss, Elizabeth. "Autobiography and Film: The Eye/I of the Camera." *Autobiography: Essays Theoretical and Critical.* Ed. James Olney. Princeton: Princeton University Press, 1980. 296–320.

Buckland, Warren. *The Cognitive Semiotics of Film.* Cambridge: Cambridge University Press, 2000.

Bulwer-Lytton, Edward. *The Last of the Barons.* Boston: Estes and Lauriat, 1892.

Burgess, Anthony. "On the Hopelessness of Turning Good Books into Films." *New York Times* 124/42820 (20 April 1975): S 2:1.

Butler, Lance St. John, ed. *Thomas Hardy after Fifty Years.* New York: Macmillan, 1977.

Card, James. *Seductive Cinema: The Art of Silent Film.* New York: Knopf, 1994.

Carrière, Jean-Claude. *The Secret Language of Film.* Trans. Jeremy Leggatt. New York: Pantheon Books, 1994.

Carroll, Lewis. *Alice's Adventures in Wonderland and Through the Looking Glass.* New York: Puffin, 1962. Originally published 1865 and 1872, respectively.

Cartmell, Deborah, and Imelda Whelehan, eds. *Adaptations: From Text to Screen, Screen to Text.* New York: Routledge, 1999.

Cartmell, Deborah, I. Q. Hunter, Heidi Kaye, and Imelda Whelehan, eds. *Pulping Fictions: Consuming Culture Across the Literature/Media Divide.* London: Pluto, 1996.

Chatman, Seymour. *Story and Discourse: Narrative Structure in Fiction and Film.* Ithaca: Cornell University Press, 1978.

"What Novels Can Do That Films Can't and Vice Versa." *Critical Inquiry* 7 (1980): 121–40.

Ciment, Michel, and Lorenzo Codelli. "Entretien avec Jan Svankmajer." *Positif* 345 (1989): 45–47.

Clifton, N. Roy. *The Figure in Film.* London: Associated University Press, 1983.

Coates, Christopher. "Thackeray's Editors and the Dual Text of *Vanity Fair.*" *Word & Image* 9.1 (1993): 39–50.

Cohen, Keith. "Eisenstein's Subversive Adaptation." *The Classic American Novel and the Movies.* Eds. G. Peary and R. Shatzkin. New York: Ungar, 1977. 245–55.

Film and Fiction: The Dynamics of Exchange. New Haven: Yale University Press, 1979.

Colby, Robert A. "'Scenes of All Sorts . . .': *Vanity Fair* on Stage and Screen." *Dickens Studies Annual* 9 (1981): 163–94.

Colpi, Henri. "Debasement of the Art of Montage." *Film Culture* 22–23 (Summer 1961): 34–37.

Congdon, Charles T. "Over-Illustration." *North American Review* 139 (1884): 480–91.

Conger, Syndy M., and Janice R. Welsch, eds. *Narrative Strategies: Original Essays in Film and Prose Fiction.* Macomb: Western Illinois University Press, 1980.

Conrad, Joseph. Preface to *The Nigger of the "Narcissus."* London: Penguin, 1987.

Conrad, Peter. *Shandyism.* Oxford: Blackwell, 1978.

Cook, David A. *A History of Narrative Film.* 3rd ed. New York: Norton, 1996.

Constanzo, William V. "Polanski in Wessex: Filming *Tess of the d'Urbervilles.*" *Literature/Film Quarterly* 9.2 (1981): 71–78.

Corliss, Richard. "The Hollywood Screenwriter." *Film Theory and Criticism.* 2nd ed. Eds. Gerald Mast and Marshall Cohen. Oxford: Oxford University Press, 1979. 692–701.

Corrigan, Timothy. *Film and Literature: An Introduction and a Reader.* New York: Prentice Hall, 1999.

Craven, Thomas. "Salome and the Cinema." *The New Republic* 33.425 (24 Jan. 1923): 225–26.

Curry, Robert. "Films and Dreams." *Journal of Aesthetics and Art Criticism* 33.1 (1974): 83–89.

Curtis, Gerard. "Shared Lines: Pen and Pencil as Trace." *Victorian Literature and the Victorian Visual Imagination.* Eds. Carol T. Christ and John O. Jordan. Berkeley: University of California Press, 1995.

Dagle, Joan. "Narrative Discourse in Film and Fiction: The Question of the Present Tense." *Narrative Strategies: Original Essays in Film and Prose Fiction.* Eds. Syndy M. Conger and Janet R. Welsch. Macomb: Western Illinois University Press, 1980. 47–59.

Debona, Guerric. "Doing Time; Undoing Time: Plot Mutation in David Lean's Great Expectations." *Literature/Film Quarterly* 20.1 (1992): 77–100.

Deleuze, Gilles, *Cinema 2: The Time-Image.* Trans. Hugh Tomlinson and Robert Galeta. Minneapolis: University Minnesota Press, 1989.

Deleuze, Gilles, and Josue V. Harari. "The Schizophrenic and Language: Surface and Depth in Lewis Carroll and Antonin Artaud." *Textual Strategies: Perspectives in Post-Structuralist Criticism.* Ed. Josue V. Harari. Ithaca: Cornell University Press, 1979. 277–95.

De Man, Paul. *Allegories of Reading.* New Haven: Yale University Press, 1979.

Dent-Read, Cathy H., and Agnes Szokolszky. "Where Do Metaphors Come From?" *Metaphor and Symbolic Activity* 8.3 (1993): 227–42.

Derrida, Jacques. *Of Grammatology.* Baltimore: Johns Hopkins University Press, 1974.

De Saussure, Ferdinand. "The Nature of the Linguistic Sign." *Critical Theory Since 1965.* Eds. Hazard Adams and Leroy Searle. Tallahassee: Florida State University Press, 1986. 546–657.

Dick, Bernard F. *Anatomy of Film.* 3rd ed. New York: St. Martin's, 1998.

Dickens, Charles. *Great Expectations.* New York: Penguin, 1965. Originally published 1860–61.

——— *Oliver Twist.* London: Penguin, 1966. Originally published 1836–37.

Dixon, Wheeler Winston. *The Cinematic Vision of F. Scott Fitzgerald. Studies in Modern Literature* 62. Ann Arbor, MI: University Microfilms International Research Press, 1986.

Dobell, Sydney. "Currer Bell." *Palladium* 1 (Sept. 1850): 161–75.

Draper, R. P., ed. *Hardy: The Tragic Novels: A Casebook.* New York: Macmillan, 1975.

Dryden, John. "A Parallel Betwixt Painting and Poetry." Preface to *De Arte Graphica* by C. A. Du Fresnoy. London: J. Hepinstall, 1745.

Du Maurier, George. "The Illustrating of Books: From the Serious Artist's Point of View." *The Magazine of Art* XIII (1890): 350–75.

Eberwein, Robert. *Film and the Dream Screen: A Sleep and a Forgetting.* Princeton, NJ: Princeton University Press, 1984.

Eco, Umberto. "Casablanca: Cult Movies and Intertextual Collage." *Modern Criticism and Theory: A Reader.* Ed. David Lodge. New York: Longman, 1988.

Edel, Leon. "Novel and the Cinema." *The Theory of the Novel.* Ed. John Halperin. New York: Macmillan, 1977. 177–88.

Effenberger, Vratislav. "Švankmajer on *The Fall of the House of Usher.*" Trans. Gaby Dowdell. *Afterimage* 13 (1987): 33.

Eighteenth-Century Fiction 10.4 (July 1998).

Eikhenbaum, Boris M. "Literature and Cinema." *Russian Formalism.* Eds. Stephen Bann and John Bowit. Edinburgh: Edinburgh University Press, 1973. 122–27.

Eisenstein, Sergei. *Film Form: Essays in Film Theory.* Trans. Jay Leyda. New York: Harcourt Brace & World, 1949.

Elliott, Eric. *Anatomy of Motion Picture Art.* Territet, Switzerland: Riant Chateau, 1928.

Ellis, John. "The Literary Adaptation." *Screen* 23 (1982): 3–5.

Elsaesser, Thomas, and Adam Barker. *Early Cinema: Space, Frame, Narrative.* London: British Film Institute, 1990.

Esrock, Ellen J. *The Reader's Eye: Visual Imaging as Reader Response.* Baltimore: Johns Hopkins University Press, 1994.

Fairfield, Sidney. "The Tyranny of the Pictorial." *Lippincott's Monthly Magazine* 55 (1895): 861–64.

Fell, John L. *Film and the Narrative Tradition.* Norman: University of Oklahoma Press, 1974.

Field, Syd. *Screenplay: The Foundations of Screenwriting.* New York: Dell Pub. Co., 1979. Reprinted 1982, 1984, 1994.

Findlay, L. M. "Aspects of Analogy: The Changing Role of the Sister Arts Tradition in Victorian Criticism." *English Studies in Canada* 3.1 (Spring 1977): 51–68.

Fine, Richard. *Hollywood and the Profession of Authorship, 1928–1940.* Ann Arbor, MI: University Microfilms International Research Press, 1985.

Fisher, Judith. "Image versus Text in the Illustrated Novels of William Makepeace Thackeray." *Victorian Literature and the Victorian Visual Imagination.* Eds. Carol T. Christ and John O. Jordan. Berkeley: University of California Press, 1995. 60–87.

Flaxman, Rhoda L. *Victorian Word-Painting and Narrative: Toward the Blending of Genres. Nineteenth-Century Studies.* Series ed. Juliet McMaster. Ann Arbor: University Microfilms International Research Press, 1987.

Forbes, Jennifer. *Reference Guide to Reviews: A Checklist of Sources for Film, Television, and Theatre Reviews.* Vancouver: University of British Columbia Library, 1976.

Foucault, Michel. *The History of Sexuality.* Trans. Robert Hurley. New York: Pantheon Books, 1978.

    This Is Not a Pipe. Trans. James Harkness. Berkeley: University of California Press, 1981.

Freud, Sigmund. *The Interpretation of Dreams.* Trans. James Strachey. *The Standard Edition of the Complete Psychological Works of Sigmund Freud.* London: Hogarth, 1953/1973.

    Jokes and Their Relation to the Unconscious. Trans. James Strachey. London: Routledge & Kegan Paul, 1960.

Friedman, Lester D. "The Blasted Tree." *The English Novel and the Movies.* Eds. Michael Klein and Gillian Parker. New York: Ungar, 1981. 52–66.

Fry, Pamela G. "Is Reading a Metaphorical Process? A Vichian Approach to Language and Thought." *Reading Psychology* 15 (1994): 273–80.

Gardner, Martin. *The Universe in a Handkerchief: Lewis Carroll's Mathematical Recreations, Games, Puzzles, and Word Plays.* New York: Copernicus, 1996.

Gaudreault, André. "Showing and Telling: Image and Word in Early Cinema." *Early Cinema: Space, Frame, Narrative.* Eds. Thomas Elsaesser and Adam Barker. London: British Film Institute, 1990.

Geduld, Harry M. *The Definitive Jekyll and Hyde Companion.* New York: Garland, 1983.

Gelder, Ken. "Jane Campion and the Limits of Literary Cinema." *Adaptations: From Text to Screen, Screen to Text.* Eds. Deborah Cartmell and Imelda Whelehan. London: Routledge, 1999. 157–71.

Géloin, Ghislaine. "The Plight of Film Adaptation in France: Toward Dialogic Process in the *Auteur* Film." *Film and Literature: A Comparative Approach to Adaptation.* Eds. Wendell Aycock and Michael Shoenecke. Lubbock: Texas Tech University Press, 1988. 135–48.

Gentner, Dedre, and Michael Jeziorski. "Analogy, Mental Models, and Conceptual Change." Project summary http://www.qrg.nwu.edu/projects/ONR-SM/analogy.htm.

"The Shift from Metaphor to Analogy in Western Science." *Metaphor and Thought.* 2nd ed. Ed. Andrew Ortony. Cambridge University Press, 1993. 447–80.

Giannetti, Louis. *Understanding Movies.* 8th ed. Upper Saddle River, NJ: Prentice-Hall, 1999.

Gibbs, Jr., Raymond W. "Why Many Concepts Are Metaphorical." *Cognition* 61 (1996): 309–19.

Giddings, Robert, and Erica Sheen, eds. *The Classic Novel: From Page to Screen.* Manchester: Manchester University Press, 2000.

Giddings, Robert, Keith Selby, and Chris Wensley. *Screening the Novel: The Theory and Practice of Literary Dramatization.* London: Macmillan, 1990.

Gneiting, Teona Tone. "The Pencil's Role in Vanity Fair." *Huntington Library Quarterly* 39 (1976): 171–202.

Goldenberg, Georg, Christa Artner, and Ivo Podreka. "Image Generation and the Territory of the Left Posterior Cerebral Artery." *Mental Images in Human Cognition.* Eds. Robert Logie and Michel Denis. New York: Elsevier Science, 1991.

Goldschmidt, Anthony. "Alice in Wonderland Psycho-Analyzed." *New Oxford Outlook* (May 1933): 68–72.

Gombrich, E. H. "Meditations on a Hobby Horse." *Meditations on a Hobby Horse and Other Essays on the Theory of Art.* London: Phaidon, 1963.

"Moment and Movement in Art." *Journal of Warburg and Courtauld Institutes* 27 (1964): 293–306.

Grierson, John. "Putting Punch in a Picture." *Motion Picture News* 34.22 (27 Nov. 1926): 2025–26.

Griffith, James. *Adaptations as Imitations: Films from Novels.* Newark: University of Delaware Press, 1997.

Grundy, Joan. *Hardy and the Sister Arts.* New York: Harper and Row, 1979.

Gunning, Tom. *D. W. Griffith and the Origins of American Narrative Film.* Urbana: University of Illinois Press, 1991.

Hall, Wendy. "Interview with Jan Švankmajer." *Animato* (July 1997). Reprinted online at http://www.illumin.co.uk/svank/biog/inter/hall.html.

Halperin, John, ed. *The Theory of the Novel.* New York: Macmillan, 1977.

Hames, Peter. "Interview with Jan Švankmajer." Trans. Karolina Vocadlo. *Dark Alchemy: The Films of Jan Švankmajer.* Ed. Peter Hames. Westport, CT: Greenwood Press, 1995. 96–118.

Hammerton, P. G. "Book Illustration." *Portfolio Papers.* Boston: Roberts, 1889. 293–311.

Hannah, Donald. "'The Author's Own Candles': The Significance of the Illustrations to *Vanity Fair.*" *Renaissance and Modern Essays.* Ed. G. R. Hibbard. New York: Barnes & Noble, 1966. 119–127.

Hardy, Thomas. *Tess of the d'Urbervilles.* New York: Oxford University Press, 1983. Originally published 1891.

Harrington, John, ed. *Film And/As Literature.* Englewood Cliffs, NJ: Prentice-Hall, 1977.

Harris, James. *Three Treatises. The First Concerning Art. The Second Concerning Music, Painting, and Poetry. The Third Concerning Happiness.* London: J. Nourse and P. Vaillant, 1744.

Harris, Margaret. "Thomas Hardy's Tess of the d'Urbervilles: Faithfully Presented by Roman Polanski?" *Sydney Studies in English* 7 (1981–2): 115–22.

Harthan, John. *The History of the Illustrated Book: The Western Tradition.* London: Thames & Hudson, 1981.

Harvey, J. R. *Victorian Novelists and Their Illustrators.* London: Sidgwick & Jackson, 1970.

Haydon, Benjamin Robert. *The Autobiography of Benjamin Robert Haydon.* Oxford: Oxford University Press, 1927.

Heaney, Liam F. "The Essence of Language: Metaphorically Speaking." *Contemporary Review* 266.1553 (1995): 313–19.

Heath, Stephen. "Narrative Space." *Contemporary Film Theory.* Ed. Antony Easthope. New York: Longman, 1993. 68–94.

Heath, Stephen, and Patricia Mellencamp, eds. *Cinema and Language.* Frederick, MD: University Publications of America, 1983.

Hedges, Inez. *Breaking the Frame: Film Language and the Experience of Limits.* Bloomington: Indiana University Press, 1991.

Hegel, Georg Wilhelm Friedrich. *The Philosophy of Fine Art. Critical Theory Since Plato.* Ed. Hazard Adams. New York: Harcourt Brace Jovanovich, 1971. 518–31.

Hitt, Jim. *Words and Shadows: Literature on the Screen.* New York: Citadel, 1992.

Hobart, Vere Henry. "Thoughts on Modern English Literature." *Fraser's Magazine* 60.355 (July 1859): 97–110.

Hodge, John. *Trainspotting and the Shallow Grave.* London: Faber & Faber, 1996.

Hodnett, Edward. *Image and Text: Studies in the Illustration of English Literature.* London: Scolar, 1982.

Homans, Margaret. "The Name of the Mother in *Wuthering Heights.*" *Bearing the Word: Language and Female Experience in Nineteenth-Century Women's Writings.* Chicago: University of Chicago Press, 1986.

Horinek, Zdenek. "The Possibilities of Theatrical Montage Successive and Simultaneous." Trans. Eva Poskocilova and Michael Quinn. *Theater Survey* 36:1 (May 1995): 77–86.

Housman, Laurence. *Arthur Boyd Houghton: A Selection from His Book in Black and White.* London: Kegan Paul, 1896.

Ingersoll, Earl G. "Cinematic Effects in Conrad's The Secret Agent." *Conradiana* 21.1 (1989): 29–36.

Intons-Peterson, Margaret J., and Mark A. McDaniel. "Symmetries and Asymmetries Between Imagery and Perception." *Imagery and Cognition.* Eds. Cesare Cornoldi and Mark A. McDaniel. New York: Springer-Verlag, 1991. 47–76.

Izod, John. "Words Selling Pictures." *Cinema and Fiction: New Modes of Adapting 1950–1990.* Eds. John Orr and Colin Nicholson. Edinburgh: Edinburgh University Press, 1992. 95–103.

Jackson, Kevin. *The Language of Cinema.* Manchester: Carcanet, 1998.

Jacobs, Hildebrand. "Of the Sister Arts; An Essay." Los Angeles, CA: The Augustan Reprint Society, 1974.

Jacobus, Mary. *Romanticism, Writing, and Sexual Difference.* Oxford: Clarendon, 1989.

Jadwin, Lisa. "Clytemnestra Rewarded: The Double Conclusion of Vanity Fair." *Famous Last Words: Changes in Gender and Narrative Closure.* Ed. Alison Booth. Charlottesville: University of Virginia Press, 1993. 35–61.

James, Caryn. "Australia's Films Display a Distinctive Gothic Darkness." *The New York Times* (28 November 1993) 28.2; 13:1.

James, Henry. "The Art of Fiction." *Partial Portraits.* New York: Haskell House, 1968. Originally published 1884 in *Longman's Magazine.*

Preface to *The Golden Bowl. The Art of the Novel.* Ed. R. P. Blackmur. New York: Scribner's, 1947. Originally published 1909.

James, Philip. *English Book Illustration 1800–1900.* London: King Penguin, 1947.

Johnson, Mark. *The Body in the Mind: The Bodily Basis of Meaning, Imagination, and Reason.* Chicago: University of Chicago Press, 1987.

Johnson, Samuel. *The History of Rasselas: Prince of Abisinnia* [sic]. Eds. Geoffrey Tillotson and Brian Jenkins. London: Oxford University Press, 1971. Originally published 1759.

Josephson, Matthew. "Masters of the Motion Pictures." *Motion Picture Classic* 23.6 (August 1926): 25.

Kalter, Joanmarie. *Actors on Acting: Performing in Theatre & Film Today.* New York: Sterling, 1979.

Katz, Bill, ed. *A History of Book Illustration: 29 Points of View.* Metuchen, NJ: Scarecrow, 1994.

Kawin, Bruce. "Right-Hemisphere Processing in Dreams and Films." *Dreamworks* 2.1 (1981): 13–17.

Kellman, Steven G. "The Cinematic Novel: Tracking a Concept." *Modern Fiction Studies* 33.3 (Autumn 1987): 467–77.

Kennedy, Victor R. "Pictures as Metaphors in Thackeray's Illustrated Novels." *Metaphor and Symbolic Activity* 9.2 (1994): 135–47.

Keyes, David. "Wuthering Heights." http://www.geocities.com/Hollywood/Cinema/ 4069/reviews/1999/wutheringheights.html, 1999.

Keyser, Lester J. "A Scrooge for All Seasons." *The English Novel and the Movies.* Eds. Michael Klein and Gillian Parker. New York: Frederick Ungar, 1981.

Kingsley, Henry. *Macmillan's Magazine* 9 (1864): 359–60.

Kipen, David. "Auteurism's Great Snow Job." *San Francisco Chronicle Magazine* (22 April 2001): 12–17.

Klein, Michael, and Gillian Parker. *The English Novel and the Movies.* New York: Frederick Ungar, 1981.

Kline, T. Jefferson. *Bertolucci's Dream Loom: A Psychoanalytic Study of Cinema.* Amherst, MA: University of Massachusetts Press, 1987.

Knight, Arthur. *The Liveliest Art: A Panoramic History of the Movies.* New York: Macmillan, 1957.

Koltnow, Barry. "Kenneth Branagh Picks Up the Pieces in Mary Shelley's Monster Classic." *Buffalo News* (5 November 1994): 10.

Konigsberg, Ira. *The Complete Film Dictionary.* New York: New American Library, 1987.

Kooistra, Lorraine Janzen. *The Artist as Critic: Bitextuality in Fin-de-Siecle Illustrated Books.* Aldershot, England: Scolar, 1995.

Kosslyn, Stephen Michael. *Image and Mind.* Cambridge, MA: Harvard University Press, 1980.

Kozloff, Sarah. *Invisible Storytellers.* Berkeley: University of California Press, 1988.

Kral, Petr [sic]. "Questions to Jan Svankmajer." *Afterimage* 13 (Autumn 1987): 22–32.

Krieger, Murray. "The Ekphrastic Principle and the Still Movement of Poetry; or *Laokoon* Revisited." *The Play and Place of Criticism.* Baltimore: Johns Hopkins University Press, 1976.

Kunzendorf, Robert G. "Mind-Brain Identity Theory: A Materialistic Foundation for the Psychophysiology of Mental Imagery." *The Psychophysiology of Mental Imagery: Theory, Research and Applications.* Eds. Robert G. Kunzendorf and Anees A. Sheikh. Amityville, NY: Baywood Publishing Co., 1990.

La Beau, Dennis. *Theatre, Film and Television Biographies Master Index.* Detroit: Gale Research Co., 1979.

Lacan, Jacques. "Situation de la psychanalyse en 1956." *Ecrits: A Selection.* Trans. A. Sheridan. New York: Norton, 1977.

Lamb, Charles. Letter to Samuel Rogers, n.d. Estimated date December 1833. *The Letters of Charles Lamb.* Ed. E. V. Lucas. New York: Dutton, 1945. 394.

"On the Genius and Character of Hogarth." *The Reflector* 3 (1811): 62.

"On the Tragedies of Shakespeare. Considered with Reference to the Fitness for Stage Representation." *The Collected Essays of Charles Lamb.* Introduced by Robert Lynd and notes by William MacDonald. New York: Dutton, 1929. 163–96.

Lane, Anthony. "Kafka's Heir." *New Yorker* (31 Oct. 1994): 48–55.

Landow, George. "Ruskin's Theories of the Sister Arts." http://landow.stg.brown.edu/victorian/ruskin/atheories/1.4.html.

Langan, Celeste. "Understanding Media in 1805: Audiovisual Hallucination in The Lay of the Last Minstrel." *Studies in Romanticism* 40 (Spring 2001): 49–70.

Larson, Randall D. *Films into Books: An Analytical Bibliography of Film Novelizations, Movie, and TV Tie-Ins.* Metuchen, NJ: Scarecrow, 1995.

Layard, George Somes. "Our Graphic Humorists: W. M. Thackeray." *The Magazine of Art* (22 February 1899): 256–62.

Lee, Rensselaer W. *Ut Pictura Poesis. The Humanistic Theory of Painting.* New York: Norton, 1967.

Leitch, Thomas M. *What Stories Are: Narrative Theory and Interpretation.* University Park: Pennsylvania State University Press, 1986.

Leonard, William Torbert. *From Theatre: Stage to Screen to Television.* London: Scarecrow, 1981. Vol. 2.

Lessing, Gotthold Ephraim. *Laocoön: An Essay upon the Limits of Painting and Poetry.* Trans. Edward Allen McCormick. Indianapolis: Bobbs-Merrill, 1962. Originally published 1766.

Lettis, Richard. "The Illustrated Dickens: 'Exactly What I Meant'." *Imagination on a Long Rein.* Ed. Joachim Möller. Berlin: Jonas Verlag, 1988. 120–24.

Lewes, George Henry. "Review of *Wuthering Heights* and *Agnes Grey*." *Leader* (28 Dec. 1850): 953.

Leyda, Jay. *Kino: A History of the Russian and Soviet Film.* London: Allen & Unwin, 1960.

Linden, George W. *Reflections on the Screen.* Belmont, CA: Wadsworth Publishing Co., 1971.

Lindsay, Vachel. *The Art of the Moving Picture.* New York: Macmillan, 1915.

"Between the Photoplays and the Stage." *Focus on Film and Theatre.* Ed. James Hurt. Englewood Cliffs, NJ: Prentice Hall, 1974. 18–28.

Lister, T. H. *The Edinburgh Review* 68.137 (1838): 77.

Lodge, David. "Thomas Hardy and the Cinematographic Novel." *Novel* 7 (1974): 246–54.

"Thomas Hardy as a Cinematic Novelist." *Thomas Hardy After 50 Years.* Ed. Lance St. John Butler. New York: Macmillan, 1977. 78–89.

Low, Rachael. *The History of the British Film.* London: Allen & Unwin, 1948–71. 3 vols.

Luhr, William. "Dickens's Narrative. Hollywood's Vignettes." *The English Novel and the Movies.* Eds. Michael Klein and Gillian Parker. New York: Frederick Ungar, 1981. 132–42.

Luhr, William, and Peter Lehman. *Authorship and Narrative in the Cinema: Issues in Contemporary Aesthetics and Criticism.* New York: Putnam, 1977.

Madsen, Roy Paul. *The Impact of Film.* New York: Macmillan, 1973.

Magill, Frank N. *Cinema: The Novel into Film.* Magill Survey. Pasadena: Salem, 1980.

Magny, Claude-Edmonde. *The Age of the American Novel: The Film Aesthetic of Fiction Between the Two Wars.* Trans. Eleanor Hochman. New York: Frederick Ungar, 1972.

Mallarmé, Stephane. "Sur le livre illustré." *Oeuvres complètes.* Eds. Henri Mondor and G. Jean-Aubrey. Paris: Gallimard, 1945.

Mamoulian, Rouben. *Sound and the Cinema.* Ed. Evan William Cameron. New York: Redgrave, 1980.

Markiewicz, Henryk. "Ut Pictura Poesis . . . A History of the Topos and the Problem." *New Literary History* 18.3 (Spring 1987): 535–59.

Mast, Gerald. *A Short History of the Movies.* Indianapolis: Bobbs-Merrill, 1981.

Mast, Gerald, and Marshall Cohen. *Film Theory and Criticism.* 2nd ed. Oxford: Oxford University Press, 1979.

Mathison, John K. "Nelly Dean and the Power of *Wuthering Heights.*" *Nineteenth-Century Fiction* (11 Sept. 1956): 106–29.

Mayer, Geoff. *Film as Text.* Milton, Queensland, Australia: Jacaranda, 1991.

McDougal, Stuart Y. *Made into Movies: From Literature to Film.* New York: Rinehart & Winston, 1985.

McFarlane, Brian. *Novel to Film: An Introduction to the Theory of Adaptation.* Oxford: Clarendon, 1996.

Words and Images: Australian Novels into Film. Melbourne: Heinemann, 1983.

Meisel, Martin. *Realizations: Narrative, Pictorial, and Theatrical Arts in 19th-Century England.* Princeton: Princeton University Press, 1983.

Mellen, Joan, ed. *The World of Luis Buñuel.* New York: Oxford University Press, 1978.

Mellencamp, Paul. "Cinematic Discourse: The Problem of Inner Speech." *Cinema and Language.* Eds. Stephen Heath and Patricia Mellencamp. Frederick, MD: University Publications of America, 1983.

Melville, Lewis. "Vanity Fair." *Bioscope* 14. 279 (15 Feb. 1912): 415–17.

Messenger, James R. "I Think I Liked the Book Better: Nineteen Novelists Look at the Film Version of Their Work." *Literature/Film Quarterly* 6.1 (1978): 125–34.

Metz, Christian. *Film Language: A Semiotics of the Cinema.* Trans. Michael Taylor. New York: Oxford University Press, 1991.

The Imaginary Signifier: Psychoanalysis and the Cinema. Trans. Celia Britton, Annwyl Williams, Ben Brewster, and Alfred Guzzetti. Bloomington: Indiana University Press, 1977.

Michalski, Milena. "Cinematic Literature and Literary Cinema: Olesha. Room and the Search for a New Art Form." *Russian Literature. Modernism and the Visual Arts.*

Eds. Catriona Kelly and Stephen Lovell. Cambridge: Cambridge University Press, 2000. 220–49.

Mill, J. S. "What Is Poetry?" *The Broadview Anthology of Victorian Poetry and Poetic Theory.* Eds. Thomas J. Collins and Vivienne J. Rundle. Peterborough, Ontario, Canada: Broadview, 1999. Originally published 1833. 1212–20.

Miller, J. Hillis. "The 'Grafted' Image: James on Illustration." *Henry James's New York Edition: The Construction of Authorship.* Ed. David McWhirter. Stanford: Stanford University Press, 1995.

Illustration. Cambridge, MA: Harvard University Press, 1992.

"*Wuthering Heights*: Repetition and the Uncanny." *Fiction and Repetition: Seven English Novels.* Cambridge, MA: Harvard University Press, 1982. 42–72.

Miller, Jonathan. *Subsequent Performances.* London: Faber, 1986.

Milligan, Spike. *Wuthering Heights According to Spike Milligan.* London: Michael Joseph, 1994.

Mills, Sara, Lynne Pearce, Sue Spaull, and Elaine Millard, eds. *Feminist Readings/Feminists Reading.* Charlottesville: University of Virginia Press, 1989.

Milne, Peter. "The Development of the Subtitle." *Photoplay* 28.5 (Oct. 1925): 132.

Mitchell, W. J. T. "Going Too Far with the Sister Arts." *Space, Time, Image, Sign: Essays on Literature and the Visual Arts.* Ed. James A. W. Heffernan. New York: Peter Lang, 1987. 1–10.

Iconology: Image, Text, Ideology. Chicago: University of Chicago Press, 1986.

Picture Theory. Chicago: University of Chicago Press, 1994.

"Spatial Form in Literature: Toward a General Theory." *Critical Inquiry* 6 (Spring 1980): 539–67.

Mitry, Jean. *Esthétique et psychologie du cinéma.* Paris: Editions Universitaires, 1963.

"Remarks on the Problem of Cinematic Adaptation." Trans. Richard Dyer. *The Bulletin of the Midwest Modern Language Association* 4 (1971): 4–5.

Möller. Joachim. ed. *Imagination on a Long Rein.* Berlin: Jonas Verlag, 1988.

Monaco, James. *How To Read a Film: The Art, Technology, Language, History, and Theory of Film and Media.* New York: Oxford University Press, 1977.

How to Read a Film: Movies, Media, Multimedia. 3rd ed. Oxford: Oxford University Press, 2000.

Moore, Robert E. *Hogarth's Literary Relationships.* Minneapolis: University of Minnesota Press, 1948.

Morris, William. *The Ideal Book: Essays and Selections on the Arts of the Book.* Ed. William S. Peterson. Berkeley: University of California Press, 1982.

Morrissette, Bruce. *Novel and Film.* Chicago: University of Chicago Press, 1985.

Moser, Thomas. "What Is the Matter with Emily Jane?: Conflicting Impulses in *Wuthering Heights.*" *Nineteenth-Century Fiction* 17 (June 1962): 1–19.

Moynahan, Julian. "Seeing the Book: Reading the Movie." *The English Novel and the Movies.* Eds. Michael Klein and Gillian Parker. New York: Frederick Ungar, 1981. 143–54.

Murphy, Brenda. *Congressional Theatre: Dramatizing McCarthyism on Stage, Film, and Television.* Cambridge: Cambridge University Press, 1999.

Musser, Charles. "The Nickelodeon Era Begins: Establishing the Framework for Hollywood's Mode of Representation." *Early Cinema: Space, Frame, Narrative.* Eds. Thomas Elsaesser and Adam Barker. London: British Film Institute, 1990. 256–73.

Nadel, Alan. "Ambassadors from an Imaginary Elsewhere: Cinematic Convention and the Jamesian Sensibility." *Henry James Review* 19.3 (Fall 1998): 279–85.

Naremore, James. *Film Adaptation.* New Brunswick, NJ: Rutgers University Press, 2000.

Nebesio, Bohdan Y. "A Compromise with Literature? Making Sense of Intertitles in the Silent Films of Alexander Dovzhenko." *Canadian Review of Comparative Literature* 23.2 (Sept. 1996): 679–700.

Nugent, Frank. Review of MGM's *Wuthering Heights. New York Times* 28 (14 April 1939): 2.

Olney, James, ed. *Autobiography: Essays Theoretical and Critical.* Princeton: Princeton University Press, 1980.

O'Pray, Michael. "Surrealism. Fantasy and the Grotesque: The Cinema of Jan Švankmajer." *Fantasy and the Cinema.* Ed. James Donald. London: British Film Institute, 1989. 253–68.

Orr, Christopher. "The Discourse on Adaptation." *Wide Angle* 6.2 (1984): 72–76.

Orr, John. "Introduction: Proust, the Movie." *Cinema and Fiction: New Modes of Adapting 1950–1990.* Eds. John Orr and Colin Nicholson. Edinburgh: Edinburgh University Press, 1992. 1–9.

"*The Trial* of Orson Welles." *Cinema and Fiction: New Modes of Adapting 1950–1990.* Eds. John Orr and Colin Nicholson. Edinburgh: Edinburgh University Press, 1992. 13–27.

Pacific Bell. *Smart Yellow Pages.* 2001.

Pantazzi, Sybille. "Author and Illustrator: Images in Confrontation." *A History of Book Illustration: 29 Points of View.* Ed. Bill Katz. Metuchen, NJ: Scarecrow, 1994. 585–600. Originally published 1976.

Park, Roy. *Hazlitt and the Spirit of the Age.* Oxford: Oxford University Press, 1971.

Pater, Walter. "Notre-Dame d'Amiens." *Miscellaneous Studies.* London: Macmillan, 1913.

"The School of Giorgione." *The Renaissance: Studies in Art and Poetry.* London: Macmillan, 1900. 130–38. Originally published 1873.

"Style." *Appreciations.* London: Macmillan, 1890. 1–36.

Patterson, Joseph Medill. "The Nickelodeons: The Poor Man's Elementary Course in the Drama." *The Saturday Evening Post* 180.21 (23 Nov. 1917): 38.

Pearson, Roberta E. *Eloquent Gestures: The Transformation of Performance Style in the Griffith Biograph Films.* Berkeley: University California Press, 1992.

Peary, G., and R. Shatzkin. *The Classic American Novel and the Movies.* New York: Ungar, 1977.

Phillips, William H. *Film: An Introduction.* Boston: Bedford/St. Martin's, 1999.

Praz, Mario. *The Hero in Eclipse in Victorian Fiction.* Trans. Angus Davidson. London: Oxford University Press, 1956.

Preminger, Alex, ed. *The Encyclopedia of Poetry and Poetics.* Princeton, NJ: Princeton University Press, 1965.

Prendergast, Roy M. *Film Music: A Neglected Art.* New York: Norton, 1977.

Pritz, Horst. *Montage in Theater and Film.* Tubingen: Francke, 1993.

Pryluck, Calvin. "The Film Metaphor Metaphor: The Use of Language-Based Models in Film Study." *Literature/Film Quarterly* 3 (1975): 117–23.

Ramsaye, Terry. *A Million and One Nights: A History of the Motion Picture.* 2 vols. New York: Simon and Schuster, 1926.

Ray, Robert B. "The Field of 'Literature and Film'." *Film Adaptation.* Ed. James Naremore. New Brunswick, NJ: Rutgers University Press, 2000.

Rea, Kenneth, ed. *A Better Direction: A National Enquiry into the Training of Directors for Theatre, Film and Television.* London: Calouste Gulbenkian Foundation, 1989.

Reynolds, Peter, ed. *Novel Images: Literature in Performance.* New York: Routledge, 1993.

Richardson, J. T. E. "Imagery and the Brain." *Imagery and Cognition.* Eds. Cesare Cornoldi and Mark A. McDaniel. New York: Springer-Verlag, 1991. 1–45.

Rigby, Elizabeth. Review of *Vanity Fair* and other novels. *Quarterly Review* 84.167 (Dec. 1848): 153–85.

Robinson, Mary F. *The Life of Emily Brontë.* London: Allen, 1883.

Ropars-Wuilleumier, Marie-Claire. *De la littérature au cinéma: genèse d'un écriture.* Paris: Armand Colin, 1970.

Rose, Rich. *Drawing Scenery for Theater, Film, and Television.* Cincinnati, OH: Betterway Books, 1994.

Rosch, Eleanor. "Principles of Categorization." *Cognition and Categorization.* Eds. Eleanor Rosch and Barbara B. Lloyd. Hillsdale, NJ: Lawrence Erlbaum, 1978.

Rotha, Paul. *The Film Till Now.* New York: Jonathan Cape & Harrison Smith, 1930.

Ruskin, John. *The Works of John Ruskin.* 39 vols. London: George Allen, 1903–12.

Salt, Barry. "Film Form 1900–1906." *Early Cinema: Space, Frame, Narrative.* Eds. Thomas Elsaesser and Adam Barker. London: British Film Institute, 1990. 31–44.

Sargent, Epes Winthrop. *Moving Picture World* (12 Aug. 1911): 363.

Scholes, Robert. "Narration and Narrativity in Film." *Quarterly Review of Film Studies* 1.111 (August 1976): 283–96.

What Stories Are: Narrative Theory and Interpretation. University Park: Pennsylvania State University Press, 1986.

Segal, S. J., and V. Fusella. "Influence of Imaged Pictures and Sounds on Detection of Visual and Auditory Signals." *Journal of Experimental Psychology* 83 (1970): 458–64.

Seger, Linda. *The Art of Adaptation: Turning Fact and Fiction into Film.* New York: Henry Holt, 1992.

Sha, Richard C. *The Visual and Verbal Sketch in British Romanticism.* Philadelphia: University of Pennsylvania Press, 1998.

Sharff, Stefan. *The Elements of Cinema: Towards a Theory of Cinesthetic Impact.* New York: Columbia University Press, 1982.

Silverman, Kaja. "History, Figuration, and Female Subjectivity in *Tess of the D'Urbervilles.*" *Novel* 18.1 (1984): 5–28.

Simpson, J. A., and E. S. C. Weiner. *The Oxford English Dictionary.* 2nd ed. 20 vols. Oxford: Clarendon, 1989.

Sinyard, Neil. *Filming Literature: The Art of Screen Adaptation.* New York: St. Martin's, 1986.

Sitney, P. Adams. *Modernist Montage.* New York: Columbia, 1990.

Sketchley, Rose D. *English Book Illustration To-day.* London: Kegan Paul, 1903.

Skrypnyk, Leonid. *Narysyz teorii mystetstva kino.* Kiev: Derzhavne vyd. Ukraine, 1928.

Slide, Anthony, and Edward Wagenknecht. *Fifty Great American Silent Films, 1912–1920: A Pictorial Survey.* New York: Dover, 1980.

Slide, Anthony, Patricia King Hanson, and Stephen L. Hanson. *Sourcebook for the Performing Arts: A Directory of Collections, Resources, Scholars, and Critics in Theatre, Film, and Television.* New York: Greenwood, 1988.

Sloan, John. "In Praise of Thackeray's Pictures." *Vanity Fair.* New York: Heritage, 1940. xiii.

Smith, Agnes. *Photoplay* (May 1927): 29.

Smith, Grahame. "Dickens and Adaptation." *Novel Images: Literature in Performance*. Ed. Peter Reynolds. New York: Routledge, 1993. 49–63.

Smith, Winston. *"Act Like Nothing's Wrong": The Montage Art of Winston Smith*. San Francisco: Last Gasp, 1994.

Sparshott, F. E. "Vision and Dream in the Cinema." *Philosophic Exchange* 1.2 (1971): 111–22.

Spiegel, Alan. *Fiction and the Camera Eye*. Charlottesville: University of Virginia Press, 1976.

Spottiswoode, Raymond. *A Grammar of the Film: An Analysis of Film Technique*. Berkeley: University of California Press, 1950.

Stam, Robert. "Beyond Fidelity: The Dialogics of Adaptation." *Film Adaptation*. Ed. James Naremore. New Brunswick, NJ: Rutgers University Press, 2000.

Stang, Richard. *The Theory of the Novel in England: 1850–1879*. New York: Columbia University Press, 1959.

Starr, Cecile. *Discovering the Movies*. New York: Van Nostrand Reinhold, 1972.

Stephenson, Ralph, and J. R. Debrix. *The Cinema as Art*. London: Penguin, 1978. Originally published 1965.

Stevens, Joan. "Thackeray's *Vanity Fair*." *A Review of English Literature*. Vol. VI. Ed. A. Norman Jeffares. London: Longmans, Green & Co., 1965. 19–38.

Stoddart, Scott F. "Redirecting Fitzgerald's 'Gaze': Masculine Perception and Cinematic License in *The Great Gatsby*." *F. Scott Fitzgerald: New Perspectives*. Eds. Jackson R. Bryer, Alan Margolies, and Ruth Prigozy. Athens, GA: University of Georgia Press, 2000. 102–14.

Stoehr, Taylor. *Dickens: The Dreamer's Stance*. Ithaca: Cornell University Press, 1965.

Stromgren, Richard L., and Martin F. Norden. *Movies: A Language in Light*. Englewood Cliffs, NJ: Prentice-Hall, 1984.

Sturgiss, Russell. "Thackeray as Draughtsman." *Scribner's Monthly* 20.2 (June 1880): 256–74.

Sullivan, Edmund J. *The Art of Illustration*. London: Chapman Hall, 1921.

Sutherland, Robert D. *Language and Lewis Carroll*. Paris: Mouton, 1970.

Svankmajer, Jan. "Švankmajer on *Alice*." *Afterimage* 13 (Autumn 1987): 51–53.

Sweeney, Patricia Runk. "Thackeray's Best Illustrator." *Costerus* 2 (1974): 83–111.

Swinburne, Charles Algernon. "Emily Brontë." *Athenaeum* (16 June 1883): 762–63.

Tallis, Raymond. "The Realistic Novel versus the Cinema." *Critical Quarterly* 27.2 (1985): 57–65.

Tambling, Jeremy. "Dickens. Digression. and Montage." *The Yearbook of English Studies: Strategies of Reading*. Ed. Andrew Gurr. Leeds, England: Modern Humanities Research Association, 1996. 43–53.

Tanner, Tony. "Colour and Movement in *Tess of the d'Urbervilles*." *Hardy: The Tragic Novels: A Casebook*. Ed. R. P. Draper. New York: Macmillan, 1975.

Taylor, Richard H., ed. *The Personal Notebooks of Thomas Hardy*. New York: Macmillan, 1978.

Teitelbaum, Matthew, ed. *Montage and Modern Life, 1919–1942*. Cambridge, MA: MIT Press, 1992.

Thackeray, William Makepeace. *Vanity Fair*. London: Bradbury & Evans, 1848. Various other editions consulted and cited in the notes.

Letter to John Leycester Adolphus. 11 May 1848. *The Letters and Private Papers of William Makepeace Thackeray*. Ed. Gordon N. Ray. Cambridge, MA: Harvard University Press, 1945.

Thompson, Howard. *The New York Guide to Movies on Television*. Chicago: Quadrangle, 1970.

Thompson, John O. "Film Adaptation and the Mystery of the Original." *Pulping Fictions: Consuming Culture Across the Literature/Media Divide*. Eds. Deborah Cartmell, I. Q. Hunter, Heidi Kaye, and Imelda Whelehan. London: Pluto, 1996. 11–28.

Thorpe, James. *English Illustration: The Nineties*. London: Faber, 1935.

Tibbetts, John C., and James M. Welsh. *Novels into Film: The Encyclopedia of Movies Adapted from Books*. New York: Checkmark Books, 1999.

Turner, G. W. "Cinematic Effects in Medieval and Modern Narrative." *Southern Review* 27.2 (June 1994): 196–206.

Turner, Mark. "Categories and Analogies." *Analogical Reasoning: Perspectives of Artificial Intelligence, Cognitive Science, and Philosophy*. Ed. David H. Helman. Boston: Kluwer, 1988.

Tyler, Parker. *The Three Faces of the Film: The Art, the Dream, the Cult*. South Brunswick, NJ: A. S. Barnes, 1967.

Vacche, Angela Dalle. *Cinema and Painting: How Art is Used in Film*. Austin: University of Texas Press, 1996.

Vasey, Ruth. *The World According to Hollywood, 1918–1939*. Madison: University of Wisconsin Press, 1997.

Vidal, Gore. "Who Makes the Movies." *New York Review of Books*. (25 Nov. 1976): 8.

Wade, Nicholas J. *Visual Allusions: Pictures of Perception*. London: Laurence Erlbaum Associates, 1992.

Wade, Nicholas J., and Michael Swanston. *Visual Perception: An Introduction*. London: Routledge, 1991.

Wagner, Geoffrey. *The Novel and the Cinema*. Rutherford, NJ: Farleigh Dickinson University Press, 1975.

Ward, Mary. "Introduction." *Wuthering Heights*. London: Smith, Elder & Co., 1900.

Watkins, Calvert, ed. *The American Heritage Dictionary of Indo-European Roots*. Boston: Houghton Mifflin, 2000.

Weightman, Gavin. *Bright Lights. Big City: London Entertained 1830–1950*. London: Collins & Brown, 1988.

Welch, Jeffrey Egan, ed. *Literature and Film: An Annotated Bibliography, 1909–1988*. New York: Garland, 1993.

Wellek, René, and Austin Warren. *Theory of Literature*. New York: Harcourt, 1942.

Whipple, E. P. "Novels of the Season." *North American Review* 67 (Oct. 1848): 354–69.

White, Gleeson. *English Illustration: The Sixties. 1855–1870*. Westminster: A. Constable, 1897.

Willemen, Paul. "Cinematic Discourse: The Problem of Inner Speech." *Cinema and Language*. Eds. Stephen Heath and Patricia Mellencamp. Frederick, MD: University Publications of America, 1983. 141–67.

Williams, Keith. "Cinematic Joyce." *James Joyce Broadsheet* 57 (Oct. 2000): 3.

Wilson, Edmund. *The Boys in the Back Room*. San Francisco: Colt, 1941.

Wollen, Peter. *Signs and Meaning in the Cinema*. London: Secker & Warburg, 1969.

Wood, Christopher. *Victorian Painting*. London: Weidenfeld & Nicholson, 1999.

Woolf, Virginia. "The Cinema." *Collected Essays*. Vol. 2. London: Hogarth, 1966. 268–72. Essay date 1926.

"Pictures." *The Moment and Other Essays*. London: Harcourt Brace Jovanovich, 1948. 173–78.

Wordsworth, William. "Illustrated Books and Newspapers." *Poetical Works of William Wordsworth*. Eds. E. de Selincourt and Helen Darbishire. Oxford: Clarendon, 1947. 75.

Wyver, John. *The Moving Image: An International History of Film, Television & Video*. London: British Film Institute, 1989.

Zukor, Adolph. *Photoplay* (June 1921): 42.

Anonymous Articles Arranged by Date

Review of William Etty's 1832 painting from Milton's *Comus*. *Athenaeum* (11 Feb. 1832): 98.

Review of *Sketches by Boz*. *The Spectator* (26 Dec. 1836): 1234.

Review of *Wuthering Heights*. *Atlas* (22 Jan. 1848): 59.

[George Henry Lewes.] "Vanity Fair: A Novel without a Hero." *Athenaeum* (12 Aug. 1848): 794–97.

Review of *Wuthering Heights*. *Britannia* (15 Jan. 1848): 42–43.

[Robert Bell.] "Vanity Fair." *Fraser's Magazine* (38 Sept. 1848): 320–33.

Review of *Wuthering Heights*. *The Examiner* (8 Jan. 1848): 21–22.

Review of Dickens's *David Copperfield* and Thackeray's *Pendennis*. *North British Review* (15 May 1851): 57–89.

"Wuthering Heights." *The Examiner* (13 May 1854): 294.

"Mr. Thackeray and His Novels." *Blackwood's Magazine* 77 (Jan. 1855): 86–96.

Review of *Extracts from the Works of W. M. Thackeray*. *Athenaeum* (12 November 1881): 623–24.

J. F. "Wuthering Heights." *Temple Bar* 81 (Dec. 1887): 562–68.

"Our Library Table." *Athenaeum* (24 September 1898): 417–18.

Palace Theatre of Varieties programs. 1898–1901.

"William Makepeace Thackeray." *Scribner's Magazine* 25 (February 1899): 236–49.

"Motion Picture Films." *Complete Illustrated Catalog of Moving Picture Machines, Stereopticons, Slides, Films*. Chicago: Kleine Optical Co., 1905. 206–07.

Film review. *Views and Films Index*. September 1906.

Review of D. W. Griffith's *A Corner in Wheat*. "Reviews of Licensed Films." *The New York Dramatic Mirror* 62.1618 (25 Dec. 1909): 15.

"Cast Mrs. Fiske Film." *The New York Dramatic Mirror* (30 June 1915): 20.

"Vanity Fair." *Variety* 29 Oct. 1915: 22.

Review of Edison's 1915 film of *Vanity Fair*. *Boston Transcript* (11 Jan. 1916).

"The Art of the Sub-Title." *The Picturegoer* May 1921: 21.

Film review. *The New York Times* (4 Sept. 1921) section 6: 3.

Review of *Shattered*. "Screen: Pictorial Efficiency." *The New York Times* (11 Dec. 1921) section 6: 3.

Preview of the 1922 film of *Vanity Fair*. *Bioscope* (26 Jan. 1922): 59.

"The Screen: A Movie of the Prairies." *The New York Times* (17 March 1923): 9.

"Hugo Ballin Edits 'Vanity Fair,' Cutting the Anachronisms." *New York Tribune* (6 May 1923) VI: 3.

"Lubitsch on Directing." *The New York Times* (16 Dec. 1923) Section 9: 5.

"Exceptional Photoplays: *Secrets of the Soul*." *National Board of Review Magazine* 1.5 (Sept.–Oct. 1926): 7–8.

"Adaptations: Novel to Film." http://www.urbancinefile.com.au/home/article_view. asp?Article_ID=3463& Section=Features. April 2000.

"Literary Cinema." http://library.thinkquest.org/2847/films.htm. 1995–2002.

Film and Television Works Cited

Alice in Wonderland. Dir. Cecil Hepworth. Hepworth Films. UK, 1903.

Alice in Wonderland. Dir. Norman Z. McLeod. Paramount. USA, 1933.

Alice in Wonderland. Dirs. Clyde Geronimi, Wilfred Jackson, Hamilton Luske. Disney. USA, 1951.

Alice in Wonderland. Dir. Jonathan Miller. BBC. UK, 1966.

Jabberwocky. Dir. Jan Svankmajer. Kratk Film Praha. CH, 1971.

Alice's Adventures in Wonderland: The World's Favorite Bedtime Story. Dir. Bud Townsend. Playboy Films. USA, 1976.

Alice's Adventures in Wonderland and Through the Looking Glass. Dir. Harry Harris. Columbia TV. USA, 1985.

Dream Child. Dir. Gavin Millar. EMI Films. USA, 1985.

Alice. Dir. Jan Svankmajer. Condor Films. CH, 1988.

Alice in Wonderland. Dir. Franco Cristofani. Film Investment Corporation of New Zealand. New Zealand, 1988.

Alice in Wonderland. Dir. Nick Willing. NBC. USA, 1999.

Bleak House. Dir. Maurice Elvey. Ideal Films. UK, 1920.

Scrooge, Or Marley's Ghost. Dir. Walter R. Booth. R. W. Paul Films. UK, 1901.

A Christmas Carol. Dir. Brian Desmond Hurst. Renown Pictures. UK, 1951.

The Cricket on the Hearth. Dir. D. W. Griffith. Biograph. USA, 1909.

The Course of True Love Never Did Run Smooth. Dir. D. W. Griffith. Biograph. USA, 1910.

Daisy Miller. Dir. Peter Bogandovich. Paramount. USA, 1974.

David Copperfield. Dir. Thomas Bentley. Hepworth Films. UK, 1913.

David Copperfield. Dir. George Cukor. MGM. USA, 1935.

Dracula Sucks. Dir. Philip Marshak. Kodiak. USA, 1979.

Love at First Bite (adapts *Dracula*). Dir. Stan Dragoti. Simon Films. USA, 1979.

Bram Stoker's Dracula. Dir. Francis Ford Coppola. Zoetrope. USA, 1992.

Frankenstein. Dir. James Whale. Universal. USA, 1931.

Mary Shelley's Frankenstein. Dir. Kenneth Branagh. Zoetrope. USA, 1994.

Great Expectations. Dir. David Lean. Rank. UK, 1946.

William Shakespeare's Hamlet. Dir. Kenneth Branagh. Columbia. USA, 1996.

Hard Times. Dir. Peter Barnes. BBC. UK, 1994.

In the Bedroom. Dir. Todd Field. Miramax. USA, 2001.

Jane Eyre. Dir. Christy W. Cabanne. Monogram. USA, 1934.

Jane Eyre. Dir. Robert Stevenson. Fox. USA, 1944.

The Last Laugh. Dir. F. W. Murnau. UFA. Germany, 1924.

Little Dorrit (Lille Dorrit). Dir. A. W. Sandberg. Nordisk Films. DN, 1924.

Mansfield Park. Dir. Patricia Rozema. Miramax. USA/UK, 1999.

The Man with the Movie Camera: A Film without Intertitles. Dir. Dziga Vertov.

Masks and Faces. Dir. Fred Paul. Ideal Film Company. UK, 1917.

William Shakespeare's A Midsummer Night's Dream. Dir. Michael Hoffman. Fox. USA, 1999.

The Name of the Rose. Dir. Jean-Jacques Annaud. France 3 Cinma. FR, 1986.

Little Nell (adapts *The Old Curiosity Shop*). Thanhouser. UK, 1912.

Oliver Twist. Dir. Frank Lloyd. First National. USA, 1922.

Oliver Twist. Dir. William J. Cowen. Monogram. USA, 1933.

Oliver Twist. Dir. David Lean. Rank. UK, 1948.

Oliver Twist. Dir. Renny Rye. BBC. UK, 1999.

Our Mutual Friend. Dir. Julian Farino. BBC. UK, 1998.

Pride and Prejudice. Dir. Cyril Coke. BBC. UK, 1979.

Psycho. Dir. Alfred Hitchcock. Shamley. USA, 1960.

William Shakespeare's Romeo + Juliet. Dir. Baz Luhrmann. Fox. USA, 1996.

Rear Window. Dir. Alfred Hitchcock. Paramount. USA, 1954.

Romola. Prod. Henry King. Inspiration. USA, 1925.

A Fair Exchange (adapts *Silas Marner*). Dir. D. W. Griffith. Biograph. USA, 1909.

The Sorrows of Satan. Dir. D. W. Griffith. Famous Players-Lasky. USA, 1926.

The Adult Version of Dr. Jekyll and Mr. Hide [sic]. Dir. Byron Mabe. Image Entertainment. USA, 1972.

Dr. Sexual and Mr. Hyde. With Tony Brzezinski. USA, 1971. [no further info]

Jekyll and Hyde... Together Again. Dir. Jerry Belson. Paramount. USA, 1982.

The Suicide Club. Dir. D. W. Griffith. Biograph. USA, 1909.

A Tale of Two Cities. Dir. William Humphrey. Vitagraph. USA, 1911.

The Only Way (adapts *A Tale of Two Cities*). Dir. Herbert Wilcox. Herbert Wilcox Productions. UK, 1926.

A Tale of Two Cities. Dir. Jack Conway. MGM. USA, 1935.

A Tale of Two Cities. Dir. Philippe Monnier. Granada. FR/GB, 1989.

Tess. Dir. Roman Polanski. Renn Productions. FR, 1979.

Trainspotting. Dir. Danny Boyle. Channel Four Films. UK, 1996.

Vanity Fair. Dir. Charles Kent. Vitagraph. USA, 1911.

Vanity Fair. Dir. Charles J. Brabin and Eugene Nowland. Edison. USA, 1915.

Vanity Fair. Dir. W. C. Rowden. Tense Moments with Great Authors Series. UK, 1922.

Vanity Fair. Dir. Hugo Ballin. Hugo Ballin Productions. USA, 1923.

Vanity Fair. Dir. Chester M. Franklin. RCA. USA, 1932.

Becky Sharp (adapts *Vanity Fair*). Dir. Rouben Mamoulian. MGM. USA, 1935.

Vanity Fair. Dir. Marc Munden. BBC. UK, 1999.

Wuthering Heights. Dir. William Wyler. MGM. USA, 1939.

Wuthering Heights. Dir. Paul Nickell. Westinghouse Television Theater. CBS. USA, 1950.

Abismos de Pasion (adapts *Wuthering Heights*). Dir. Luis Buñuel. Plexus Films. Mexico, 1953.

Dil Diya Dard Liya (adapts *Wuthering Heights*). Dir. A. R. Kardar. Kary Productions. Bombay, 1966.

Wuthering Heights. McGraw-Hill Text Films. USA, 1967.

Wuthering Heights. Dir. Robert Fuest. Paramount. USA/UK, 1970.

The Semaphore Version of Wuthering Heights. Monty Python Series. BBC. UK, 1970.

"Wuthering Heights/House of Dolls." *Fantasy Island.* Dir. Philip Leacock. Columbia TV. Air date 9 Jan. 1982.

Arashi ga oka (aka *Onimaru*: adapts *Wuthering Heights*). Dir. Kiju Yoshida. Seiyô, Films. Japan, 1988.

Emily Brontë's Wuthering Heights. Dir. Peter Kosminsky. Paramount. USA, 1992.

The Piano. Dir. Jane Campion. Miramax. AUS, 1993.

Emily Brontë's Wuthering Heights. Dir. David Skynner. London Weekend Television. UK/USA, 1998.

Index